THE NUCLEAR PRESENT

A Guide to Recent Books on
Nuclear War, Weapons, the
Peace Movement, and Related
Issues, with a Chronology of
Nuclear Events, 1789–1991

by

GRANT BURNS

The Scarecrow Press, Inc.
Metuchen, N.J., & London
1992

British Library Cataloguing-in-Publication data available

Library of Congress Cataloging-in-Publication Data

Burns, Grant, 1947-
    The nuclear present : a guide to recent books on nuclear war,
weapons, the peace movement, and related issues : with a chronology of nuclear events, 1789-1991 / by Grant Burns.
        p.   cm.
    Updates: The atomic papers. 1984
    Includes indexes.
    ISBN 0-8108-2619-4 (acid-free paper)
    1. Nuclear arms control--Bibliography. 2. Nuclear weapons--Bib-
liography. 3. Nuclear warfare--Bibliography. 4. Nuclear industry
--Bibliography. I. Burns, Grant, 1947- . Atomic papers. II.
Title.
Z6464.D6B855 1992 JX1974.7
016.3271'74--dc20   92-32440

In Memory of Louis Slotin
1911–1946

Contents

Contents

The Nuclear Present

The Nuclear Present brings the user of my bibliography *The Atomic Papers* up to date, well into 1991, on significant English-language books appearing on nuclear weapons and related topics since Scarecrow's publication of that bibliography in 1984. A number of titles have been picked up from before 1984 that did not appear in *The Atomic Papers*, but there is nothing listed here, save for a very few re-issued books or subsequent editions, originally published before 1980. I have for the most part relied on the collections at the libraries of Michigan State University and the University of Michigan for access to the books.

The Nuclear Chronology included here permits the reader to obtain a fairly detailed sense of the historical record of nuclear weapons, including testing, manufacture, use, and movements for arms control and disarmament. The Chronology begins with Martin Klaproth's discovery of uranium in 1789, and ends with the Korean agreement on a nuclear weapons ban of December 31, 1991. The Periodical Review will facilitate identification of useful and important journals, magazines, and newsletters specifically concerned with nuclear weapons, strategy, and the peace movement.

This guide identifies important works of nuclear non-fiction that have come out over the past decade, and especially those published after 1984. It should serve all but major research libraries as an aid to collection development, and should help almost any researcher investigating nuclear weapons issues. I have generally omitted nuclear fiction from my coverage, partly because of time constraints, partly because of the fine bibliographic work recently done in this area by such authors as Paul Brians and David Dowling.

I have tried to provide accurate and fair descriptions of the work covered. Frequent brief quotations from the books within the annotations should help give a sense of the authors' styles and perspectives. The annotations will, from time to time, indicate my agreement with or aversion to the messages being presented. Readers will come to their own conclusions, which will in many instances not coincide with mine.

Grounds for Optimism: The Second Russian Revolution

The remarkable period following the failed Soviet hard-liners' coup attempt of August, 1991, renders some of the books noted in this bibliography of much more historical than current events interest. In the postwar decades, the prospect of nuclear war between the United States and the U.S.S.R. waxed and waned. With the former Soviet Union on its way to what promises to be a loose confederation of independent states, with communism a fading memory in both Eastern Europe and in the former Soviet states, and with the likelihood of steadily growing cooperation across a broad range of concerns between the West and these former communist nations, the specter of an East-West nuclear war has never seemed so evanescent.

However much comfort one takes in the recent Soviet events, one must remember that nuclear weapons still abound. One of the most unsettling aspects of the botched Soviet coup was the question of nuclear control. For a disconcerting time, there existed some real anxiety, both in the Soviet Union and abroad, as to what "authority" prevailed over the vast Soviet nuclear arsenal. Since only a minute portion of that arsenal devoted to mischief at the hands of a renegade political-military faction could precipitate global havoc, the issue of "Who's in charge?" is a pressing one. Present efforts to tighten control of the former Soviet nuclear weaponry emphasize the pressure.

If command and control of the nuclear superpowers'

arsenals is a point of concern even when the outlook for their political and economic relations is reasonably promising, then long-term considerations for nuclear peace are equally significant. Some of the former Soviet states, such as the Ukraine, are on record as having no interest in maintaining nuclear forces on their territory. It is well within reason to believe that all land-based Soviet nuclear weapons will eventually be relegated to Russian soil, which already houses the great majority of the former Soviet nuclear forces.

As much as one may admire the heroism of Boris Yeltsin's stand against the coup plotters, one cannot have every confidence that in a democracy as fledgling as that of the Russian Republic, and one born in such material privation, the rule of law and freedom will long endure. One must have every hope for its success, but the vehicle of Russian democracy, with its tentative new role in the world community, could yet go astray and take with it a still-overwhelming nuclear capability.

Assuming that the new independent states emerging from the bureaucratic wreckage of the Soviet Union manage to weather the near-term struggle for bread that competes with their struggle for freedom and democracy, there remains a menace to nuclear peace in the Third World. Pakistan and India simmer in their long-term hostility, with war a distinct possibility, and nuclear war a real threat within that possibility. What would be the effect on the international scene, to say nothing of the effect on the Indian and Pakistani populations, should these two countries "exchange" a dozen or so warheads? What will be the result if an ambitious, marginally sane dictator of the Saddam Hussein school obtains the nuclear firepower that Hussein himself has long sought? Will the late 1991 agreement on nuclear weapons between North Korea and South Korea help lead to an effective solution to the tensions between these two nations, or will it melt away in the heat of those tensions?

As the nuclear present evolves, the greatest threat to world, as well as regional, nuclear peace lies in the hands of nuclear tyros and terrorists. No observer can dismiss the catalytic function that a deranged leader or small group could serve with a handful of nuclear bombs. Given a sufficiently unfortunate series of events, such individuals might well wrest general nuclear war from an international situation otherwise justifying optimism as well as hope.

Close to five decades of muddled thinking about nuclear weapons have left humanity with a fine mess to clean up. Yet, in comparison to the international tone of the early 1980s, the environment has changed dramatically, even profoundly, for the better. Humanity has not escaped the nuclear woods, but has reached a clearing that permits regrouping in the sunlight, and movement ahead in a spirit of cooperation that only a few years ago was all but unimaginable. The books described in this bibliography will help the reader understand how and why the world reached this point in the nuclear present. What the nuclear future holds must remain opaque until it arrives, but, for all the menace and intimidation yet residing in the world's nuclear forces, not since the first white light of the Atomic Age has there seemed as much justifiable reason to be optimistic that the future exists.

"Talking WW III Blues"

In 1962 the Cuban Missile Crisis brought the United States and the Soviet Union within a whisker of nuclear war. Shortly afterward, a little-known folksinger recorded "Talking World War III Blues," a satiric song in which he portrayed himself wandering the streets of New York City after the war that almost happened. At one point he forgets the desolation in favor of romantic urges: "I spied me a girl — before she could leave, I said let's go play Adam & Eve! I took her by the hand, my heart was thumpin'...." But the young lady demurs. "Hey, man, you crazy or somethin'?" she asks. "Remember what happened the last time they started." She is in no hurry to help initiate a chain reaction that would lead to WW IV.

viii

American Nuclear Mythology

The shadows of the atomic bombs that helped hasten the end of World War II have darkened international relations since 1945. Lurking within every international disagreement is the possibility of nuclear confrontation and the unleashing of violence whose potential consequences defy rational comprehension. The event triggering a global nuclear war could be a direct point of contention between the United States and another nuclear power; it could be, like the Cuban Missile Crisis of 1962, a situation in which the superpowers are "eyeball to eyeball" from the opening bell.

It could also be an event with far fewer direct connections among the nuclear powers. It could be an Asian border dispute, a U.S. or Russian or French military intervention that goes wrong in a Third World nation; it could be an act of nuclear terrorism that provokes an injudicious response. It could be a head of state's series of miscalculations, bad decisions, and personal reluctance to lose face by showing discretion rather than tenacity in a crisis. There are so many ways for the world, or a sizable piece of it, to end with a bang.

In 1984, during the nadir of recent U.S.–Soviet relations, when Ronald Reagan was making jokes about introducing legislation to outlaw Russia and about how "the bombing begins in five minutes," students at Brown University approved a campus referendum calling upon the University to stock cyanide capsules in the campus health facility for distribution in the event of nuclear war. That same year, 70 percent of northern New Jersey high school students questioned believed that they would die in a nuclear war within 20 years. These gloomy insights into the recent outlook of American youth suggest that if Americans as a people have created a mythology to explain the nuclear threat, the creation has not done a very good job. If a myth leaves one that uncomfortable about the issue it purports to explain and rationalize, it is not a successful myth.

American nuclear mythology features some distinctive contentions. The first of these explains the use of the atomic bomb on Japan. According to this myth, the bombing of Hiroshima and Nagasaki ended the war in the Pacific and saved many thousands of lives that would have been lost in an American invasion of Japan. Perhaps both contentions are true; there is no way to measure their accuracy. Some scholars, such as Gar Alperovitz, have questioned these rationales for the use of the Bomb on Japan, contending that even without the Bomb's use Japan would have soon surrendered following the Soviet Union's entry into the war. There is some question as to whether an invasion of Japan would, in fact, have been required without the atomic attacks.

There is no question now, however, that the atomic bombing of Japan is secure in its place in American nuclear mythology. The mushroom cloud left in the Enola Gay's wake symbolizes not only the end of World War II but the dawn of the Nuclear Age; it is an historical event as heavy with mythical meaning as Moses' descent from Mt. Sinai with the Ten Commandments in hand was to the ancient Hebrews.

When the Hiroshima bomb, coyly christened "Little Boy" as if the diminutive name somehow would deny the weapon's power, leveled that city and killed some 80,000 people (give or take a few thousand; people went right on dying from the effects of the Hiroshima and Nagasaki bombings for decades to come), it put Americans into a unique position. They alone possessed the most destructive force available to humanity, having pried it away from the very heart of matter. They alone had assumed the responsibility for loosing this force on other human beings. It was a terrible burden for a people who, in their subscription to another myth, liked to think of themselves as the champions of freedom and justice for all. Many Americans found the atomic immolation of the Japanese cities unsettling even as they welcomed the end of a long, cruel war.

The use of the Bomb and a monopoly over its

possession brought a variety of curious responses in American life. The American nuclear mythology envisioned the Bomb as having been used for a morally honorable cause, but this aspect of the myth is only the most obvious. Somewhat less obvious was the effort to diminish the Bomb's implications by incorporating its trappings into daily life. If the Bomb could be reduced to objects as trivial as a child's prize in a box of cereal, a promise in *Popular Mechanics* of a car powered by a tiny atomic reactor reposing in the family garage, or an endless supply of electric power "too cheap to meter," then the stupendous threat to the future embodied by the Bomb was, surely, not out of hand.

As a boy in the 1950s, I once had the opportunity to choose the new paint colors for my room. From the catalog, I selected a nice blue for the ceiling, and something called "A-Bomb Red" for the walls. For several years, then, I slept within my A-Bomb Red walls and thought they were just fine. At school, along with millions of other children of the 1950s, I participated in the "duck & cover" atomic raid drills; at home, the threat of global devastation was, at least in the form of the paint on my walls, reduced to a mere sample chip in the paint vendor's catalog.

The Bomb Has Its Secrets

A very substantial part of the early American nuclear mythology concerned the "secret" of the Bomb. Americans got it into their heads that the process of nuclear fission was somehow their secret to have and to hold. "Atomic secrets" is a term that appeared with regularity in journalism of the period. Americans' great fear was that the Russians would somehow purloin their "secrets" and build their own Bomb. Clearly they could not build an atomic bomb without stealing "secrets" from the U.S., because they weren't bright enough or "advanced" enough otherwise.

When the Soviet Union detonated its first atomic bomb in 1949, the secret was out and American confidence in its mythology of superiority and control was shattered. There are no "atomic secrets." There have never been any "atomic secrets." The dynamics of nuclear reactions have existed unchanged since the instant of creation, and have been there for anyone with the curiosity, the resources, and the determination to learn them.

Nature does not harbor secrets, but that fact of existence did not keep Americans from a bolt of outrage over the Soviet nuclear achievement. Part of the outrage found a release in the execution of Julius and Ethel Rosenberg for atomic espionage in 1953. No one now can doubt that Soviet scientists would have developed the bomb regardless of the Rosenbergs' assistance, but identifying the people who gave away the American "secret" was in keeping with the terms of nuclear mythology. America saw the Rosenbergs as betraying the myth; they had to die.

Two Minutes till Midnight

One of the most interesting periods of American nuclear mythology followed immediately the announcement of the Russian bomb. In the early years of the Soviet nuclear capability, years when the United States maintained an overwhelming strategic advantage and when the likelihood of a Soviet attack on the United States was nearly non-existent (only a phalanx of Soviet leaders completely out of touch with reality would have attempted such an attack), many Americans reacted to the Soviet nuclear "threat" as though war was coming soon. The conviction of the coming war was as certain as that expressed on those fundamentalist bumper stickers announcing that "Jesus Is Coming Soon."

Although there is some difference of opinion about what "soon" means in religious eschatology, there seemed little doubt about it in the nuclear case. Atomic war was a here-and-now proposition. The Soviet bombers would be winging over the North Pole not in some distant future when everything went wrong, but tomorrow. Or this afternoon. The perception of the threat's awful proximity can hardly be overstated. Elmer Davis's *Two Minutes till Midnight* was a 1955 book on the war's approach; in despair over the Soviet perfection of nuclear weapons, Davis, along with many citizens from the U.S. Congress to Main Street, believed that atomic war was around the next corner. Over half the respondents to a University of Michigan Survey Research Center study of U.S. adults in 1952 believed it either "likely" or "very likely" that another world war was on the way. Over half believed that if war did come, it would occur within five years.

This face of the myth left no room for comfort. It explained what was happening -- the ultimate battle between good and evil -- but it didn't help anyone except weapons producers breathe easier. The nuclear myth required modification to placate atomic anxiety, and this modification dawned in the myth of the winnable atomic war, a war that would leave the United States supreme and pretty much intact as it banished the evil forces of communism.

In its Oct. 27, 1951 issue, *Collier's*, a popular magazine with a circulation in the millions, devoted an entire issue to the coming war. In "Preview of the War We Do Not Want: Russia's Defeat & Occupation, 1952–1960," the authors imagined the U.S. a nuclear victor, with Moscow incinerated along with Washington, D.C. No one stateside would miss Moscow, and the loss of Washington, often derided as something resembling a national asylum for the helpless, probably wouldn't wring too many tears from the average American. With artists' lurid full-color impressions of the annihilation of these two great cities, the *Collier's* issue portrayed a limited, winnable nuclear war which, when concluded, would leave the world free to enjoy an apotheosis of American values.

U.S. atomic bomb plants worked twenty-four hours a day. The U.S. and the Soviets built H-bombs, then intercontinental ballistic missiles. John Kennedy based part of his campaign for the Presidency on a wholly bogus "missile gap" alleging that the U.S. was seriously behind the Soviet Union on this front. In the early 1960s, the U.S. had 200 missiles with nuclear warheads. The Russians had about 70.

Around the time of the missile gap that wasn't, some Americans bought into another myth vigorously promoted by the Kennedy administration, and later resurrected by the Reagan administration, the myth that if they took a few simple precautions they could survive nuclear war. Fallout shelters were big news; the FHA offered loans of up to $2,500 for the construction of home shelters. IBM offered interest-free loans to its employees for home shelter construction. My father ordered a set of plans from the government; he let them gather dust on the coffee table for a few months, then tossed them out. In the end he was too sensible a man to tear up the back yard because the civil defense officials assured him it was a good idea.

Through all of this nuclear to-do evolved the myth of nuclear deterrence, which contends that if we have a lot of bombs we're safe, and if we have a lot more bombs, we're safer yet, because the enemy will be afraid to use theirs on us. The myth that the Bomb makes us safe through deterrence is one of the central myths of the nuclear age, cherished now by generations of nuclear strategists, most of whom have never worn a military uniform nor been the target of hostile fire, and who have built countless academic careers by elaborating endlessly and arcanely on the fundamentally simple nature of deterrence.

Back to the Future

History has a way of doubling back on itself. American nuclear mythology took a major reverse step a few years ago when the idea of the winnable "limited" nuclear war came back into favor. The notion really took off with the advent of the Reagan administration, but it was well established by 1979 when Jimmy Carter issued Presidential Directive 59, outlining a revision of

U.S. nuclear targeting strategy designed to facilitate nuclear warfighting rather than war avoidance. At about the same time, some interesting strategists such as Colin Gray and Keith Payne were producing articles like "Victory Is Possible," which appeared in the journal *Foreign Policy* in 1980. In their piece, Gray and Payne wrote that "the United States must possess the ability to wage nuclear war rationally."

Although generally unknown to the public, this notion has been embraced by the U.S. military and political community. In the nuclear war plan known as SIOP (Single Integrated Operational Plan), the U.S. created a systematic scheme for waging nuclear war involving all branches of the service simultaneously. It was a "rational" plan by rational men who believed that victory was possible, and who ignored not only the very likely prospect of any nuclear war escalating beyond control, but the long-term environmental consequences of such a war as well. When Gray and Payne wrote about nuclear victory, the nuclear winter theory had not yet been devised, but there was no shortage of studies on the environmental implications of nuclear war. Gray and Payne disregarded them.

Where the idea of a survivable, even winnable, nuclear war might have made some marginal sense in the early 1950s, today it makes none. Before recent arsenal cuts, the U.S. and the U.S.S.R. possessed some 60,000 nuclear warheads. If even a modest portion of this arsenal, or the one that remains, were let fly, the belief that either survival or victory would be possible strains credibility.

American nuclear mythology has consisted of a series of half-baked rationalizations, strategic misconceptions, and wishful thinking. When one vision, one myth, has failed, another has supplanted it, only to be tossed out in turn in the continuing scramble for something that makes sense within the traditional context of nationalism, militarism, and anti-communism. The posture historically assumed by U.S. nuclear strategists would, if subjected to intense public scrutiny, leave most Americans in dismay and high anxiety. Most Americans do not know about the Single Integrated Operational Plan. Most do not know about their government's preparations for "limited" and protracted nuclear warfighting. Most believe in the myth that the U.S. would not initiate a nuclear war that would inevitably bring devastation to the U.S., when in fact American leaders are on record as indicating otherwise.

That close to 50 percent of those responding to a Gallup poll taken in late January of 1991 favored using nuclear weapons on Iraq suggests that the efforts of the U.S. government to keep the public in the dark about the reality of nuclear weapons and their effects have been successful. In 1953, President Eisenhower instructed the Atomic Energy Commission to keep the public "confused" about weapons testing to facilitate an unimpeded testing program. The public was confused then, and is confused now.

What can dispel the vapors of a fraudulent nuclear mythology? Remembering that the "global village" posited by McLuhan is the one that we all live in might be advantageous.

To return to Adam and Eve, it might be useful to bear in mind an episode from Rod Serling's old "Twilight Zone" series. In 1961, the "Twilight Zone" featured an episode called "Two," starring Elizabeth Montgomery, later of "Bewitched" fame, and Charles Bronson, later of *Death Wish* fame. Any boy who painted his walls A-Bomb Red in 1960 was bound to watch the "Twilight Zone," and I did. In "Two," Bronson and Montgomery portray survivors of a final war between the U.S. and the Soviet Union. Montgomery is a member of the invading Soviet forces, Bronson an American soldier. The two are thrown together; this American Adam and this Russian Eve, struggling to live in a post-nuclear Eden, must overcome their conditioned enmity to enhance the prospects for their mutual survival. The lesson was clear, and remains so. It is the same lesson Albert Einstein tried to deliver in his advocacy of world government after the destruction of Hiroshima and Nagasaki.

Will the citizens of the world recognize the terrible gamble that nuclear deterrence constitutes, a gamble that, if lost even once, means the end of the game? Will they accept the truth pointed out by former nuclear weapons researcher Herbert York, among many other authorities, that the best nuclear deterrence buys is a measure of time to devise a more stable, less potentially lethal basis for relations among nuclear weapon states? Or will wishful thinking and the acceptance of the latest strain of nuclear mythology serve as a substitute for critical thinking, as it has served so impotently since August 6, 1945?

One trembles at the choice, and dreams along with Bob Dylan's narrator in "Talking World War III Blues" of a devastated land where "everybody sees himself walking around with no one else."

So What Does a Librarian Do About It?

The first action a librarian takes is to make sure that when library users come looking for information and opinion on an important topic, they can easily find it. When I began buying books for the University of Michigan-Flint Library in areas concerned with nuclear war and related topics, I proceeded with some uncertainty. There could be no question of the importance of the issues, but would the books find their way into students' hands? In a research library it is the norm for a given book to sit on the shelf, little or rarely used. In a relatively small library primarily devoted to serving undergraduates, there can be few spots on the shelves dedicated to the luxury of deadweight, and few justifications for spending a meaningful portion of a limited acquisitions budget to acquire that weight.

My fears were, I am happy to report, groundless. These books have been used, often heavily used. The UM-Flint reference librarians receive rather few questions about nuclear war, but a demand for information and opinion on the topic clearly exists among our users. Unvoiced demand is no doubt a common phenomenon among library users, whether the subject involves nuclear winter or surfing; librarians cannot assume that because the questions on the topic aren't coming thick and fast at the reference desk, the public is either happy with the parsimonious materials at hand or is simply indifferent and uninterested. Aside from the occasional display of book jackets and the preparation of bibliographies for the library's "free literature" table, the library staff has made no unusual effort to promote the use of these items; the demand is strong enough that users seek them out on their own.

Will this be the experience in all libraries? Probably not. I suspect, however, that it will be a very common one. Like many other topics, nuclear war may be one that library users would prefer not to discuss with the staff, even if they are keenly interested in it. There is, after all, something more than a little embarrassing about belonging to a race of creatures that not only defiles its own nest with pollution of every sort, but could willfully obliterate it altogether.

I am pleased, by the way, to note that the American Library Association Council has adopted resolutions addressing nuclear and related issues. Item 50.11 in the *ALA Policy Manual* urges libraries to make information on disarmament and conflict resolution readily accessible, and 50.12 advocates that libraries "establish balanced up-to-date collections . . . on national security in the nuclear age, on nuclear arms, and the movements for disarmament and a nuclear moratorium." It is good to know that one's concerns as a citizen of the earth are shared in a professional manner by one's colleagues.

It has been said that a poem is never finished. Neither is a bibliography. Somewhere in eternity a room waits for poets and bibliographers to commiserate over the hopelessly open-ended nature of their work. The chief point, however, is not the bibliographer's vain satisfaction in having achieved utter comprehensiveness or infallible commentary. The point is to bring the books to the reader's attention.

xviii

Only by dwelling on the issues they address can humanity hope to see the light that will lead it through the Nuclear Age in good health.

CHAPTER 1

Reference Works

I. Bibliographies

1-1 *Arms Control, Disarmament, and International Security*. Regina Books, 1988. Biannual.

An unannotated bibliography of over 2,000 items, including books, periodical articles, pamphlets, government documents, dissertations, and other materials. The format is an expanded version of the bibliographical section of the periodical *Arms Control Today* (see item 9-9), and of the topics and themes in Richard D. Burns' *Arms Control and Disarmament: A Bibliography* (ABC-Clio, 1977). In spite of the absence of annotations, a valuable aid to the researcher aiming for in-depth access to the literature. Sponsored by the Center for the Study of Armament and Disarmament at California State University, Los Angeles, and the Arms Control Association of Washington, D.C.

1-2 Atkins, Stephen E. *Arms Control and Disarmament, Defense and Military, International Security, and Peace: An Annotated Guide to Sources, 1980-1987*. ABC-Clio, 1989. 411p.

Atkins, arms control bibliographer for the University of Illinois Library, has compiled a fine guide to the literature. Arranges close to 1,600 items in the four main categories noted in the title, and breaks down the literature in each main area by genre, including annuals and yearbooks, bibliographies, dictionaries, digests, encyclopedias, journals, newsletters, monographs, and other types. Annotations are single paragraphs of almost uniform length (100-120 words); subject, author-title indexes, and a publisher list enhance access. Includes numerous entries for material on nuclear weapons and nuclear war. An impressive effort that will serve researchers at any level. Unfortunately, the book's painfully high price ($75) will deter not only most individuals but many libraries from acquiring it.

1-3 Burns, Grant. *The Atomic Papers: A Citizen's Guide to Selected Books and Articles on the Bomb, the Arms Race, Nuclear Power, the Peace Movement, and Related Issues.* Scarecrow Pr., 1984. 309p.

This bibliographer's first attempt to wrestle with the nuclear issue in a substantial way. Arranged by subject in eighteen categories, it manages in its 1,130 entries to identify and briefly comment on most of the important English-language books on nuclear matters, 1945-1983. Its virtues include its status as one of the first book-length bibliographic treatments of the topic and its handy division by subject, and its brief guide to nuclear fiction. Subject and author indexes.

1-4 Canadian Institute for International Peace and Security. *Canada and International Peace and Security: A Bibliography: Covering Materials from January 1985 through December 1989.* The Institute, 1990. 434p.

Cites over 10,000 items, including theses, government documents, and other elusive material. The chronological period is, obviously, rather tight, and the emphasis is understandably on Canadian materials. A must for Canadian libraries supporting research in peace and security issues, desirable for other libraries.

1-5 Carroll, Berenice A.; Fink, Clinton F.; Mohraz, Jane E. *Peace and War: A Guide to Bibliographies.* ABC-Clio, 1983. 580p.

The authors of this guide clearly labored at length to unearth the almost 1,400 bibliographies in both English and other languages annotated here. The focus is on the U.S. and Western Europe, the bulk of the citations to items published in the twentieth century. Within the great range of materials, which includes books, articles, parts of books, and other sources, the authors note approximately 100 bibliographies concerned in whole or in part with nuclear weapons and nuclear war. Many other entries focus on arms control and disarmament. Author and subject indexes.

1–6 Champion, Brian. *Advanced Weapons Systems: An Annotated Bibliography of the Cruise Missile, MX Missile, Laser and Space Weapons, and Stealth Technology.* Garland, 1985. 206p.

Champion, an Alberta, Canada, librarian, turned to some three dozen periodicals in which he found close to 650 articles on the weapons he notes in his title. His annotations are succinct and informative. Most citations are to material from the late 1970s and early 1980s, but some reach back into the 1950s. Both scholarly and popular periodicals are represented. Will be useful to those tracing the history of these weapons.

1–7 Cot, Jean-Pierre, et al. *Repertory of Disarmament Research.* United Nations Institute for Disarmament Research, 1982. 449p.

Among its almost 6,500 entries, this directory contains over 2,000 unannotated citations to books and articles and other materials on nuclear war, weapons and disarmament published 1970–1980. Arrangement is by publication year and topic. The focus is international, with numerous references to non-English language material; coverage is thorough. The last section of the book provides a listing of national and international research institutes. Chiefly of value to in-depth studies of the period. Name index.

1-8 Duguid, Terry, et al. *Defense and Arms Control.* CSP Publications, 1986. 266p.

A compilation of references to resources on the relationship between scientific and technological development and international peace and security. Although the emphasis is on Canadian sources, much of the material is available in the U.S. Lists publications (books and periodicals), teaching aids (films, curriculum materials), organizations, and individual Canadian researchers and educators. Includes many references specifically pertinent to nuclear concerns. Entries for organizations and films are annotated.

1-9 Eiss, Harry. *Literature for Young People on War and Peace: An Annotated Bibliography.* Greenwood, 1989. 131p.

In addition to his coverage of other war and peace literature, Eiss lists and describes approximately three dozen books on nuclear war that he deems appropriate for children. The books selected include both fiction and non-fiction. Also contains entries for a number of books regarding nuclear war that Eiss selected for their merits as instructional aids for teachers and other adults.

1-10 Gay, William and Pearson, Michael. *The Nuclear Arms Race.* American Library Association, 1987. 289p.

Gay, a philosopher, and Pearson, a sociologist, address much more than this book's title implies. Indeed, the title is wholly inadequate to indicate their scope, which includes the evolution of nuclear weapons, nuclear policies, probability and consequences of nuclear war, debate over strategic theories, and other issues. They characterize their discussions of these topics as a primer, in two respects: they intend to inform the reader on the basics, and to prepare him or her for further research or other action.

The presentation of the basics is more than adequate, and each individual topic's treatment is buttressed by an extensive, partially annotated bibliography of books, articles, and government documents. An appendix provides an annotated guide to indexes, abstracts, bibliographies, and other reference works, an annotated list of scholarly journals and other periodic sources. A first-rate point of departure for students of nuclear issues. Glossary, indexes.

1-11 Green, William C. *Soviet Nuclear Weapons Policy: A Research and Bibliographic Guide.* Westview, 1987. 399p.

Assesses both Western and Soviet literature on nuclear weapons policy; substantially annotates over 600 periodical articles and books published since the late 1940s, although most have appeared since 1970. Set up in three main sections: an analytical essay, "The Interpretation of Soviet Nuclear Weapons Policy," the bibliographic guide, and a guide to the primary Soviet source material. Intended chiefly for Sovietologists and strategic analysts, but any researcher investigating the topic would find this volume useful. Indexes.

1-12 Hoover, Robert A. *The MX Controversy: A Guide to Issues & References.* Regina Books, 1982. 116p.

In the book's first half, Hoover capably summarizes the MX history up to 1981; in the second portion he includes 360 unannotated citations to scholarly books and articles on or related to the MX published from the middle '70s to 1981. He groups the citations into such categories as "Limited Nuclear War," "MX and SALT," "MX Basing Alternatives," etc. A good tool for easy identification of early literature on the MX and its attendant controversies. Index.

1-13 Larson, David L. *The "Cuban Crisis" of 1962: Selected Documents, Chronology, and Bibliography.* 2d ed. Univ. Press of America, 1986. 461p.

Larson, a political scientist, points out in his brief preface to this edition of a work first published in 1963 that the significance of Cuba as a player between the superpowers has not ended. The main portion of the book contains 101 documents (eight additional ones compared to the first edition, including six previously classified letters between John F. Kennedy and Khrushchev) related to the 1962 crisis. They feature statements by government officials (U.S., Soviet, Cuban, and others), letters, and speeches. Among the several appendices is a concise review of the crisis. A long chronology, running from 1686 to 1985, helps place the crisis in deep historical context, and a selected bibliography, expanded since the first edition, leads to many additional works. A welcome tool for any student or scholar.

1–14 Lawrence, Robert M. *Strategic Defense Initiative: Bibliography and Research Guide.* Westview, 1987. 352p.

A most useful guide to SDI issues as they stood at the time of this book's publication. The author sets forth both the case for and the case against SDI in meaty narrative sections, and provides abstracts of over 80 important books, articles, and government documents, as well as citations to approximately 900 other publications, ranging from news magazines to scientific journals. Appendices contain the texts of documents and treaties related to SDI and an SDI glossary.

1–15 Markarian, Edward. *Psychosocial Aspects of the Threat and Prevention of Nuclear War: An Annotated Bibliography.* California State University, Los Angeles, Center for the Study of Armament and Disarmament, 1988. 69p.

A nice little annotated bibliography of 279 books, articles, and essays grouped into such categories as "Behavior, Psychology, and Nuclear War," "Perceptions of Nuclear War," and "Eduction and Nuclear War." Publication dates range from the 1940s into the 1980s; journals cited include both those in the fields of psychology and in other disciplines. Author index.

1-16 Musto, Ronald G. *The Peace Tradition in the Catholic Church: An Annotated Bibliography.* Garland, 1987. 590p.

Follows the author's *The Catholic Peace Tradition* (Orbis, 1986) with a nearly-1500 item record of the literature on that tradition. The citations include books and periodical articles in both English and foreign languages. The subject scope is comprehensive, embracing just war theory, the role of international law, mystical and contemplative aspects of Catholicism, and many other issues. Items cited are primarily from the twentieth century; annotations range from a sentence or two to several paragraphs. There is a fair quantity of material covered dealing with nuclear concerns, and the diligent user will be rewarded. The absence of a subject index somewhat limits the volume's effectiveness.

1-17 Newman, John and Unsworth, Michael. *Future War Novels: An Annotated Bibliography of Works in English Published Since 1946.* Oryx, 1984. 101p.

Although not nearly as comprehensive in its treatment of nuclear war fiction as some items listed under "Literary Studies" in Chapter 2, this book remains useful. The authors list and annotate close to 200 novels ranging from pulp fiction to serious literature; a large number of the entries concern nuclear war. The annotations are long enough to permit adequate plot sketches and some critical commentary. The chronological arrangement, by decades, has some advantages. Indexes.

1-18 Norton, Augustus R. *NATO, a Bibliography and Resource Guide.* Garland, 1985. 252p.

One section of this bibliography focuses on approximately 200 unannotated citations to books and articles on "Nuclear Tactics, Strategy and Doctrine" for the alliance as a whole; another on "National Nuclear Strike Forces" with 70 entries. It also includes sections on SALT and on "General Disarmament and Force Reductions." References are to English-language primary and secondary sources; in all, approximately 4,000 citations cover the whole of NATO concerns in a country-by-country, period-by-period format. Author index.

1–19 *Nuclear America, a Historical Bibliography.* ABC-Clio, 1984. 184p.

Beginning with "The Road to Hiroshima" and concluding with "Nuclear Reactors and Public Reaction," *Nuclear America* presents abstracts of over 800 articles drawn from ABC-Clio's Information Services' data base. All entries concern the U.S. directly. The chronological coverage includes material published 1973–1982. Abstracts range from a dozen or so to about 120 words. Between the above-mentioned chapters one finds those also devoted to the development of nuclear weapons, the strategic balance, and arms control. The range of periodicals cited is extensive, and includes some foreign journals. Good subject index.

1–20 *Nuclear Warfare: Science & Medical Subject Analysis with Reference Bibliography.* Abbe Publishers, 1987. 159p.

An oddly-executed unannotated bibliography on medical and related literature on nuclear war issues. The 331 citations are accessed by a "Subject and Research Categories" index which precedes them. Time range of the citations seems to be 1980–85. In libraries without access to *Medline* or *Index Medicus*, this book would possess some utility—though, one suspects, of a marginal sort.

1-21 Pacific Information Centre for the South Pacific Regional Environmental Programme. *Nuclear Issues in the South Pacific: A Bibliography.* Pacific Information Centre, Univ. of the South Pacific, 1987. 351p.

Useful for anyone doing in-depth analysis of nuclear questions in the South Pacific, this unannotated bibliography lists over 5,000 books, articles, newspaper articles, audio-visual items, and unpublished works. In the first body of entries, "Monographs and Analytic Entries," it is not altogether clear what the chronological scope is, although the bulk of the 2,389 citations are to items from the 1970s and 1980s. Following an author-title index to this section, one finds most of the remaining citations referring to articles in the *Fiji Times* and the *Fiji Sun*, with coverage beginning in the early 1970s and ending in 1987. Includes directories of individuals and organizations interested in the Pacific's nuclear role.

1-22 Scrivener, David and Sheehan, Michael. *Bibliography of Arms Control Verification.* Gower, 1990. 161p.

In four main sections covering compliance issues, verification, verification in Soviet writings, and general issues, the authors bring together approximately 1,500 unannotated citations to books, reports, government and United Nations documents, dissertations, and articles. At the very least, an author index would have been agreeable, but there is none. Subject access is enabled by division of the broad categories mentioned into narrower subtopics. Periodicals cited range from the *Readers Digest* to *Jane's Defence Weekly* and *Cornell International Law Journal.* The majority of the citations appear to refer to material from the 1980s, but there are references to some items from as far back as the 1950s.

1-23 Smith, Myron J. *The Soviet Air and Strategic Rocket Forces, 1939-1980: A Guide to Sources in*

English. ABC-Clio, 1981. 321p.

Cites but does not annotate over 3,000 books, articles, reports and documents published 1940–1979 on the Soviet air and rocket forces, with a large number of entries devoted to nuclear issues. Periodicals cited represent a broad mix of popular, professional, and scholarly sources, from *Vital Speeches* to *Time*, *Air Force Magazine*, and *Foreign Affairs.* Includes citations to translated Russian materials. Author index.

1–24 Vance, Mary A. *Nuclear Nonproliferation: A Bibliography.* Vance Bibliographies, 1989. 20p.

This pamphlet lists approximately 200 citations to English-language material on nuclear proliferation. The range of items runs from pamphlets of a few pages to multi-volume sets, and includes U.S. government documents, U.S. and foreign periodical articles, books, U.N. documents, and congressional hearings. Publication dates are 1980–1988. Absence of annotations is a hindrance, but the bibliography would still be useful for in-depth research. The emphasis is on scholarly and professional publications.

Dictionaries

1–25 Ali, Sheikh Rustum. *The Peace and Nuclear War Dictionary.* ABC-Clio, 1989. 294p.

Less comprehensive than Semler, et al. (see below), but benefits from some discussion of the historical significance of the terms in question. Covers approximately 300 terms in thorough entries. Good index.

1–26 Colen, Donald J. *The ABCs of Armageddon: The Language of the Nuclear Age.* World Almanac, 1988. 208p.

Informed by the author's dismay and anger over what he considers the misguided, wrongheaded decisions that have placed civilization on the edge of the nuclear precipice. "What we have done in the name of security is appalling," writes the former defense contractor PR man. He defines 250 pieces of nuclear and defense terminology from his insider's perspective. His discussions of the terms are generally supported by references, and Colen's forthright opinions, rather than undercutting his presentation, lend it color and personality. Glossary of acronyms, bibliography, index.

1-27 Elliot, Jeffrey M. and Reginald, Robert. *The Arms Control, Disarmament, and Military Security Dictionary.* ABC-Clio, 1989. 349p.

More an encyclopedia than a dictionary, with entries of several hundred words under 268 terms arranged in nine categories, from general "War and Peace" to "Nuclear Weapons" and "Arms Control and Disarmament." The index leads the reader not only to the main entry for a given term, but to secondary entries where it receives additional discussion. A useful guide to terminology in any educational setting.

1-28 Farrell, James J. *The Nuclear Devil's Dictionary.* Usonia Pr., 1985. 125p.

A capable work of satire whose inspiration is Ambrose Bierce's classic, *The Devil's Dictionary.* The first feature that will draw in readers is the inclusion of almost four dozen editorial cartoons, with the work of seven Pulitzer Prize-winning cartoonists represented. The cartoons draw the reader to the real business, Farrell's accurate and often acerbic definitions of 385 nuclear terms. "Fallout," for example, is "crop dusting for people." "Posterity" consists of "the descendants whose rights to life we abort by our atomic rites of death." Farrell, a history professor, has taught on the role of nuclear weapons in American culture.

1-29 Green, Jonathon. *The A-Z of Nuclear Jargon.* Routledge & Kegan Paul, 1986. 199p.

In his commentary on the 500+ terms defined here, Green is clear about his antinuclear position, but his definitions are also clear and colorful. Entries range from a succinct few lines to a discursive several pages. Includes helpful cross-references and a bibliography.

1-30 Josephson, Harold, et al. *Biographical Dictionary of Modern Peace Leaders.* Greenwood Pr., 1985. 1,133p.

In this volume's 700+ biographical essays, the authors seek "to define the parameters of peace advocacy, present and clarify the wide variety of ideas and approaches that comprise the antiwar effort, and offer information about the many individuals who either contributed to the organized peace effort or who influenced others to question war and organized violence through their writings and personal activity."

The designation "modern" does not prevent the inclusion of many long-deceased peace advocates, some born in the 18th century, many in the 19th. Signed entries are of several hundred words, and contain bibliographies. A listing of biographees by the 41 nationalities represented is a nice touch, and an index facilitates access to many subjects referred to in the essays. Includes a 7-page chronology of the peace movement, 1815-1983.

1-31 May, John. *The Greenpeace Book of the Nuclear Age: The Hidden History, the Human Cost.* Pantheon, 1989. 378p.

A comprehensive and detailed account of civilian and military nuclear accidents since the Bomb's invention. Following a helpful introduction that provides fundamental information on nuclear weapons and reactors, the book marches chronologically through the international range of nuclear glitches, blunders, and catastrophes that have so far occurred, into 1989.

Major incidents, such as the loss of H-bombs over Palomares, Spain in 1966, the sinking of the nuclear attack submarine "Thresher" in 1963, and the fire at the British Windscale nuclear plant in 1957 receive several pages of coverage. Other incidents receive shorter but still informative attention. The bibliography is arranged by subject and date, e.g., "1952-1958 British Nuclear Tests," "1980 September 18/19 Titan II Missile Fire, Arkansas." A well-executed and troubling guide to the history of unintentional nuclear folly. Index.

1-32 Robertson, David. *Guide to Modern Defense and Strategy: A Complete Description of the Terms, Tactics, Organizations and Accords of Today's Defense*. Gale, 1987. 324p.

Published in England as *A Dictionary of Modern Defence and Strategy*, which describes it better than the term "guide." It contains approximately 400 readable entries for often obscure terms. "The main aim of the book," says Robertson in his preface, "is to set out the policy implications and theoretical arguments that lie behind the concepts and physical specifications." His lengthy entries, most a half-page or longer, succeed in this regard. The utility of the book is improved through bold-facing of terms for which entries appear elsewhere in the dictionary. Contains a large number of terms pertinent to nuclear war and weapons.

1-33 Semler, Eric; Benjamin, James; Gross, Adam. *The Language of Nuclear War: An Intelligent Citizen's Dictionary*. Perennial Library, 1987. 325p.

As the authors' preface states, this dictionary "encompasses words describing weapons, strategies, treaties, science, organizations, slang terms, effects, and history. In particular we have emphasized terms that may shape the nuclear debate in coming years."

The work of three Dartmouth College students, the book clearly discusses over 500 terms. The selected bibliography does not, however, lend credence to the authors' claim to have read "most" of the material written on nuclear war. The absence of such influential and widely disparate authors as Bernard Brodie and Colin S. Gray indicates some major gaps in their embrace of the literature. A useful item nevertheless. Bibliography, acronym list.

1-34 Waldman, Harry. *The Dictionary of SDI*. Scholarly Resources, 1988. 182p.

A generally useful, if sometimes confusing, aid for those investigating SDI and related technologies. Waldman, an SDI proponent with a background in ABM systems, may sometimes assume too much about the lay reader's knowledge of obscure acronyms in his definition of some 1,000 terms. The definitions range from a sentence to a page or more. Copiously illustrated by Douglas Holdaway. Includes the text of President Reagan's 1983 "Star Wars" speech, as well as the texts of the ABM Treaty and other U.S.-Soviet agreements. Although there is, as to be expected, some overlapping of terms covered by other dictionaries noted here, Waldman's is worthwhile because of its strong focus on the major development in strategic technology of the 1980s.

Directories and Handbooks

1-35 *American Defense Annual*. Lexington Books, 1986-

Addressed to the lay reader, this annual edited (up through the 1990/91 edition) by Joseph J. Kruzel focuses on policy more than technology, although there is a fair helping of technical information on specific weapons. A good part of the overview is devoted to strategic forces and nuclear strategy. The volume is not an attempt at a neutral compilation of "facts." It is composed of essays on various aspects of American defense by different authorities, each, presumably, with individual points of view that need to be corroborated and corrected by comparison with other sources. The same is true, of course, of any source of information, no matter how diligent the attempt to achieve pure objectivity. The annual includes a briefly-annotated list of recent books on defense.

1-36 Burke, Patrick, ed. *The Nuclear Weapons World: Who, How & Where.* Greenwood, 1988. 383p.

A follow-up to the Oxford Research Group's *How Nuclear Weapons Decisions Are Made* (item 3-72), this directory sheds further light on that murky subject. It covers nuclear decision making in the U.S., the Soviet Union, the United Kingdom, France, China, NATO, and the Warsaw Treaty Organization. The effective format divides each chapter in two, the first half devoted to identifying and describing institutions in which decisions are made, the second half to a biographical guide to over 700 individuals involved in the process. Includes subject and name indexes. Glossary.

1-37 Campbell, Christopher. *Nuclear Facts.* Hamlyn, 1984. 192p.

Pictures, drawings, maps and other illustrative material bring to the eye images of weapons systems that generally are confined to the mind's conjuring. What *does* an MX missile look like? What sort of artillery equipment can launch a tactical nuclear projectile? The guide is strictly a hardware item: the more critical issues of arms control, disarmament, and the consequences of nuclear war not part of these pictures. Glossary, index.

1-38 Cochran, Thomas B., et al., eds. *Nuclear Weapons Databook.* Ballinger, 1983-. Vol. 1: *U.S. Nuclear Forces and Capabilities,* 340 p.; Vol. 2 (1984), *U.S. Nuclear*

Warhead Production, 223 p.; Vol. 3 (1987), *U.S. Nuclear Warhead Facility Profiles*, *132 p.; Vol. 4 (1989), Soviet Nuclear Weapons*, 433p.

Together with his co-editors, most frequently William M. Arkin, who has worked with him on the first four volumes in this series, Thomas Cochran has put together a massive compilation of data on nuclear weapon production, systems, and capabilities. In his foreword to the first volume, Princeton physicist Frank von Hippel called it "the most authoritative and complete reference work available on U.S. forces and capabilities." The ensuing volumes have maintained the standards of rigorous investigation set by the first. Anyone seeking information on warheads, missiles, contractors, aircraft, surface ships and submarines, with specifications, cost, and commentary is well advised to turn to this series. (Further volumes are planned.)

All volumes in the series are noteworthy; the latest, on Soviet forces, may be the most so, given the difficulty of obtaining information. An indication of the thoroughness of approach characterized by the work is the latest volume's table of "Known Soviet Underground Nuclear Explosions, 1961-1987," which not only lists over 400 such explosions, but gives their precise time of occurrence, general location, latitude and longitude, seismic data, and yield in kilotons. Sources are cited throughout the series, which features many illustrations, including photos, charts, maps, etc. Indexes.

1-39 Conetta, Carl, ed. *Peace Resource Book 1988-1989: A Comprehensive Guide to the Issues, Organizations, and Literature*. Ballinger, 1988. 440p.

A comprehensive guide to national and local peace groups; most entries for approximately 300 national groups are briefly annotated. The shorter portion of the guide is devoted to a bibliography, "Guide to Peace-Related Literature," with individual sections on nuclear weapons and nuclear policy, arms control, and other subtopics. The bibliography contains roughly 900 entries for books and articles; most entries have short annotations. The bulk of the citations are to work from the 1980s, but there are references to some earlier items of importance. A nice guide, especially for its voluminous listing, state by state, of thousands of local peace groups. Unfortunately, none of the book's entries are identified by item number, an oversight that makes certain kinds of systematic use difficult. This volume succeeds *Peace Resource Book* (Ballinger, 1986), and the *American Peace Directory 1984* (Ballinger, 1984).

1-40 Day, Alan J., ed. *Peace Movements of the World.* Longman, 1987. 398p.

Identifies and provides information on over 800 national and international peace movements. Most entries include information on organizational aims and objectives, publications, affiliations, membership, etc. A good share of the entries, however, offer only name and address. The bulk of the entries, which seek to cover only groups with a primary interest in peacemaking, refer to Western European, North American, and British groups, but entries also appear for groups in Eastern Europe, the U.S.S.R., Africa, Asia, and other areas. Arrangement is by country. Less comprehensive as a guide to the American peace movement than *Peace Resource Book.*

1-41 Day, Samuel H., ed. *Nuclear Heartland: A Guide to the 1,000 Missile Silos of the United States.* Progressive Foundation, 1988. 95p.

The heart of this book is its third chapter, a state-by-state guided tour of ICBM sites in Wyoming, Nebraska, Colorado, the Dakotas, Montana, and Missouri. Precise instructions will take the traveler to each site. Other parts of the book discuss the ICBM buildup and "the awakening" of the public to the threat represented by these missiles, but it is the detailed directions to the silos themselves that gives the book its unique quality. Suitable as a guide for protestors or for those seeking an offbeat, albeit depressing, vacation itinerary.

1-42 Engstrom, Elmer, et al. *Comprehensive Test Ban Negotiation, 1954 to 1981: Including the History of Limited Test Ban Treaty, Threshold Test Ban Treaty, Peaceful Nuclear Explosions Treaty.* 2d ed. Arms Control Reporter(?), 1988. 69p.

A chronological history of the comprehensive test ban, first suggested in 1954 by Indian Prime Minister Nehru. The straightforward chronology also covers the various treaties referred to in the title. Briefly describes important events. Bibliography.

1-43 Goldblat, Jozef. *Agreements for Arms Control: A Critical Survey.* Taylor & Francis, 1982. 387p.

A comprehensive handbook on arms control, with analysis and assessment of existing agreements and negotiations current at the time of publication. The nearly 80 agreements, many involving nuclear issues, appear in their complete texts, with references to their sources. Goldblat precedes the agreements with several chapters on the history of arms control, discussion of obligations entailed in arms control agreements, and observations on verification. Particularly because of the gathering in one place of many agreements reported in otherwise scattered places, this collection is helpful. Bibliography, index.

1-44 _____. *Arms Control Agreements: A Handbook.* Praeger, 1983. 328p.

A revised and abridged version of the above book. The main business at hand is contained in chapter five, "Arms Control Agreements: The Texts and Parties," in which Goldblat provides texts of and signatories to a large number of agreements, from the Hague Declaration on asphyxiating gases of 1899 to agreements on conventional weapons in 1981. Bibliography.

1-45 Green, Marguerite. *Peace Archives: A Guide to Library Collections of the Papers of American Peace Organizations and of Leaders in the Public Effort for Peace.* World Without War Council, 1986. 66p.

Profiles collections and services of 30 major archival institutions and identifies approximately 80 individual peace collections in the U.S. Includes a short bibliography of search aids.

1-46 Menos, Dennis. *Arms Control Fact Book.* McFarland, 1985. 140p.

Part glossary, part organizational directory, part chronology, and part guide to international participation in arms control treaties and alliances, this little red book contains a good deal of useful information. The glossary covers slightly over 100 terms, but the entries are typically of several hundred words each. The organizational section features similarly informative entries for some fifty organizations active in arms control and disarmament, most of them in the U.S. The ten-page chronology notes "Key Arms Control Events," 1925-1985. Although the book is dated in spots, these three main sections are still handy. Bibliography, index.

1-47 Meyer, Robert S. *Peace Organizations Past and Present: A Survey.* McFarland, 1988. 266p.

Meyer identifies four approaches to peace—historical, personal, instructional, and structural—and distributes his descriptions of close to 100 organizations among these categories. The United Nations and the League of Nations fall into the first group; the Peace Corps and Jewish Peace Fellowship, e.g., in the second; and the World Federalist Association, e.g., in the last. The largest group follows "instructional approaches." Here are entries for the Center for Defense Information,

Council for a Livable World, the U.S. Committee Against Nuclear War, among nearly fifty other groups. Entries are substantial and informative, running one, two, or more pages. The groups identified are, to be sure, a very small portion of the peace organizations that now exist, or have existed. Bibliography, index.

1-48 *The Military Balance.* International Institute for Strategic Studies, 1959-. Dist. in U.S. by Brassey's U.S.

Over half of this annual now attends, quite appropriately, to military forces in the Third World. And, as its coverage of the Third World enlarges, the editors continue to refine the guide's precision to allow a more effective comparison of forces among individual nations. It groups national entries geographically; provides numerical breakdowns on nuclear delivery vehicles, military manpower, budgets, and other data. A more useful document for analysis of Soviet forces, among others, than the Pentagon's annual piece of self-service, *Soviet Military Power.*

1-49 Polner, Murray, ed. *The Disarmament Catalogue.* Pilgrim Pr., 1982. 209p.

A not completely well-organized guide to books, organizations, periodicals, films, and other resources of use to those investigating various aspect of war and disarmament, interspersed with poems, statements from individuals and groups, article reprints, and other material. A lot of useful information here, but the grab-bag format gets in the way of efficient retrieval. Absence of an index doesn't help, either.

1-50 Rogers, Paul. *Directory of Nuclear, Biological and Chemical Arms and Disarmament.* Tri-Service, 1990. 147p.

This directory ably offers succinct yet substantive information on numerous aspects of arms control, from descriptions of a few hundred words each of individual weapons systems, including nuclear, of the U.S., U.S.S.R., and other original "Nuclear Club" members, to outlines of the histories and functions of significant arms agreements such as SALT I and the ABM Treaty. A welcome distillation of a vast quantity of information into a form graspable by the non-specialist. The index allows quick access to data on a wide range of nuclear weapons.

1-51 _____. *Guide to Nuclear Weapons.* Berg, 1988. 123p.

A handy little guide to nuclear weapons and delivery systems. In addition to the older members of the "Nuclear Club," Rogers surveys new and aspiring nuclear powers Israel, South Africa, India, Pakistan, Argentina, Brazil, Iran, Iraq, Libya, and Taiwan. Good index.

1-52 Sayer, Karen and Dowling, John, eds. *1984 National Directory of Audiovisual Resources on Nuclear War and the Arms Race.* Univ. of Michigan Media Resources Center, 1984? 55p.

May be the best available guide to both fiction and nonfiction films on nuclear war issues; it is, at any rate, the best to come to this bibliographer's attention. It identifies and succinctly describes over 400 films, videotapes, slide shows, and filmstrips; it includes documentaries, feature films, animated works, university and television network productions, and out-of-print items. Production dates range from 1946 to 1984. Includes information on distributors, prices, etc., some of which is no doubt dated. Good subject index.

1-53 *SIPRI Yearbook: World Armaments and Disarmament.* Various publishers, 1972-. Annual.

Long one of the major sources of up-to-date information on the world military scene, this guide from the Stockholm International Peace Research Institute addresses weapons and technology, global military expenditures, developments in arms control and the arms trade, and many other issues. Extensive attention goes to nuclear and related topics, from U.S. and Soviet weapon programs to ballistic missile proliferation in the Third World. A wealth of statistics and interpretation by recognized authorities makes each volume in the series the latest that the serious researcher cannot do without. The average volume runs to 600 pages or more, and features plentiful references. Published as *World Armaments and Disarmament: SIPRI Yearbook* until 1987.

1-54 Social and Human Sciences Documentation Centre and the Division of Human Rights and Peace. *World Directory of Peace Research and Training Institutions 1988.* 6th ed. Berg, 1988. 271p.

A valuable guide for the serious scholar of peace and international relations covering more than 650 institutions in country-by-country listings. The typical entry provides address, telephone, founding date, staff size, areas of interest, publications, and a short description of activities. The focus of the institutions is on peace research, not peace activism. Index.

1-55 *Strategic Survey.* International Institute for Strategic Studies, 1967-.

Provides the International Institute's review and assessment of security-related events on an international scale. It opens with an essay outlining perspectives on the year's events, focuses first on the Soviet Union and the U.S., and then moves into a region-by-region discussion of security issues in Europe, Africa, the Middle East, Asia, and other locales. Weapons, arms control, and domestic conflict receive close attention; a fairly detailed chronology, following the same national and regional subdivisions as the main body of the text, completes the volume. The absence of an index is something of an irritant, but the systematic arrangement mitigates that problem to some extent.

1–56 Trzyna, Thaddeus C., ed. *International Peace Directory.* California Institute of Public Affairs, 1984. 63p.

A handy if rather dated directory listing and describing approximately 100 peace organizations from more than two dozen countries. Almost a third of the listings refer to U.S. groups. Entries include notes on purposes and projects, publications, staff, etc. Apparently the good intentions of following this volume with a more comprehensive one have flickered out.

1–57 *The United Nations Disarmament Yearbook.* Department for Disarmament Affairs, United Nations, 1976–. Annual.

In its 14th volume (1989) at this writing, the *Yearbook* reviews the year's developments across the broad range of disarmament, arms control, and related issues. Most of the material focuses on the U.N. role in these processes. Like its predecessors, vol. 14 devotes a large part of its space to nuclear topics, including disarmament, prevention of nuclear war, non-proliferation, nuclear-weapon-free zones, and other subjects. Indispensable as a record of U.N. activity in these areas.

1–58 United States Arms Control and Disarmament Agency. *Documents on Disarmament.* 1960–. Annual.

A chronological arrangement of papers on arms control and disarmament. A massive compilation, the current utility of the volume seriously suffers from its tardy appearance: the latest volume, for 1985, did not come out until May of 1989. It remains useful for historical review, however, for it features hundreds of pertinent documents on issues in disarmament, including the nuclear variety. Speeches, interviews, federal reports, U.N. resolutions, correspondence from heads of state, and many other types of documents are included. Sources range from governmental to television programs and popular magazines, and include numerous foreign statements. The volume concludes with a chronological list of documents, a bibliography of federal publications, a list of persons cited, and an index.

1-59 _____. *Arms Control and Disarmament Agreements.* Transaction Books, 1984. 290p.

Originally published by the U.S. Arms Control and Disarmament Agency in 1982, this guide contains all major arms control agreements since WW II in which the U.S. was a participant, up to the 1981 "Convention on the Physical Protection of Nuclear Material." Includes among many others the "Hot Line" agreement and the Limited Test Ban Treaty (both 1963), the Outer Space Treaty of 1967, and the Prevention of Nuclear War Agreement of 1973. Each treaty text is preceded by a helpful narrative discussion. Notes.

1-60 Walmer, Max. *An Illustrated Guide to Strategic Weapons.* Prentice Hall, 1988. 118p.

Good color photographs and illustrations of, the cover promises, "every major modern nuclear weapon," with detailed data on development and deployment, along with concise information on dimensions, range, weight, throw weight, warhead, guidance, propulsion, and accuracy.

1-61 Williams, Robert C. and Cantelon, Philip L., eds. *The American Atom: A Documentary History of Nuclear Policies from the Discovery of Fission to the Present, 1939-1984.* Univ. of Penn. Pr., 1984. 333p.

Gathers primary documents illustrating the development of American nuclear policies and responses to those policies. The main focus of the 173 documents is on nuclear weapons, with numerous items concerning the Manhattan Project, the hydrogen bomb, deterrence, nuclear testing, and arms control. Included are treaties, White House statements, memoranda, personal letters, and other materials. Many of the "big names" are represented, such as Szilard, Oppenheimer, Groves, Truman, Dulles, and Reagan. A useful and engrossing collection. Index.

1-62 Woodhouse, T., ed. *The International Peace Directory.* Northcote, 1988. 189p.

The main portion of this directory provides information on approximately 600 peace organizations, including address, phone, publications, membership, and objectives. The majority of the organizations are in the West, with 161 in the U.S. Easy to use country-by-country format. Indexes by membership type and issues covered further enhance the book's handiness.

Encyclopedia

1-63 *World Encyclopedia of Peace.* Pergamon Pr., 1986. 4 vol.

A significant contribution to the peace movement and its scholars, this set is the only real, up-to-date encyclopedia devoted to the topic. A suggestion of its stature lies in the designation of Linus Pauling as Honorary Editor-in-Chief and in the "Dedication" by United Nations Secretary-General Javier Perez de Cuellar. The first two volumes contain signed articles, with bibliographies, on a wide range of peace-related topics; the articles are substantial. "Conscientious Objection" runs to five pages, "Nonalignment" consumes seven pages. Numerous articles bear directly on nuclear war and nuclear weapons.

The third volume contains the texts of close to 40 major treaties and a biographical directory of Nobel Peace Prize laureates; the fourth provides an annotated directory of international peace institutes and organizations and an unannotated bibliography of books and journals. Subject and name indexes cover the entire set.

CHAPTER 2

Nuclear Weapons and Nuclear War

I. Overviews and General Histories

2-1 Ackland, Len and McGuire, Steven, eds. *Assessing the Nuclear Age: Selections from the Bulletin of the Atomic Scientists.* Educational Foundation for Nuclear Science; Dist. by Univ. of Chicago Pr., 1986. 382p.

Since 1945, the *Bulletin of the Atomic Scientists* has been one of the major periodical sources for important contributions to the dialogue on nuclear war and peace. The 41 essays here appeared for the most part in the journal's 40th anniversary issue. A dozen others were added from later issues to bring coverage of current topics such as SDI, verification, treaty compliance, and proliferation up to date. Broad divisions group the essays under the topics "Retrospectives," "Atomic Culture," "The Arms Race," "The United States," and "Futures." The anthology would make an excellent source of readings for a college class; many of the essays would be useful at the secondary school level. Bibliography, index.

2-2 Allison, Graham T., et al., eds. *A Primer for the Nuclear Age.* Univ. Pr. of America, 1990. 142p.

Contains fourteen short essays by a variety of scholars "designed to provide a broad overview in a short period of time." Given the short attention span of humanity at large, this may be the best way to help focus any reader's thinking on such issues as nuclear weapons' historical development, nuclear doctrine, domestic influences on nuclear weapons policy, proliferation, and terrorism. The book would make a good text to inspire further reading and discussion at the early undergraduate or high school levels.

2–3 Beukel, Erik. *American Perceptions of the Soviet Union as a Nuclear Adversary: From Kennedy to Bush.* Pinter, 1989. 408p.

A thorough analysis of the title topic, with a methodical discussion of interests, deterrence, the political significance of nuclear forces, negotiations, and the Soviet view from 1961 to 1989. Beukel hopes to show how the nuclear issue has been related to and how it has manifested itself in different political relations and issues. His closing remarks suggest that both American and Soviet approaches to nuclear topics are closely tied to deeply-held historical and ideological attitudes. This link mitigates against either an overly-cheerful and optimistic reaction to positive nuclear developments as signs of an enduring trend, or an overly-gloomy estimation of the long-term outlook when U.S.-Soviet relations are antagonistic. The book will be slow going for most readers. Bibliography, index.

2–4 Blumberg, Stanley A. and Panos, Louis G. *Edward Teller: Giant of the Golden Age of Physics.* Scribner's, 1990. 306p.

Of all the atomic scientists responsible for the Bomb and its effects, probably no one is easier to dislike than Teller. This enthusiast of nuclear weapons ("Father of the H-bomb"), consistent SDI booster and wielder of obscene metaphors ("It's a boy!" he once exulted upon a successful H-bomb test) undeniably remains a major figure in things nuclear. This biography falls a little short of hagiography, but not by much. The concluding remarks about the octogenarian Teller "pressing his weakened body" into the breach of current events "because I have no choice" catches the authors' reverent tone fairly well. The book's strengths are its readability and its basis in interviews with Teller and many of his peers, and access to Teller's papers. Notes, bibliography, index.

2-5 Bottome, Edgar M. *The Balance of Terror: Nuclear Weapons and the Illusion of Security, 1945-1985.* Revised ed. Beacon Pr., 1986. 291p.

Updates *The Balance of Terror: A Guide to the Arms Race* (Beacon, 1971). Along with minor changes in the original text, contains two new chapters, one on "Turbulence in American Foreign Policy" in the 1970s, the other on "Ronald Reagan: Myth and Reality in the Nuclear Age." The original portion of the book focuses on the early years of the arms race, the massive retaliation and collective security policies of the Eisenhower administration, a study in the "myth creation" of the so-called "missile gap" (1957-61), the Kennedy administration policies of flexible response and second-strike counterforce, and the Johnson-Nixon period up to 1970.

Bottome describes the two superpowers as "imperial systems in decline"; he calls on Americans to understand and reject the imperial goals of U.S. foreign policy as a prerequisite to reversal of the arms race. "It is time for a change," he writes, "for an end to U.S. reliance on nuclear weapons and on intervention in the affairs of other countries to conduct its foreign policy." Glossary, notes, index.

2-6 Boyer, Paul S. *By the Bomb's Early Light: American Thought and Culture at the Dawn of the Atomic Age.* Pantheon, 1985. 440p.

Boyer, a professor of history at the University of Wisconsin, offers an engrossing account focusing on the Bomb's enfolding in popular American culture, 1945-1950, from the movement for world government to the sudden high-profile status of the atomic scientists to the Bomb's manifestations in literature, advertising, psychology, and other areas of national life. "All the major elements of our contemporary engagement with nuclear reality took shape literally within days of Hiroshima," he claims. The book is his attempt to return to the beginning, for "unless we recover this lost segment of our cultural history, we cannot fully understand the world in which we live, nor be as well equipped as we might to change it." Boyer did the bulk of his research in books, newspapers, and other print materials of the period covered. Among the book's bonuses are some wonderful, outlandish and appalling illustrations—photographs, cartoons, etc.— revealing popular Bomb consciousness of the late 1940s. Don't miss the mushroom cloud cake celebrating completion of the 1946 atomic tests at Bikini. Bibliography.

2-7 Bundy, McGeorge. *Danger and Survival: Choices about the Bomb in the First Fifty Years.* Random House, 1988. 735p.

Bundy, a security adviser to President Kennedy during the Cuban Missile Crisis, presents an informed assessment of the Bomb's career and influence. He reviews such issues as the failed international control of nuclear weapons, the attitudes toward their existence held by both U.S. and Soviet leaders, and the evolving nature of nuclear deterrence. Of special interest are his discussions of the Cuban Crisis and our current relationship with the Bomb. Bundy argues that the flirtation with nuclear war over the Cuban missile sites set the tone for superpower relations down to the present day.

Bundy focuses on the superpowers, for it is they who hold the cards to "danger and survival on a planetary scale." They have come this far without destroying each other or the rest of the world, and, although the danger remains mortal, we understand it better today than ever. "Our survival in the first fifty years of danger," writes Bundy, "offers encouragement to renewed pursuit of truth, resolute practice of courage, and persistence in lively hope."

2–8 Clarfield, Gerard H. and Wiecek, William M. *Nuclear America: Military and Civilian Nuclear Power in the United States, 1940–1980.* Harper & Row, 1984. 518p.

An accessible and capable history taking into its scope the development of the Bomb, its use on Japan, nuclear power in the Cold War, the "Atoms for Peace" program, the controversy over atomic fallout in the 1950s, the arms race, and other issues. The authors' personal opinion of the effort to control nuclear power is clear: "We are tormented by visions of the end of human life," they write, "a universal dance of death that will make the epidemiological catastrophes of the Middle Ages seem like the sniffles by comparison. This is the price we pay for demanding to ride the chariot of the sun." Their stance reverses that adopted by some writers, such as Colin S. Gray, who use the medieval plague to prop up arguments that nuclear war would not be all that much more unpleasant than previous human disasters. Notes, index, interesting annotated bibliography.

2–9 Cohen, Avner and Lee, Steven. *Nuclear Weapons and the Future of Humanity: The Fundamental Questions.* Rowman & Allanheld, 1986. 496p.

An attempt to provide a collection of essays discussing "fundamental questions" about nuclear weapons. These questions involve culture, rationality, human nature, morality, and political and social philosophy. The editors call for basic changes in the nuclear-thinking process that takes into consideration these phenomena; comfortable adherence to nuclear deterrence as matter of expedient habit isn't sufficient. The majority of the 27 contributors are philosophers; most of the others are political scientists. They strive to address the editors' call for a deep rethinking of nuclear issues. A massive book with tiny print that will not often appeal to any but advanced students, although that is unfortunate, for there is much here in the way of careful, considered thinking that could reward the less-than-expert reader. Notes, index.

2-10 Dennis, Jack, ed. *The Nuclear Almanac: Confronting the Atom in War and Peace.* Addison-Wesley, 1984. 546p.

Contains over two dozen scholarly essays prepared by members of the MIT Faculty Coalition for Disarmament, providing an overview of nuclear issues, including the Bomb's development, effects, proliferation, nuclear weapons technology, physics background, etc. Among the contributors: Herbert York, Kosta Tsipis, Bernard T. Feld, Paul C. Warnke, and many others. A manageable one-volume guide to the issues. Many illustrations and charts. Index.

2-11 Drell, Sidney D. *Facing the Threat of Nuclear Weapons.* Univ. of Washington Pr., 1989. 120p.

Three lectures aimed at helping develop a better understanding of nuclear weapons policy. "Challenge to Survival" discusses the effects of nuclear war, moral issues, deterrence, the MX, and an insistence on the need for U.S. public demand for effective arms control. "The Imperative of Arms Control" dwells on verification, testing, and nuclear disengagement (ending reliance on nuclear weapons), while "The Scientist's Dilemma" discusses questions raised by considering the careers of Joel Oppenheimer and Andrei Sakharov. The book includes the famous "open letter" to Drell from Sakharov, "The Danger of Thermonuclear War," which appeared in the summer, 1983 issue of *Foreign Affairs.* The clarity of Drell's thought and prose make this book a compelling one. Notes.

2-12 Ehrlich, Robert. *Waging Nuclear Peace: The Technology and Politics of Nuclear Weapons.* State Univ. of New York Pr., 1985. 397p.

An overview of nuclear war issues such as weapons

effects, the arms race and arms control, nuclear winter, civil defense, proliferation, and others. Ehrlich, a physicist, has intended this work as a textbook; with "Study Questions" following each chapter. He tries to help readers see facts objectively and unemotionally, and succeeds to a considerable degree in this objective. Notes, index.

2-13 Feldbaum, Carl B. and Bee, Ronald J. *Looking the Tiger in the Eye: Confronting the Nuclear Threat.* Harper & Row, 1988. 315p.

A good history of nuclear weapons and related issues for younger readers, perhaps from ages 12-16, depending on their reading skills. The authors have done a nice job of weaving quotations from important figures--politicians, scientists, military leaders--in nuclear history into their account. They cover the race for the first A-bomb, the arms race between the U.S. and the Soviet Union, the Cuban Missile Crisis, arms control, and other nuclear subtopics. The message of the book is in its title, whose opening phrase comes from a 1953 statement by J. Robert Oppenheimer: "I believe that until we have looked this tiger in the eye, we shall be in the worst of all possible dangers, which is that we may back into him." Many good photos, good bibliography of suggested readings. Notes, index.

2-14 Freedman, Lawrence. *The Price of Peace: Living with the Nuclear Dilemma.* Firethorn Pr., 1986. 288p.

Freedman, who has written extensively on nuclear issues, gathers here eleven of his essays and lectures on the topic, focusing on such questions as the "myth" of flexible response, European nuclear force negotiations, SDI (whose good sense he questions), and disarmament and the future of Europe. Readable, though of an academic tone. Notes, index.

2-15 _____. *U.S. Intelligence and the Soviet*

Strategic Threat. 2d ed. Princeton Univ. Pr., 1986.
25p.

The first edition (Westview, 1977) of this work and the
second are essentially identical except for the new
foreword. Freedman examines in detail the ways U.S.
intelligence has estimated the threat, or lack of same,
posed by Soviet forces. His discussion proceeds from
the early years of the Cold War, through the ABM
debates of the 1960s, the SALT talks, and new
weapons technologies of the 1970s.

Freedman contends that calculations of the "Soviet
threat" have depended "not only on estimates of what
the Soviet Union is attempting to do, but also on a
sense of the vulnerabilities in the U.S. military
position." The prevailing strategic doctrine in the
U.S., and attitudes toward defense budgets and arms
control, are as important as the Soviet force structure
itself. A revised version of the author's doctoral
thesis. Notes, bibliography, index.

2-16 Graham, Thomas W. *American Public Opinion on
NATO, Extended Deterrence, and Use of Nuclear
Weapons: Future Fission?* Univ. Pr. of America, 1989.
148p.

Graham, of the Center for Science and International
Affairs at Harvard University, analyzes the data
contained in public opinion polling on the Bomb and
related matters since the end of WW II, and briefly
discusses implications for federal policy on such
topics as a declared No First Use statement and
appropriate response in the event of a Soviet attack
on Europe. The most interesting part of the book, and
its largest part by far, is the compilation of poll
questions and responses draw from the Gallup
organization, Louis Harris & Associates, the Roper
Organization, and many other opinion pollsters. The
questions and answers appear in reverse chronological
order, 1987-1945. An enlightening look at the history
of public opinion on the Bomb. Notes.

2-17 Hamilton, Michael S., et al. *Nuclear Weapons in the University Classroom: An Interdisciplinary Teaching Reference.* Univ. Pr. of America, 1990. 151p.

The authors, all university faculty members, discuss questions about pedagogy in courses concerning nuclear weapons, review existing (sparse) literature on teaching the topic, and point out the advantages of a political science and sociological approach to nuclear weapons teaching. The longest portion of the book is an unannotated bibliography of 800 readings and films compiled from 75 American college and university syllabi for courses on nuclear arms. The bibliography's divisions group entries into such categories as "General Texts," "Nature of the Threat," and "Strategic Doctrine." A book of some use, especially in identifying important recent periodical literature.

2-18 Hansen, Chuck. *US Nuclear Weapons: The Secret History.* Aerofax (Dist. by Orion Books), 1988. 232p.

Referring to the U.S. detonation of over 850 nuclear bombs by mid-1987 as an "orgy of nuclear self-indulgence hidden from public view," Hansen sets out to bring details of the orgy into the public eye. He does this with hundreds of photographs, tables, charts and other material illustrating the history of American nuclear weapons. In chief support of his research were U.S. government documents, many obtained through Freedom of Information Act requests. A contributor to the *Nuclear Weapons Databook* series (see item 1-39), Hansen also drew heavily from this series and from declassified documents provided by the Defense Nuclear Agency's Nuclear Test Personnel Review program. A good aid to detailed investigation of the U.S. nuclear arsenal and its history. Notes, index.

2-19 Hewlett, Richard G. and Holl, Jack M. *Atoms for Peace and War, 1953-1961: Eisenhower and the Atomic Energy Commission.* Univ. of California Pr., 1989. 696p.

This third volume in the official history of the A.E.C. follows Hewlett's and Oscar E. Anderson's *The New World, 1939–1946* (Penn State, 1962), and Hewlett's and Francis Duncan's *Atomic Shield, 1947–1952* (Penn State, 1969). Although much of this story has already been told in a variety of places, some of it, thanks to the authors' access to previously classified material, has not. Most academic and large public libraries should have all volumes in the series. As an official history, however, the treatment is less than suitably energetic in addressing some troubling aspects of A.E.C. endeavors, such as oversight of U.S. nuclear weapons facilities' health and safety issues. Additionally, these official studies have been attacked for their authors' use of documents deliberately withheld from public dissemination to facilitate preparation of a history based on these "classified" materials. Notes, index. Includes an essay on sources by Roger M. Anders.

2–20 Holroyd, Fred, ed. *Thinking About Nuclear Weapons: Analyses and Prescriptions.* Auburn House, 1985. 409p.

Prepared for a course on nuclear weapons at the Open University, and would still be a useful supplementary textbook for a college course. The range of viewpoints is broad, from unilateral disarmament advocates to SDI and "limited" nuclear war enthusiasts, and the selections are well chosen. Contributions include excerpts from books and reprinted articles. Interesting in light of current nuclear ambitions in the Third World is the essay by Thomas F. Dorian and Leonard S. Spector, "Covert Nuclear Trade and the International Nonproliferation Regime." Acronym glossary, index.

2–21 Kegley, Charles W., Jr. and Wittkopf, Eugene R., eds. *The Nuclear Reader: Strategy, Weapons, War.* St. Martin's, 1985. 332p.

An anthology of nuclear writings "designed to expose the range of opinion and prescription regarding these urgent matters." Focuses primarily on the competition between the U.S. and the Soviet Union. The selections have been culled from books and periodicals, and effectively introduce the reader to many nuclear issues, including deterrent strategy, ballistic missile defense, and the effects of nuclear war. The editors drew on the work of many "name" writers, such as Theodore Draper, Albert Wohlstetter, Freeman Dyson, Desmond Ball and Keith Payne, among numerous others. Although additional reading would be required in some areas (SDI, for example), the book could still serve as a useful text for an undergraduate class. Notes, index.

2-22 McKay, Alwyn. *The Making of the Atomic Age.* Oxford Univ. Pr., 1984. 153p.

McKay, a chemist and nuclear power advocate, furnishes a brief, readable history of the nuclear era, including the earliest steps into radioactivity, the Manhattan Project and its counterparts, for what they amounted to, in Germany and Japan. Bibliography, index.

2-23 Morris, Charles R. *Iron Destinies, Lost Opportunities: The Arms Race between the U.S.A. and the U.S.S.R., 1945-1987.* Harper & Row, 1988. 544p.

Arguing that "not even the most enthusiastic advocate of nuclear deterrence would argue that 10 billion tons of TNT equivalent explosive power is the essential minimum for deterrence," Morris proposes to answer the question, "How did we get here?" That is, why have we saddled ourselves with that incredible load of explosives? A good study of the history of arms uncontrolled, from the beginning of the Nuclear Age to SDI. Morris's attention to both political and technical aspects of the arms race is exhaustive, and sometimes fatiguing. Whether he answers the question he set out is uncertain, but his history of the march of nuclear pathology is comprehensively drawn. Bibliography, index.

2-24 Newhouse, John. *War and Peace in the Nuclear Age.* Knopf, 1989. 486p.

As Newhouse writes in his "Acknowledgments," "This book covers a lot of ground--from the stirrings of the 'new physics' early in the century to events of June, 1988, notably the last meeting between Ronald Reagan and Mikhail Gorbachev." The broad subject and historical scope of the book sometimes leaves the issues of nuclear war and weapons in the wings, but as the title implies, their shadows fall on the stage even when the immediate topic is something else. Newhouse is only guardedly hopeful, and not particularly optimistic, about the prospects for the nuclear future: "The superpowers could and should have reordered their priority concerns years ago. Yet even now, as the need for a different and more realistic view of national security is widely perceived and accepted, the nuclear age continues, as it began, in a bog of official and bureaucratic discord." Notes, bibliography, index.

2-25 Nunn, Jack H. *The Soviet First Strike Threat: The U.S. Perspective.* Praeger, 1982. 292p.

An outgrowth of work done for a doctorate at MIT, this book examines the tenacious grip of U.S. fears over the perceived threat of a Soviet disarming first strike. Nunn looks at antecedents of the threat in sea and air strategies, at the hypothetical "Eight Hour War" of the mid-1950s, the "Thirty Minute War" of the late '50s, and the specter of the successful first strike "in a nuclear world of plenty" (1961-). He calls the focus on the first-strike threat an inordinate result that was "principally a product of the U.S. sense of vulnerability . . . a misreading of Pearl Harbor, where surprise was tactical at best. This particular variation of the disarming first strike became the yardstick for judging the adequacy of both deterrence and national security."

Nunn argues that an attempt at a pre-emptive strike in any but an atmosphere of severe crisis is implausible, given the risk and devastation associated with nuclear war, as well as the huge arsenals available to both side, which render effective first-strike knockout blows impossible. An interesting examination of a fear that, though increasingly irrational, has long served as a driving wheel of U.S. nuclear strategy. Bibliography, index.

2-26 Schloming, Gordon C. *American Foreign Policy and the Nuclear Dilemma.* Prentice Hall, 1987. 284p.

Schloming is critical of U.S. behavior, which he finds not much superior to Soviet, because he believes that "America *ought* to measure itself by exceptional standards." In this textbook he surveys the nuclear-related issues of U.S. foreign policy, including strategy, arms control, and Soviet-American rivalry, and offers suggestions for "restructuring national security." Of special interest is his chapter on "Nuclear Theology," with its examination of a litany of U.S. nuclear beliefs, e.g., that the U.S. will respond only defensively, that escalation can be controlled, and that democracy would survive a nuclear war. Chapter-ending study questions and suggested readings are plentiful. Glossary, bibliography, index.

2-27 Sedacca, Sandra. *Up in Arms: A Common Cause Guide to Understanding Nuclear Arms Policy.* Common Cause, 1984. 130p.

A bit dated; the book reflects the intense nuclear anxiety of the early 1980s--but still a useful introduction for the citizen seeking a base of understanding in nuclear issues. Discusses the balance of Soviet and American nuclear forces, methods of dealing with the Soviets, the role of technology in affecting the risk of nuclear war, and how citizens can influence nuclear arms policy. Clearly written and attractively produced. Bibliography, index.

2-28 Segal, Gerald, et al. *Nuclear War and Nuclear*

Peace. St. Martin's, 1983. 162p.

Convinced that much of the nuclear debate is dominated by an unproductive match between extremist positions, the authors try to stake out a centrist position. Their final prescription includes recognition that the nuclear age will probably remain nuclear for many decades, that much can be done through arms control to reduce tension and danger, and that "we must never forget that the sources of war are to be found in political relations and not in some mechanical outcome of an arms race." Bibliography, index.

2-29 _____. *Nuclear War and Nuclear Peace.* 2d ed. Macmillan, 1988. 173p.

In four main parts: "Strategy and Survival," "Untying the Nuclear Knot," "Europe Between the Superpowers," and "Britain and the Bomb." The authors individually dwell on such questions as the Soviet threat (or lack of same), difficult topics in arms control, disillusionment with nuclear strategy, and whether Britain should possess a strategic nuclear deterrent. Control and reduction, rather than elimination, of nuclear weapons is a theme of the book. "There are no utopian solutions to the threat of nuclear war for two basic reasons," states the conclusion. Having been invented, nulcear weapons cannot be uninvented, and they are themselves tools in a political process. The authors walk a middle line between despair and blind optimism; they renounce the possibility of achieving "some mechanical outcome of an arms race," (read "SDI" there), and state that "there is no substitute for old-fashioned statecraft calming the impulses to war."

2-30 Smoke, Richard. *National Security and the Nuclear Dilemma: An Introduction to the American Experience.* Addison-Wesley, 1984. 271p.

In this introduction to nuclear issues, Smoke identifies the "dilemma" of national security as lying in the fact that, "in spite of enormous efforts, America is less secure today that it was several decades ago." He tries to answer questions about the growth of U.S. nuclear forces, the relationship between American strategy and the evolving technology of nuclear weapons, and efforts toward effective arms control and reduction. Along the way he discusses Sputnik and the "Missile Gap," SALT and subsequent Soviet and American nuclear buildups. Clearly written, appropriate for both college and upper-level high school students, but understandably marked by the bleak pessimism at large during the U.S.-Soviet relations that prevailed during the book's composition. Smoke's concluding sentence: "The prospect before the American people is continuation of the arms race, with all its costs, absurdity, and danger, almost without hope of any end." Glossary, suggested readings, index.

2-31 _____. *National Security and the Nuclear Dilemma: An Introduction to the American Experience.* 2d ed. Random House, 1987. 323p.

Like the first edition, this one assumes little background on the reader's part. Smoke takes an historical, evolutionary approach, showing how issues have developed since 1945, with focuses on the political and technological background, the Cold War, Sputnik and the Missile Gap, SALT II, Soviet and American buildups, SDI and other topics. Smoke's systematic approach will be a great help to those new to the issues; so much of the literature on nuclear weapons immerses the newcomer in a narrow portion of the territory, making it difficult to grasp the great ebb and flow of events and ideas that have brought the world to its present nuclear condition. Smoke holds the reader's hand on an instructive trip through that ebb and flow. Glossary, index, suggestions for further reading.

2-32 Snow, Donald M. *The Necessary Peace: Nuclear Weapons and Superpower Relations.* Lexington Books, 1987. 147p.

Snow contends that the superpowers' possession of nuclear weapons has provided a stabilizing and tranquilizing effect; it "has made war between them far less likely than would have been the case in the absence of nuclear weapons." He lays out the effects nuclear weapons have had on world politics, describes the dynamics of U.S.-Soviet relations, and of the stability the two countries have achieved. He also examines the Reagan vision of a world shielded from nuclear attack, and Gorbachev's "apparent interest in a nuclear-disarmed world," especially as these two viewpoints affect the present "stable system." Bibliography, notes.

2-33 Szumski, Bonnie. *Nuclear War: Opposing Viewpoints.* Greenhaven Pr., 1985. 249p.

An effective book for raising questions and issues in the high-school classroom; contains a large number of pro and con arguments from well-known authorities (Richard Pipes, Paul Ehrlich, Carl Sagan, and Daniel O. Graham are a few) addressing major nuclear topics, such as human survival in nuclear war, civil defense, arms control, and space weapons. Out of the pro-con molds is a nevertheless useful section, "How Would Nuclear War Begin?" outlining six scenarios, from superpower initiation to computer error. Contributions were drawn from a wide variety of books and periodicals.

2-34 Tetlock, Philip E., et al., eds. *Behavior, Society, and Nuclear War.* Oxford Univ. Pr., 1989-.

The National Academy of Sciences created the Committee on Contributions of Behavioral and Social Science to the Prevention of Nuclear War in 1985 in response to a perceived need "to move beyond the academy's traditional focus on technical issues to explore the potential contributions of behavioral and social science research to the issue [of nuclear war]." This volume is the first in a planned series intended to review work in specific areas to see how it bears on defense and foreign policy issues. It features five essays on such diverse topics as crisis decision making, the causes of war, and public opinion and nuclear weapons. Contributors are chiefly political scientists, although at least one sociologist and one psychologist are also on board. All contributions are in-depth examinations of pertinent literature. Notes, index.

2-35 Tsipis, Kosta. *Arsenal, Understanding Weapons in the Nuclear Age.* Simon & Schuster, 1983. 342p.

Describing the American public as "totally and deliberately excluded from policy decisions which are vital for its very survival," Tsipis seeks to disprove the belief common among nuclear strategists and weapons experts that the weapons themselves are too complicated for the average person to comprehend. His discussion of nuclear weapons and their delivery systems, along with the physics involved in the weapons' performance, is accessible and informative, and should help improve the tone and content of the public nuclear debate that Tsipis believes essential to the survival of humanity. Index.

2-36 Warf, James C. *All Things Nuclear.* Southern California Federation of Scientists, 1989. 302p.

Warf, a Group Leader on the Manhattan Project from 1942-1947, was a founding member of the Federation of Atomic Scientists, now the Federation of American Scientists. He has taught at the University of Southern California for 40 years. This book is a nice compilation that any curious reader could turn to for quick information salted with the author's firm belief in the necessity of adopting promptly policies that will help avoid nuclear war, war which "would represent blind, brutal calamity, with no meaning, just suffering and death." The detailed index heightens the book's utility as a quasi-reference volume. Warf covers all the big topics—nuclear weapons, targeting, the arms race, effects of nuclear war, and ways to peace, among others. Contains some striking prose, as well.

2-37 Yakovlev, Aleksandr N. *On the Edge of an Abyss: From Truman to Reagan: The Doctrines and Realities of the Nuclear Age.* Progress Publishers, 1985. 399p.

A Soviet reaction to the U.S. military buildup of the Reagan administration. Yakovlev insists that in the mid-'80s American political scientists, "especially right-wing conservatives," launched an intense assault on the principles of peaceful co-existence to justify "the maniacal plans for nuclear attacks, plans still locked up in Pentagon safes." It isn't appealing to agree with a writer whose tone is that of the propagandist, but considering the crackpot advocacy of "limited" nuclear war advanced by some U.S. political scientists in the 1980s, it is hard to do otherwise. Yakovlev proceeds from this point of view to an examination of the U.S. role in world affairs and the American attitude toward the Soviet Union. An interesting position paper on superpower relations at the time. Translated from the Russian *Ot Trumena do Reigana.* Notes.

2-38 York, Herbert. *Making Weapons, Talking Peace: A Physicist's Odyssey from Hiroshima to Geneva.* Basic Books, 1987. 359p.

From his work on the Manhattan Project as a very young scientist to his role as chief negotiator at the Comprehensive Test Ban discussions under Jimmy Carter, York has obtained an in-depth view of the nuclear weapons world. In this autobiography, he ranges across the whole of that world and its history. With many of his colleagues, York believed in 1945 that the Bomb made war obsolete. His youthful optimism deteriorated to the point that in 1970 he wrote of the world being "doomed" unless the arms race were reversed.

At the date of this book, York's view has moderated between euphoria and despair, with his early faith in a technological solution to the threat of war displaced by a belief in the need for political and social solutions. He points to the inherent dangers but also the apparent stability of nuclear deterrence, and expresses hope that the time purchased through deterrence will allow humanity to achieve an international climate permitting deterrence to be relegated to history, in favor of a situation in which one lost gamble will not mean the end of the game. A good, inside look at the nuclear age by a participant whose thinking has remained flexible. Notes, index.

II. Development of the Bomb

2-39 Badash, Lawrence, et al., eds. *Reminiscences of Los Alamos, 1943-1945.* Reidel, 1980. 188p. Dist. in the U.S. by Kluwer Boston.

Originating in the editors' hopes of helping rectify the considerable gap in first-hand accounts of the Los Alamos nuclear weapons site history, this volume gathers ten papers by participants in the Manhattan Project. The papers were first delivered as lectures in 1975 at the University of California-Santa Barbara. Transcribed question-and-answer sessions with the audience follow several of the papers. Both historians and interested lay readers will find the collection useful. Index.

2-40 Hacker, Barton C. *The Dragon's Tail: Radiation Safety in the Manhattan Project, 1942-1946.* Univ. of Calif. Pr., 1987. 258p.

The result of an official research project initiated by the Department of Energy's Nevada Operations Office. In writing his study of the Manhattan Project's radiation safety management, Hacker relied chiefly on documents from the Project and related programs, but also drew heavily on interviews with participants and eyewitnesses. (The 80+ interviewees are listed separately.) Hacker concludes that, given the standards of the times, radiation safety guidelines were acceptably maintained and followed. A nicely-researched investigation of this facet of the Bomb's development; includes coverage of radiological issues in Operation Crossroads, the U.S. nuclear testing at Bikini in 1946. Bibliography, index.

2-41 Jones, Vincent C. *Manhattan, the Army and the Atomic Bomb.* Center of Military History, U.S. Army; U.S. Government Printing Office, 1985. 660p.

On the Army's organization and administration of the bomb-building Manhattan Project, 1939–1946 (at which latter date the Atomic Energy Commission assumed responsibility for atomic energy in the U.S.). Jones, a long-time historian with the U.S. Army Center of Military History, takes a broad chronological approach, with topical treatment of individual developments. He describes the formation of the Manhattan District engineer organization, the building and operation of plants for the production of fissionable materials, the administration of support activities, and the building, testing, and use of the Bomb. Jones relies primarily on archival records from the Manhattan Project; his examinations of personal papers, interviews and correspondence, and published sources help round out the research on this massive official history. Many interesting black & white photos. Notes, bibliography, index.

2-42 Kurzman, Dan. *Day of the Bomb: Countdown to Hiroshima.* McGraw-Hill, 1986. 560p.

The human story of the Bomb, from its conception by physicist Leo Szilard in 1933 to its use on Hiroshima. Kurzman, a foreign correspondent with the *Washington Post*, generally writes with absorbing skill of major characters, such as Szilard, atom spy Klaus Fuchs,

and Manhattan Project director Maj.-Gen. Leslie
Groves, and "minor" ones, too, including Hiroshima
residents. Sometimes his itch to convey his characters'
feelings allows him to presume too much about their
interior lives. Bibliography.

2-43 Lawren, William. *The General and the Bomb: A
Biography of General Leslie R. Groves, Director of the
Manhattan Project.* Dodd, Mead, 1988. 324p.

Groves set forth his own story in *Now It Can Be Told*
(Harper, 1962). Convinced that Groves's book "was
more remarkable for its restraint than for its
revelations," especially regarding his role with
Manhattan Project scientists such as J. Robert
Oppenheimer, Lawren, a science journalist, found his
convictions confirmed through his examination of
Groves's personal papers in the National Archives. "In
the end I came to see it as my job not so much to
praise Groves as simply to resurrect him, to try to
restore him to the position he so obviously earned at
the very front and center of the history of the
bomb." Readable; less concerned with passing moral
judgment than in setting straight the historical
record, as Lawren sees it. Index.

2-44 MacPherson, Malcolm. *Time Bomb: Fermi,
Heisenberg, and the Race for the Atomic Bomb.* Dutton,
1986. 316p.

MacPherson concentrates on the years 1938–1942, and
on the physicists Enrico Fermi and Werner Heisenberg.
Fermi fled the Italian fascists for America; Heisenberg
was the top German physicist of his era. Both were
involved in work on the uranium pile, whose success
facilitated Bomb development. MacPherson finds
compelling parallels between the two men, up to their
employment on Bomb research by opposing sides in
the war. They attended the same schools, studied
under the same teachers, won Nobel Prizes before the
age of 40, and were well acquainted. A readable,
apparently well-researched (though not foot-noted)

account of the Bomb's generation, with special insights on the lure of scientific work, regardless of the purposes to which it will be put. Bibliography, index.

2-45 Nichols, Kenneth D. *The Road to Trinity.* Morrow, 1987. 401 p.

Army Corps of Engineers General Nichols and first general manager of the Atomic Energy Commission, reflects on the Manhattan Project, in which he served as district engineer, as well as on the A.E.C. of the early 1950s. A good look inside the beginning of the nuclear era by one who helped shape it; contains some reflections on the Three Mile Island and Chernobyl disasters, which have not dulled the author's appetite for nuclear power. Nichols also advocated the use of atomic weapons during the Korean War. Bibliography, index.

2-46 Rhodes, Richard. *The Making of the Atomic Bomb.* Simon & Schuster, 1986. 886p.

This huge history of the Bomb combines exhaustive research—there are close to 800 endnotes and a long bibliography—with consistent readability. Technical, political, and psychological considerations receive the author's attention. Especially affecting ("horrifying" might be a better word) is his concluding chapter, "Tongues of Fire," in which he quotes extensively from survivors of the bombings, and otherwise details the effects of nuclear attack. Although he looks straight on at the threat of the Bomb, Rhodes still finds grounds for hope that a way may be found to escape the nuclear dilemma. "Change is possible because the choice is bare: change is the only alternative to total death." Nearly 130 black & white photos, most of which this writer had not previously seen, illustrate the men, women, and materials of the developing nuclear age. A superb work that received the National Book Award in 1987.

2-47 Snow, C.P. *The Physicists*. MacMillan, 1981. 192p.

The first draft of a book C.P. Snow planned to expand considerably, completed shortly before his death in 1980. Written largely from memory rather than research, the work is a readable history of the scientists who made the Bomb possible, from Michael Faraday to Einstein and Oppenheimer. Includes many good photographs of prominent atomic scientists, such as a full-page photo of the Curies in their laboratory. Index.

2-48 Szasz, Ferenc M. *The Day the Sun Rose Twice: The Story of the Trinity Site Nuclear Explosion, July 16, 1945*. Univ. of New Mexico Pr., 1984. 233p.

The first nuclear explosion took place on the date indicated in this book's title at 5:30 a.m. at the Trinity Site, 120 miles from Albuquerque. Szasz's study of the site, the test, and its aftermath takes advantage of declassified materials not available to earlier writers, such as *New York Times* reporter William L. Laurence (*Dawn Over Zero*, Knopf, 1946), the only journalist to witness the test, and Lansing Lamont (*Day of Trinity*, Atheneum, 1965). Szasz discusses site and test preparations, the blast, and its aftereffects, including the radiation sickness of local cattle. A good account, supplemented with a number of photographs of the site, and one of the nuclear "gadget" that changed the world on its detonation. Notes, bibliography, index.

2-49 Wiggan, Richard. *Operation Freshman: The Rjukan Heavy Water Raid, 1942*. William Kimber, 1986. 176p.

Operation Freshman was an unsuccessful Allied attempt to attack the source, in Southern Norway, of the heavy water supplies being produced for Nazi Germany's research on the atomic bomb. Subsequent efforts did succeed in denying German scientists their heavy water supply. Wiggan relates the story of Operation Freshman relying on official records, secondhand accounts, Norwegian eyewitness reports, and other sources, but not first hand reports from the men who attempted to carry out the mission, for none of them returned. Photos, bibliography, index.

2–50 Wilcox, Robert K. *Japan's Secret War*. Morrow, 1985. 236p.

Could the Japanese have launched a nuclear attack on the American west coast, given a bit more time to pursue their research on the Bomb? According to Wilcox, the Japanese had, in fact, successfully tested an atomic bomb, developed in or near Konan, Korea. Reportedly the Japanese test bomb was detonated on August 12, 1945; it had been developed by the Japanese Navy for use in Kamikaze attacks. In a readable, quasi-novelistic style, Wilcox tells the tale of the alleged Japanese bomb, drawing on information from numerous books, articles, government documents, and interviews. The account's absence of footnotes is an unfortunate hindrance to its credibility, and Wilcox's assertions fly in the face of conventional wisdom about the Japanese bomb research efforts, generally regarded as pathetic. Bibliography, index.

2–51 Wilson, Jane S. and Serber, Charlotte, eds. *Standing by and Making Do: Women of Wartime Los Alamos*. Los Alamos Historical Society, 1988. 130p.

Los Alamos was a secret, made-to-order village in the Jemez Mountains of north-central New Mexico; it was the heart of American nuclear weapons research in WW II. In 1943, families of the scientists and other Los Alamos staff members began moving to the village, which was in a very real sense a closed community, sealed off and guarded from the outside world. This book helps tell the stories of the women of Los Alamos, narrated in their own words. Schoolteachers, housewives, a science librarian and others help the reader learn how it was. Numerous photos, including one of each of the collection's nine contributors.

2–52 Wyden, Peter. *Day One: Before Hiroshima and After.* Simon & Schuster, 1984. 412p.

A good contribution to the literature of the Bomb and its effects, Wyden's book is both a well-researched and readable treatment. He covers the men who made the Bomb, the decision to use it, target selection, the bombing and its aftermath. Details are plentiful, thanks in part to the author's thorough consultation of secondary sources and especially to his yeoman's work in collecting interviews, including more than 70 with American and British scientists, most of whom worked at Los Alamos during the war, and approximately 80 with residents of Hiroshima, Kyoto, and Tokyo. Notes, bibliography, index.

III. Hiroshima and Nagasaki

2–53 Akizuki, Tatsuichiro. *Nagasaki 1945: The First Full-Length Eyewitness Account of the Atomic Bomb Attack on Nagasaki.* Quartet Books, 1982. 158p.

The author was a 29-year old doctor working in a small TB hospital in a Franciscan monastery on the northern edge of Nagasaki when the second atomic bomb fell. Thanks to the author's status as a physician, his account of the bombing and its aftermath benefits from a degree of informed observation; his account is especially telling of the helplessness faced by would-be agents of relief in nuclear war. Translation of *Nagasaki Gembakuki.*

2–54 Barker, Rodney. *The Hiroshima Maidens: A Story of Courage, Compassion, and Survival.* Viking, 1985. 240p.

Barker chronicles the experiences of a group of twenty-five young Japanese women injured and disfigured in the atomic bombing of Hiroshima. The women were brought to Mount Sinai Hospital in New York City, where they received reconstructive surgery. While in New York, they stayed with Quaker families; one of these families was the author's, who was a young boy at the time. He bases the book chiefly on extensive interviews conducted over a five-year period in Japan and the U.S.; he talked with nearly all of the women and host families. The women have never enjoyed the "Hiroshima Maidens" appellation; they refer to each other as the *satsukikai*, literally, the "Azalea Association," linking this May-blooming flower to the month they arrived in the U.S. for treatment. Human interest stories many never change the world, but this one is indeed moving. Photographs, bibliography.

2-55 Braw, Monica. *The Atomic Bomb Suppressed: American Censorship in Japan, 1945-1949*. Liber Forlag, 1986. 183p.

A doctoral dissertation prepared for the Lund, Sweden, University Dept. of History; analyzes the conduct of American censorship in Japan during the occupation, especially regarding control of information about the atomic bombings. Braw contends that the suppression of A-bomb data was in some respects erratic, in some strict, in the second case particularly involving Japanese scientific studies, such as physicians' reports. She relies on interviews with A-bomb survivors, documents from the American archives of the Occupation, and other primary and secondary materials. "In all Occupation research," she writes, "it is as if Hiroshima and Nagasaki did not exist." An interesting study of the period and of the political and military reasons for the American suppression of Bomb-related information. Notes, bibliography.

2-56 Burchett, Wilfred G. *Shadows of Hiroshima*. Verso, 1983. 123p.

Burchett claims to have been the first Western journalist in Hiroshima after the bombing; he wrote an early dispatch on the attack for the London *Daily Express*. Indeed, Burchett's Sept. 5 Hiroshima dispatch for the *Express* preceded William L. Laurence's first *New York Times* report by eight days. The book is an interesting look at early efforts to control news coverage of Hiroshima, as well as at Burchett's first return to Hiroshima, in 1971, and his subsequent concern over victims of the Bomb, both Japanese and U.S. atomic test veterans, and his identification of Hiroshima as a central symbol in the peace movement. Notes.

2–57 Chisholm, Anne. *Faces of Hiroshima.* Jonathan Cape, 1985. 182p.

The author sought out the twenty-five women known as the "Hiroshima Maidens," most of whom were Hiroshima schoolgirls in 1945, and who were badly burned and disfigured by the Bomb. They were later treated with plastic surgery in the U.S., but remained in many ways scarred, both physically and psychologically. Chisholm sought these women because of her belief that "They could say not only what it was like to be burned in an atomic explosion, but what it was like to live on as an involuntary symbol of the world's first experience of nuclear war." A valuable document of nuclear consequences, with many quotations from the victims in the context of Chisholm's historical treatment.

2–58 Clark, Ian. *Nuclear Past, Nuclear Present: Hiroshima, Nagasaki, and Contemporary Strategy.* Westview, 1985. 146p.

In a close examination of the atomic bombings, Clark argues that we have grasped the wrong truths about them. These wrong truths include, among others, the notion that first use of atomic weapons was determined by a rational process; that tight control prevailed over the missions when in fact it did not; and that the bombings saved many lives. "What Hiroshima and Nagasaki teach us is that nuclear decision making, like most other forms of policy making, is likely to be non-rational." He claims that "we delude ourselves if we think nuclear war is susceptible of traditional termination or of victory." A detailed departure from the conventional wisdom about the first two nuclear attacks. Bibliography, index.

2–59 Clarke, Hugh V. *Last Stop Nagasaki!* Allen & Unwin, 1984. 135p.

Based on the experiences of Australian POWs in two Nagasaki camps in 1945, where they received relatively good treatment in comparison to prisoners in some other Japanese camps. The last third of the book is given to a discussion of the atomic bombing and its effects on the POWs, as well as on the citizens of Nagasaki. There were still nearly 170 POWs in a camp some 1,700 meters from the bomb's epicenter; many of the prisoners' accounts of the bombing are quoted at length. The book is a minor but meaningful addition to the atomic attack literature. Highlighted by many photos, including those of POWs at work on Japanese war projects.

2–60 *Fire from the Ashes: Short Stories About Hiroshima and Nagasaki.* Readers International, 1985. 204p.

Nine stories inspired by the bombings, ranging from Masuji Ibuse's "The Crazy Iris," first published in 1951, and Tamiki Hara's "Summer Flower," from 1947, to Kyoko Hayashi's 1978 story "The Empty Can." It is a good collection featuring both the work of those who directly experienced the Bomb, such as Hayashi, and those who did not, such as Ibuse. All the contributors are accomplished writers, many of them prizewinners. Ibuse, for example, won the Order of Cultural Merit for his novel of Hiroshima, *Black Rain* (Kodansha, 1970).

2–61 *After Apocalypse: Four Japanese Plays of Hiroshima and Nagasaki.* Translated by David G. Goodman. Columbia Univ. Pr., 1986. 325p.

Each of the plays in this volume offers a different perspective on the experience of the Bomb, moving progressively further from a literal recitation of the event. "The Island," a 1955 work by Hotta Kiyomi, gives a realistic portrait of the effect of the Hiroshima bombing on Japanese society. In Tanaka Chikao's "The Head of Mary" (1958), the bombing of Nagasaki is seen from a Catholic point of view as an effect of God's will in history; it features a group of bomb survivors who scheme to steal the remains of a statue of the Virgin that stood before a Nagasaki cathedral prior to the bombing. Betsuyaku Monoru's "The Elephant," an existential drama, dwells on the contrast between a dying bomb victim's still-vigorous will and a healthy relative's hopeless passivity. Satoh Makot's "Nezumi Kozo: The Rat" (1969) concludes the quartet by presenting the bombings as dramatic examples of the human drive for self-destruction. An interesting collection with a helpful supplementary text by the editor. Notes.

2-62 Harper, Stephen. *Miracle of Deliverance: The Case for the Bombing of Hiroshima and Nagasaki.* Stein and Day, 1986. 224p.

The book's main title quotes Winston Churchill's description of the Bomb on hearing that its test explosion equalled 20,000 tons of TNT. Describing postwar debate over the atomic bombings as coming "from the comfortable long term view," Harper discusses the plans for the invasion of Japan (Operation Zipper), which various authorities estimated would cost between 500,000 and one million Allied casualties. A readable history of the end of the war in the Pacific, with a focus on the role of the Bomb. Not altogether free of errors: that could not have been a "B-52" from which observers watched the Nagasaki bomb. Bibliography, index.

2-63 Hersey, John. *Hiroshima.* Knopf, 1985. 196p.

A new edition of Hersey's classic 1946 account of the Hiroshima bombing as experienced on the ground. This edition contains a long additional chapter, "The Aftermath," which brings the story up to date.

2-64 *Hibakusha, Survivors of Hiroshima and Nagasaki.* Kosei Pub. Co., 1986. 206p.

"No one close to the great fireball blast survived, but those at some distance did, some for a brief nightmare of living hell and others for many years . . . a nightmarish hell that shall haunt them all the days of their lives."—from the foreword by George Marshall. Here are twenty-five first-person accounts of atomic bomb survivors, the "Hibakusha." Grueling, agonizing pieces of human suffering, their intensity often magnified by the calm tone that comes with several decades between the event and the recounting.

2-65 Kanda, Mikio, ed. *Widows of Hiroshima: The Life Stories of Nineteen Peasant Wives.* St. Martin's, 1989. 183p.

A record of the editor's interviews with Japanese peasant wives who lost their husbands and children in the Hiroshima bombing. In the literature of the Bomb, dry accounts of the weapons' theoretical effects and even drier speculation on the merits or demerits of strategies predominate. Even visionary treatments like Schell's *The Fate of the Earth* are at least one step removed from the real thing, the fundamental suffering caused by the bombs. For that reason, no one's grasp of nuclear issues is complete or even adequate without a good stretch of time spent with works such as this one. Try to read these accounts of the Bomb's aftermath without a heart turning to lead. "The way my husband died was like all the tortures of this world made into one," says one woman. And when another says "I'm living out my last days, thankful for every new day that's granted to me," the effect is not as much one bringing admiration for the persistence of effort, as horror at the useless, pointless suffering that necessitates the effort.

2–66 Kohchi, Akira. *Why I Survived the A-Bomb*. Institute for Historical Review, 1989. 228p.

The author lived with his family in Hiroshima at the time of the bombing. His account of the attack will be familiar to those who have read other first-hand treatments, but is no less affecting for its familiarity. The book is, however, perhaps more interesting in its discussion of events in Japan preceding Hiroshima's bombing than it is in coverage of that event itself. Kohchi contends that "our fate was in the hands of a few who, in inflicting death on the many, successfully realized their own personal ambitions. Nothing else, let alone the future of mankind or the world, was in their minds." Kohchi singles out Brig. Gen. Curtis LeMay for particular opprobrium. LeMay assumed command of the B-29 raids on Japan in March, 1945, and promptly carried out a major shift in U.S. bombing strategy from narrowly-focused assaults on military and industrial targets to indiscriminate bombing of population centers. This change included the March 10, 1945 incendiary raid on Tokyo, which burned to death approximately 130,000 people.

2–67 Lifton, Betty Jean. *A Place Called Hiroshima.* Photographs by Eiko Hosoe. Kodansha International, 1985. 151p. Distributed in the U.S. by Harper & Row.

A frequently riveting black & white photo essay on Hiroshima, interweaving images of past and present in an effort to bring forth the meaning of the nuclear threat. Lifton's text complements the photos, and contains many affecting pieces. Not the least of these is the story of Yama-no-Obaasan, "the old woman of the mountain," who was so devastated upon the slow, terrible death of her daughter-in-law that she decided to purify herself by living for three years in a cave. "'I prayed for Ryoko and for the world,' she said. 'I hoped that when I returned to Hiroshima, I would have special powers to help the hibakusha.'" ("Hibakusha"—"explosion injured persons"—is the

Japanese term for atomic bomb survivors.)

2-68 Minear, Richard H., ed. and trans. *Hiroshima: Three Witnesses*. Princeton Univ. Pr., 1990. 393p.

Contains the work of three accomplished Japanese writers who were in Hiroshima the day of the bombing. They are fabulist Hara Tamiki, novelist Ota Yoko, and poet Toge Sankichi. All three were long-term residents of the city. Tamiki's "Summer Flowers" first appeared in 1947 in a Japanese literary journal. The essay describes the attack and its aftermath, as well as the Hiroshima scene before the attack. In one passage of awful irony, Tamiki describes Japanese schoolgirls watching American B-29s pass overhead. "Beautiful, aren't they!" exclaimed the girls.

In "City of Corpses," a memoir written by Ota Yoko in 1945 immediately after the bombing, she speaks of "the discovery of a new hell" in radiation sickness. Toge Sankichi contributes some two dozen powerful poems reflecting on the bombing. This, from "Flames": "After that concentrated moment/of the explosion,/pure incandescent hatred/spreads out, boundless."

A very nicely executed book, with informative introductions to each author's work, a glossary, guide to names and places, maps, and bibliography.

2-69 Nagai, Takashi. *The Bells of Nagasaki*. Kodansha International, 1984. Distributed by Harper & Row. 118p.

A brief but affecting eyewitness account of the Nagasaki bombing and its aftermath. The author was a pro-war nuclear scientist at a Nagasaki medical school. After the Bomb, he persevered in spite of his injuries to bring relief to the stricken. His depictions of what he saw on his rounds are gripping. Nagai, who died in 1951 from his exposure to the Bomb, experienced a religious conversion in which he came to see Nagasaki's destruction as a form of atonement for the crimes of war.

2-70 Nakazawa, Keiji. *Barefoot Gen: A Cartoon Story of Hiroshima.* New Society, 1987. 286p.

The author was a 7-year old child in Hiroshima in 1945. This autobiographical comic-format account of the Hiroshima attack focuses for the most part on pre-Bomb Hiroshima, following Gen, the young hero, in his adventures in a society at the rag end of a losing war effort. Nakazawa emphasizes Gen's experiences as a child from a family led by a hot-tempered, yet strongly antimilitaristic father. The conflict between the values Gen's father insists upon and his nation's determined refusal to lay down the gun in an obviously futile cause creates significant tension in the book. The reader knows, of course, what is coming at the end, but rather than undercutting the drama, this foreknowledge makes for an even stronger sympathy with the characters, and a greater horror at their impending fate. Expertly drawn in black and white.

2-71 _____. *Barefoot Gen: The Day After.* New Society, 1988. 190p.

The second volume in the story of Gen and his family begins immediately after the bombing in the radioactive rubble of Hiroshima. Gen's father and younger brother and sister die, yet he and his mother and baby sister must ignore the ruin and cut short their grieving to tend to the business of their own survival. Gen maintains a determined, survivor's attitude in spite of the devastation all around, devastation from the atomic bombing and also from the unremitting B-29 raids that have brought Japan to the edge of exhaustion.

2-72 _____. *Barefoot Gen: Life After the Bomb.* New Society, 1989. 164p.

The third volume in the saga of Gen finds the boy and his mother and infant sister struggling for continued survival in the aftermath of the bombing. Food and shelter are top priorities. In one of the book's most moving sections, Gen takes a job caring for a young art student seriously injured in the bombing. The student's own family cannot bear to be in the same room with him because of his repulsive, festering wounds and because they fear that they will be infected by his radiation sickness. Gen, too, is nearly overcome by the ghastly sick room, but his desperate need for money to help care for his mother, and his innate humanity, lead him to nurse the victim and to provide the compassion that the family cannot offer. In spite of this selfless conduct, Gen is far from an idealized character: he is a boy of many moods, including anger, a treatment that helps cement the story securely in reality.

2–73 Perlman, Michael. *Imaginal Memory and the Place of Hiroshima.* State Univ. of New York Pr., 1988. 214p.

Chiefly of concern to those interested in archetypal psychological theories (there are numerous references to Carl Jung in the text), this book dwells on the nature of memory and nuclear imagery and myths. By "imaginal memory," Perlman "refers both to that aspect of memory that involves some kind of imagining, and to a specific practice of remembering images elaborated in this book." Not always overwhelmingly clear, but interesting, especially in its discussion of atomic bombing victims' perceptions of the Bomb and its effects. Notes, index.

2–74 Rosenblatt, Roger. *Witness: The World Since Hiroshima.* Little, Brown, 1985. 101p.

Four views of what happened on and after August 6, 1945, from the perspectives of an Hiroshima schoolboy who became director of the Hiroshima Peace Memorial Museum; a physicist aboard the monitoring plane the "Great Artiste," which accompanied the "Enola Gay" on its mission; Richard Nixon, whom Rosenblatt interviews; and of the general public's reaction to the bomb: "What people saw initially in Hiroshima seems to have scared them more profoundly than they realized they could be scared." The sum of this book is less than its parts: all four "witnesses" make some interesting observations, but, aside from indicating that humanity must somehow accommodate the Bomb or perish, the author does not produce an especially insightful or otherwise productive conclusion.

2–75 Selden, Kyoko and Selden, Mark, eds. *The Atomic Bomb: Voices from Hiroshima and Nagasaki.* M.E. Sharpe, 1989. 257p.

Four novellas, poetry, memoirs, photographs, and other recollections of the bombings as experienced by those who were there. Like all the work produced by the atomic attack survivors, the material here brings into pointed, human reality the consequences of nuclear weapons use. It stands in powerful and painful emotional contrast to the many arid, rationalistic treatises on deterrent theory and nuclear strategy that have abounded since 1945. Bibliography.

2–76 Shigematsu, Itsuzo and Kagan, Abraham, eds. *Cancer in Atomic Bomb Survivors.* Plenum, 1986. 196p.

Presents the results obtained to publication date of epidemiological and pathological studies of atomic bombing victims carried out by such groups as the Atomic Bomb Casualty Commission (now the Radiation Effects Research Foundation) and university staffs in Hiroshima and Nagasaki. The volume consists of thirteen studies by individuals associated with these organizations; they focus on cancer mortality, types of cancer, survivor sampling and method of cancer detection in Hiroshima and Nagasaki, animal experiments, and other topics. Notes, index, statistical tables.

2-77 Shiotsuki, Masa. *Doctor at Nagasaki: My First Assignment Was Mercy Killing.* Kosei Pub. Co., 1987. 191p.

When the bomb fell on Nagasaki, the author was stationed 19 kilometers away from the hypocenter at Omura Naval Hospital. He was a 25-year old intern who had begun duty a month before the attack. "It was almost as though I had been brought to Omura for the express purpose of encountering the atomic bomb." His encounter begins with the explosion, which occurred as he gave a demonstration on a patient for a superior. The impossibility of meeting the medical demands of nuclear victims comes through plainly in his account. "All I could do was grit my teeth and try in some way to relieve their pain." He assisted in committing euthanasia; "My own torment will continue until the moment I too lose consciousness in death." Dr. Shiotsuki devoted the remainder of his life to informing his medical colleagues and the public at large about the effects of the Bomb. This translation of his memoir, first published in 1978, a year before his death, also includes an interesting foreword by Tatsuichiro Akizuki (see item 2-53), a doctor at a Catholic t.b. sanitarium considerably closer to ground zero than Shiotsuki's facility.

2-78 Shohno, Naomi. *The Legacy of Hiroshima: Its Past, Our Future.* Kosei Pub. Co., 1986. 150p.

Not to be confused with Edward Teller's *The Legacy of Hiroshima* (Greenwood, 1975, c. 1962). The author, a university science student whose parents lived in Hiroshima when the bomb fell, describes the "horrendous destruction" he saw when he traveled to the city to search for his parents. He writes of the city's ruin because "one must have accurate knowledge of nuclear weapons and nuclear war, fully absorb the experiences of the survivors of Hiroshima and Nagasaki, and inform as many people as possible about these things." His systematic account covers the immediate effects of the explosion, the deaths of loved ones, varieties of injuries, and the rending of the social fabric. Shohno advocates "a completely new way of thinking" as the only way to solve "the seeming endless repetition of war and violence in human history." His book should help many readers adjust their ways of thinking. Includes an annotated bibliography of works on the bombing of Hiroshima and Nagasaki.

2-79 Thomas, Gordon and Witts, Max M. *Ruin from the Air: The Enola Gay's Atomic Mission to Hiroshima.* Scarborough House, 1990. 386p.

An expanded version of a book first published by Hamish Hamilton in 1977. Its distinguishing feature is its day-by-day chronological treatment of the Bomb and its first use, beginning at Sept. 1, 1944 with an account of Col. Paul Tibbets's assignment to pilot the plane that dropped the Hiroshima bomb. Scenes shift from American (Washington, DC; Los Alamos; Wendover AFB) to Japanese, including pre-attack Hiroshima. In addition to the many human-interest vignettes in the book concerning Americans responsible for the bombing, there are some gripping glimpses of Japanese reaction. One of the most notable depicts Capt. Mitsuo Fuchida, leader of the attack on Pearl Harbor, flying into Hiroshima shortly after its destruction, unaware of what had happened. Fuchida landed his navy bomber in a daze after coming in over a city that "was simply not there any more." Fuchida, "the man who had literally led Japan into World War Two, continued to wander aimlessly through the wasteland." Based on many interviews in addition to archival sources and published material. Photos, notes, bibliography, excellent index.

IV. Nuclear Weapons, Nuclear War, and Their Effects

2-80 *ANCOC Common Core: NBC Reading Book.* U.S. Army Sergeants Major Academy, 1985. 282p. Su. Docs. No. D 101.2:N88.

A revealing example of the Army's preparation for a variety of future war environments, including chemical, biological, and nuclear. The nuclear portion of this indoctrination and training manual covers approximately 65 pages, and dwells on nuclear weapon effects, individual and unit defensive measures, fallout prediction, and radiological monitoring of personnel, food, and water. Few readers could doubt the soldiers' increased confidence at being informed that "A properly constructed foxhole provides excellent protection against both initial and residual radiation," or question the instruction to dig one's hole "so that it will withstand the blast wave." Above all, after being on the receiving end of a nuclear blast, the good soldier should "Stay calm, check for injury, check weapons and equipment for damage, and prepare to continue the mission."

2–81 Arkin, William M. and Fieldhouse, Richard W. *Nuclear Battlefields: Global Links in the Arms Race.* Ballinger, 1985. 328p.

Arkin and Fieldhouse focus "on the factors that would determine what a nuclear war would look like, how it would progress, and what its targets would be." They approach the task from a desire to correct existing public ignorance about these matters, ignorance that military and civilian policy makers encourage and exploit. Through maps, tables, and text, the authors do a thorough job of showing what the targets are in the U.S. and around the world, and explain the way in which the "nuclear weapons infrastructure" works. One of the book's most valuable features is its appendices, giving systematic information on the location, organization, and activity of nuclear weapons facilities of the U.S., Soviet Union, U.K., and China. The U.S. itemization is on a state–by–state basis and consumes, including notes, 77 pages of small print. An exhaustively researched study. Glossary, bibliography, and indexes, including geographical index.

2-82 Ball, Desmond. *Can Nuclear War Be Controlled?* International Institute for Strategic Studies, 1981. 51p.

The emphasis here is on the vulnerability of command and control systems in nuclear war. Given the susceptibility of the command structure—Ball estimates that it would require only 500–1000 warheads to pretty effectively demolish it—the idea that nuclear war could be effectively controlled and terminated once it passed a low level of intensity is doubtful. He argues that "it is likely that decision-makers would be deterred from initiating nuclear strikes no matter how limited or selective the option available to them" because of the impossibility of controlling the war or of removing "residual uncertainties" regarding large-scale use of nuclear weapons. Notes.

2-83 Barabanov, M. V., et al. *Disastrous Effects of Nuclear War: Socio-Economic Aspects.* Nauka Publishers, 1985. 62p.

Three Soviet economists and one physicist provide an alarmed reaction to their perceptions of U.S. nuclear adventurism at the most dreary point of recent U.S.-Soviet relations. "They keep talking prooflessly about a possibility of using a limited war with small losses as an instrument of national policy. In so doing they forget about the complexities of links existing between conflict situations in the modern world . . . which would directly lead to the escalation of a limited nuclear conflict into an all-out nuclear holocaust." The authors try to demonstrate the scope of the global catastrophe that would follow nuclear war. Translation of the Russian *Gubitel'nye Posledstviia Iadernoi Voiny.*

2-84 Blair, Bruce G. *Strategic Command and Control: Redefining the Nuclear Threat.* Brookings Institution, 1985. 341p.

Blair is uniquely qualified to discuss the command and control of nuclear weapons thanks to his experience as a Minuteman launch control officer. His concern is that communications channels between those responsible for the physical act of launching nuclear warheads and those responsible for the decision-making regarding such launch are at risk; specifically, the Strategic Air Command, which has at its behest most of the U.S. nuclear force, follows such a stylized routine for action in the event of an apparent Soviet attack that SAC blunders could initiate a nuclear war. Blair's solution to the problem lies in reduced stress on the obsession with a rapid reaction to a perceived first strike; by lengthening the time of response, the command system can more reasonably be expected to produce rational decision.

The most disturbing note rung by Blair suggests that the presumably carefully-tailored system enabling U.S. response to nuclear attack—the command, control, and communications system—might well be thrown into chaos by such attack. Thus, even before the nature of a Soviet attack, or appearance of attack, becomes clear, the U.S. could feel compelled to launch a full-scale second strike that would obviate the already dim possibility of containing nuclear war at a limited level. Notes, index.

2–85 Blair, David, ed. *First and Final War: A Basic Information Manual on the Effects of Nuclear War Applied to Australasia.* Oxford Univ. Pr., 1986. 80p.

What would happen "down under" in the event of nuclear war; covers medical and environmental consequences. Many photos, maps of potential zones of destruction. Bibliography.

2–86 British Medical Association's Board of Science and Education. *The Medical Effects of Nuclear War: The Report.* Wiley, 1983. 188p.

Using an estimated (and rather modest, given available arsenals) 200–megaton nuclear attack on Great Britain as their basis for extrapolation, the British Medical Association working group responsible for this study posits casualties, fatalities, and the ability of the medical community to deal with them. That ability, the group concludes, is nonexistent. Bibliography, index.

2-87 Budyko, Mikhail I., et al. *Global Climatic Catastrophes*. Springer-Verlag, 1988. 99p.

Over half of this study, which also concerns natural climatic catastrophes, is devoted to the climatic effects of nuclear war. The authors urge an expansion of the investigations under way concerning ecological consequences of the use of modern weapons, along with reduction and elimination of weapons posing the threat of ecological annihilation. A translation of *Global'nye Klimaticheski Katastrofy*.

2-88 Bunge, William. *Nuclear War Atlas*. Blackwell, 1988. 204p.

A geographer and socialist who would prefer "revolution without annihilation" offers a frequently-interesting vision of the effects of nuclear war. Less a true atlas than a textual argument supplemented with occasional, rather small, maps illustrating such events as the nuclear immolation of the Chicago area. Bunge also dwells on what he considers the pernicious mindset underlying the "Star Wars" project and on the more attractive potentials of a peaceful future. Bibliography, index.

2-89 Canfield, Catherine. *Multiple Exposures: Chronicles of the Radiation Age*. Univ. of Chicago Pr., 1989. 304p.

A detailed and interesting history of humanity's often-deadly flirtation with ionizing radiation, from Roentgen's discovery of X-rays to U.S. space shuttle missions involving large and, should a shuttle crash, potentially disastrous loads of plutonium. Canfield discusses some of the Radiation Age's most portentous events, such as the fate of the employees of U.S.

Radium Corporation, who became contaminated in the
1920s by the radium they used to paint numerals on
watch dials. She also dwells on nuclear accidents,
nuclear testing, the Manhattan Project, fallout and
attendant disease and injury, attempts at legislation
and control, and other issues. Notes, bibliography,
index.

2-90 Carter, Ashton B., et al., eds. *Managing Nuclear
Operations.* Brookings Institution, 1987. 751p.

A massive study jointly sponsored by the Brookings
Institution and the Center for Science and
International Affairs at Harvard University. Focuses
on the management of nuclear "operations," including
peacetime safety and security considerations, crisis
alert, war termination, the psychological climate of
nuclear command, delegation of nuclear command
authority, strategic defense, and many other topics.
Groups over twenty essays into three main categories:
"Nuclear Operations," "The Command System," and
"Policy Perspectives." Not a good starting point for
the uninitiated. Notes, index.

2-91 Cassell, Christine, et al., eds. *Nuclear Weapons
and Nuclear War: A Source Book for Health
Professionals.* Praeger, 1984. 553p.

Composed for the most part of reprinted articles and
excerpts from books on nuclear war and its effects,
with the emphasis on medical, ecological, psychological,
and long-term effects. Most of the selections are from
the early 1980s, and represent a good cross-section of
writing being done at the time. The volume remains
applicable in spite of the passage of a decade since
most of its contents were composed, and will be of
interest not only to medical and health professionals
but to public policy makers and lay readers as well.
Notes, index.

2-92 Clarke, Magnus. *The Nuclear Destruction of Britain*. Croom Helm, 1982. 291p.

Underpinning this analysis of the probable collapse of British society under the multiple crises of nuclear war (from immediate to long-term effects) is the assumption that adequate preparation would enable its survival. This preparation would involve a comprehensive, publicly-disseminated war-survival strategy. "Britain will not survive nuclear war, not because collapse is, in any sense, inevitable," concludes Clarke, "but because its traditional 'blind eye' to war in peacetime has ceased to be appropriate." Not precisely a treatise advocating more vigorous civil defense, but a blend of speculation about the threat of Soviet attack and Great Britain's options under that threat. Bibliography.

2-93 Clarke, Robin, et al. *London Under Attack: The Report of the Greater London Area War Risk Study Commission*. Blackwell, 1986. 397p.

The GLAWRS was commissioned by the Greater London Council in 1984, and, with the assistance of over 40 authors producing more than 30 separate research papers, worked up this exceptionally detailed study of the hypothetical effects on London of five nuclear war scenarios. These range in severity from a modest attack on UK nuclear forces to a 90-megaton attack on the UK, including a 10.35-megaton attack on London itself. The study describes environmental, medical, psychological, economic and other consequences of these attacks, and notes civil defense measures that may (or may not) be called for. The authors acknowledge that at the upper end of the megaton scale, civil defense measures would be useless. Packed with maps and statistics, including a "Casualties by Borough" series of tables which provides figures for citizens who could be presumed seriously injured or dead as a result of flash burns, blast and fall-out. Carefully prepared, restrained in tone, altogether chilling. Index.

2-94 Cuddihy, Richard G. and Newton, George J. *Human Radiation Exposures Related to Nuclear Weapons Industries*. National Technical Information Service, 1985. 162p.

This report summarizes events leading to releases (accidental or planned) of radioactivity into the environment from nuclear weapons industries, estimates the levels of radiation exposure and health risks to those affected, reviews scientific aspects of litigation resulting from such exposure, and recommends improved ways to evaluate and manage future radiation mishaps. The discussion includes events at weapons test sites from Trinity onward, at the Rocky Flats, CO, nuclear weapons facility, and a number of nuclear weapons accidents. A carefully-researched study which suffers, however, from its appearance before revelations in the late 1980s about the generally scandalous environmental and safety conditions throughout the U.S. nuclear weapons production system. Notes, glossary.

2-95 Denborough, Michael, ed. *Australia and Nuclear War*. Croom Helm Australia, 1983. 270p.

Published at the height of the Reagan administration's enthusiastic gutting of constructive social programs to fund the U.S. military buildup; small wonder that the book opens with the statement that "Planet Earth is galloping towards destruction due to our irrationality." The twenty contributors to this collection "examine nuclear war from an Australian point of view, with the aim of encouraging debate in our community about the most important problem that the world has ever had to face." The contributors include Australian government figures, filmmakers, health officials, and a representative of the German Greens, among others. Their essays concern the nuclear arms race, the consequences of nuclear war (especially for Australia), and methods of nuclear war prevention.

Some Americans like to fantasize about buying a one-way ticket to Australia, or New Zealand, should nuclear war seem imminent, but the idea of escaping Down Under is a hollow one. As J.A. Ward writes in his essay, "Can We Survive a Nuclear Attack Upon Australia," "The importance of the United States military bases in Australia make it almost inevitable that our country will be attacked in a major nuclear war between the superpowers." Index.

2–96 Diacon, Diane. *Residential Housing and Nuclear Attack*. Croom Helm, 1984. 146p.

Relying on extensive examination of the literature, consultation with housing agencies, government departments, public service bodies, and questionnaire surveys, the author depicts what she believes could reasonably be expected to happen to the UK's residential structures in a nuclear war. She includes discussion of past and present civil defense methods, and measures one might take to enhance the prospects of individual survival, ranging from recommended shelter supplies to the possibility of moving to a second home in a presumably "safe" area when the nuclear front begins to look dicey.

Whatever the measures, Diacon's conclusions are bleak, with her estimation that the "vast majority" of houses in the UK would be destroyed in a large nuclear attack (which for the compact geography in question would need be no more than a vigorous counterforce attack). She charges that government figures on the damage nuclear attack would bring are underestimated, and that the potential for rebuilding after attack would be "extremely limited." Numerous tables and maps. Bibliography, index.

2–97 Dotto, Lydia. *Planet Earth in Jeopardy: Environmental Consequences of Nuclear War*. Wiley, 1986. 134p.

Based on the 2-volume *The Environmental Consequences of Nuclear War* (item 2-100). This reduction of that weighty work discusses immediate blast effects along with long-term consequences in the climate, agriculture, ecosystems, and "the human response," which, the report estimates, would include the deaths, from a major nuclear war, of 1,000-4,000 million people in the "chronic phase" of nuclear winter and starvation. A handy little book that could be used effectively in college classes or upper-level secondary schools. Bibliography.

2-98 *Effects of Nuclear War on Health and Public Services: Report of the WHO Management Group on Follow-up of Resolution WHA36.28: "The Role of Physicians and Other Health Workers in the Preservation and Promotion of Peace...".* 2d edition. World Health Organization, 1987. 179p.

This concise volume, loaded with charts, maps and graphs illustrating effects of nuclear war, examines the physical characteristics of nuclear explosions, their effects, and a variety of nuclear war scenarios. The climatic, biological, psychosocial, and short-term health consequences of nuclear war all receive attention. The primary conclusions: "It is obvious that the health services in the world could not alleviate the situation in any significant way," and, therefore, "The only approach to the treatment of health effects of nuclear warfare is primary prevention, that is, the prevention of nuclear war."

2-99 Ehrlich, Paul, et al. *The Cold and the Dark: The World after Nuclear War.* Norton, 1984. 229p.

An early, major treatment of the nuclear winter theory, closely following the seminal article on the topic (Turco, Toon, Ackerman, Pollack & Sagan's "Nuclear Winter: Global Consequences of Multiple Nuclear Explosions," *Science* 222: 1283-92, 1983). Based on presentations at the Conference on the Long-Term Worldwide Biological Consequences of Nuclear War held in Washington, DC in late 1983. The conference focused on atmospheric, climatic, and biological consequences; the two major presentations, by Carl Sagan and Ehrlich, are followed by panel discussions. Includes eight clearly reproduced color plates illustrating an artist's interpretation of the environmental effects of nuclear war: urban dislocation, devastated agricultural resources, and destruction of aquatic environments. A book that helped mark a turning point in the way many scientists and others envisioned the consequences of nuclear war. Notes, index.

2–100 *Environmental Consequences of Nuclear War.* Wiley, 1985. Volume 1: Pittock, A. Barrie, et al. *Physical and Atmospheric Effects*, 359p.; Volume 2: Harwell, Mark A. and Hutchinson, Thomas C. *Ecological and Agricultural Effects*, 523p.

A major project of the Scientific Committee on Problems of the Environment of the International Council of Scientific Unions, involving a large number of scientists, this set thoroughly examines the potential environmental effects of nuclear war, taking into account thermal irradiation, air shock waves, blast damage, radiation, various types of nuclear bursts (e.g., water, high–altitude); discusses nuclear war scenarios, dust and smoke, urban fire development, post–nuclear chemical pollution, the vulnerability of ecosystems to climatic changes, long–term agricultural effects, etc. An invaluable tool for the exploration of nuclear weapon effects. Notes, glossary, index.

2–101 Firth, Stewart. *Nuclear Playground.* Univ. of Hawaii Pr., 1987. 176p.

Firth presents the Pacific as a region where World War III could well begin, thanks to the presence of plentiful numbers of U.S. and Soviet nuclear–armed forces. His real concern, however, is the historical nuclear abuse of the South Pacific and its peoples by the nuclear powers. He discusses the testing that endangered the Australian Aborigines and the island dwellers—the Bikinians, the Enewetakese, the Rogelapese, and others, who "have experienced a radioactive environment at first-hand." Their experience, he notes, "might one day be ours." His study examines both the past and present of the nuclear Pacific, with attention to the movement for a nuclear-free Pacific. Concludes with an interesting Epilogue, a description of a nuclear war beginning in the Pacific, told from the perspective of an imaginary future historian. Notes, bibliography, index.

2-102 Fisher, David E. *Fire & Ice: The Greenhouse Effect, Ozone Depletion, and Nuclear Winter.* Harper & Row, 1990. 232p.

An irreverent and readable discussion of three technologically-induced possibilities for working serious havoc on the future of earth and humanity. Fisher, a professor of geochemistry, furnishes a brief but useful discussion of nuclear winter, laying out the theory and responses to it, including the *National Review's* predictable characterization of nuclear winter as the brainchild of communist propagandists. Fisher's concluding statement is typical of his tone: "The catastrophes are coming, but they're not upon us yet. The game, as they say, isn't over until the fat lady sings, and she hasn't started singing yet. But if you listen carefully you can hear her offstage, in the wings, beginning to warm up." Notes, bibliography.

2-103 Greene, Jack C. and Strom, Daniel J., eds. *"Would the Insects Inherit the Earth?": And Other Subjects of Concern to Those Who Worry About Nuclear War.* Pergamon Professional Publishers, 1988. 78p.

Based on material developed for a course held at Southeastern Louisiana University in 1984. In the foreword, Lauriston S. Taylor sets the tone with a contention wildly divergent from almost all respected authorities on nuclear strategy and the consequences of nuclear war: "The worst nuclear war that can be conceived today could leave in this country [the U.S.] perhaps fifty million survivors." That is assuming that effective civil defense measures are taken. The book is composed of responses by various experts in radiology, biology, civil defense and other fields to questions about radiation, nuclear winter, agricultural effects of nuclear attack, and other nuclear war concerns. There is a good deal of interesting information here; as for the insects, one authority says "I think I would put my money on one of the little fungus gnats or chironomid flies."

Cites the usual notions about the "effective" Soviet civil defense program. (Who, after all, can doubt that a nation that could not begin to effectively distribute a record wheat harvest, as the Soviet Union could not in 1990, would fail to provide for its population's post-nuclear survival?) *The* place to go to learn about the edibility of irradiated livestock. Tip: don't use the organ meats.

2–104 Greene, Owen, et al., eds. *Nuclear Winter: The Evidence and the Risks.* Polity Pr., 1985. 212p. Dist. by Basil Blackwell.

An effective early book on nuclear winter, detailing the theoretical effects and outlining policy implications. The point of view is strictly one in opposition to continued reliance on nuclear weapons. Notes, index.

2–105 Gregory, Shaun. *The Hidden Cost of Deterrence: Nuclear Weapons Accidents.* Brassey's, 1990. 255p.

On the causes, dangers, and responses to nuclear weapons accidents. Although the author believes that the nuclear powers have addressed safety and security measures at least well enough to prevent accidental explosion of a nuclear weapon, "empirical evidence clearly demonstrates that nuclear weapons

accidents are continuing to occur around the world."
Shaun looks at nuclear weapons safety decade-by-
decade, 1940s-1980s, considering the human and
technical factors in the accidents, and the accident
response and control approaches of the U.S., the U.K.,
and the U.S.S.R. A chapter enumerating nuclear
weapon accidents from 1950-1988 provides brief details
of these accidents; an appendix lists a large number
of accidents involving nuclear capable aircraft, 1980-
1988. Glossary, notes, bibliography.

2-106 _____ and Edwards, Alistair. *A Handbook of
Nuclear Weapons Accidents.* School of Peace Studies,
Univ. of Bradford, 1988. 218p.

The heart of this book is a 49-page itemized list of
accidents involving nuclear weapons belonging to the
U.S., the U.K., and the U.S.S.R. Each entry identifies
the weapon owner, the weapon or system, the location
of the accident, gives a brief description of the
accident, a categorization by type of accident
(detonation, theft, accident with potential for creating
risk of nuclear war, etc.), and the source of
information. Among accidents in the most serious
category, on at least two occasions in 1971, submarine
emergency communications transmitter buoys
accidentally released from U.S. Polaris submarines
signalled that the subs had been sunk by enemy
action. Index.

2-107 Grinspoon, Lester, ed. *The Long Darkness:
Psychological and Moral Perspectives on Nuclear
Winter.* Yale Univ. Pr., 1986. 213p.

Eight prominent contributors, including Robert J.
Lifton, Carl Sagan, and Henry Steele Commager, write
on aspects of nuclear winter ranging from policy
implications and evolutionary considerations to nuclear
winter and the will to power. The book grew out of a
symposium in Los Angeles of the Scientific Program of
the 1983 annual meeting of the American Psychiatric
Association; the tone varies from the academic to the

readily accessible. Index.

2-108 Harwell, Mark A. *Nuclear Winter: The Human and Environmental Consequences of Nuclear War.* Springer-Verlag, 1984. 179p.

Examines the effects of a hypothetical nuclear war involving the "exchange" of approximately 5,000 megatons of nuclear warheads on the major industrialized nations, including the detonation of multiple warheads on some 300 metropolitan areas in the U.S. with populations of 100,000 and up. The consequences forecast include initial effects (local and global fallout, blast effects, etc.), and intermediate and long-term consequences of reduced temperatures and diminished sunlight. Projections include deaths of up to three-fourths of the U.S. population and a billion deaths worldwide from short-term effects; long-term climatic effects suggest the real possibility of no human survivors in the Northern Hemisphere, and the potential resides in "certain key atmospheric parameters" for a similar effect in the Southern Hemisphere. Bibliography, index.

2-109 London, Julius and White, Gilbert F., eds. *The Environmental Effects of Nuclear War.* Westview, 1984. 203p.

Addresses numerous aspects of nuclear war, including blast, heat, local fallout, radiation dispersal patterns and time of residence in the atmosphere, long-term radiological consequences for human beings, urban fires, ozone destruction. Glossary, maps, charts, notes.

2-110 Lynch, Allen. *Political and Military Implications of the "Nuclear Winter" Theory.* Institute for East-West Security Studies (distributed by Westview), 1988. 49p.

A brief but potent examination of the nuclear winter theory drawing on both U.S. and Soviet literature.

Lynch leaves no doubt about the catastrophic environmental potential of nuclear war, or about the wishful notion advanced by some strategists that a nuclear war could be limited to a level short of all consuming. Bibliography.

2-111 McNaught, L.W. *Nuclear Weapons and Their Effects.* Brassey's, 1984. 136p.

A textbook for professional soldiers on the effects of nuclear weapons and protective measures that might be taken in the field. There is some fascinating material here, such as methods of contending with flash blindness; these include the option of wearing an opaque patch over one eye to protect it from potential flash, thus leaving the victim only half-blind, to "a spare man in the cockpit or vehicle." Presumably the spare man keeps his eyes covered at all times until after a blast has taken place. The book's chief interest for the civilian is one of reinforcing the reality of nuclear warfighting plans. Although seemingly a fantasyland to most, the nuclear battlefield is one seriously anticipated by military planners. Glossary, index.

2-112 Midgley, John J. *Deadly Illusions: Army Policy for the Nuclear Battlefield.* Westview, 1986. 220p.

Midgley explains the growth of the U.S. Army's battlefield nuclear capabilities as the result not of confidence in either military or civilian circles that the Army could fight using nuclear weapons, but of "internally generated bureaucratic pressures to acquire advanced weapons and to retain these weapons under Army control." He begins with the origins of the nuclear battlefield in the 1940s, and proceeds to cover developments of the 1950s through 1970s. He concludes that the Army's plans for fighting with nuclear weapons on the battlefield "are based on an illusion of victory in an extended nuclear campaign." Notes, bibliography, index.

2-113 National Research Council. Committee on the Atmospheric Effects of Nuclear Explosions. *The Effects on the Atmosphere of a Major Nuclear Exchange.* National Academy Pr., 1985. 193p.

The mealy-mouthed euphemism "nuclear exchange" means a "war," not something like what takes place at the K-Mart customer service desk. This report came in response to a 1983 Department of Defense request; it takes into consideration a war in which approximately one-half of the world's nuclear arsenal is detonated, and estimates the ensuing effects from dust, fires, chemical, and other interactions in the atmosphere. The report concludes that such a nuclear war could cause "dramatic perturbations of the atmosphere lasting over a period of at least a few weeks," quite likely severely affecting "great portions" of the land masses in the northern temperate zone. Notes, index, numerous statistical tables, charts.

2-114 *Nuclear Winter and National Security: Implications for Future Policy.* Air Univ. Pr., 1986. 76p. Su. Docs. No. D 301.26/6: N88/2.

A combination of civilian and military scholars examine the issue of nuclear winter through a range of scenarios from "high level" (only a massive nuclear war could lead to nuclear winter) to "low level" (the atmosphere is so sensitive to nuclear debris that only a small number of weapons could precipitate nuclear winter). It is an interesting exercise, concluding with a very mixed reaction from Lt. Col. Dennis M. Drew, who probably speaks for many when he mentions his optimism that, with the final effect of nuclear weapons intimated in the nuclear winter theory, "the scourge of nuclear weapons . . . might finally be eliminated"— but "It may be that we will be trading the degree of international order imposed by nuclear weapons for the potential chaos of a world less dominated by the superpowers."

2-115 Openshaw, Stan; Steadman, Philip; Greene, Owen.

Doomsday: Britain after Nuclear Attack. Blackwell, 1983. 296p.

A detailed account of the possible effects of nuclear attack on Great Britain, both nationally and locally. The book opens with an estimation of the size of attack the UK would probably receive, discusses nuclear strategies, war scenarios, and the portion of the Soviet arsenal directed at Britain, and then dwells on both the immediate and long-term consequences of attack. The authors also provide a highly critical analysis of the British Home Office's notions of the effects of nuclear attack, and a gloomy assessment of British civil defense in both its existing form and in its future incarnation. They hold that "even much greater investment and much more elaborate civilian defenses offer little hope. We have condemned official attempts to conceal the truth about these questions, and to exaggerate the extremely marginal effectiveness of civil defense measures." Numerous maps and tables. Notes, index.

2-116 Peterson, Jeannie, ed. *Nuclear War, the Aftermath.* Pantheon, 1983. 196p.

Using a global war scenario in which less than half the total explosive power of the Soviet and American nuclear arsenals is used, the *Ambio* Advisory Group prepared a special report for that magazine on the consequences of such a war. The report appeared as *Ambio* 21: no. 2-3, 1982. This book expands on the *Ambio* report with chapters on epidemiology ("The Future is Sickness and Death"), the medical consequences of radiation, atmospheric and agricultural effects, and, among others, economic consequences ("Back to the Dark Ages"). There are, of course, almost countless uncertainties regarding nuclear war, but, as the conclusion states, "In any case societies as we know them today will most certainly cease to exist." Research on nuclear winter was in its early stages when this book was in preparation, so the full range of atmospheric consequences of nuclear war is not treated;

nevertheless, the effects described paint a somber enough picture of a planet scourged by the Bomb. Many charts, tables and illustrations. Contributors include military analysts, physicians, biologists, physicists, and other experts.

2–117 Pry, Peter V. *The Strategic Nuclear Balance*. 2 vols. Crane Russak, 1990.

Pry, a CIA employee, analyzes the U.S.–Soviet strategic balance, discusses and criticizes various ways of judging the balance, and proposes some new methods. All things considered, he believes that regardless of what method one uses to calculate the balance, any calculation based on various possible nuclear wars, many of which Pry investigates, inevitably leaves the Soviet Union a "winner," enabling the U.S.S.R. "to enforce a final war outcome favorable to the Soviet Union." Will be of interest to chart and number–loving advocates of more and better U.S nuclear weapons and better delivery vehicles. William R. Van Cleave sets the stage for Pry's wallowing in alleged U.S. nuclear inferiority when, in his foreword, he sanguinely alludes to the self–serving Pentagon annual, *Soviet Military Power*, as a volume worth taking at face value. Notes, indexes.

2–118 Rogers, Paul, et al. *As Lambs to the Slaughter: The Facts About Nuclear War*. Arrow Books, 1981. 289p.

Published when the imminence of nuclear war seemed more pressing than at any time since the Cuban Missile Crisis, this book is a good source of the British peace advocate's view of the situation then prevailing. The authors discuss "the slide to nuclear war," the nuclear arsenals of the U.S., the U.S.S.R., and the U.K., the short and long–term effects of nuclear war on Britain, and what the concerned individual might do, including becoming well informed. Notes.

2–119 Sagan, Carl and Turco, Richard. *A Path Where No Man Thought: Nuclear Winter and the End of the Arms Race.* Random House, 1990. 499p.

Astronomer Carl Sagan and atmospheric sciences professor Richard Turco contributed to one of the most important scientific papers of the Nuclear Age, "Nuclear Winter: Global Consequences of Multiple Nuclear Explosions," published in "Science" magazine in 1983. The paper stimulated an intense and continuing debate over the potential environmental consequences of nuclear war.

Here Sagan and Turco review the theory of nuclear winter. The theory holds that even a limited U.S.–Soviet nuclear war could, as a result of the immense fires started in both urban and rural settings, throw enough fire debris into the atmosphere to significantly reduce the amount of sunlight and heat reaching the earth's surface.

The result would be "the cold and the dark," with plummeting temperatures in the northern hemisphere and the destruction of agriculture; the catastrophe could spread to the southern hemisphere as well. Scientists not noted for recklessness have indicated that a full-blown nuclear winter could destroy all life on earth.

To escape the nuclear winter threat, Sagan and Turco advocate a major shift in nuclear strategy. Rather than relying on the endless replication of nuclear capabilities that has marked superpower deterrent strategy for most of the post-war era, they suggest a "minimum sufficient deterrence," or MSD, "a strategic arsenal small enough to avoid nuclear winter, but large enough to provide a real measure of deterrence."

They discuss "rough sketches" of routes to minimum sufficient deterrence, including rigorous protocols for inspecting the dismantling and destruction of nuclear warheads, unhindered space-based surveillance of weapons deployments, continuous on-site monitoring of all places where fissionable material is mined or refined, and mobile inspection teams in both the U.S. and the U.S.S.R. which will be provided rapid access to any sites deemed suspicious.

A fine overview of the nuclear winter theory, and a politically hopeful response to the questions about human survival that the theory provokes. Numerous color illustrations, notes, index.

2-120 Sederberg, Peter C., ed. *Nuclear Winter, Deterrence and the Prevention of Nuclear War.* Praeger, 1986. 200p.

A collection of a dozen papers presented at a conference on Nuclear Winter and the Prevention of Nuclear War at the University of South Carolina in 1984. Given the date, these are early examinations of the nuclear winter theory, to the extent that they focus on the issue. Curiously, given the topic, only one contributor represents the biological or environmental sciences. The rest are political scientists. Notes, index.

2-121 Solomon, Fredric, and Marston, Robert Q., eds. *The Medical Implications of Nuclear War.* National Academy Pr., 1986. 619p.

In his forward to this collection of 30 papers presented at a symposium held at the National Academy of Sciences in Washington, DC in September, 1985, Dr. Lewis Thomas, President Emeritus of the Memorial Sloan-Kettering Cancer Center, angrily describes the content of the typical newspaper or news magazine at a time when mass destruction looms: they're full of "the harangues by statesmen hungry for television, the talk of new talks, arms control talks, treaty violation talks . . . endless bewildering columns on the SDI and talk about the SDI. Wretched, dishonest, evasive talk, political talk, with no mention anywhere of burnt blasted vaporized human beings in the billions and half the planet frozen and irradiated."

In this volume, one finds plentiful discussion of those conveniently ignored topics. Many well-known physicians, psychologists and scientists treat the environmental consequences of nuclear war, including health consequences, medical resource needs and availability, and psychological concerns. Generally accessible to the average reader. Notes, glossary, index.

2-122 Steadman, Philip and Hodgkinson, Simon. *Nuclear Disasters & the Built Environment.* Butterworth, 1990. 134p.

This report to the Royal Institute of British Architects aims to give a comprehensible assessment of the effect on the built environment of disasters arising either from nuclear accident or attack. The latter concern occupies approximately half the book. Following an overview of potential nuclear attacks on Britain, the book describes in detail damage that would be sustained by buildings and their components in such attacks. Extensive use of photos, charts, and maps augments the text. The authors note that little or nothing can be done to protect existing buildings from nuclear attack, and accuse the British government of evasiveness, if not outright lying, in its recommendations for civil defense. Current and alert to other recent studies, the volume also discusses computer programs for predicting the effects of attack. Bibliography, index.

2-123 Stephenson, Michael and Hearn, Roger, eds. *The Nuclear Case Book.* F. Muller, 1983. 144p.

Although dated and written chiefly from a British point of view, this compilation of nuclear information (e.g., an annotated directory of nuclear weapons) and opinion (e.g., Alun Chalfont's essay, "Arguing About War and Peace") still contains a good deal of interesting material. Most interesting, perhaps, are the various maps illustrating a number of nuclear war scenarios, including a dual theater Central American-

Middle East war, and U.S.-Soviet nuclear confrontation over Iran and Pakistan. Index.

2-124 Thompson, James A. *Psychological Aspects of Nuclear War*. Wiley, 1985. 127p.

Readable and brief, this statement was adopted by the Council of the British Psychological Society at its October, 1984 meeting. After the obligatory depiction of the physical effects of nuclear war, the book goes into some detail on human response to disaster, nuclear decision making, and conflict resolution. One of the volume's most significant and prescient statements appears very early: "The limitations of our psychological frameworks and our lack of experience of large-scale disasters combine to give any attempt to conceptualize such an event a measure of unreality." It is an acknowledgement that is too often absent from speculation about nuclear war among professional strategists, particularly among those who envision a survivable nuclear war, or even one in which "victory is possible." Bibliography, index.

2-125 Tritten, James H. *Soviet Naval Forces and Nuclear Warfare: Weapons, Employment, and Policy*. Westview, 1986. 282p.

Tritten examined approximately 300 Soviet documents published 1956-1985 in an effort to determine how the Soviet navy would function in a nuclear war with the U.S. The book is not without interest as a close examination of public statements by Soviet officials, but their nature as public statements renders their revelatory quality somewhat suspect. Tritten, however, argues that "the Soviets are not as sophisticated in their manipulation of the West as they are often credited with being." He advocates U.S. pursuit of strategic defenses, even if imperfect, as a way to improve deterrence of war. Contains a bibliography of Soviet documents and statements consulted. Index.

2–126 Tucker, Anthony, and Gleisner, John. *Crucible of Despair: The Effects of Nuclear War.* Menard Pr., 1982. 62p.

Closely related in its origins to *As Lambs to the Slaughter* (item 2–118), which, like this book, finds early 1980s British governmental publicity about the virtues of civil defense less indicative of a concern for the people than of a fatalistic assumption that nuclear war is both inevitable and imminent. This book sets forth the effects of nuclear attack that one could expect, contrary to the palliatives of the British government. Short on horror footage, long on dispassionate numbers. "If civil defence as a concept is merely a dangerous illusion, and if it is inconceivable that there could be medical service or 'treatment' after a nuclear war, what is the alternative? It is to make the true situation perfectly clear to the public and to the authorities and to put every effort into prevention."

2–127 U.S. Congress. House. Committee on Science and Technology. Subcommittee on Natural Resources, Agriculture Research, and Environment. *The Climatic, Biological, and Strategic Effects of Nuclear War: Hearing before the Subcommittee on Natural Resources, Agriculture Research, and Environment of the Committee on Science and Technology, House of Representatives, 99th Congress, Second Session, Sept. 12, 1984.* U.S. Government Printing Office, 1985. 237p. Su. Docs. No. Y 4.Sci 2-98/126.

Early hearings in response to the nuclear winter theory, featuring testimony and prepared statements from Carl Sagan, Harvard geologist Stephen Jay Gould, Edward Teller, climate authorities from the U.S. and the U.S.S.R., and other experts. There are some very interesting exchanges among Sagan, Gould, and Teller indicating that Teller, who has been critical of the nuclear winter theory, nevertheless agrees with the other two scientists that even a modest drop in temperature in the northern hemisphere as a result of nuclear war would prove catastrophic for agricultural production, and thus for human life. The document also contains several pertinent reproduced articles from the journals *Science*, *Scientific American*, *Nature*, and *Foreign Affairs*.

2-128 U.S. Congress. Joint Economic Committee. Subcommittee on International Trade, Finance, and Security Economics. *The Consequences of Nuclear War: Hearings before the Subcommittee on International Trade, Finance, and Security Economics of the Joint Economic Committee, Congress of the United States, 98th Congress, Second Session, July 11 and 12, 1984.* U.S. Government Printing Office, 1986. 297p. Su. Docs. No. Y 4.Ec 7-W 19/2.

Hearings highlighted by a lengthy (47 pages) prepared statement by Carl Sagan on "Nuclear War and Climatic Catastrophe," and by a collection of eight articles on the environmental and economic consequences of nuclear war. The document also contains testimony by Sagan, Paul Warnke, and spokesmen from the Federal Emergency Management Agency and the U.S. Arms Control and Disarmament Agency.

2-129 U.S. General Accounting Office. *Nuclear Winter: Uncertainties Surround the Long-Term Effects of Nuclear War: Report to Congress.* GAO, 1986. 55p. Su. Docs. No. GA 1.13-NSIAD-86-62.

An examination of the scientific and policy implications of nuclear winter by the GAO. The agency reviewed literature and interviewed scientists, researchers, and policy analysts both in and out of government. GAO concludes that nuclear winter is a plausible theory requiring additional research in fire effects from various war scenarios before adjusting nuclear policies. Bibliography, list of interviewees (including the ubiquitous Carl Sagan and Edward Teller, among other prominent individuals).

2-130 Velikhov, Yevgeni, ed. *The Night After: Climatic and Biological Consequences of a Nuclear War, Scientists' Warning*. Mir Publishers, 1985. 165p.

The work of the Soviet Scientists' Committee for the Defence of Peace Against Nuclear Threat. In his long introduction, Velikhov, Vice-President of the U.S.S.R. Academy of Sciences, reviews some of the body of international literature on the long-range climatic effects of nuclear war, and closes with worried remarks on the implications of the Reagan administration's SDI visions. The volume contains five essays on the long-term effects of nuclear war, including a piece on "Natural Analogs of a Nuclear Catastrophe," such as volcanic eruptions and massive wildfires.

Following the essays are abstracts of scientific reports from a 1983 Moscow conference on nuclear war, with supplemental documents on the prevention of nuclear war from international as well as Soviet sources. A high point of the book is its imaginative and effective set of opening illustrations, juxtaposing a painting of an infant sleeping in its mother's arms during a wheat harvest with images of Durer's famous "Four Horsemen of the Apocalypse." The message is clear, as is that of the book.

2-131 Wade, Nicholas. *A World Beyond Healing: The Prologue and Aftermath of Nuclear War*. Norton, 1987. 190p.

Although not as resolutely gloomy as some writers on the question of society's ability to recover from nuclear war, Wade still provides chilling discussions of the immediate and long-term effects of nuclear war. His final chapter, "Rethinking Nuclear War," contains some interesting observations on the possible effects of nuclear winter theory on nuclear strategy, including movement to smaller, more accurate weapons able to destroy their targets without creating an overabundance of extraneous effects. "Improved" weaponry or not, Wade concedes that "the United

States and the Soviet Union must reconsider the calculus of terror and strive for a form of coexistence that does not require the present world's destruction as its guarantee." Notes, index.

2–132 Zuckerman, Ed. *The Day after World War III.* Viking, 1984. 407p.

A popular treatment of nuclear business, frequently informed with cynical humor. Civil defense, a protracted nuclear war, the quest (led by Edward Teller) for the "clean" bomb (low fallout-producing), the development of the hydrogen bomb, notes on AT&T's National Emergency Control Center, plans for postwar tax collection and transportation, and other topics receive Zuckerman's bemused and skeptical attention. Neither systematic nor persuasive in the sense of mounting an argument, the book is still a revealing portrait of the official obtuseness and wishful thinking that has aided in achieving the degree of nuclear anxiety the world enjoys today. Notes, index.

V. Testing, Testing: From Nevada to Christmas Island

2–133 Arnold, Lorna. *A Very Special Relationship: British Atomic Weapon Trials in Australia.* Her Majesty's Stationery Office, 1987. 323p.

Neither a defense of nor an argument against nuclear weapons, this official history's concern is why Britain adopted defense policies that entailed nuclear weapons tests, and why more than half the tests, including all the earlier ones, took place in Australia. It covers the five series of tests in Australia ("Hurricane," 1952; "Totem," 1953; "Mosaic," 1956; "Buffalo," 1956; "Antler," 1957), but not the "Grapple" series, which took place in the Christmas Islands in 1957–58. Arnold evaluates the achievements and costs of each test series, with attention to radiation safety standards both at the time of the tests and from present-day perspectives.

The origins of Great Britain's nuclear force are dealt with far more extensively in a number of other books, but the systematic discussion of the Australian testing makes this treatment useful. Notes, bibliography, photos, index.

2-134 Ball, Howard. *Justice Downwind: America's Atomic Testing Program in the 1950s.* Oxford Univ. Pr., 1986. 280p.

Although he begins with a brief account of the development of the Bomb and the relationship between the Atomic Energy Commission and national security, Ball's real concerns are the effects of American nuclear testing on those who lived downwind from the explosions, and the responses of these "Downwinders" to the tests. He discusses at length the aftermaths of numerous tests, 1950–1958, the medical controversy over radiation exposure and cancer, and legal remedies sought by Downwinders for their complaints.

The book includes a fair number of illustrations, including a map outlining high fallout exposure areas from blasts at the Nevada Test Site. The map shows a wide area of contamination in Nevada, Arizona, and Utah; the area contains several cities. Appendices offer further material of interest, such as excerpts from a patronizing 1957 A.E.C. booklet, "Atomic Testing in Nevada" ("Your best action is not be worried about fallout," it counsels), and selections from the Downwinders' newsletter, *Testing News.* Bibliography, index.

2-135 Blakeway, Denys. *Fields of Thunder: Testing Britain's Bomb.* Unwin, 1985. 243p.

A much more critical study of the British nuclear testing in the Pacific than Arnold's *A Very Special Relationship* (item 2-133). Blakeway accuses those responsible for the tests of "lackadaisical attitudes" regarding the safety of those exposed to radiation, including thousands of military veterans involved in the testing as well as civilians. Blakeway focuses on safety transgressions and inept or indifferent conduct by officials, arguing that the tests were carried out in haste, and that the scientists responsible felt strong political pressure to achieve workable results at improvident speed. "The real victims of the tests," writes Blakeway, "are often forgotten in the orgy of righteous indignation against the authorities responsible. They are the ex-servicemen and their widows, and the Australian Aborigines . . . there is no doubt that the men 'fortuitously' exposed to radiation were guinea pigs in an extensive and often mismanaged operation." An appendix lists and details British nuclear tests in Australia and at Christmas Island, 1952–1958. Notes, index.

2–136 Danielsson, Bengt and Danielsson, Marie-Therese. *Poisoned Reign: French Nuclear Colonialism in the Pacific.* Penguin, 1986. 323p.

First published in 1977 as *Mururoa, Mon Amour*, this study by two long-time residents of Tahiti links the French history of nuclear testing at the Moruroa atoll with its effort to retain colonial power in French Polynesia. It is a detailed examination of the history of French nuclear abuse in the Pacific, involving considerable evident use of documentary sources; unfortunately, the book's utility is hindered by its complete lack of adequate scholarly apparatus in the way of footnotes, bibliography, and indexes.

2–137 Dibblin, Jane. *Day of Two Suns: U.S. Nuclear Testing and the Pacific Islanders.* Virago, 1988. 299p.

Journalist Dibblin tells the story of the inhabitants of the Marshall Islands, whose daily lives since 1946 have been routinely interfered with by American weapons testing. Between 1946 and 1958, the U.S. set off over sixty nuclear bombs in the Marshalls; in the mid-1980s, testing related to the Strategic Defense Initiative took place there. The book discusses two communities victimized by atomic testing: the people of

Rongelap atoll, exposed to fallout, and those of Kwajalein atoll, who were evicted from their land so that it could provide a target for missiles launched from the west coast of the U.S. Dibblin dwells on not only the islanders' victimization, but on their struggles to obtain justice and freedom from nuclear oppression.

2-138 Falin, Valentin, ed. *The Last Nuclear Explosion: Forty Years Struggle Against Nuclear Tests (A Historical Survey)*. Novosti Press Agency, 1986. 285p.

Opening with references to the space shuttle Challenger's explosion and the Chernobyl disaster, Falin remarks that "even that which is most improbable nevertheless happens." Readers interested in a look at nuclear testing from Soviet perspectives will find the first hundred pages here of merit. In "Forty Years of Struggle Against Nuclear Tests," Falin sets forth those perspectives. Also of use is the following collection of 121 documents related to nuclear testing, 1946–1986. The documents include statements from U.S. and Soviet leaders, test announcements, government resolutions and proposals.

2-139 Fradkin, Philip L. *Fallout: An American Nuclear Tragedy*. Univ. of Arizona Pr., 1989. 300p.

If the atomic testing in Nevada during the 1950s was not performed willy-nilly, it was at best conducted without prudent regard for the potential long-term health effects of the radioactive debris that the bombs rained across the country. Fradkin describes early tests like Shot Harry (May 19, 1953), soon known as "Dirty Harry" for the huge quantity of fallout it generated, occurring in an official atmosphere of indifference toward health effects. Fradkin, a former reporter for the *Los Angeles Times*, goes about his work with the clarity and doggedness of a good journalist as he discusses the tests, their unintended victims, and the legal ramifications of their claims. It is easy to judge well in hindsight, but, given the enormous power of the Bomb and its known effects at the time, the cavalier approach apparently taken by the testers is inexcusable.

2-140 Fuller, John G. *The Day We Bombed Utah: America's Most Lethal Secret.* New American Library, 1984. 268p.

A journalistic treatment of the alleged effects of nuclear weapons testing on Utah and its citizens. Fuller pays close attention to tests in the early 1950s, including the May 19, 1953 "Dirty Harry" test, the most radiologically filthy of all the tests conducted in Nevada. Fuller follows the legal history of the case; the A.E.C. was charged with obscuring evidence and intimidating witnesses, and with negligence in conduct of the tests. Fuller gives a dramatic sense of what it was, and has been, like for the ranchers and other everyday citizens of Utah to live under the shadow of the Bomb in their own back yards. One wishes, however, that Fuller had provided formal references to pertinent documents supporting his assertions. Index.

2-141 Lerager, Jim. *In the Shadow of the Cloud: America's Atomic Vets.* Fulcrum, 1988. 116p.

A photographic record of the U.S. military victims of atomic testing. Lerager notes that approximately 235,000 U.S. servicemen were exposed to nuclear test blasts, 1945-1960. Another 115,000 were stationed at Hiroshima and Nagasaki after the war, where they saw firsthand the effects of atomic bombardment. Lerager's artful yet unpretentious black & white photographs of atomic veterans and their families, invariably posed in a homey setting (at the kitchen table, on the front porch, in the living room) face pages with text quietly describing the health problems of the veterans and their families, especially those of their children.

The book is not an attempt to offer scientific proof that these atomic veterans owe their infirmities and suffering to their exposure to the Bomb and its trappings; it is, rather, an accumulating record of the terrible price so many average citizens seem to have paid for their patriotism, their loyalty, and their trust in a government that assured them no harm would come to them if they followed orders and did their jobs. In their own way, the photos and accompanying text, portraying the insidious long-term effects of radiation exposure, are as emotionally draining as photos taken of Hiroshima and Nagasaki victims.

2-142 Miller, Richard L. *Under the Cloud: The Decades of Nuclear Testing*. Collier Macmillan, 1986. 547p.

Over 100 aboveground nuclear test bursts took place at the Nevada site, 1951-1963. Each left a path of fallout in its wake, carried by the wind across the continent. "Like the soldiers maneuvering in the desert," says Miller, "every person alive during the 1950s and early 1960s lived under the atomic cloud. This book is the story of how it happened and why." His story is a well-researched account of the testing and its effects. His investigation enabled the integrated presentation of some extremely interesting data in several appendices. One appendix, for example, lists a large number of specific subsurface and aboveground tests, with yield, height of burst, and other details, and lists state-by-state, city-by-city, the fallout recipients of each blast. Another appendix provides maps of fallout trajectories across the U.S. from over 70 tests. The maps and other data reinforce Miller's portrayal of the entire population as living "under the cloud." Notes, index.

2-143 Oulton, Wilfrid E. *Christmas Island Cracker: An Account of the Planning and Execution of the British Thermo-Nuclear Bomb Tests, 1957*. T. Harmsworth, 1987. 412p.

British Air Vice Marshal Oulton offers a chatty, enthusiastic memoir of British H-bomb testing in which he participated. Based in part on many interviews with others who took part in the project. The focus is almost entirely on getting the job done rather than on what the job means. It is also the sort of account in which blue eyes are "piercing" and in which, if one exclamation point will suffice, three are presumably better!!! Lots of interesting photos, though. Glossary, index.

2-144 Robinette, C. Dennis, et al. *Studies of Participants in Nuclear Tests: Final Report, 1 September 1978 - 31 October 1984.* Medical Follow-Up Agency of the National Research Council, 1985. 45p.

An important document for the consideration of those pressing for legal redress for atomic test veterans, not because it lends support to such efforts, but because it does not. A committee of six experts selected by the National Research Council included a geneticist, an epidemiologist, a cancer specialist and other authorities from the University of Wisconsin, Harvard, the University of Texas, and other institutions. They examined the health records, including expected deaths in comparison to those expected in the population at large, of some 46,000 participants in one or more of five nuclear test series in the early to mid-1950s. Their findings, discussed here in detail, lead them to conclude that "there is no consistent or statistically significant evidence for an increase in leukemia or other malignant disease in nuclear test participants." Notes, tables.

2-145 Robinson, Derek. *Just Testing.* Collins Harvill, 1985. 204p.

A study of the aftermath of British nuclear weapons testing in the 1950s, when, according to the author, twenty thousand servicemen witnessed those tests. Robinson claims "a minimum figure of 200" deaths among this group beyond the normal expectancy, especially from radiation-induced cancers such as leukemia. He condemns the British government's "thirty years of violent neglect" of these test victims.

The book includes a large number of statements from former servicemen interviewed about their experiences with testing. Robinson analyzes data obtained from close to 800 questionnaire respondents from among the atomic veterans, and finds some disquieting information. E.g., of the group, sixty reported children born deformed or otherwise handicapped. Includes a list of deceased British atomic veterans, their ages, and causes of death. Cancer predominates.

2–146 Smith, Joan. *Clouds of Deceit: The Deadly Legacy of Britain's Bomb Tests.* Faber and Faber, 1985. 176p.

A journalist who began her investigations of British nuclear testing and its victims while working for the *Sunday Times* pursues the issues in depth in this book. She speaks of "the contagion of secrecy and distrust" that has enveloped government actions concerning the bomb and its test victims, and contends that the British media caved in to government pressure during the time of the tests.

2–147 Symonds, J.L. *A History of British Atomic Tests in Australia.* Australian Government Publishing Service, 1985. 593p.

The author, who served with the Australian Atomic Energy Organization, prepared this history under commission of the Australian Department of Resources and Energy. Given the author's background and the official nature of the undertaking, the book's conclusions can be expected to find little to condemn in the British testing of the 1950s. The book, relying extensively on government documents, meets that expectation, in contrast to various unofficial studies of British testing. Because of the official imprimatur on this book, along with Symonds' access to documents that would prove elusive to other researchers, it deserves reading, preferably in conjunction with less sanguine evaluations of the subject.

2-148 Titus, A. Costandina. *Bombs in the Backyard: Atomic Testing and American Politics.* Univ. of Nevada Pr., 1986. 214p.

Titus provides a concise overview of atomic development in the U.S., and dwells on the testing both above and below ground carried out in Nevada. She shows how the A.E.C. and the military used promises of civilian benefits and the fear of communist encroachment to convince the public that testing was A Good Thing. By far the book's best passages describe what now seems the almost unbelievable equanimity with which Nevada test area residents accepted the nuclear presence in their "backyard," not only accepted, but revelled in it as an exciting tourist attraction. Titus also gives sympathetic attention to the efforts of radiation victims to obtain legal compensation for their suffering. Good illustrations. Don't overlook the cheesecake treat, "Miss Atomic Bomb" posing for her Sands Hotel PR shot. Notes, bibliography, index.

VI. The Cuban Missile Crisis

2-149 Blight, James G. *The Shattered Crystal Ball: Fear and Learning in the Cuban Missile Crisis.* Rowman & Littlefield, 1990. 199p.

A psychological perspective on the crisis by a psychologist. Blight borrows his main title from a chapter in the Harvard Nuclear Study Group's *Living with Nuclear Weapons* (Harvard, 1983), "The Shattered Crystal Ball: How Might Nuclear War Begin?" The Harvard group examines a number of scenarios that might precipitate nuclear war. Blight argues that for at least 48 hours during the Cuban crisis, both Soviet and American leaders "could honestly have said that nuclear war was not only possible, but probable." Blight believes that vicarious participation in the terror springing from this belief can yield useful insight on the continuing avoidance of nuclear war. He takes a phenomenological perspective: what was it like to be in the places of leaders who stood at the verge of seeing their decisions and maneuvers spin out of control into nuclear disaster? Blight's major thesis is "that fear in the missile crisis was not only connected to the outcome, but that it actually *produced* [his emphasis] the learning required to escape the predicament without a war." A unique, well-written and highly interesting approach to the Cuban Missile Crisis. Notes, index.

2-150 _____ and Welch, David A. *On the Brink: Americans and Soviets Reexamine the Cuban Missile Crisis.* Hill & Wang, 1989. 400p.

A fascinating and eye-opening exercise in oral history in which the authors, of the Harvard University Center of Science and International Affairs, brought together American and Soviet participants in the Cuban Missile Crisis, along with scholars of the event, for exchanges and reflections. The resulting conversations point to a number of significant conclusions: effective nuclear "crisis management" is not possible—avoidance of such a crisis is essential; the Soviets were convinced that the U.S. planned to invade Cuba, and make up for the Bay of Pigs fiasco; maintenance of effective superpower communications is vital. Not the least interesting datum is the Soviet acknowledgment that they could not have launched over twenty nuclear warheads at the U.S. from their own soil had the crisis reached flashpoint. The U.S. claimed at the time that the Soviets had over 300 warheads at their disposal. Bibliography.

2-151 Brune, Lester H. *The Missile Crisis of October 1962: A Review of Issues and References.* Regina Books, 1985. 147p.

A succinct but broadly-based scholarly study of the missile crisis that mixes criticism and praise of the nations and individuals involved. The author does a good job of taking into consideration the reactions to the crisis at the time as well as those of later vintage, and places the crisis within the context of both foreign and domestic policies. Brune's bibliographic essay on works concerning the crisis takes up half the book, and, among the books, U.S. documents, articles and other items covered one finds references to both scholarly and general-interest materials. A valuable tool to facilitate an in-depth analysis of the crisis.

2-152 Garthoff, Raymond L. *Reflections on the Cuban Missile Crisis.* Revised edition. Brookings Institution, 1989. 236p.

Garthoff's account of the crisis relies on both English and Russian-language sources, as well as on his personal access to individuals involved in the crisis thanks to his status at the time as a member of the Foreign Service and as a special assistant to the State Department for the Soviet Bloc. Always a thoughtful writer on U.S.-Soviet relations, Garthoff clearly suggests the incredible good luck that helped the superpowers avert disaster in spite of some gross failures of communication between them, and within their own chains of command. His analysis shows that the crisis, generally regarded as having been resolved in October of 1962, continued at a lower level of intensity well into November. Notes, index.

2-153 Medland, William J. *The Cuban Missile Crisis of 1962: Needless or Necessary.* Praeger, 1988. 167p.

A quick guide to the various schools of thought concerning the crisis, schools that the author identifies as "traditional," "Sovietologist," "right-wing revisionism," and so on. By no means comprehensive in its treatment of the literature, but Medland's abstracts of close to fifty articles and books on the crisis will still be useful to students.

2-154 Pope, Ronald R., ed. *Soviet Views on the Cuban Missile Crisis: Myth and Reality in Foreign Policy.*

Univ. Press of America, 1982. 285p.

A presentation and "dissection" of both official and unofficial Soviet views of the crisis, generally identified by the Soviets as "the Caribbean crisis." The assorted documents, with Pope's commentary provided in footnotes, include correspondence between John F. Kennedy and Khrushchev, Khrushchev's official explanation of the crisis and its resolution, and Anatolii A. Gromyko's official account. Considering that mutual perceptions play as important a role in nuclear superpower relations as objective reality, this book is a valuable addition to the literature of the crisis. Maps, bibliography, index.

VII. The Arms Race

2-155 Barnaby, Frank and Thomas, Geoffrey, eds. *The Nuclear Arms Race, Control or Catastrophe?: Proceedings of the General Section of the British Association for the Advancement of Science, 1981.* Frances Pinter, 1982. 250p.

The essays here, most by authors well known in the field, combine an overview of the usual areas of concern (deterrence, nuclear weapons effects, prospects for nuclear war) with the not untouched but less-frequently plowed ground on the relationship between scientists and the fruits of their nuclear weapons work. Contributors include Jozef Rotblat, former British foreign secretary David Owen, a Los Alamos weapons researcher who took up the study of the medical effects of radiation, and Egbert Boeker of the Free University, Amsterdam, who argues for a neutral, denuclearized Europe. Notes.

2-156 Carlton, David and Schaerf, Carlo, eds. *Perspectives on the Arms Race.* Macmillan, 1989. 336p.

The proceedings of the 11th International School on Disarmament and Research on Conflicts, held in San

Miniato, Italy, in August of 1986. Eighteen essays in three categories: the general arms race, the Strategic Defense Initiative, and regional aspects of the arms race. Contributors hail from the UK, the US, Brazil, Italy, Yugoslavia, and other nations. Among the most interesting essays are those dealing with China's defense policy, the origins of the SDI "pipedream," which takes into account Pres. Reagan's pre–White House career (Reagan was the only California governor to ever visit the Livermore Laboratory), and the role of US pressure groups such as the National Institute for Public Policy (Fairfax, VA), led by "limited" nuclear war proponents and ABM Treaty antagonists Keith Payne and Colin S. Gray. Notes, index.

2–157 Craig, Paul P. and Jungerman, John A. *Nuclear Arms Race: Technology and Society*. McGraw–Hill, 1985. 461p.

A textbook divided into three main parts: the nuclear status quo and how it was reached; the technical background of the nuclear arms race; and exploration of the consequences of the arms race, nuclear defense, proliferation, and psychological and economic factors. Although it generally seeks the balanced treatment of a textbook intended to enlighten rather than persuade, the authors are not without their own prescriptions for a nuclear remedy. They set these forth concisely in their concluding chapter. Bibliography, index.

2–158 Dodson, Bert. *Nuke: A Book of Cartoons*. McFarland, 1988. 128p.; *Nuke II: Another Book of Cartoons*. McFarland, 1990. Approx. 144p.

If there is laughter to be found in the nuclear arms race (and people being what they are, they'll laugh at or about anything, especially the things that scare them), Bert Dodson finds the nuclear funnybone in these two collections of comic strips. The "hero" of the majority is a pointy-headed warhead ("Nuke") who finds himself caught up in debates over SDI, hunting, industrial "progress," weapons proliferation, nuclear accidents, and other hot topics. *Nuke II* moves away from Nuke a bit more than the first book in favor of other characters (bunnies, gophers, real-life politicos like George Bush and Ronald Reagan), but addresses similar issues. The artwork is capable, the sensibility ranges from whimsical and wistful to satirically mordant, and the effect is satisfying.

2-159 Easlea, Brian. *Fathering the Unthinkable: Masculinity, Scientists, and the Nuclear Arms Race.* Pluto Pr., 1983. 230p.

Easlea, a mathematical physicist, focuses on "the overall 'masculine' nature of modern science and particularly weapons science." His thesis is that masculine behavior plays a major role in "underwriting" the nuclear arms race, and that this behavior originates in "an unsatisfactory sexual division of labour between men and women in both the 'domestic' and 'public' domains, in particular in the domestic domain of childbirth, baby and infant care and in the public domain of control over nature." (One cannot help but think of Edward Teller's famous announcement of a successful H-bomb test with the grotesque declaration, "It's a boy!")

Easlea portrays the scientists and others who continue to perfect new and more terrible weaponry as satisfying a culturally-conditioned masculine satisfaction in creating danger for themselves and for others. The "others" are the vast majority of the population who seem to have no control over the boys behind the bombs. A useful perspective supported with numerous references to both contemporary and historical authorities. Notes, index.

2-160 Gertcher, Frank L. and Weida, William J. *Beyond Deterrence: The Political Economy of Nuclear Weapons.* Westview, 1990. 362p.

The main topic here is the way economic and political

incentives result in a continuing demand for further nuclear weapon production. The authors examine among other areas nuclear proliferation in the Middle East ("a tinderbox," they say), South Africa, and other nations. They discuss the possible effects of strategic defense, the "nuclear weapon infrastructure" in the U.S., the Soviet Union, and elsewhere, the impact of U.S. regional defense spending on the inertia for nuclear weapons, and the reallocation of nuclear weapon resources to non-defense applications. A useful book for advanced students investigating the link between nuclear weapons and the intense competition, in the U.S. and other nations, for available resources. Notes, bibliography, index.

2-161 Holland, Lauren H. and Hoover, Robert A. *The MX Decision: A New Direction in U.S. Weapons Procurement Policy?* Westview, 1985. 289p.

The MX has been deployed to this point in existing Minuteman silos whose vulnerability is in question. The authors found the bureaucratic politics perspective generally underlying weapons procurement unsatisfactory in explaining MX decision-making. Their investigations led them to see MX policymaking as the result of interplay among several factors "that may never converge again," including, among others, a weapon system capable of massive impacts, lack of consensus on the objectives informing the system's development, a system that is technically flawed, and a project for which an opposition movement operates in several decision-making areas simultaneously. A detailed study of the controversial history of the weapon dubbed the "Peacekeeper" by Ronald Reagan. Glossary, bibliography, index.

2-162 Huisken, Ronald. *The Origin of the Strategic Cruise Missile.* Praeger, 1981. 202p.

The cruise missile was a significant player in two of the past decade's most important nuclear developments: NATO deployment of cruise and Pershing

II missiles, and their subsequent scrapping, with several Soviet missile classifications, under the INF Treaty. Huisken, a defense analyst with the Australian government at the time of this book's publication, discusses the technical characteristics of the cruise, the history of such prototypes as the Snark and Regulus missiles, submarine and air-launched versions, and the missile's role in nuclear strategy. The cruise, he argues, became an inevitable part of U.S. armaments with the June, 1977 cancellation of the B-1 bomber. Notes, index.

2-163 Inglis, David R. *To End the Arms Race: Seeking a Safer Future.* Univ. of Mich. Pr., 1986. 268p.

Inglis, a theoretical physicist and veteran of bomb research, has written on arms control and other nuclear topics since the early 1950s. This collection assembles over 30 of his essays published 1951-1978 on a full range of nuclear issues, from testing and disarmament planning to antiballistic missiles and "Attitudes and Decisions." *Bulletin of the Atomic Scientists* is the most frequent source of the essays; others include *New Republic, Saturday Review,* and *Centennial Review.* As Norman Cousins says in his foreword, Inglis is "eager to see strong public support for the establishment of governmental policies at home or abroad that promote approaches and policies for bringing the weapons under control and for strengthening the concept of workable world order."

2-164 Kurtz, Lester R., et al. *The Nuclear Cage: A Sociology of the Arms Race.* Prentice-Hall, 1988. 335p.

Kurtz, of the University of Texas at Austin, is no optimist about the future of humanity, but his work in putting together this textbook on the arms race and means of "coping with the nuclear threat" suggests that he has not completely thrown in the towel. The book adequately introduces a range of nuclear issues, from how the bombs work to reflections on the peace movement. Kurtz takes his metaphor of "the nuclear cage" from Max Weber's "iron cage," used to describe the nature of bureaucratic institutions. Notes, bibliography, index.

2-165 Laird, Robbin F. *The Soviet Union, the West, and the Nuclear Arms Race.* New York Univ. Pr., 1986. 236p.

Laird examines in this book's ten essays the development of post-war Soviet nuclear weapons policies, the evolution of American policies, and the positions of France and Britain. The focus on Western Europe at a time when the Berlin Wall still stood inevitably casts some of this book in a different light, but the historical overview Laird provides of the strategic moves and countermoves between East and West is concise and helpful. Notes, index.

2-166 Levi, Barbara G., et al., eds. *The Future of Land-Based Strategic Missiles.* American Institute of Physics, 1989. 287p.

One of this book's virtues is that, unlike almost any other collection of individually-written papers on a topic, this one begins with a list of "findings" on which all contributors agree. Among these findings: if land based missiles are not upgraded, the U.S. strategic arsenal may evolve toward a diad of strategic bombers and submarines; even in vulnerable basing, single warhead missiles contribute significantly to crisis stability; terminal defense might provide partial survivability of ICBMs, but raises several arms control issues. Anyone looking for an in-depth discussion of the ICBM's past and present will find this volume fruitful, whether concerning strategic doctrine and ICBMs, evaluation of future basing options, or research on vulnerability, command and control, or engineering of missile silos. The study group responsible for the work consists of ten physicists and engineers with extensive background in strategic issues. Notes, illustrations.

2-167 Osmar, Nils. *A Cartoon History of the Nuclear Arms Race.* Starwind Pr., 1984. 24p.

A simply-presented account of the nuclear arms race in black & white comic-book format. The wonderful simplicity and stark clarity of this historically accurate treatment contrast in telling fashion with the endless volumes of arcane exegesis produced by scholars of the Nuclear Age. Anyone able to read at a reasonable elementary-school level could grasp Osmar's account, but it is in no way patronizing or condescending. The chief problem will be in obtaining a copy of the comic. Bibliography.

2-168 Powaski, Ronald E. *March to Armageddon: The United States and the Nuclear Arms Race, 1939 to the Present.* Oxford Univ. Pr., 1987.

Powaski points out that each U.S. president since Truman has promised to pursue restraint in the growth of superpower arsenals as well as seeking to halt nuclear proliferation, yet each has, in fact, increased the destructive force of the American arsenal and has allowed acquisition of nuclear weapons capability by non-nuclear states. He seeks to account "for this discrepancy between presidential words and actions," and in the process examines each nuclear presidency from Roosevelt to Reagan. Among the factors he identifies in the discrepancy is the continuing American reliance on power politics (military force is the ultimate means of obtaining national objectives), the dynamics of the Cold War, the influence of the military-industrial complex, and other phenomena. Notes, bibliography, index.

2-169 Prins, Gwyn, ed. *Defended to Death: A Study of the Nuclear Arms Race.* Penguin, 1983. 387p.

An overview of the arms race beginning with World War I. "The authors of this book do not deny that there is a 'Soviet threat,' but there is also an American threat, a French threat, and a British threat, and all these threats are the same: it is the possession of nuclear weapons that threatens the possessor with destruction by those of the other power, which fears destruction by the first party's weapons." The bias is antinuclear; there is a good examination of the cruise and Pershing II missiles and perhaps too relenting an attitude toward Soviet contributions to the arms race. Bibliography, index.

2–170 Rosenblum, Simon. *Misguided Missiles: Canada, the Cruise, and Star Wars.* J. Lorimer, 1985. 234p.

As the subtitle notes, the author examines the cruise missile (tested in Canada) and SDI from Canadian perspectives, and doesn't like what he sees. He urges Canada's abandonment of its participation in the development of nuclear weapons "as a sign that the endless escalation of nuclear weaponry can be checked."

2–171 Schroeer, Dietrich, and Hafemeister, David, eds. *Nuclear Arms Technologies in the 1990s: Washington, DC, 1988.* American Institute of Physics, 1988. 476p.

The 1988 conference proceedings of the American Institute of Physics. The eighteen papers address the environmental effects of nuclear war, the nuclear arms race between India and Pakistan, verification technologies, strategic defense, nuclear arms policies, and other issues. The majority of the contributors are scientists, with a few exceptions in the fields of international relations and strategy. Not a volume that will be high on the selection list for most libraries, given its generally unexceptional offerings compared to more rigorously-compiled anthologies covering similar territory.

2–172 Schwartz, William A. and Derber, Charles, et al. *The Nuclear Seduction: Why the Arms Race Doesn't Matter, and What Does.* Univ. of Calif. Pr., 1990. 294p.

The authors constitute the Boston Nuclear Study Group, which formed with the original intention of responding to the Harvard Nuclear Study Group's *Living with Nuclear Weapons* (Harvard Univ. Pr., 1983), a mainstream statement on the problem. The Boston Group's response evolved into an attempt to avoid both mainstream and predictable opposition points of view; their analysis suggests that the global nuclear debate "largely focuses on a set of marginal issues and with only a few exceptions ignores the real risk factors for nuclear war." They identify the "seductive" aspects of the nuclear world as the giant weapons systems, so obvious, so frightening, and so easily fixated upon. The real source of danger, however, lies in the Third World, "where the superpowers and their clients confront each other every day, often hidden from public view, and where they periodically collide in terrifying crises that threaten to provoke worldwide catastrophe."

Whether the authors' thesis is especially novel is debatable, but their discussions of Third World superpower adventurism, with a large number of case studies, the link between U.S. foreign policy and nuclear war, nuclear misperceptions of leadership, and other nuclear issues merits attention. The authors rely on an interesting word, "weaponitis," coined by political scientist Samuel Huntington in 1983, to describe the preoccupation with the weaponry in exclusion of focus on the actual problem(s).

2–173 Smith, Theresa C. and Singh, Indu B. *Security vs. Survival: The Nuclear Arms Race.* L. Rienner, 1985. 195p.

Eight essays drawn from lectures presented at Rutgers University in an effort by the University to answer a perceived obligation to equip ordinary individuals with information and opinion needed to help determine the merits of the nation's nuclear policies. The biggest "name" here is Herman Kahn, who writes on central nuclear war. Others address military spending and the U.S. economy, medical consequences of nuclear war, "limited" nuclear war, and other topics. Glossary, index.

VIII. Asia and the Pacific

2-174 Coates, Ken, ed. *China and the Bomb.* Spokesman; Dist. by Humanities Pr., 1986. 111p.

An essay by the editor precedes a modest collection of official statements made over a period of two decades-plus, along with a handful of articles by spokesmen of various Chinese public organizations. Coates writes of China's vulnerability to Soviet nuclear attack in his brief review of the Chinese nuclear position. A slight book, but one that offers quick access to some pertinent points of view. Anyone using this book, however, will want to turn to meatier treatments of China and the bomb, especially John Lewis's *China Builds the Bomb* (item 2-177).

2-175 Hayes, Peter; Zarsky, Lyuba; Bello, Walden. *American Lake: Nuclear Peril in the Pacific.* Penguin, 1987. 529p.

"This book," says the preface, "tells the story of American and Soviet plans for nuclear war in the Pacific." The first portion of the study examines the authors' view of the imminence of American nuclear attacks on Korea and China in the 1950s; the second surveys American and Soviet military forces in the region; the third, "Charting a New Pacific," visualizes means by which the Pacific might be wrested from the nuclear domain. The authors set out such approaches as a nuclear-free zone in the region, non-intervention zones, and "people's diplomacy." The chapter "Nuclear Epitaph?" is a believable scenario for nuclear war originating in Korea and proceeding in rapid increments, through miscalculation, technical glitches and fatalism to envelop the globe. Notes, index.

2-176 Landais-Stamp, Paul and Rogers, Paul. *Rocking the Boat: New Zealand, the United States and the Nuclear-Free Zone Controversy in the 1980s.* St. Martin's, 1989. 185p.

Two peace scholars investigate the New Zealand–U.S. relationship as it concerns the former's participation in the U.S. military program, specifically regarding nuclear weapons. New Zealand Prime Minister David Lange was elected to office in 1984 partly on the basis of his promise to ban nuclear-powered and nuclear-armed warships from New Zealand harbors. The book concentrates on the period 1984–1987, when the U.S. brought heavy pressure on New Zealand to rescind the nuclear ban. The authors see the ban in the context of long-term developments in the Pacific. An interesting examination of the superpower-ally status, although Stuart McMillan's *Neither Confirm Nor Deny* is probably a better treatment. Bibliography, index.

2-177 Lewis, John W. and Litai, Xue. *China Builds the Bomb.* Stanford Univ. Pr., 1988. 329p.

China set off its first nuclear bomb on Oct. 16, 1964. This in-depth study of the nation's bomb-building project covers the period 1955–1967. The treatment takes into account both the real or perceived threat of American nuclear aggression and the project's debt to Soviet assistance, which provided major elements required for China to fulfill its nuclear aspirations. The authors portray the Bomb as a national goal of the highest priority; the Chinese government called the first test "a major achievement of the Chinese people in their struggle to strengthen their national defense and oppose the U.S. imperialist policy of nuclear blackmail and nuclear threats." It may be fortunate that this study was prepared in a time of relative openness in the Chinese regime, for some of the official histories and memoirs on which it is based might have resisted efforts to procure them in China's renewed insularity. Includes an appendix briefly describing the contributions of some three dozen "Key

Figures in China's Nuclear Weapons Program." Another appendix lists China's nuclear tests, 1964–1978. Bibliography, index.

2–178 McMillan, Stuart. *Neither Confirm Nor Deny: The Nuclear Ships Dispute between New Zealand and the United States.* Praeger, 1987. 177p.

A good discussion of the domestic and international repercussions of New Zealand's decision to turn away U.S. vessels bearing nuclear weapons. McMillan, who writes on international and strategic affairs for the New Zealand paper *The Press*, focuses on the concerns involved in the country's decision and the U.S. refusal to modify its policy on confirmation or denial of the presence of nuclear weapons aboard its naval vessels. In a balanced analysis, he argues that both nations nicely illustrate Barbara Tuchman's characterization of nations as expressed in *The March of Folly* (Knopf, 1984) as having a limitless capacity to act stupidly toward one another and toward their own interests. Notes, index.

2–179 Pugh, Michael C. *The ANZUS Crisis, Nuclear Visiting and Deterrence.* Cambridge Univ. Pr., 1989. 285p.

Pugh describes New Zealand's denial of visiting rights to U.S. nuclear warships as neither a David and Goliath clash nor as "preposterous grandstanding by a socialist government under the sway of misguided or even malevolent pacifists," although both interpretations received widespread acceptance. He finds instead that New Zealand's decision, "rather than a contagious threat," is symptomatic of separatist trends in the Western Alliance. He contends that a major issue at stake "is the extent to which the United States places a greater value on nuclearism than the political goals which nuclear deterrence is said to safeguard." He examines U.S. responses and reprisals, anti-nuclear activism in New Zealand, environmental, regional security, and other issues tied to the decision. Notes, bibliography, index.

2–180 Ryan, Mark A. *Chinese Attitudes toward Nuclear Weapons: China and the United States During the Korean War*. M.E. Sharpe, 1989. 327p.

Originated as a dissertation for Georgetown University. Ryan argues that some basic Chinese attitudes toward nuclear weapons and war developed during the Korean War; these attitudes relate to nuclear disarmament and proliferation, civil defense, and the likely repercussions of nuclear war. Ryan finds a tendency in the West to have overestimated Chinese fear of nuclear weapons, and makes some interesting observations on Chinese v. American perceptions of various nuclear issues, especially civil defense. From 1962 into the Reagan years, the U.S. approach to CD was pretty much hands off, partly in response to a belief that CD preparations are provocative. China made a significant commitment to CD, and believed that this commitment helped hold the Soviets at bay during tensions of the late 1960s and early '70s. Ironically, with the efficacy of CD at its lowest point historically, the notion of "a few shovelfuls of dirt" as a way to avoid the Bomb's effects made a limited resurgence under Reagan, and the fantasy of the invincible nuclear shield of "Star Wars" represented the ultimate in civil defense.

IX. Behind the Scenes at the Bomb Factories

2–181 Coyle, Dana, et al. *Deadly Defense: Military Radioactive Landfills*. Radioactive Waste Campaign, 1988. 169p.

In this treatment of the radioactive waste problems associated with weapons production, testing, and storage, the authors contend that massive releases of radioactive pollution "are endemic to the entire nuclear weapons production apparatus." The book discusses something of the history of the Bomb and its waste production, profiles thirteen U.S. nuclear weapons plants and the Nevada Test Site, dwells at length on the Oak Ridge Reservation and the Fernald (OH) Feed Materials Production Center, and discusses health effects of radiation.

The pollution record described here is astounding and appalling. The Fernald plant alone has reportedly released close to 400,000 pounds of uranium dust into the air, soil and water. Contributors have professional backgrounds in geology, journalism, physics, medicine, and avocational backgrounds as activists. Based on their examination of citizen action efforts at Hanford, Livermore, and Rocky Flats, they contend that people can effectively mobilize to combat nuclear weapons pollution. Includes a large, foldout map delineating nuclear materials' transportation routes among the U.S. weapons facilities.

2-182 Del Tredici, Robert. *At Work in the Fields of the Bomb*. Harper & Row, 1987. 192p.

106 black & white photographs by the author, some striking, some pedestrian, but all pertinent to the nuclear world. Minuteman missile launch operatives, a train loaded with radioactive whey powder contaminated by the Chernobyl accident, a uranium mill, neutron bomb inventor Sam Cohen, and 2,000 jars of human organs from people irradiated by the Nagasaki bomb (stored in hopes that they will one day provide useful information about radiation damage) are a handful of the subjects portrayed. Interviews and field notes collected by the author during his project follow the photographs.

2-183 Loeb, Paul. *Nuclear Culture: Living & Working in the World's Largest Atomic Complex*. New Society, 1986. 260p.

A disturbing look at the lives of the men and women who work the Hanford Nuclear Reservation in Washington State. Loeb focuses in a sympathetic, anecdotal manner on the Reservation's 13,000 atomic workers who labor in a complex that is half the size of Rhode Island and one of the nation's major nuclear weapons facilities. Loeb interviews many of the citizens of the adjacent towns—Richland, Kennewick, and Pasco—that feed Hanford its employees; they discuss their impressions of earning their bread by the grace of the Bomb, and deliver their rationalizations for doing so. A worthy companion to Mojtabai's *Blessed Assurance.*

2-184 Mojtabai, A.G. *Blessed Assurance: At Home with the Bomb in Amarillo, Texas.* Houghton Mifflin, 1986. 255p.

The Pantex plant in Amarillo is the final assembly site for all U.S. nuclear weapons. Mojtabai's is a sensitive human interest story of the men and women of Pantex and Amarillo, with two chief attitudes under consideration: the technocratic ("Steady Technological Progress") and the apocalyptic ("End Time"). As befits the title ("Blessed Assurance, Jesus Is Mine!" is a popular hymn in Amarillo churches), the greater part of the book is devoted to the religious apocalyptic outlook, including such remarkable perversions of Christian doctrine as the Rapture, through which the "saved" will be wafted to Heaven in their corporeal forms—they'll just disappear from planet earth— before the nuclear "Tribulation" begins below. A basic item for those exploring the psycho–religious epiphenomena of the Bomb.

2-185 Parfit, Michael. *The Boys Behind the Bombs.* Little, Brown, 1983. 298p.

Parfit's consistent treatment of himself in this book as a third person ("Michael drove on a wet highway between hills that were bright with new grass, poppies, and mustard.") may be taken as needlessly coy, as a clever narrative device, or as an easily-overlooked quirk, but his investigation of the old–boy nuclear weapons network reads almost like a novel.

Not, alas, a particularly interesting one in most places, for its subjects, weapons men all, come across as unexceptional technocrats. Lack of a name index is a real irritant.

2-186 Rosenthal, Debra. *At the Heart of the Bomb: The Dangerous Allure of Weapons Work*. Addison-Wesley, 1990. 244p.

Based on 260 hours of interviews with close to 100 people who work or have worked in the two nuclear weapons design facilities in New Mexico. Forty-one interviewees were from Los Alamos, the rest from Sandia. Engineers, technicians, scientists, the Los Alamos priest, researchers and assorted others speak through these pages; Rosenthal is not averse to offering her own opinions: "They believe we can prepare indefinitely for both genocide and suicide without ever giving in to the temptation to try it." Relaxed, anecdotal, yet disciplined prose, with occasional unobtrusive footnotes. A far more satisfying look at "the boys behind the bombs" than Michael Parfit's book of that title. Bibliography, index.

2-187 U.S. Congress. House. Committee on Energy and Commerce. Subcommittee on Transportation and Hazardous Materials. *Environmental Crimes at DOE's Nuclear Weapons Facilities: Hearing before the Subcommittee on Transportation and Hazardous Materials of the Committee on Energy and Commerce, House of Representatives, 101st Congress, First Session, October 5, 1989*. U.S. Government Printing Office, 1990. 118p. Su. Docs. No. Y 4.En 2/3-101-106.

A hearing on the situation at U.S. weapons plants, described as "out of control" by subcommittee chairman Thomas A. Luken, in a "de facto state of environmental lawlessness which has existed at DOE plants over the last 4 years which has resulted in the defiling and the desecrating of the land and water and air at the facilities and the surrounding areas." Witnesses called include DOE contractors, the

Inspector General of the DOE, and representatives of citizens' groups at Rocky Flats, CO, and Fernald, OH. The most interesting statements are those from citizens who describe and lament the nuclear-weapons-related environmental blunders—or crimes—that have taken place in their neighborhoods.

2-188 U.S. Congress. House. Committee on Energy and Commerce. Subcommittee on Oversight and Investigations. *Nuclear Weapons Facilities: Hearing before the Subcommittee on Oversight and Investigations of the Committee on Energy and Commerce, House of Representatives, 99th Congress, Second Session, on Adequacy of Safeguards and Security at Department of Energy Nuclear Weapons Production Facilities, March 6, 1986.* U.S. Government Printing Office, 1987. 217p. Su. Docs No. Y 4.En 2/3-99-143.

An assembly of prepared statements, testimony, and reproduced documents concerning security of U.S. nuclear weapons production facilities from terrorist attack. The document opens with chairman John D. Dingell's remarks on theft of plutonium and bomb components from the Savannah River facility, and his accusation that a previous assurance of adequate security was "a lie." Witnesses representing the Dept. of Energy discuss security provisions at the various weapons facilities around the country. Contains numerous photos of scenes from these facilities, and a number of passages marked "DELETED" for security purposes.

2-189 Weeramantry, C.G. *Nuclear Weapons and Scientific Responsibility.* Longwood Academic, 1987. 227p.

The author, a professor of international law, argues that nuclear weapons' indiscriminate effects make them "illegal," and that those who help develop them are legally responsible for them. Forceful but not splenetic, opinionated but under control, this analysis of the social responsibility of nuclear weapons scientists is a worthwhile contribution to the literature on this troubling issue. The scientist, he writes, "must be more conscious of the power he wields. He must also be more conscious of the responsibility that goes with that power." A number of appendices contain statements by nuclear scientists indicating some of the consciousness of the results of their work of the sort desired by the author. Notes, index.

X. Western European Perspectives

2-190 Botti, Timothy J. *The Long Wait: The Forging of the Anglo-American Nuclear Alliance, 1945-1958.* Greenwood Pr., 1987. 274p.

The U.S. and Great Britain required several years after WW II to develop a close working relationship in nuclear weapons. Not until well into the Eisenhower administration did the U.S. enter a period of enthusiastic "nuclear collaboration" [Botti's term] with Great Britain. On July 3, 1958, the two nations agreed on a long-term nuclear alliance. "What finally forced the door open," writes Botti, "was the Eisenhower administration's New Look defense policy and emphasis on nuclear weapons to deter Soviet aggression and defend Western Europe." (The New Look was Eisenhower's emphasis on nuclear weapons as a whole.) Botti's is a detailed, scholarly study of the nuclear weapons interactions between the U.S. and Great Britain during the period covered, based on research in archival sources as well as in published materials. Notes, bibliography, index.

2-191 Boutwell, Jeffrey D. *The German Nuclear Dilemma.* Cornell Univ. Pr., 1990. 247p.

Another worthy contribution to nuclear area studies that has been undercut to some extent by political developments since the work's conclusion. Boutwell completed this study before the reunification of Germany. Nevertheless, readers looking into the history of the deployment of tactical nuclear weapons in Western Europe will find the book worth their time. Boutwell examines the situation from the 1940s into the late 1980s, and reflects at length on the INF issue, NATO nuclear policy, the Afghan crisis and the peace movement, and inter-German relations, 1980-1989. He identifies the core of the dilemma referred to in the title as the need for a reliance on nuclear deterrence to entail a credible threat to actually use the weapons. Helmut Schmidt, West German chancellor, has long been an advocate of deterrence, yet has publicly dismissed the possibility of using nuclear weapons. Notes, bibliography, index.

2-192 Buteux, Paul. *The Politics of Nuclear Consultation in NATO, 1965-1980*. Cambridge Univ. Pr., 1983. 292p.

A systematic attempt to examine the impact of nuclear weapons on NATO. Addresses the role of the alliance in determining how political issues arising among the allies are resolved. The focus is on consultation and the Nuclear Planning Group, which originated in a proposal by Robert S. McNamara in 1965 to develop a committee of allied defense ministers who would seek improved consultation among the allies on nuclear planning. Bibliography, index.

2-193 Cioc, Mark. *Pax Atomica: The Nuclear Defense Debate in West Germany During the Adenauer Era.* Columbia Univ. Pr., 1988. 251p.

In the 1950s, NATO's most extensive nuclear installation (some 3,400 U.S.-built warheads and 240 facilities) went into West Germany as a deterrent to Soviet aggression, whose imminence seemed to be suggested by the North Korean action against South Korea. NATO offered to train West German soldiers in the use of nuclear-capable systems, but many observers feared a resurgent German military machine, with the fingers of former Nazi generals "on the nuclear trigger." This study of a major public policy issue up to the middle 1960s originated as a doctoral dissertation. Ample illustrations include editorial cartoons that help provide a good sense of the era's attitudes. Notes, bibliography, index.

2–194 Cuthbertson, Ian M. and Robertson, David. *Enhancing European Security: Living in a Less Nuclear World*. Macmillan, 1990. 223p.

The authors look forward to substantial reduction in conventional forces and the elimination of nuclear weapons as playing a significant deterrent role in Europe. They maintain, however, that military readiness will remain a meaningful instrument in European affairs even as the superpower military presence in Europe declines. They propose, among other measures, that long–range, high–technology weapons be banned from Europe; that to assure effective cuts in conventional forces, U.S. and Soviet units currently deployed in Europe be demobilized, not merely withdrawn, and that severe restrictions be placed on armor, mobile weapons, and aircraft infrastructure support. The book contains useful insights regarding the difficult, nuts & bolts bargaining that must take place to help secure non-nuclear stability in contemporary Europe. Notes, index.

2–195 Freeman, J.P.G. *Britain's Nuclear Arms Control Policy in the Context of Anglo–American Relations, 1957–1958*. Macmillan, 1986. 317p.

In this revised doctoral dissertation, Freeman studies successive British governments' nuclear arms control policies during the years indicated, a period that saw such important steps as the Partial Test Ban Treaty halting atmospheric testing in 1963, and the Non-Proliferation Treaty of 1968, which Great Britain was the first nation to ratify. Freeman's central theme "is that Britain's attitude to nuclear arms control and disarmament was conditioned primarily and fundamentally by the perceived requirements of her security and by the restraints imposed by her relationship with the U.S." He discusses test ban negotiations under Macmillan and Eisenhower, then Macmillan and Kennedy; the Campaign for Nuclear Disarmament, British scientists and nuclear arms control, the quest for the NPT, and other issues. A good volume to follow Botti's *The Long Wait*. Notes, bibliography, index.

2–196 Holm, Hans–Henrik and Petersen, Nikolaj, eds. *The European Missiles Crisis: Nuclear Weapons and Security Policy*. F. Pinter, 1983. 274p.

Eight essays, all but one by European academicians and officials addressing problems surrounding NATO's 1979 decision to deploy cruise and Pershing II missiles at the same time as pursuing negotiations on intermediate range nuclear forces. The book's long introduction, by Ib Faurby and the editors will be especially helpful to those seeking an historical overview of the Euromissile crisis. "The INF Issue— History and Implications" provides just such a perspective. Bibliography, index.

2–197 Hopmann, P. Terrence and Barnaby, Frank, eds. *Rethinking the Nuclear Weapons Dilemma in Europe*. Macmillan, 1988. 374p.

Proceedings of a 1985 conference in Racine, Wisconsin involving participants from several European countries and the U.S. The volume's 21 papers are in six main divisions: "Nuclear Weapons in Europe"; "'No First Use' of Nuclear Weapons in Europe"; "Alternatives to Nuclear Deterrence in Europe"; "Crisis Management and War Avoidance in Europe"; "Conventional Arms, Arms Control and the Nuclear Threshold"; and "The Domestic Political Context." Notes, index.

2–198 Howorth, Jolyon and Chilton, Patricia, eds. *Defence and Dissent in Contemporary France*. St.

Martin's, 1984. 264p.

Ten essays on post-war French defense policies and critical responses to those policies, with an emphasis on nuclear issues. Contributors are British and French scholars; they look at the historical context of French defense policy, French nuclear weapons, the French peace movement, and other issues. Notes, bibliography.

2-199 Malone, Peter. *The British Nuclear Deterrent: A History.* St. Martin's, 1984. 200p.

Written from the point of view that "Britain's nuclear weapons programme has been a rather striking success," and is one that should be operationally independent. Discusses technical issues, political questions, "the American connection," NATO and cost considerations, and the Thatcher government's decision to procure a new generation of submarines equipped with the American Trident missiles beginning in 1980. A question that comes to mind is whether Britain's nuclear force has, in fact, deterred the Soviet Union in any measurable respect. If it has not, then its success might be less striking than Malone believes. Bibliography, notes, index.

2-200 Marsh, Catherine and Fraser, Colin, eds. *Public Opinion and Nuclear Weapons.* Macmillan, 1989. 220p.

Eleven essays by social scientists expressing a diversity of personal positions. The publics of concern here are chiefly those of Great Britain and Europe; specific targets of opinion include deterrence, SDI, disarmament, and the role of the nuclear debate in the 1983 British election. Notes, index.

2-201 Miall, Hugh. *Nuclear Weapons: Who's In Charge?* Macmillan, 1987. 167p.

Seeks to answer the question, why do we continue to build new nuclear weapons? Miall argues that decision-making processes leading to nuclear weapons, processes that are theoretically controlled by the public through constitutional agencies, possess a life of their own. Miall first examines the nuclear scientists, defense contractors, government officials and others who design, build, and administer the weapons, then discusses the public accountability of these individuals. Because of Miall's British perspective, and his discussion of the U.S. not as the prime mover on the nuclear stage but as one of several players, along with his discussions of those other players, the book may be of particular use to American readers. Index.

2-202 Pierre, Andrew J., ed. *Nuclear Weapons in Europe*. Council on Foreign Relations, 1984. 118p.

A useful little book that addresses questions beyond those raised by the INF controversy raging at the time of the book's publication. These include whether the security of Western Europe should depend on the U.S., what role American nuclear weapons based on the continent should have, whether NATO should adopt a "No First Use" policy, and the appropriate place of arms control in Western security policy and the future evolution of East-West relations. The four essays comprising the book include William G. Hyland's "The Struggle for Europe: An American View"; Lawrence D. Freedman's "U.S. Nuclear Weapons in Europe: Symbols, Strategy, and Force Structure"; Paul Warnke's "The Illusion of NATO's Nuclear Defense"; and Karsten D. Voight's "Nuclear Weapons in Europe: A German Social Democrat's Perspective."

2-203 Ramsbotham, Oliver. *Modernizing NATO's Nuclear Weapons: "No Decisions Have Been Made."* Macmillan, 1989. 257p.

Scilla E. McLean contends in the foreword that recent advances in nuclear arms reduction between the superpowers "have lulled the public into a false sense of security." The author studies NATO's and the

Warsaw Pact's nuclear weapons modernization programs, discusses objections to modernization, shows the range of opinion existing on the question throughout NATO, and presents arguments for and against modernization as he perceives them. He urges full attention to the issues in national parliaments as a way to the "universally desired" result: "the evolution of international security arrangements which will enable nuclear weapons to be safely and steadily marginalized, to the point where they will no longer be deployed side-by-side with conventional forces in Europe at all." Notes, index.

2-204 Ruston, Roger. *A Say in the End of the World: Morals and British Nuclear Weapons Policy, 1941-1987*. Oxford Univ. Pr., 1989. 272p.

Ruston examines the rationales offered by British governments for their reliance on nuclear weapons, how they have handled the moral problems involved, and whether their rationalizations stand up to scrutiny. He deals mostly with official arguments, reasons offered in both public and private for important policy decision, and reviews not only Great Britain's nuclear history, but the issues of "just war," appeasement, and strategic bombing. Ruston systematically undercuts the rationales advanced concerning Britain's status as a world power, equal footing with the U.S., a necessary counter to Soviet weapons, a cheap defense compared to conventional forces, and the ability to resist nuclear blackmail. Notes, bibliography, index.

2-205 Sabin, Philip A.G. *The Third World War Scare in Britain: A Critical Analysis*. Macmillan, 1986. 191p.

Sabin, an antinuclear activist in the late 1970s and early 1980s, found his estimation of nuclear war's imminence growing less anxiety-provoking as he learned about the political and historical background of the nuclear age. He came to believe, with most defense experts, "that there is actually very little risk of a major East/West conflict in the foreseeable future." In this book, with the help of data from public opinion polls, he investigates the exacerbated fears of nuclear war common in Great Britain in the early 1980s. He urges a more open approach to the debate over nuclear policies as one way to help avoid further intensification of nuclear anxieties. Bibliography, index.

2-206 Schwartz, David N. *NATO's Nuclear Dilemmas.* Brookings Institution, 1983. 270p.

Schwartz traces the events leading to the 1979 NATO decision to deploy the Pershing II and ground-launched cruise missiles; his investigation entails discussion of "NATO's Nuclear Addiction" over the long term, from the Truman and Eisenhower administrations on, with substantial attention to the dubious trust Western Europe could place in the "guarantee" of an American nuclear response to Soviet aggression in Europe. A valuable, concise history. Bibliography, index.

2-207 Sigal, Leon V. *Nuclear Forces in Europe: Enduring Dilemmas, Present Prospects.* Brookings Institution, 1984. 181p.

Another effort to dissect the dilemmas of NATO's 1979 decision to deploy intermediate range cruise and ballistic missiles. Sigal's study concerns contradictions in NATO strategy, including those in the military rationale for the new deployments, the antinuclear mood and movement in Europe, and the relationship between battlefield nuclear weapons and stable deterrence. Sigal's own position on the situation then prevailing: "If nothing is done to reverse the present direction, the problem of how to prevent nuclear weapons from being used -- inadvertently, accidentally, or deliberately -- will become all the more unmanageable." Notes, index.

2-208 Simpson, John. *The Independent Nuclear State: The United States, Britain, and the Military Atom*. 2d edition. Macmillan, 1986. 341p.

A chronological account and overview of the history of British military research, development, and production work in atomic energy, with a focus on the links between the British and American nuclear weapon and submarine programs. Simpson identifies six major periods in the stages of nuclear dependency and interdependency between the two nations; the most important of these took place from 1958–1964, with reciprocal Anglo–American interaction leading to the rapid development of a British nuclear stockpile and a switch to the use of U.S.-made strategic delivery systems. Simpson argues that "the possibility of recapturing non-nuclear innocence disappeared during the decade between 1955 and 1965, without the majority of the British population or their legislators being fully aware of it." The study features extensive reliance on U.K. and U.S. archival materials. Notes, bibliography, index.

XI. Literary Studies

2-209 Bartter, Martha A. *The Way to Ground Zero: The Atomic Bomb in American Science Fiction*. Greenwood Pr., 1988. 278p.

Bartter's is an often-fascinating work on the American science fiction of the Bomb. She gives considerable space to a discussion of pre-Bomb fiction envisioning new and apocalyptic methods of war, and investigates the sociological and psychological aspects of science fiction's efforts to contend with the threat of nuclear destruction. The long bibliography is a good guide to both short stories and novels. Her most intense coverage of a given author, or authors, is a comparison of the fiction of Theodore Sturgeon and Robert A. Heinlein. It is unfortunate that, given the historical aversion of most libraries to maintaining files of such periodicals as *Amazing Stories* and

Astounding Science-Fiction, much of the short fiction (and Bartter has zealously identified some 250 short stories, in addition to over 100 novels) will prove problematic for many readers to obtain. Bibliography.

2-210 Brians, Paul. *Nuclear Holocausts: Atomic War in Fiction, 1895-1984.* Kent State Univ. Pr., 1987. 398p.

A survey of novels and stories published in English depicting nuclear war (or something very much like it) and its aftermath. Together with books by others noted in this section, Brians' work makes a major rectification of the relative absence of critical attention to the fiction of nuclear war. Brians divides the book between a very good annotated bibliography of the fiction and his essays on how nuclear fiction has treated such topics as the long-term consequences of nuclear war, causes of nuclear war, and "The History of the Holocaust." His annotations in the bibliographic portion are generally substantial and critical; a "Timeline" provides a year-by-year guide to nuclear or quasi-nuclear fiction in English. A supplementary checklist itemizes works of fiction in which nuclear war is narrowly averted; another lists "doubtful cases" in which nuclear war may or may not have occurred, and others focus on nuclear testing and atomic reactor disasters. Title and subject indexes complete the thorough access. An indispensable guide to nuclear fiction that will probably come to be regarded as a seminal work on the topic.

2-211 Dowling, David. *Fictions of Nuclear Disaster.* Univ. of Iowa Pr., 1987. 239p.

Dowling begins his exploration of nuclear fiction with a statement that "the literature of nuclear disaster is moral in the sense that it ponders what we ought to be and ought to do." When done well, he continues, this literature "rejuvenates mainstream fiction and reminds science fiction of its roots in technological man's investigation of himself."

The book is a useful account with good description of novels and stories featuring liberal use of substantial quotations from the works themselves. A good part of Dowling's purpose is to show the range of literary responses to the nuclear threat, beginning with H.G. Wells's visionary novel of 1914, *The World Set Free.* Dowling correctly notes that some (indeed, one would have to say many) of the responses prove "bizarre or grotesquely inadequate," but, as he suggests, this flaw is part and parcel of the times and their prevailing . perceptions. Good fiction deliberately prompts reevaluation of such perceptions; fiction that is not so good can still prove helpful toward that end, even if unintentionally. Dowling's study takes into consideration some 250 novels and stories, almost all of them American or British. Bibliography, index.

2–212 Smith, Jeff. *Unthinking the Unthinkable: Nuclear Weapons and Western Culture.* Indiana Univ. Pr., 1989. 190p.

An examination of nuclear weapons from the perspective of cultural history, employing literary and other texts. Smith concentrates on literature and film, although his selections in both areas are curiously limited—he cites only four films, for example, and ignores the fiction of nuclear war, which has produced some outstanding works. Nevertheless, his reflections on various positions in the nuclear debate, observations on "remote causes" of the nuclear dilemma in the Middle Ages and in 19th century industrialization, do bring viewpoints to the issue seldom found in nuclear literature. Bibliography, index.

2–213 Weart, Spencer R. *Nuclear Fear: A History of Images.* Harvard Univ. Pr., 1988. 535p.

An original and highly imaginative investigation of nuclear imagery in films, novels, television and other sources since the turn of the century. Physicist-historian Weart's analysis involves political, historical, psychological, and broad cultural considerations. He does his best to wrestle with this exhausting topic; if he emerges less than victorious on every front, his struggle is nevertheless admirable and illuminating. One laments, however, the book's absence of illustrations. A very valuable aid in grasping the origins, meanings, and influences of popular images of the atom and the Bomb. Bibliography, notes, index.

XII. Civil Defense

2-214 Campbell, Duncan. *War Plan UK*. Paladin Books, 1983. 445p.

Journalist Campbell spent over five years investigating Great Britain's plans for civil defense, which he argues in his introduction has become, in Britain as in many other nations, "a central symbol in the nuclear disarmament debate. It is a symbol precisely because official civil defense policies are constructed more with a view to public relations on behalf of the Bomb, than to actual civil protection." He looks at the history of civil defense in Great Britain, 1949-1972, the post-1972 "protect and survive" government line, and at the disaster nuclear war would bring to the overwhelming majority of British citizens, regardless of the government's "fraudulent" civil defense plans. Notes, glossary, index.

2-215 Dowling, John and Harrell, Evans M. *Civil Defense: A Choice of Disasters*. American Institute of Physics, 1987. 231p.

The editors and nine other authors, all physicists or mathematicians with an interest in nuclear education, examine a number of facets of civil defense, including the history of American attitudes toward the topic, sheltering from a nuclear attack, implications of nuclear winter, political and psychological issues, and long-range recovery from nuclear war. There is much information here, some differences of opinion, a filmography by Dowling, and a substantial quantity of references to pertinent literature. Numerous illustrations. Index.

2-216 Leaning, Jennifer and Keyes, Langley, eds. *The Counterfeit Ark: Crisis Relocation for Nuclear War*. Ballinger, 1984. 337p.

Sponsored by the Physicians for Social Responsibility, this collection contains fifteen essays on what the editors consider the useless charade of "crisis relocation"—movement of large parts of the population to supposedly safer territory should nuclear war threaten—planned by the Federal Emergency Management Agency. Contains selections from official civil defense documents whose undertone of wishful thinking contrasts with what would prove the logistically insurmountable problem of actually protecting a significant portion of the public from nuclear war. Notes, index.

2-217 Perry, Ronald W. *The Social Psychology of Civil Defense*. Lexington Books, 1982. 127p.

An attempt to predict U.S. citizens' likely response to a warning to evacuate under the Federal Emergency management Agency's controversial Crisis Relocation Plan (CRP). CRP is a plan to move vulnerable population away from nuclear target areas 5-7 days before the bombs start falling. The author, who has a background in managing the consequences of environmental hazards, turns to evacuation in natural disaster in his efforts to obtain some grasp of how the public would behave in the very unnatural event of a nuclear war. He concludes that CRP could become effective public policy, provided the federal government vigorously addresses technical problems and the problems of disseminating information to the public. Bibliography, index.

2-218 Royal United Services Institute for Defence

Studies. *Nuclear Attack: Civil Defence: Aspects of Civil Defence in the Nuclear Age: A Symposium*. Brassey's, 1982. 284p.

A pre-nuclear winter awareness survey of civil defense programs presumed to be in effect ("The total centralisation of economic activity in the USSR is the greatest single factor for an enhanced Civil Defence capability.") but which may now, like the wonderfully centralized Soviet economy, be moribund. Not necessarily a Pollyanna vision of the ease of surviving nuclear war; the contributors do acknowledge such war's devastating effects. Those interested in riding out the Big One may find some useful suggestions. One tip: "It is important to have a good supply of painkillers." Alcohol, too, would be helpful, "if taken in large enough quantities." No doubt. Index.

2-219 Tyrrell, Ivan. *The Survival Option: A Guide to Living through Nuclear War*. J. Cape, 1982. 237p.

An interesting exercise in survivalism. Aimed chiefly at readers in Great Britain, but those of a survivalist mindset in the U.S. would find useful information here, whether regarding shelters, food storage, water, what to do after emerging from your hiding place, etc. One post-emergent activity: "Open up discussions with the nearest farmers and, if it will help, participate in their work, trading your group's labour for a future share in the produce." Tyrrell does not clarify just where it is these farmers will appear from in a post-attack world. Index.

XIII. Legal Considerations

2-220 Cohen, Maxwell and Gouin, Margaret E., eds. *Lawyers and the Nuclear Debate: Proceedings of the Canadian Conference on Nuclear Weapons and the Law*. Univ. of Ottawa Pr., 1988. 419p.

The Canadian Conference on Nuclear Weapons and the

Law grew from a 1985 decision to conduct a "worldwide, world-class conference representing the main political and legal cultures of every continent" which would provide "a professional and doctrinal mirror for the nuclear age and its war/peace problems." Participants in the conference were a truly international group; most were legal professionals, although a few, such as Edward Teller, represented other persuasions. Panels formed dealt with eight major topics, among them "Science and Weapons of Mass Destruction in the Nuclear Age," "Legal Constraints on Nuclear Proliferation," and "The Responsibility of the Legal Profession." Chiefly of interest to legal scholars. Bibliography.

2-221 Dewar, John, et al., eds. *Nuclear Weapons, the Peace Movement and the Law*. Macmillan, 1986. 255p.

Originates in a set of lectures at the University of Warwick School of Law in 1983 and 1984, and in papers presented at the 1984 International Conference on the Legality of Nuclear Weapons held in Coventry and organized by the Campaign for Nuclear Disarmament. The majority of the contributors are lawyers; in the collection's fourteen essays, they examine nuclear first-use issues, the relevance of laws of war in the nuclear age, the responsibilities of the legal profession, and the uses of law in conjunction with the peace movement. The Greenham women's protest and nuclear missiles in the Netherlands receive close attention. Although the book's focus is on Western Europe, numerous U.S. cases appear in the "List of Cases and Legislation" that opens the book, and there are many points in the text concerned with the situation in the U.S. Bibliography, index.

2-222 Meyrowitz, Elliott L. *The Prohibition of Nuclear Weapons: The Relevance of International Law*. Transnational, 1990. 333p.

"We would be more secure as a people, not less," writes the author, "if our governmental leaders were to try to conform national policy to the minimal obligations of international law." In spite of the Bush administration's invocation of such law as a rationale for its conduct of the Persian Gulf War, respect for the rule of law among nations has never been a serious obstacle in the path of U.S. conduct abroad. Perhaps a broadcasting of Meyrowitz's views would help. Describing the need for a discussion of the legality of the use of nuclear weapons as "both inevitable and urgent," Meyrowitz first reviews historical limitations on weapons and methods of warfare, outlines the official U.S. position, and summarizes the opinions of various scholars. He offers a lengthy assessment of the Baruch Plan of 1946, the original failed effort to place atomic weapons under international control. The book is basically an argument in support of nuclear disarmament and reliance on reason and law rather than violence in international relations. Notes, bibliography, index.

2-223 Pogany, Istvan, ed. *Nuclear Weapons and International Law*. Avebury, 1987. 253p.

Nine essays, chiefly by British legal scholars, addressing the central question of the legality of nuclear weapon deployment and use, as well as questions regarding the development of SDI, non-proliferation, nuclear testing, and other matters. On the main question, are nuclear weapons "legal," the reader finds here some contrasting views. Will be of most interest to legal authorities and advanced scholars. Notes, index.

2-224 Raven-Hansen, Peter, ed. *First Use of Nuclear Weapons: Under the Constitution, Who Decides?* Greenwood, 1987. 252p.

After the decision was made, there would not likely be many left who would trouble themselves with reflections on the constitutionality of it all. This collection of papers by legal scholars and congressional experts debates whether the Chief

Executive has a Constitutional right to go nuclear on his own initiative, or whether Congress should, as proposed by the Federation of American Scientists, have the responsibility of authorizing the Executive nuclear order. Some ponderable thoughts on both sides of the fence. Bibliography, index.

2–225 Singh, Nagendra and McWhinney, Edward. *Nuclear Weapons and Contemporary International Law.* 2d edition. Kluwer Academic, 1989. 611p.

An ambitious effort to examine the legal aspects of nuclear weapons, especially regarding disarmament. A comprehensive historical treatment that will be forbidding to any but legal scholars in the whole, yet in its parts, with attention to such issues as nuclear weapons and treaty laws, the contemporary law of disarmament, and the dynamics of international law-making and the nuclear disarmament process, less expert readers will find useful information and ideas. Contains numerous appendices illustrating legal agreements on weaponry; some of these, such as the Hague Declaration on Asphyxiating Gases, appear in French, but not, inexplicably, in English. The first edition of this work appeared in 1959. Notes, bibliography, index.

XIV. Spies

2–226 Kessler, Ronald. *The Spy in the Russian Club: How Glenn Souther Stole America's Nuclear War Plans and Escaped to Moscow.* Scribner's, 1990. 275p.

In 1986, Glenn Souther, a U.S. Navy photographer with top secret clearance, defected from the U.S. and obtained asylum in the Soviet Union. A 1989 obituary on one KGB staffer Mikhail Yevgenyevich Orlov in the Soviet army newspaper *Red Star* identified Orlov as Souther, leading observers to deduce that Souther/Orlov, who enlisted in the Navy at 18, had been a deep-cover agent. Apparently overwhelmed by cultural shock on his attempted transition to Soviet life, Souther reportedly killed himself, and was buried in a Moscow cemetery reserved for heroes. The Soviet media praised Souther for his noble efforts on behalf of the U.S.S.R. These efforts apparently included passage of U.S. nuclear war plans to the Soviets. Although a major aspect of Kessler's study focuses on security questions, the psychological issues at hand are equally interesting. How did a boy raised in the American heartland (Indiana) come to lie in a hero's grave in Moscow? The "Russian Club" of the title refers to a school club Souther belonged to while in college in Vermont. Notes, glossary, index.

2–227 Moss, Norman. *Klaus Fuchs: The Man Who Stole the Atom Bomb*. St. Martin's, 1987. 216p.

Recent re-evaluation of the role Klaus Fuchs played in helping the Soviet Union obtain the Bomb suggests that his assistance was actually worthless, an ironic twist to his sorry tale. What finally matters in the matter of Fuchs is not what he did, but what he thought he was doing.

In 1950, socialist true believer Klaus Fuchs confessed to British authorities that while working on nuclear weapons for Britain and the U.S. from 1942–1949, he systematically fed information on the Bomb to the Soviet Union. Fuchs served 9 nears of a 14-year sentence; on his release, he moved to East Germany to direct a nuclear physics laboratory. It was Fuchs's information that led to the apprehension in the U.S. of Harry Gold, David Greenglass, and Julius and Ethel Rosenberg.

Moss goes into greater analysis of Fuchs's personality than the treatment by Robert C. Williams (item 2–229). Without being overly cozy with Fuchs and his agenda, Moss elucidates some of the psychological background that influenced Fuchs in his actions, and indicates that greed or a desire for personal advancement were not the spurs to his spying. Notes, index.

2–228 Sharlitt, Joseph H. *Fatal Error: The Miscarriage of Justice that Sealed the Rosenbergs' Fate.* Scribner's, 1989. 274p.

An interesting review of the Rosenberg case based on the belief that their trial and executions were illegal, carried out under the wrong law. Sharlitt accepts the conclusion that the couple carried on atomic espionage for the Soviets, but that the law to which they were subject was the Atomic Energy Act of 1946, rather than the Espionage Act of 1918. Under the right law or not, the Rosenbergs went to the electric chair. The Rosenbergs were executed for what J. Edgar Hoover called "the crime of the century." (It was hardly that: the Soviet Union would have developed the Bomb regardless of any assistance received from these individuals.) Sharlitt questions the severity of the punishment, charging that the Rosenbergs' contributions to the Soviet nuclear effort were much exaggerated in comparison to what other atomic spies produced. Bibliography, index.

2–229 Williams, Robert C. *Klaus Fuchs, Atom Spy.* Harvard Univ. Pr., 1987. 267p.

This study, meticulously researched, is a fascinating account of a man characterized as possessing "a marvelous ability to think in abstract terms," yet simultaneously "helpless when it comes to either observe or evaluate reality." It also offers insights on governmental perceptions of security assurance. Appendices contain the texts of Fuchs's original confessions, as well as Harry Gold's statements to the FBI. Notes, bibliography, index. (See also item 2–227).

CHAPTER 3

Strategy

3-1 Abshire, David M. *Preventing World War III: A Realistic Grand Strategy.* Harper & Row, 1988. 331p.

The author, a U.S. ambassador to NATO, sees the relative power of both the U.S. and the U.S.S.R. declining into the next century, with Japan, Europe, and China "each generating its own gravitational field." He considers it vital to develop new approaches to nuclear deterrence, citing Henry Kissinger's September, 1979 speech in which Kissinger said that "our European allies should not keep asking us to multiply strategic assurances that we cannot possibly mean or if we do mean, we should not want to execute because if we execute, we risk the destruction of civilization." Nuclear strategies of escalation, Abshire believes, increasingly lack credibility and military logic; he calls for a withdrawal from a strategy of incredible first use to one of credible denial and retaliation. Notes, index.

3-2 Abt, Clark C. *A Strategy for Terminating a Nuclear War.* Westview, 1985. 253p.

Abt's conception of nuclear war termination focuses on replacing the threat of city bombardment in response to nuclear attack with a plan he calls "RIACTE" (Retaliatory Invasion and Cities Targeting Exclusion). The book's final chapter presents a scenario of the RIACTE termination strategy in action. Important elements of the strategy include fewer and smaller nuclear weapons, used slowly; postponed revenge; dispersal of military forces out and away from cities (the "exclusion" portion of the policy), and the retaliatory invasion by small U.S. and Allied units along all 15,000 miles of the Soviet border, chiefly along the northern and Siberian borders and in the Far East. The invasion strategy, designed for maximum control (versus the almost certain run-amuck anarchy that would accompany nuclear warfighting) is based on "the traditional Russian hatred of foreign invasion. . . . It assumes that the Soviet leadership would rather terminate a nuclear war, which at the time of the invasion it is clearly not 'winning' in the classical sense, than deal with the very real possibility of an even partially successful invasion of the Soviet homeland."

A fascinating book in which Abt makes a noble effort to defend his ideas; it is difficult in the end, however, to read it as more than the fanciful, if sincere, material of a fictional alternate history. Index.

3-3 Aldridge, Robert C. *First Strike! The Pentagon's Strategy for Nuclear War*. South End Pr., 1983. 325p.

A veteran engineer who worked for the Lockheed Corporation on sea-based missiles, Aldridge found himself at a moral crossroads when his work seemed to conflict with U.S. treaty obligations. He quit his Lockheed job in 1973. His subsequent investigation of American nuclear strategy and weaponry convinced him that the nation was attempting to prepare for a "successful" first strike on the Soviet Union. Here he amplifies on the observations leading him to that conclusion. His discussion concentrates on specific weapons systems (e.g., the Trident, the MX, cruise missiles) that he sees as elements of a planned first-strike arsenal. Notes, glossary, index.

3-4 _____. *Nuclear Empire*. New Star Books, 1989. 160p.

Here Aldridge continues his admonitions about U.S. nuclear war plans. He outlines what he considers the American public's hoodwinking about the reality of U.S. nuclear warfighting plans, the effects of the U.S. "nuclear empire" around the world, weapons and programs supporting a first strike capability, and the threat posed by U.S. command and control problems. He also discusses a comprehensive test ban as "a quick and efficacious way out of the arms race," and various other approaches to halting the nuclear menace. Disturbing, yet not hopeless. Notes, glossary, index.

3-5 Allison, Graham T.; Carnesale, Albert; Nye, Joseph S., Jr., eds. *Hawks, Doves, and Owls: An Agenda for Avoiding Nuclear War*. Norton, 1985. 282p.

A followup to the Harvard Nuclear Study Group's *Living with Nuclear Weapons* (Harvard Univ. Pr., 1983), this book is the product of a long-term project of Harvard's John F. Kennedy School of Government. It examines issues of nuclear weapons acquisition, nuclear strategy, diplomacy, and arms control regarding one criterion: "net effects on the likelihood of a major nuclear war between the United States and the Soviet Union."

The editors' objectives are to develop a framework for studying the risks of nuclear war and to identify ways of reducing its likelihood. Following description of five "Paths to Nuclear War" by as many contributing authors (Paul Bracken on accidental war, Richard K. Betts on surprise attack, Fen Osler Hampson on escalation in Europe, Francis Fukuyama on escalation in the Middle East and Persian Gulf, and Henry S. Rowen on "catalytic" war—a third party draws the U.S. and Soviet Union into nuclear war), the editors describe three strategic caricatures, the birds cited in their title. They align themselves for the present with owls, who see war's cause not in provocation or appeasement, but in loss of control in crisis situations. Their "Agenda for Action" entails maintenance of a credible nuclear deterrent, obtaining a credible conventional deterrent, enhancing crisis stability, developing procedures for war termination, and, finally, reducing reliance on nuclear deterrence over the long haul. A most interesting and quite readable book, and one sure to cause arguments.

Notes, glossary, index.

3–6 Arbatov, Aleksei G. *Lethal Frontiers: A Soviet View of Nuclear Strategy, Weapons, and Negotiations.* Praeger, 1988. 296p.

A translation of *Voenno-strategicheskii Paritet i Politika SShA.* Arbatov, a specialist in strategic weapons and arms negotiations, illuminates from a Soviet perspective the history of U.S.-Soviet interaction in strategic affairs. He discusses the emergence of strategic nuclear parity, the deterioration of detente, the conflict between the Reagan administration's pursuit of a new strategic superiority and the realities of strategic balance, and the "new era" in Soviet-American relations commencing with the Reagan-Gorbachev summit of 1987 in Washington, D.C., when the two leaders signed the INF Treaty. Speaking of the "new realities," Arbatov emphasizes that attempts to preserve strategic advantage "block the search for compromise at the negotiating table and provoke countermeasures from the opponent, which lead to counter-countermeasures and fuel the arms race to the detriment of the security of all sides." A useful, clearly-translated book that will give most readers a fresh point of view on superpower relations. Bibliography, index.

3–7 Beres, Louis Rene. *Reason and Realpolitik: U.S. Foreign Policy and World Order.* Lexington Books, 1984. 143p.

Beres, a political scientist who has worked extensively in the areas of nuclear weapons, nuclear war, and human rights, contends that the "balance of power" touted by such statesmen as Henry Kissinger as the basis for international peace is entirely wrongheaded, and that the American embrace of this so-called balance in its strategy of realpolitik exacerbates the global arms race, is economically destructive, contributes to environmental pollution, and promotes violations of human rights. Beres argues that the goal of foreign relations "must be nothing less than the erection of a new pattern of thinking that defines national interests in terms of strategies that secure and sustain the entire system of states." In his focus on nuclear war, Beres criticizes the U.S. for its contribution to proliferation, for its subscription to "omnicide," and for its advocacy of "enhanced" civil defense during the Reagan administration. Notes, index.

3-8 Betts, Richard K. *Nuclear Blackmail and Nuclear Balance.* Brookings Institution, 1987. 240p.

Taking available data from declassified documents and other sources, Betts examines the role of nuclear weapons in the crises of the Cold War. His list of cases in which U.S. and Soviet leaders tried to exploit risks of nuclear war to obtain their objectives includes, among others, the Berlin Blockade of 1948, Soviet-Chinese border clashes of the late 1960s, the Suez Crisis of 1956, and, of course, the Cuban Missile Crisis. Betts, who believes that tempting nuclear fate is imprudent, discusses the different theories involving potential losses and the likelihood of provoking nuclear war that come into play in such threats, as well as the dynamics of threatening behavior brought about by the greater strategic parity that has come to prevail between the U.S. and the U.S.S.R. Notes, index.

3-9 Blackaby, Frank, et al., eds. *No-First-Use.* Taylor & Francis, 1984. 151p.

Produced under the auspices of the Stockholm International Peace Research Institute, *No-First-Use* investigates the arguments advanced by advocates and opponents of such a nuclear policy, and then discusses the political and military implications of such a stance. The two main departure points are articles reprinted from the journal *Foreign Affairs.* They include the seminal 1982 essay, "Nuclear Weapons and the Atlantic Alliance," in which McGeorge Bundy,

George F. Kennan, Robert S. McNamara, and Gerard
Smith called for a no-first-use policy by the West,
and "Nuclear Weapons and the Preservation of Peace,"
a hostile reaction to the former piece by Karl Kaiser
and others. Discussions papers are furnished by
Lawrence Freedman, Daniel Frei, Paul C. Warnke, and
others. Mikhail A. Milshtein, of the Institute of U.S.
and Canadian Studies, Academy of Sciences of the
U.S.S.R., also contributes an essay illuminating the
Soviet viewpoint. The variety of arguments available
here makes the book especially useful. Index.

3-10 Bobbitt, Philip. *Democracy and Deterrence: The
History and Future of Nuclear Strategy*. St. Martin's,
1988. 350p.

Bobbitt, a law professor at the University of Texas,
claims that two views of nuclear deterrence have
become locked "as if imprisoned in amber." One view
relies on the countervalue deterrent, based on the
assumption that the use of nuclear weapons inevitably
means the extermination of the developed world; the
other assumes nuclear warfighting as something that
could be pursued to a point short of general
annihilation. In the end, argues Bobbitt, "The fate of
the world does not hang on whether the U.S. and
U.S.S.R. reduce their weapons or on whether they
freeze their technologies." What happens, rather, will
depend on "whether Euro-Japanese security is
enhanced, from their perspective, by our strategies,
military and diplomatic; whether the public can be
made to understand and support such steps as do
enhance the extended commitment when it has been
told more or less constantly that it is the number of
weapons and the advance of technology that causes
(or cures) the problem; and whether democratic
governments can consciously unite these elements—
public and expert—that are already but unhappily
linked." Bibliography.

3-11 _____ et al., eds. *US Nuclear Strategy: A
Reader*. New York Univ. Pr., 1989. 525p.

A good compilation of two-dozen-plus essays and articles on the history of American nuclear strategy, beginning with pre-Hiroshima deterrence and moving into "The Future of Nuclear Strategy." Many of the major contributors to nuclear strategy—Bernard Brodie, John Foster Dulles, Robert S. McNamara, Herman Kahn, and Henry Kissinger—are here. So are Colin S. Gray and Keith Payne, with yet another reprint of their nuclear warfighting clarion call "Victory Is Possible" (originally published in *Foreign Policy's* summer, 1980 issue). Includes a bibliography of recommended reading in various strategic areas.

3-12 Booth, Ken, and Baylis, John. *Britain, NATO and Nuclear Weapons: Alternative Defence versus Alliance Reform*. Macmillan, 1989. 374p.

Booth and Baylis split this book's length, each advocating his own preferred response to Great Britain's security needs. Booth, who opens his case for alternative defense with the statement "The Cold War is over, and we have won it. The West is secure, and its societies enjoy considerable material comfort," argues that a non-nuclear policy allied with non-provocative defense and a commitment to common security "would represent the optimum contribution by Britain to the changing character of the international landscape." Baylis, on the other hand, questions whether it is reasonable to expect a fundamental change in the European security system in the foreseeable future. He argues in behalf of "cautious evolutionary reform rather than radical reform," and addresses questions about the validity of nuclear deterrence, political and military problems of non-nuclear strategies, and revisions in NATO's strategic concept. Notes, index.

3-13 Branch, Christopher I. *Fighting a Long Nuclear War: A Strategy, Force, Policy Mismatch*. National Defense Univ. Pr., 1984. 77p. Supt. of Docs. No. D 5.409-84-5.

In light of the U.S. strategic shift from the idea of nuclear war as a massive, rapidly-concluded phenomenon to "one premised upon multiple nuclear exchanges in a longer war," the author, a U.S. Air Force Colonel, questions whether U.S. nuclear forces have kept pace with declared strategy. Col. Branch believes that U.S. forces have not, in fact, kept up with the strategic environment, and calls for enhancement of strategic weapons and their support systems; "the credibility of this Nation's strategic defense posture is at stake." Notes.

3-14 Brodie, Bernard; Intriligator, Michael D.; Kolkowicz, Roman. *National Security and International Stability.* Oelgeschlager, Gunn & Hain, 1983. 441p.

A good source of useful contributions from some of the leading strategists of the time, including Brodie himself, Desmond Ball, Edward N. Luttwak, Klaus Knorr, Thomas C. Schelling, and others. Although co-editor Brodie died in 1978, this volume was assembled to reflect his views that "we need people who will challenge, investigate, and dissect the prevailing dogmas" of foreign policy and strategic studies. The collection also focuses on the need to stress the political rather than the technological aspects of strategy, and the need to understand that strategy frequently does not lend itself to scientific analysis because of the inevitable value judgments it entails.

Among topics dealt with are nuclear warfighting, terrorist use of nuclear weapons, and changing attitudes toward deterrence. Case studies focus on such issues as the H-bomb decisions, the ABM debate, and MIRV'd warheads. Most readers will find plenty to agree and argue with here, as well as inspiration for more serious thinking on the topics of concern. Notes, index.

3-15 Buzan, Barry, ed. *The International Politics of Deterrence.* F. Pinter, 1987. 205p.

The results of a study on deterrence commissioned by the U.N. General Assembly in 1984. Following essays by a diverse group representing seven nations, the heart of the book sets out the arguments, counter-arguments and comments regarding nuclear deterrence concerning the non-aligned nations, the Warsaw Pact, and NATO. With the Warsaw Pact having become what Secretary of Defense Richard Cheney called "a fiction" in late 1990, and with German unification secure, the heart of the book no longer beats audibly, but the differing positions are still worth pondering. NATO experts believe that deterrence has contributed to peace; Warsaw Pact representatives believe peace has prevailed in spite of deterrence; experts from non-aligned nations agree only that deterrence may have played a role in the postwar European peace. Bibliography.

3-16 _____. *An Introduction to Strategic Studies: Military Technology and International Relations.* Macmillan, 1987. 325p.

There is some conflict here between the book's presentation as an "introduction" and the familiarity it assumes with issues and terminology. Nevertheless, the good index will assist the reader in obtaining insights, as offered by Buzan, on a wide range of nuclear issues. Essentially a literature review, with discussion of the many subtopics of the Bomb, from proliferation to deterrence, the arms race and arms control and disarmament. The bibliography is reasonably thorough, although the absence of some obvious choices (Bernard Brodie's *Strategy in the Missile Age*, Henry Kissinger's *Nuclear Weapons and Foreign Policy*) is a little surprising. On the other hand, as Buzan notes, "I could not possibly read everything." That's the truth; no one can, but Buzan has done a more comprehensive job than most.

3-17 Catudal, Honore M. *Nuclear Deterrence: Does It Deter?* Humanities Press International, 1986. 528p.

Catudal announces in his preface that a growing body of evidence suggests that "nuclear deterrence does not deter—at least not as we think it does." He describes nuclear deterrence as a dangerous panacea. His treatment of deterrence takes into account the origins of U.S. strategic policy, the evolution from the doctrine of mutual assured destruction to the notion of limited nuclear warfighting, European nuclear issues, civil defense, and three case studies: the first atomic bombing, the Korean War, and the Cuban Missile Crisis. His major conclusions on the errors of deterrence theory include the assertions that American policymakers have consistently taken an oversimplified view of the world (especially during the Cold War); they have relied on vague nuclear deterrence strategies in situations calling for conventional approaches; seduced by the Bomb, they have relied on its threat too readily, in lieu of managing or avoiding conflict through diplomacy. Notes, bibliography, index.

3–18 _____. *Soviet Nuclear Strategy from Stalin to Gorbachev: A Revolution in Soviet Military and Political Thinking.* Humanites Press International, 1989. 413p.

In this sequel to the above book, Catudal tries to illuminate Soviet strategic thinking, particularly regarding the connections among ideology, political imperatives, and military views and doctrine. A valuable examination of the history of Soviet nuclear doctrine which counters the monotonous worst–case anticipations of many American strategists and takes into consideration the new opportunities in arms control and disarmament emerging under the leadership of Gorbachev. Includes the text of the INF Treaty between the U.S. and the Soviet Union. Bibliography, index.

3–19 Charles, Daniel. *Nuclear Planning in NATO: Pitfalls of First Use.* Ballinger, 1987. 177p.

Explores the terrain of military operational plans for nuclear weapons in Europe, which the author describes as "the fuse mechanism of global nuclear war." Charles looks to a state policy of "no first use" by NATO as a desirable means of maintaining stability. At this juncture, the main fuse of nuclear war, global or otherwise, certainly seems to lie in the Middle East, where far different dynamics prevail than in the long-standing but rapidly eroding NATO-Warsaw Pact standoff. Notes, index.

3-20 Cimbala, Stephen J., ed. *Challenges to Deterrence: Resources, Technology, and Policy.* Praeger, 1987. 305p.

A collection of fifteen essays by various authorities examines nuclear deterrence within four broad categories: 1) The evolving strategic environment; 2) Risks and challenges to stability; 3) Implications for U.S. strategy of the geopolitical dimensions of deterrence; 4) Issues of cost and strategy for future force structures. Within these categories the contributors (historians, political scientists, mathematicians and other intellectuals) focus on such issues as U.S. Army combat orientation, trends toward crisis instability, nuclear war in the Middle East, Japan's role in deterrence, and such weapons systems as the Trident submarine and the Midgetman ICBM. Notes, index.

3-21 _____. *First Strike Stability: Deterrence After Containment.* Greenwood Pr., 1990. 213p.

An energetic effort to come to grips with the latest developments in U.S.-Soviet relations following the Eastern European breakaway from the Soviet sphere of control, along with progress (or apparent progress) in arms negotiations. In spite of these very encouraging developments, warns Cimbala, "War remains possible on account of the unforeseeable, inadvertent, and uncontrollable uncertainties that plague decision making and military planning in Washington, Moscow, and elsewhere." He believes that the risk of nuclear war is largely independent of variables, such as force sizes, under the control of policy makers. His discussion of the "post Cold War" relationships of the nuclear superpowers is most interesting and, even without being informed by an awareness of the present stumbling negotiations on strategic arms and conventional force reduction, tempers one's bliss at positive developments.

Cimbala's reflections on the inadequacy of U.S. nuclear strategy to deal with inadvertent nuclear war, or nuclear war by escalation (rather than by deliberation) show that the strategic situation is one that in no sense encourages complacence or indolence. Notes, bibliography, index.

3–22 _____. *NATO Strategy and Nuclear Escalation.* Pinter Publishers in assoc. with John Spiers, 1989. 276p.

Cimbala studies NATO in relation to the new Soviet thinking, the question of reliance on conventional defense, extended deterrence (linkage of U.S. strategic weapons to European security), U.S. maritime strategy and the possibility of inadvertent nuclear war, SDI, and war termination. Cimbala makes a case that "NATO is not as well served as it might be by ambiguous doctrines of escalation and escalation control, and by plans which are partly dependent on those doctrines." A densely written meditation on the elusive topic of what would happen if nuclear war started. The text features helpful summary conclusions at the end of each chapter. Notes, index.

3–23 _____. *Nuclear Endings: Stopping War on Time.* Praeger, 1989. 295p.

As he frequently does, Cimbala turns his attention here to the prospects of calling nuclear war to a halt. He argues in favor of dwelling on nuclear war termination for, among other reasons, "to improve strategic war planning," to augment nuclear deterrence (if we think we can stop it before we're completely destroyed, we'd be more willing to start it, and thus could not be trusted so much to sit on our nuclear hands by an adventurous enemy). Bibliography, index.

3-24 _____. *Nuclear Strategizing: Deterrence and Reality*. Praeger, 1988. 306p.

Cimbala dwells on the link between nuclear deterrence and "rationality." He refers to the rationality of superpower deterrent relationships as "the rationality of coping." Through coping, policy makers seek to avoid military or political events that would bring themselves or their nations trouble. Cimbala points out that the rationality of coping cannot be anticipated in a nuclear war or near-war situation; as a parallel, he cites the Three Mile Island crisis in which what was happening remained obscure to decision makers for days, with the "why" of the event opaque for even longer. Nuclear strategy is not strategy, in Cimbala's opinion, but "strategizing," "what one does when unable to use strategy." Strategy or strategizing, this book is, like much of Cimbala's other work, a densely written analysis of contemporary nuclear reality, or realities, and will reward the diligent reader with a better understanding of many subtopics, from "nuclear surprise" to "scientism," which, in Cimbala's view, is to science as strategizing is to strategy. Notes, index.

3-25 _____. *Rethinking Nuclear Strategy*. SR Books, 1988. 278p.

Cimbala examines nuclear deterrence by denial (preventing one's opponent from obtaining the objectives for which he is fighting at a cost tolerable to one's self), retaliation (costs of attacking are seen to outweigh gains to be achieved), and control (accidental or unauthorized attack by one's own forces is preventable, and one's own system is not vulnerable to a command decapitation by the enemy). He discusses technological problems, pro and con arguments on SDI, theater nuclear forces, the question of prompt retaliation vs. delayed response, and "intelligent wars," which he defines as "the competitions to develop and successfully apply artificial intelligence and other cognitive aids to the solution of military problems." Notes, index.

3-26 _____. *Strategic Impasse: Offense, Defense, and Deterrence Theory and Practice.* Greenwood Pr., 1989. 266p.

Cimbala again devotes time to war termination in his essays on controlling escalation in Europe, in Third World conflicts, and in relation to Soviet perceptions. He draws his title from his opening assertion, "Nuclear weapons are useful, but nuclear war is not. This is the fundamental contradiction from which the nuclear impasse springs."

The weapons are "useful" because they help prevent war (although one can hardly note an absence of costly wars around the world throughout the Nuclear Age). They have, at any rate, apparently helped prevent a U.S.-Soviet war. Cimbala believes that the superpowers will not choose to move away from deterrence based on the threat of offensive retaliation, a position in keeping with the Bush administration's recent revision of the SDI program away from the original vast defense against thousands of Soviet missiles to a far more modest system and, one would think, one far less discomforting to Soviet observers; the Bush SDI plan at this writing is seen as a way to intercept small missile attacks from terrorists or Third World nations.

Cimbala warns against complacency in Europe, for given such potential trouble points as Baltic nationalism and NATO disarray, "out-of-area problems could spill back into conflict that may ultimately involve the superpowers and their respective coalitions." Notes, bibliography, index.

3–27 _____, ed. *Strategic War Termination*. Praeger, 1986. 227p.

The eleven contributors to this volume "focus on the theory and practices of war avoidance and war termination after deterrence has failed but before escalation has totally escaped control." The individual chapters examine models of U.S. and Soviet counterforce first strikes, the relationships between deterrence and war termination, the conduct of a protracted global war, countercommand attacks, and other aspects of nuclear war. The contributors agree that nuclear war would be difficult to control, "but that this difficulty is a feeble excuse for not trying," and that "war termination rather than victory might be the appropriate objective for conventional as well as nuclear wars." An interesting collection, with George H. Quester, Colin S. Gray, Clark C. Abt and the editor among the contributors. Notes, index.

3–28 _____. *Uncertainty and Control: Future Soviet and American Strategy*. Pinter, 1990. 183p.

In this discussion of escalation, inadvertent war, and U.S.–Soviet conflict, Cimbala returns to his theme of war termination. Superpower command systems are not adequate, he believes, to control or stop a limited nuclear war (or perhaps not even a conventional war); as war prevention seems more secure, "the control of regional war in Europe or direct U.S.–Soviet conflict elsewhere remains beyond procedural, technical and political reach," and American and Soviet military doctrine and leadership are unprepared to stop what they have so far been able to avoid beginning. Cimbala investigates a number of hypotheses as to why these observations are so. A good investigation of a topic too seldom addressed, although one might wish that the book focused a little less on the NATO–Warsaw Pact dynamic and a bit more on potential Third World flash points for U.S.–Soviet antagonism. Notes, index.

3-29 _____ and Douglass, Joseph D., Jr., eds.
Ending a Nuclear War: Are the Superpowers Prepared?
Pergamon-Brassey's, 1988. 198p.

The editors and contributors to this volume contend
that for the U.S. and the West in general, failure to
adequately connect matters of force and policy have
led to an environment of "technologism" and "strategic
fatalism." Together, the two qualities produce an
atmosphere which makes a nuclear war once begun
impossible to finish short of utter destruction. The
contributors see two fundamental requirements for
effective war termination: a survivable command
system and a survivable reserve force. They rely on
their analysis of Soviet military and political thought
to point out weaknesses in those of the West, and the
approach makes interesting if not always convincing
reading. Given the evaporation of Soviet control over
Eastern Europe and Soviet withdrawal in general from
the world stage, claims advanced here about the
"ultimate strategic goal of Soviet politics" being "the
establishment of dictatorships of the proletariat
throughout the world" seem a little dubious. Notes,
index.

3-30 _____ and Dunn, Keith A., eds. *Conflict
Termination and Military Strategy: Coercion,
Persuasion, and War.* Westview, 1987. 196p.

The eleven essays here evolved from a conference
held in 1985 at the Naval War College. Conference
participants came from both academia and government.
Several of the essays specifically concern cessation of
nuclear hostilities, such as William O. Staudenmaier's
"Conflict Termination in the Nuclear Era," but others
also address nuclear questions. Raymond L. Garthoff's
"Conflict Termination in Soviet Military Thought and
Strategy" is a welcome antidote to that tiresome
iteration from the American right about the alleged
Soviet commitment to "victory" in a nuclear war.
Notes.

3–31 Clark, Ian and Wheeler, Nicholas J. *The British Origins of Nuclear Strategy, 1945–1955*. Clarendon Pr., 1989. 263p.

Those looking into Great Britain's nuclear history will want to consult this concise book. One of the questions American readers in particular may wonder about is why, with what might seem to be the protection offered by the American "nuclear umbrella," did Britain feel compelled to develop an independent nuclear force? The authors address that question and others. Notes, bibliography, index.

3–32 Cleveland, Harlan and Bloomfield, Lincoln, eds. *Prospects for Peacemaking: A Citizen's Guide to Safer Nuclear Strategy*. MIT Pr., 1987. 159p.

A better than usual collection of five essays on nuclear and related matters initiated by the "Prospects for Peacemaking" program, a 1984 undertaking involving Minnesota citizens and experts who together explored the nuclear threat and means of reducing it. The essays cover "A Citizen's Approach to Soviet–American Relations," by Marshall Shulman, "The Use and Nonuse of Nuclear Weapons," by John M. Lee, who advocates a "minimizing" policy based on No First Use, No Firing On Warning, and No Immediate Response, as well as essays on arms control and the problem of command and control in crisis. Former Secretary of State Dean Rusk concludes with a good essay, "Rethinking National Security and Arms Control." Notes, index.

3–33 Commission on Integrated Long-Term Strategy. *Discriminate Deterrence: Report of the Commission on Integrated Long-Term Strategy*. U.S. Gov't. Printing Office, 1988. 69p. Supt. of Docs. No. D 1.2:D 48.

Co-chaired by Fred Ikle and Albert Wohlstetter, the Commission on Integrated Long-Term Strategy allowed that "to help defend our allies and to defend our interests abroad, we cannot rely on threats expected to provoke our own annihilation if carried out," and that NATO nuclear weapons should come into play "mainly as an instrument for denying success to the invading Soviet forces." The report also recommends an enhanced ability to defeat aggression through a "discriminating, non-nuclear force," and that capacities for "discriminate nuclear strikes to deter a limited nuclear attack on allied or U.S. forces, and if necessary to stop a massive invasion" are also desirable. Counting among its members such strategic heavyweights as Zbigniew Brzezinski, Samuel P. Huntington, and Henry Kissinger, the commission stresses that excessive attention has been devoted to two major strategic scenarios, an all-out Warsaw Pact attack on Central Europe and a Soviet nuclear attack on the U.S.

3-34 David, Charles P.. *Debating Counterforce: A Conventional Approach in a Nuclear Age.* Westview, 1987. 260p.

Inspired, or perhaps appalled, by developments within American circles of strategic thought in the 1980s, a Canadian professor of international relations discusses what he sees as the nuclear debate that exists between "the Apocalyptics" and "the Conventionalists." The Apocalyptics see nuclear weapons as so potentially devastating that their only use can be as a deterrent to attack; the Conventionalists would adopt conventional military strategies, including those of an offensive nature, to nuclear weapons, possibly involving nuclear attack on the enemy's own forces ("counterforce"). David writes that conventional nuclear strategy calls into question the basis of deterrence holding that "if either side wins an atomic war, both lose."

The conventionalists enjoyed a decade in the sun during the Reagan tenure of office, when few months could pass without another administration adjunct appearing in print or elsewhere with comments on how the U.S. could "win" or "prevail" in a nuclear war. David believes that successful attempts to "conventionalize" nuclear weapons use considerably augment the threat of an all—out U.S.-Soviet nuclear war. Bibliography, index.

3-35 DeLeon, Peter. *The Altered Strategic Environment: Toward the Year 2000.* Lexington Books, 1987. 113p.

The author examines three new conditions that have recently entered the domain of strategic doctrine: the possibility of a nuclear winter, the implications of SDI, and the greatly enhanced ability of conventional weapons to assume roles formerly the strict province of nuclear weapons. He also identifies a fourth emerging factor, the growing public awareness of and readiness to be a part of the nuclear weapons debate. He argues that because of the importance of all these points, "the altered strategic environment" cannot be tentatively drawn without an inter-related discussion of these factors. As for that environment, he cautiously sees it as moving toward a strengthened strategic balance, new incentives for arms control, and a more complex approach to U.S.-NATO relations. Notes, index.

3-36 Douglass, Joseph D. and Hoeber, Amoretta M. *Conventional War and Escalation: The Soviet View.* Crane, Russak, 1981. 63p.

The authors disagree with current contentions that the Soviet Union has come to agree with the prevailing notion that "nuclear war is impossible" insofar as a meaningful route to rational objectives. They claim that "no such shift in interest from nuclear toward conventional war in Europe can be identified either in Soviet military writings or in their force pronouncements." They attempt to give substance to this idea through a discussion of Soviet military literature, none of which was originally published after 1974, and most of which appeared well before that date.

3-37 Dyson, Freeman J. *Weapons and Hope.* Harper & Row, 1984. 340p.

First serialized in *The New Yorker* (Feb., 1984), physicist Dyson's examination of the nuclear scene rests on the optimistic view of weapons technology, both offensive and defensive, that it will come to lessen the probability of nuclear war given politically judicious accommodation of technological possibilities. His "live and let live" nuclear doctrine, known in strategic quarters as "parity plus damage-limiting," involves gradual disarmament leading to a point at which the introduction of antiballistic defenses would render the remaining offensive weapons obsolete.

Arranged in four main parts, "Questions," "Tools," "People," and "Concepts," the book moves from setting up a rhetorical framework ("Can we survive nuclear war?" "Are we, as a society, prepared to face the risks and uncertainties of living in a non-nuclear world?") to an investigation of seven alternative strategic doctrines which have developed around nuclear weapons. The "live and let live" doctrine treats nuclear weapons as bargaining chips "to be negotiated away as rapidly as possible. It commits us firmly to the path of negotiating nuclear weapons all the way down to zero, or as close to zero as the Soviet Union will allow." A provocative, if not wholly convincing, argument. Notes, index.

3-38 Edwards, A.J.C. *Nuclear Weapons, the Balance of Terror, the Quest for Peace.* State Univ. of New York Pr., 1986. 275p.

The phrase "balance of terror," which came into being in the 1950s, describes the state of mutual nuclear fear felt by East and West when thinking about one another's nuclear arsenals. It is the balance of terror which creates deterrence, the threat of "mutual assured destruction" of both sides should either prove rash enough to use nuclear weapons for other than deterrent or bargaining purposes. After reviewing the nuclear history leading to the terrible balance, Edwards concludes that, however dreadful and expedient it may be, no preferable and attainable alternative yet exists for maintaining peace. He believes that "even an imperfect balance between the two sides seems likely to keep the world at peace, barring gross mismanagement by either side." Unfortunately, gross mismanagement has been known to occur in the course of human events. Notes, index.

3-39 Falk, Jim. *Taking Australia off the Map: Facing the Threat of Nuclear War.* W. Heinemann Australia, 1983. 290p.

Falk opens with a nuclear war scenario originating in the Middle East. The war spreads quickly to East and West, and to Australia, where a one-megaton bomb detonates over Sydney. It is a gripping portrait of a city undergoing devastation thanks to distant events over which its citizens have little or no control, and sets the tone for Falk's worried analysis of the growing nuclear dangers of the 1980s. He touches on the erosion of deterrence as the dominant nuclear strategy, the introduction of new weapons, and the difficulty of controlling nuclear events once set into motion. The book's title does double-duty: it suggests what would happen to Australia in a nuclear war, but also urges a change in Australian strategic entanglements that might remove the continent from primacy as a target on the nuclear map. Falk identifies Australia's deep involvement in the nuclear fuel cycle and the U.S. nuclear weapons system as the twin anchors of Australia's jeopardy, and insists that "we must find a way to disengage from each of these." Notes, index, photos.

3-40 Ford, Daniel F. *The Button: The Pentagon's Strategic Command and Control System.* Simon & Schuster, 1985. 270p.

From the North American Aerospace Defense Command headquarters in Cheyenne Mountain, CO, to the specially modified jetliners code-named "Looking

Glass" which began an around-the-clock airborne nuclear war command post in 1961, Ford details the U.S. command and control system for nuclear war in straightforward, readable prose. He makes it clear that, should the threat of nuclear war become imminent, the U.S. could very well choose to initiate the "exchange," in hopes of achieving crippling damage before its own communications system deteriorated past effectiveness. (Presumably the Soviets have a similar point of view.) A revealing treatment accessible to most readers. Notes, index.

3-41 Freedman, Lawrence. *Britain and Nuclear Weapons.* Macmillan, 1980. 160p.

A handy, short overview of the evolution of British nuclear weapons policy and the forces that have influenced it. Freedman concentrates on politics and weapons systems, up to the 1979 deployment decision on cruise and Pershing II missiles. Notes, index.

3-42 _____. *The Evolution of Nuclear Strategy.* 2d edition. St. Martin's, 1989. 522p.

The bulk of this book has not changed from its first edition in 1981, although a new chapter outlines developments of "The Reagan Administration and the Great Nuclear Debate," including the rise of antinuclear protest, the "second detente," SDI, and other issues. Overall, it is an arresting examination of nuclear strategy since the beginning of the age. Readable, thorough discussions of the advent of the Bomb, the development of deterrence, the fear of surprise attack (still, it seems, the unwarranted expectation of the average person when thinking about the nuclear threat), assured destruction, etc. Freedman argues that "strategy" has become an essentially meaningless term when applied to the nuclear face-off; contemporary stability depends not on strategy but on its antithesis, on threats that things will get out of hand, that bad decisions and accidents could trigger events beyond control or understanding. "Those who have responsibility for unleashing nuclear arsenals live by the motto that if they ever had to do so they would have failed. Remarkably, up to now, they have succeeded. C'est magnifique, mais ce n'est pas la strategie." Notes, bibliography, index.

3-43 Garden, Timothy. *Can Deterrence Last?: Peace through a Nuclear Strategy.* Buchan & Enright, 1984. 128p.

The author was Group Captain in the Royal Air Force, with an academic background in physics and international relations. This book is a brief, clearly stated account of the principles of nuclear deterrence, informed by the basically optimistic notion that deterrence has seemed to work in the past, and will be able to continue working. Possibly most useful as a quick country-by-country overview of nuclear strategies adopted by Bomb Club members, including the U.S., the Soviet Union, Great Britain, France, China, India, and Israel. Notes, index.

3-44 Garthoff, Raymond L. *Deterrence and the Revolution in Soviet Military Doctrine.* Brookings Institution, 1990. 209p.

Another counter by Garthoff to the standard charge made by American conservatives that the Soviets believe that nuclear war can be won, and are preparing accordingly. Garthoff, who makes extensive use of Soviet sources, characterizes strategic moves made under Gorbachev as further evidence of the U.S.S.R.'s commitment to nuclear deterrence as a defensive stance. These moves include both concrete actions, such as the Soviet nuclear test moratorium of 1985 and 1986, and arms control and reduction proposals tendered to the U.S. Notes, index.

3-45 Garvey, Gerald. *Strategy and the Defense Dilemma: Nuclear Policies and Alliance Politics.*

Lexington Books, 1984. 136p.

Princeton University political scientist Garvey charges that the U.S. "has been living off of old intellectual capital," and must rethink its strategic concepts to achieve a posture combining effective global military capability with affordability. Among his remedies is a policy that would remove the link between employment of strategic nuclear forces as a result of conflict overseas; would redesign the U.S. strategic force to meet a narrowly-defined mission of primary deterrence, i.e., deterrence of any strike against U.S. territory; and would link international economics to overseas security by urging beneficiaries of a U.S. military presence "to adopt more agreeable trade, monetary, and investment policies." A provocative book with some controversial contentions. Notes, bibliography, index.

3-46 Gray, Colin S. *Nuclear Strategy and National Style.* Abt Books, 1986. 363p.

"Central to every major element in this book," writes Gray, "is the idea that the United States and the Soviet Union have a distinctive national style, reflecting a strategic culture, that has a significant impact on their separate ways of strategic deliberation and defense preparation." In dense prose and small type, Gray seeks to identify and analyze those styles.

Lurking beneath his analysis is the assumption that it is a good idea to prepare to fight a nuclear war with the idea of "victory" in mind, and that, indeed, nuclear victory is possible. His assertions of how things are is questionable; whether the Soviet Union was, as he claims, an "imperial" state in 1986 was debatable; in 1991, such a claim is insupportable. A book on nuclear strategy published in 1986 that scarcely mentions the prospect of nuclear winter seems, furthermore, to willfully ignore elements of nuclear possibility that would render the author's notions about "recovery" from nuclear war implausible.

When he writes of this recovery ability, Gray states that "Contrary to appearances, perhaps, I am not seeking to trivialize or even to 'conventionalize' the phenomenon of nuclear war." Yet by comparing nuclear war to previous historical disasters, that is what he seems to do, implying that the qualitatively unique disaster of nuclear war can somehow be compared in kind with events such as the plague that took a long time to achieve their full human effect, that touched only a relatively small part of the world, and that had little or no effect on nature itself.

"There is reason to believe," he optimistically states, "that it [the civilized world] could survive nuclear wars through suitable provision of active and passive defenses in the context of U.S. adoption of a true 'classical strategy.'" On the other hand, one might remind Gray that "civilization" requires cities, and that "nuclear wars" (how many would Gray look forward to?) could probably be assumed to reduce most cities of any consequence to rubble.

Unfailingly interesting, Gray is seldom convincing unless one has a taste for imaginary bloody victory. Gray's influential contributions to the Reagan era's fight-to-win nuclear vision make his work an important stopping point on the way to grasping the present nuclear setting.

3-47 Guertner, Gary L. *Deterrence and Defense in a Post-Nuclear World.* St. Martin's, 1990. 177p.

Although he sees no likelihood of a nuclear-free world, Guertner is optimistic that political decisions and technological innovations can help the U.S. and the Soviet Union move "to a higher plateau" where there will be fewer incentives for a continued arms race. He asserts that "powerful nations must eventually base their military strategies on weapons that can be used. This overwhelmingly simple strategic logic will push us into the post-nuclear era." An interesting study focusing narrowly on the superpowers, with attention paid to such issues as

Soviet incentives for conventional deterrence, the relative merits and demerits of future weapons deployments, and the relationship between strategic stability and conventional deterrence. Guertner has taught strategy at the U.S. Army War College, and has served as scholar-in-residence of the U.S. Arms Control & Disarmament Agency. Glossary, notes, index.

3-48 Halperin, Morton H. *Nuclear Fallacy: Dispelling the Myth of Nuclear Strategy.* Ballinger, 1987. 173p.

Halperin, director of the Center for National Security Studies and a former National Security Council member, had last roamed the fields of nuclear strategy fifteen years before writing this book. In his return to the subject, he opens by pointing out that "at any instant, 5,000 of the 25,000 nuclear devices in the American arsenal are ready to be fired within minutes at any potential adversary anywhere in the world." He challenges the assumption that nuclear warheads are "weapons" that can be used to fight and win wars. "No one knows how to win a nuclear war," he writes. "Yet nuclear devices are integrated into all aspects of U.S. military strategy worldwide." Halperin provides a brief history of American nuclear policy, discusses twenty case-by-case instances of the "mythology" of U.S. nuclear threats, and surveys issues of European nuclear strategy and arms control. He urges presidential initiative in rejecting the bomb as a usable weapon, and proposes that strategic weapons be designed for survivability rather than alacrity of response in attack. Bibliography, index.

3-49 Haley, Edward, et al., eds. *Nuclear Strategy, Arms Control, and the Future.* Westview, 1985. 372p.

Brings together classic statements on nuclear strategy and arms control made by Soviet and U.S. policymakers, military thinkers, and opinion leaders during the last forty years. The editors define "classic" as causing "everything" to change because the statement was made, "or the statement embodied

the beliefs of many people in and out of government."
The emphasis is on statements by both civilian and
military leaders, with a large section given to
statements by Soviet representatives. Covers the
whole of the nuclear era, with individual sections
devoted to the development of U.S. nuclear strategy,
the nature of Soviet strategy, intermediate-range
nuclear force controversies, arms control, and morality
and nuclear weapons. A total of 58 statements from
such sources as the National Security Council, the
Joint Chiefs of Staff, George F. Kennan, Robert S.
McNamara, Leonid Brezhnev, the Scowcroft Commission,
and many others. A valuable source for following
major developments in the nuclear age. Glossary.

3-50 _____ and Merritt, Jack, eds. *Nuclear Strategy,
Arms Control, and the Future.* 2d ed. Westview, 1988.
378p.

The timeliest portions of this collection focus on arms
control and strategy in the future. A better-than-
average anthology of nuclear-related writings with a
wide range of selections and diverse points of view.
Intended as a textbook; the book's format, with its
strong emphasis on chronological perspective and its
organization into major subtopics, will help students
obtain a good historical grasp of the issues. Notes,
glossary.

3-51 Herken, Gregg. *Counsels of War.* Knopf, 1985.
409p.

Author of *The Winning Weapon: The Atomic Bomb in
the Cold War, 1945-1950* (Knopf, 1981), Herken here
recounts the nuclear era through interviews with
scientists, strategists, and policy makers. He "attempts
to trace the course of thinking about the unthinkable
from Hiroshima to the present time as a way of
explaining not only where we are but how we got
there." He posits a 360-degree turn in American ideas
about nuclear war, at least among those responsible
for nuclear decisions. From the protracted, "winnable"

nuclear war described in *Collier's* in 1951, we have traveled through the acceptance of MAD right back to the previously discredited notion (and one discredited during a time of substantially inferior destructive power on both sides) of possible victory through nuclear war. Herken agrees with the late Bernard Brodie, author of the magisterial *Strategy in the Missile Age* (Princeton, 1959) that the nuclear debate has reached a dead end and needs reorientation to the fundamental question posed by Clausewitz on strategy: "De quoi s'agit–il?"—"What is it all about? What is it for?" Well researched and well written, Herken's book is commended to any reader seeking a mastery of the great historical ebb and flow of nuclear thinking.

3–52 Ifestos, Panayiotis. *Nuclear Strategy and European Security Dilemmas: Towards an Autonomous European Defence System?* Avebury, 1988. 496p.

Ifestos, an economist and Greek diplomatic representative to the European Economic Community headquarters, 1979–1988, examines European defense from both historical and contemporary perspectives. He emphasizes nuclear strategy, the security attitudes of France and Britain in a nuclear context, the U.S. nuclear "guarantee" to Western Europe, SDI, and other strategic issues bearing on Europe. In the closing section, Ifestos discusses problems, obstacles and prospects for an autonomous European defense. Dense with footnotes and forbidding to the eye, this book will deter all but the most intrepid readers. Bibliography, index.

3–53 Jervis, Robert. *The Illogic of American Nuclear Strategy*. Cornell Univ. Pr., 1984. 203p.

Jervis notes in his preface that expert discussion of the details of nuclear strategy often ignores the "fundamental questions" whose answers must support firm analysis. In a book designed for both experts and concerned citizens, he argues that the influence of nuclear weapons on global politics has led to revolutionary relationships between foreign policy and military force, since neither nuclear-armed superpower can protect itself from destruction without the other's cooperation. Jervis believes that deterrence will be maintained as long as a belief in the "inevitability" of war does not come to the fore; it is, therefore, important for the U.S. to convince the Soviets that war is not inevitable, even in grave crisis. He examines the U.S. "countervailing strategy," based on the assumption that the U.S. must be ready to meet and block Soviet force at any level of violence; and discusses the issues and contradictions of this strategy, which, he contends, "contributes to, and perhaps springs from, the American tendency to shoot ourselves in the foot by creating unnecessary problems that require great efforts to dispel."

Jervis offers no magic recipe for improving global security in the nuclear age. He indicates that—to invoke Einstein's famous statement—a new way of thinking is required to adequately deal with the paradoxes of deterrence. Meanwhile, we can probably live with deterrence if we don't make a fetish of responding to Soviet force at every level."

3-54 _____. *The Meaning of the Nuclear Revolution: Statecraft and the Prospect of Armageddon.* Cornell Univ. Pr., 1989. 280p.

Jervis believes that nuclear weapons have changed the way nations behave, and argues that "large-scale violence is no longer a viable tool of statecraft." His emphasis is on superpower relations in his discussion of strategic theory, morality, and international strategy, and the psychological aspects of crisis stability. Jervis's prose is clear and his observations insightful. Especially in his final chapter, "The Symbolic Nature of Nuclear Politics" and in his "Conclusions: Winning and Losing—Clausewitz in the Nuclear Era," he argues persuasively that the security of nations is an interdependent matter, that, contrary to former Green Bay Packer coach Vince Lombardi's remarks about winning being "the only thing," in the nuclear world winning is losing: the intelligent player looks for a tie. One of the first books to turn to for an enlightening way of looking at contemporary issues of war and peace.

3–55 _____, et al. *Psychology and Deterrence.* Johns Hopkins Univ. Pr., 1985. 270p.

Those who embrace nuclear deterrence on the ground that it can be trusted to appeal to reason will find their assumptions challenged in this volume, in which five political scientists investigate psychological aspects of deterrence. The most important contributions are those of Robert Jervis, who argues that a number of psychological factors hinder deterrence, and Richard N. Lebow, who analyzes the clarity (or opacity) of international communications. Emotion, time, ambiguous data, and other factors all complicate what seems to be the inherently irrational process of political decision making. (A very recent and dramatic addition to the book's roster of case studies, which include the 1973 Yom Kippur War and the Falkland Islands War, might well be Iraq's apparent failure to believe what, to Western ears, seemed the very credible threat to use force should Iraq not abandon Kuwait.) Bibliography, index.

3–56 Kaku, Michio and Axelrod, Daniel. *To Win a Nuclear War: The Pentagon's Secret War Plans.* South End, 1987. 357p.

Based extensively on recently declassified Pentagon documents, this book shows how the U.S. has planned to start nuclear war since the close of WW II. The authors note over two dozen incidents, ranging from U.S.-Soviet antagonism over Iran in 1946 to the Iranian crisis of 1980, in which the U.S. engaged in nuclear threats, planning, or maneuvers. They divide their study into three eras of nuclear strategy: massive pre-emption (1945–1960); MAD (Mutual Assured Destruction, 1960–1974); and Counterforce (1974–

present). They focus on the Berlin crises (in 1948, plan "BROILER" called for hitting 24 Soviet cities with 34 nuclear bombs), first-strike planning under President Kennedy, and the link between SDI and first-strike capability, among other topics. The portrait of the U.S. policy makers at the highest level as more concerned with how to fight a nuclear war than with how to prevent one is disturbing, and a late chapter, "Pre-War Situation," outlining some of the attitudes toward nuclear war by Reagan administration officials, is positively chilling. For those who have surveyed nuclear literature in depth, there may be little new here, but the book brings together an historical picture of U.S. nuclear strategy that will leave most readers on edge. Notes, bibliography, index.

3-57 Kelleher, Catherine, et al., eds. *Nuclear Deterrence: New Risks, New Opportunities.* Pergamon-Brassey's, 1986. 238p.

A collection of papers presented at a conference at the University of Maryland in 1984. Broad topics include arms control, nuclear winter, nuclear deterrence, and the global military balance. Readers might find among the most interesting pieces George H. Quester's "Nuclear Winter: Bad News, No News, or Good News?" in which he asks whether nuclear winter might not be viewed "as the final sealing of a necessary deterrent bargain between the superpowers," and Zhang Jingyi's "The Current Nuclear Dilemma: A Chinese View," in which he speaks of the "historical mission" "to emancipate people's thinking from the yoke of 'nuclear fetishism' so that the peace, stability, and security of the human society are based on a scientific, rational, and correct strategy." Notes, index.

3-58 Kenny, Anthony. *The Logic of Deterrence.* Firethorn Pr., 1985. 103p.

In the first part of this short book, Kenny concludes that the actual fighting of a nuclear war could be neither rational nor morally defensible; in the second part, he contends that nuclear deterrence policies of both East and West are "murderous, dangerous and extravagant," and in the third argues that there is room for progress in disarmament between the "illusory hopes" invested in multilateral negotiations and the "impractical idealism" of unilateral disarmament. He suggests that the West's nuclear weapons be used only as bargaining counters to obtain balanced and eventually total reduction of Soviet forces; the explicit, official policy under this strategic regime is that the nuclear weapons of the West would never be used in any but this bargaining mode. Brief bibliography.

3-59 Kolkowicz, Roman, ed. *The Logic of Nuclear Terror*. Allen & Unwin, 1987. 289p.

Some major authorities on nuclear strategy, including among others George H. Quester, Lawrence Freedman, Colin S. Gray, and Joseph S. Nye, Jr., examine historical and theoretical problems of deterrence, Soviet and American perspectives, and the future of deterrence. Among the most interesting contributions is that of Ken Booth, a political scientist at the University College of Wales, Aberystwyth. His essay, "Nuclear Deterrence and 'World War III': How Will History Judge?" is a penetrating critique of the disarray and shallowness of strategic thinking; his discussion of the semantics of strategy (how much changes, e.g., when the terms at the heart of the subject—"war," "strategy," and "weapon" are preceded by the adjective "nuclear"), the ideology of nuclear deterrence, and "the strategic fundamentalists" deserve reading by anyone approaching the topic of nuclear strategy. Notes, index.

3-60 _____ and Mickiewicz, Ellen, eds. *The Soviet Calculus of Nuclear War*. Lexington Books, 1986. 276p.

Ten essays from an academic symposium held at Emory University in 1984 attempting "to examine assumptions commonly made not only about our own strategy, and the mission capability to support it, but primarily about that of our adversary." Of particular note may be Dale R. Herspring's prescient essay, "The Soviet Union and the East European Militaries: The Diminishing Asset," in which he discusses both the qualitative disparities between Eastern European and Soviet weapons systems and questions regarding the political reliability of Warsaw Pact nations. Given the collapse of the Warsaw Pact and the demise of European communism, this is one of the book's few contributions that connects well with current events. Among other essays are those concerning Soviet arms negotiation positions, ballistic missile defense, and the control of nuclear war.

3–61 Kozar, Paul M. *The Politics of Deterrence: American and Soviet Defense Policies Compared, 1960–1964.* McFarland, 1987. 169p.

A capable discussion of the superpower policies of the period, whose signal event was the Cuban Missile Crisis, a crisis that, although the U.S. "won" by intimidating the Soviet Union into withdrawal of its missiles from Cuba, it lost through the event's provocation of a more heated arms race. In his conclusions, Kozar speaks of the "mistrust and misperception" that characterized superpower relations of the early 1960s; should deterrence fail, it will probably be a result of mistrust and misperception revisited on a grand scale. A suitable book for newcomers to the topic. Notes, bibliography, index.

3–62 Kull, Steven. *Minds at War: Nuclear Reality and the Inner Conflicts of Defense Policymakers.* Basic Books, 1988. 341p.

An experienced psychotherapist focuses on the psychological processes of making defense policy, and on what happens when policymakers try to accommodate the international changes wrought by nuclear weapons. His attention turns to both American and Soviet officials; he finds in both two streams of thought regarding nuclear weapons. One seeks to adapt to nuclear reality through a basic re-evaluation of the role of force in international relations; the other insists on incorporating nuclear weapons into a traditional orientation toward the military's role. Kull concludes that, in spite of the resistance of the traditionalists, the awareness of nuclear reality is slowly creating a "regime of mutual restraint" between the superpowers, although the possibility of nuclear war remains, through a combination of unfortunate and improbable events. Kull's many interviews with both American and Soviets gives the book human immediacy. Notes, index.

3-63 Laird, Robbin F. *France, the Soviet Union, and the Nuclear Weapons Issue*. Westview, 1985. 142p.

Laird examines French perceptions of the Soviet threat to Europe, and discusses French nuclear weapons deployments in the 1980s and 1990s and their effects on European security. He believes that the French "starving" of conventional forces to feed the nuclear variety damages internal relations of the Western Alliance, and that a Franco-German security relationship "is at the heart of any Europeanization of the Alliance." The French, he says, will continue to insist on the independence of their nuclear deterrent, yet this independence will become increasingly difficult to maintain as the French nuclear force grows in importance to Western defense efforts. "There is no easy way out of this dilemma, a dilemma that the Soviets hope to exacerbate." Laird illustrates an irony in the French notion of "independence" through analysis of Soviet documents indicating that the Soviets see France's military forces as part of NATO. Notes, index.

3-64 _____ and Herspring, Dale R. *The Soviet Union and Strategic Arms*. Westview, 1984. 160p.

This survey of Soviet attitudes toward and policies on nuclear weapons takes into consideration a broad spectrum of Soviet thought. The authors help orient the reader with an opening treatment of post-war Soviet military policy to 1984. They see the Soviet military system, in a global environment of assured destruction in a strategic war, evolving into one with an emphasis on the utility of weaponry functioning below the all-out strategic level. Notes, index.

3–65 _____ and Jacobs, Betsy A., eds. *The Future of Deterrence: NATO Nuclear Forces after INF.* Westview, 1989. 200p.

Several experts on military and security issues speculate on what happens on the NATO nuclear scene following the INF Treaty. Despite its publication date, the book is already dated by the crumbling of the Warsaw Pact and the growth of democratic movements in Eastern Europe. Nevertheless, the various discussions of NATO's nuclear forces, especially in relation to questions about the long-term credibility of extended American nuclear deterrence, provides the book a good measure of utility. Notes, index.

3–66 Laqueur, Walter and Sloss, Leon. *European Security in the 1990s: Deterrence and Defense after the INF Treaty.* Plenum, 1990. 214p.

The authors examine Western European defense in the aftermath of the INF Treaty, attempting to visualize the situation as it may exist in the next ten years, with speculation on future requirements for theater nuclear forces, the options of alternative or nonprovocative defense, and other issues. More than half the book consists of documents pertaining to European security, 1948–1989, and this may be, for most readers, its chief appeal. Close to forty statements, treaties, speeches, and other items, from the North Atlantic Treaty to a May, 1989 statement by President Bush on conventional arms, provide a documentary overview of European security issues in the Nuclear Age. Index.

3–67 Lawrence, Philip K. *Preparing for Armageddon: A Critique of Western Strategy*. St. Martin's, 1988. 190p.

Assigns blame for the nuclear predicament "squarely on the U.S. In virtually every area where there has been technological upgrading [regarding the nuclear threat] the innovator has been America." Lawrence also holds the Soviet Union guilty of nuclearism, however, by joining the U.S. in fostering a belief in the efficacy of nuclear warfighting. He criticizes nuclear deterrence as inherently immoral, for it depends on the intention of committing an immoral act, specifically, "mass murder." Bibliography, index.

3–68 Lebovic, James H. *Deadly Dilemmas: Deterrence in U.S. Nuclear Strategy*. Columbia Univ. Pr., 1990. 252p.

An in-depth discussion of the psychology and politics of U.S. strategy; opens with the statement that "This book is about the *failure* of U.S. nuclear strategy." Lebovic attributes this failure to the strategy's inability to competently direct arms control, weapons development and deployment, and nuclear targeting. In his analysis, he argues that a consensus on nuclear arms between the U.S. and the Soviet Union is possible, but policy makers must desist from their habit of mistaking "the tidy world of strategy for the real world." Especially interesting is a chapter on U.S. assumptions and perceptions regarding Soviet intentions. Probably of most benefit to advanced students. Notes, bibliography, index.

3–69 Lebow, Richard N. *Nuclear Crisis Management: A Dangerous Illusion*. Cornell Univ. Pr., 1987. 226p.

Lebow investigates the shaky nature of decision making and stability in times of nuclear crisis. He contends that U.S. officials take an inflexible approach that exacerbates the dangers of situations already

pregnant with disaster, and that this official way of
thinking and reacting has not caught up to the
delicate balances of nuclear reality. Index.

3–70 MacKay, Louis and Fernbach, David. *Nuclear-Free
Defence: A Symposium*. Heretic Books, 1983. 223p.

The editors posed a number of questions to specialists
in disarmament and defense and to political activists
in other areas; they asked about what "defense"
means, acceptable and unacceptable forms of
resistance, military threats that might be faced by a
nuclear-free and non-aligned Britain, non-nuclear
defense options, etc. Presented in a question-and-
answer format. An interesting glimpse into radical
conceptions of what might constitute morally
acceptable and meaningful defense policies.
Bibliography.

3–71 MacLean, Douglas, ed. *The Security Gamble:
Deterrence Dilemmas in the Nuclear Age*. Rowman &
Allanheld, 1984. 170p.

The outgrowth of a conference on nuclear deterrence
held at the University of Maryland in 1983. Some
interesting contributions here, including Gregg
Herken's "The Nuclear Gnostics," a capsule history of
nuclear strategy, and George H. Quester's "Traditional
and Soviet Military Doctrine: Tendencies and Dangers."
Other of the eleven essays discuss the U.S. Catholic
bishops' position on deterrence, "existential
deterrence," and "moral perplexities" of deterrence.
Notes, index.

3–72 McLean, Scilla, et al., eds. *How Nuclear Weapon
Decisions Are Made*. St. Martin's, 1986. 264p.

Relying exclusively on unclassified sources and on
published information, the contributors to this
anthology intend it not as a scholarly analysis of
decision making, but as a manual for those who want

to understand the basics of nuclear decision making in the U.S., the Soviet Union, the United Kingdom, France, and China, as well as in NATO and the Warsaw Treaty Organization. Each nation or organization receives attention to various components of its decision-making organs; the U.S. chapter, for example, considers the intelligence community, the Departments of Energy and Defense, the State Department, Congress, defense contractors, think tanks and pressure groups. A number of flow charts and organizational diagrams assist in the project. A helpful guide. Index.

3–73 McNamara, Robert S. *Blundering into Disaster: Surviving the First Century of the Nuclear Age.* Pantheon, 1986. 212p.

McNamara, the prime mover of American strategic thought in the 1960s, based his view of nuclear weapons on the belief that they had no applicable military use; their only function was to prevent opponents' weapons from being employed. The result of this view, a strategic standoff based on the prospect of Mutual Assured Destruction should either side attack the other, formed the substance of American nuclear strategy for many years. In spite of the past decade's growing enthusiasm in American strategic circles for what Colin S. Gray and Keith Payne call the "rational" nuclear war, the prospect of MAD still plays a major role.

This book, based on lectures given at Duke University, is essentially a restatement of McNamara's long-espoused opinions along these lines, but it is a restatement with considerable refinement of his original approach to nuclear weapons. An advocate of nuclear buildup in the 1960s, McNamara now proposes major cuts in the nuclear arsenal toward a state of deterrence obtained "at the lowest possible level" of potential destruction, down to a few hundred warheads from the present levels of some 30,000 per superpower. McNamara stresses the importance of healthy East–West relations, and furnishes a harsh assessment of the SDI as a provocative and wrong-headed measure.

The worst thing about the book is its title, which implies far worse than McNamara suggests is possible through intelligent, careful reevaluation of the U.S. nuclear stance. Bibliography, index.

3-74 Martel, William C. and Savage, Paul L. *Strategic Nuclear War: What the Superpowers Target and Why.* Greenwood Pr., 1986. 249p.

The authors developed a computer model of a nuclear war through which they projected the outcome of counterforce (military) and countervalue (population) "exchanges" between the superpowers. Their concluding chapter of "Reflections and Recommendations" wraps up their findings fairly concisely. They question the counterforce capability of the U.S. nuclear arsenal, in contrast to the Soviet forces' dedication to this objective. They recommend U.S. disavowal of a first-strike attack, establishment of a strategic planning staff, creation of a bipartisan commission on nuclear policy, and accelerated investigation of how to end an accidental nuclear war. They urge that all Soviet cities be removed from the U.S. targeting list, that targeting be restricted to strategic counterforce targets, and that the ICBM be dropped from the U.S. nuclear triad, reducing the U.S. force to bombers and submarine-launched ballistic missiles. They make these recommendations with the objectives of rendering nuclear war both less likely to occur and, if it occurs, less likely to bring about all-encompassing ruin. An engrossing study that shows how serious inquiry can be conducted with an inexpensive desktop computer. Bibliography, index.

3-75 Martin, Laurence W. *The Changing Face of Nuclear Warfare.* Daily Telegraph, 1987. 155p.

Martin surveys the state of contemporary nuclear strategy. An easy-to-read book with a large number of excellent color illustrations that bring to vivid reality Martin's discussions of nuclear terrorism, Third World conflict, nuclear proliferation, global arsenals, strategic defense, and other nuclear-related matters. Martin concludes that "The most rational future for nuclear strategy at both the theatre and strategic levels is . . . probably the continued maintenance of deterrent forces with a capability for limited action." He acknowledges, however, that if such action commences, "the best hopes of nuclear deterrence will have failed and the world will have reached a desperate plight." Glossary, index.

3-76 Miller, Steven E., ed. *Strategy and Nuclear Deterrence: An International Security Reader.* Princeton Univ. Pr., 1984. 297p.

Notable for its inclusion of one of Bernard Brodie's last exercises in the area, "The Development of Nuclear Strategy," based on an address given at the National Conference, Inter-University Seminar on Armed Forces and Society, University of Chicago. The ten articles were all first published in the journal *International Security*, 1978–1983. They dwell on deterrence and its failure, the evolution of American strategy, and the political implications of nuclear weapons. Aside from an opportunity to spend some useful time in the presence of Brodie's restraint— nuclear warfighting is not necessary for deterrence— the collection features yet another of the painfully influential Colin S. Gray's meditations on the merits of using the Bomb, "Nuclear Strategy: The Case for a Theory of Victory." Notes.

3-77 Morgan, Patrick M. *Deterrence: A Conceptual Analysis.* 2d ed. Sage, 1983. 240p.

The second edition of a work frequently used as a textbook employs the most straightforward definition of deterrence: "Deterrence involves manipulating someone's behavior by threatening him with harm," and brings this definition to the world stage by saying, "In international politics we find ourselves in an age when deterrence as the foundation of national security ultimately rests on a readily available capacity to wreck many of the world's greatest civilizations." Morgan joins many other authors in arguing that, however well deterrence seems to have worked on the nuclear level, its continuing success becomes less likely the more it is relied upon, and that escaping the era of traditional nuclear deterrence intact will depend on luck, accident, and improbability. Continued survival must involve dismantling the international deterrent apparatus while emphasizing other, more constructive, kinds of relationships. Notes.

3-78 Nacht, Michael. *The Age of Vulnerability: Threats to the Nuclear Stalemate*. Brookings Institution, 1985. 209p.

Nacht outlines seven dilemmas highlighting the sense of vulnerability that the nuclear age has created. These include what he regards as the dominant trait of the Russian national character, "a pervasive insecurity"; the paradox of the American character, in which a perceived need to be the most powerful military force competes with a desire to be the chief agent of world peace; technological improvements in weaponry increasing the susceptibility of all stationary and many mobile targets; the tenuous relationship between the superpowers' state policies and what their policies would be in a nuclear war; arms control negotiations that fail to control threats to either side's forces; the position between entrapment and abandonment felt by American allies; and the spur to nuclear proliferation resulting from the intensity of the U.S.-Soviet nuclear competition. Nacht argues that the U.S.-Soviet nuclear stalemate has served us well, and that, in spite of the above areas of vulnerability, "the nuclear stalemate remains in place. It will take truly revolutionary technological innovation or a massive exercise of human stupidity before this stalemate is seriously threatened." Notes, index.

3-79 Nolan, Janne E. *Guardians of the Arsenal: The Politics of Nuclear Strategy.* Basic Books, 1989. 320p.

This discussion of the political aspects of nuclear strategy, especially of the gap between political and operational assumptions about such strategy, opens with one of the best accounts of "The Speech," Ronald Reagan's March 23, 1983 "Star Wars" blockbuster. As have other authors, Nolan depicts Reagan's announcement of his SDI vision as coming as a total surprise to his most senior advisers and Cabinet members; drafts of the speech were apparently cleared neither by the Secretary of Defense nor by the Secretary of State. Like other auditors of the speech, including its authors, these officials reacted with "genuine astonishment" at the President's description of the end of the nuclear threat. (The President's speechwriters had merely left an "insert" space in their text, presumably for the deposit of one of his warm anecdotes or homilies).

The "Star Wars" speech was "an invitation to highly politicized chaos," a chaos in which the Pentagon proceeded to carry out an expansion and modernization of U.S. nuclear forces. In her treatment of SDI and the history of nuclear strategy, Nolan seeks to reveal the "blatant contradiction" between abstract beliefs about nuclear weapons held by political leaders and the actual, pragmatic planning for the use of nuclear weapons in war. This contradiction creates a lack of accountability in the political process which may, ironically thanks to the public debate on strategic defense, be approaching a point of correction. A book intended for the general public; succeeds in its goal of creating a point of departure for a wider debate on the problems it addresses. Notes, bibliography, index.

3-80 Osgood, Robert E. *The Nuclear Dilemma in American Strategic Thought.* Westview, 1988. 138p.

Osgood analyzes the various schools of American strategic thought since 1946. He identifies such groups as "maximalists," who advocate flexible and limited nuclear response, "abolitionists," who would banish nuclear weapons, and "rejectionists," who subscribe to deterrence based on assured obliteration of the aggressor. He dismisses the abolitionists as hopelessly out of touch with reality; he himself inclines to the maximalist view. In his analysis, Osgood makes helpful observations on the work of many prominent writers on nuclear strategy. Nontechnical, brief, and readable, the book could serve readers at several levels of sophistication. Bibliography, index.

3-81 Pringle, Peter and Arkin, William. *SIOP, the Secret U.S. Plan for Nuclear War.* Norton, 1983. 287p.

"SIOP"--Single Integrated Operation Plan--is the acronym for the U.S. plan for conducting nuclear war with the Soviet Union. The "single" aspect is its uniqueness in calling for use of the nuclear weapons of the U.S. Army, Air Force, and Navy; it is "integrated" through its embrace of all the nuclear contingency plans of the various U.S. regional commands, along with the nuclear forces of Great Britain. Using Freedom of Information Act material and recently declassified documents, the authors attempt to present a comprehensive outline of U.S. nuclear war plans, which they finally dismiss as the "mere symbol of a bygone age when being able to coordinate the threat of a massive nuclear response was thought to be good enough to deter the Soviet Union." An illuminating portrait of the surreal, but at the same time too real, world of nuclear weapons control and command systems. Notes, glossary, index.

3-82 Quester, George H. *The Future of Nuclear Deterrence.* Lexington Books, 1986. 333p.

Quester, of the University of Maryland's Department of Government and Politics, places considerable confidence in nuclear deterrence and mutual assured destruction as effective peace-keeping strategies, and here tries to lay out his case for these concepts, which have come under attack from both the left and the right. "The overall point of this book is that the problems of the future of nuclear deterrence are indeed manageable, that we can survive to do another taking stock [of the situation] in 2005, and another in 2025, and that the concepts and mechanisms of nuclear deterrence as we have known them will indeed play a major role in carrying us forward." Quester addresses such subtopics as "responsible retaliation," the tension between deterrence and traditional morality, nuclear winter, substitution of conventional for nuclear weapons, and the future of NATO. Index.

3–83 Reule, Fred J., et al. *Dynamic Stability: A New Concept for Deterrence.* Air Univ. Pr., 1987. 106p. Supt. of Docs. No. D 301.26/6: St 1/2.

Lt. Col. Reule, chief of the Airpower Research Institute's Nuclear Studies Group, assumes with his co-authors that deception and mobility will be used to create non-targetable land-based missile forces, and that with such non-targetable strategic forces on both sides, a condition of "dynamic stability" would prevail. "The central issue," writes Reule, "would no longer be how many strategic weapons and delivery systems a country has, but how they are based." Under the envisioned system, advantages of a first strike or quick escalation to counterforce strike would be reduced or eliminated. Should war occur, the time available for decision making would be enhanced, and incentives would appear for smaller offensive force structures. Notes.

3–84 Rhodes, Edward J. *Power and Madness: The Logic of Nuclear Coercion.* Columbia Univ. Pr., 1989. 269p.

Rhodes explores the logic of power in a superpower environment in which mutual assured destruction is the shadow lurking behind every lower-level conflict. He believes that effective nuclear deterrence can be achieved with fewer weapons, and that, properly understood, "the logic and power of MADness permits us to escape the current coupling, counterforce, and strategic defense debates and to build consistent policies on the basis of a logically coherent strategy." He seeks to describe the qualities required of the U.S. nuclear force not only to deter Soviet "surgical" nuclear strikes on U.S. targets, but massive attack on the U.S. and major nuclear or conventional aggression against close U.S. allies.

3–85 Sagan, Scott D. *Moving Targets: Nuclear Strategy and National Security*. Princeton Univ. Pr., 1989. 237p.

Sagan joins the conservative crowd that takes to heart old (and sometimes mouldering) Soviet writings suggestive to the reader looking for confirmation of his preconceptions that the U.S.S.R. believes that "victory is possible" in nuclear war. Given this view, which most experts in tune with contemporary Soviet thinking on nuclear war dismiss, it may be reasonable to propose with Sagan that the U.S. develop a nuclear strike force able to wipe out Soviet leadership and reserve forces if it wants to preserve deterrence. On the other hand, it might not, since such a threat would quite likely undermine the stability one seeks to preserve. Bibliography.

3–86 Schneider, Barry R.; Gray, Colin S.; Payne, Keith B., eds. *Missiles for the Nineties: ICBMs and Strategic Policy*. Westview, 1984. 169p.

Eight essays on the future of the ICBM, with contributions from representatives of the conservative National Institute for Public Policy, a former Air Force officer, and from the editors themselves. Among the topics addressed are superhardened ICBM silos, SDI and ICBM modernization, small mobile missiles, deep basing, and Soviet responses to U.S. missile initiatives. A not uninteresting discussion of an essentially useless weapon, "useless" in that, should either the U.S. or the Soviet Union feel compelled to launch its ICBMs, contemporary civilization will almost certainly find itself obliterated. Notes, index.

3-87 Schwartzman, David. *Games of Chicken: Four Decades of U.S. Nuclear Policy.* Praeger, 1988. 233p.

Economist Schwartzman discusses nuclear strategies of presidential administrations in the nuclear age. He condemns the U.S. as the prime mover of the arms race, and argues that U.S. strategic planning has historically placed far too much emphasis on "the Soviet threat" of conventional aggression, with a strategic policy that heightens the risk of a preemptive first strike through an excessive reliance on counterforce weaponry such as the MX.

3-88 Scowcroft, Brent, et al., eds. *Defending Peace and Freedom: Toward Strategic Stability in the Year 2000.* Univ. Pr. of America, 1988. 216p.

The proceedings of a meeting of the Working Group on Strategic Stability and Arms Control of the Atlantic Council of the United States. Assesses the chief elements of strategic stability "in terms consistent with both the necessities and opportunities of this century's closing years." Members of the Working Group included the editors as well as such individuals as former Assistant Secretary of Defense and Assistant Secretary of State William Bundy, Soviet expert Raymond Garthoff, *New Republic* senior editor Charles Krauthammer, and many others of diverse backgrounds. The book consists of ten essays on arms control, reduction of dependence on nuclear weapons, confidence-building measures, and other issues. In the book's featured paper, whose title is the same as the book's, the Working Group makes specific prescriptions for enhanced stability, conventional defenses, arms control, and crisis management. This policy paper benefits from appended comments and dissent by several group members.

3-89 Shenfield, Stephen. *The Nuclear Predicament: Explorations in Soviet Ideology.* Routledge & Kegan Paul, 1987. 126p.

Dismisses as inaccurate the standard conservative contention that the Soviet Union's stated hopes for peace are merely part of a campaign to lull the West while the Soviets prepare for nuclear victory. Shenfield points to conflicting Soviet opinions on the threat of nuclear war and the commitment to preserve and spread socialism, with the school of thought under Gorbachev setting the campaign for the spread of socialism on the back burner in favor of a more cooperative international climate in which to pursue national objectives. An informed and thoughtful examination of Soviet beliefs and attitudes and their effects on policy; relies extensively on Soviet sources. Bibliography.

3-90 Shoemaker, Christopher C. and Spanier, John. *Patron-Client State Relationships: Multilateral Crises in the Nuclear Age.* Praeger, 1984. 211p.

The authors note that, although much attention has been paid to "bipolar" superpower crises, when the U.S. and the Soviet Union directly confronted one another, with nuclear war the terminal point should the confrontation escape control, relatively little study has been given "bipolycentric" crises. These crises begin with conflicts among regional states that can, in spite of what may be questionable merits, draw the superpowers into direct antagonism. The frequency of these crises has been increasing, owing to such changes as the development of numerous new non-Western states, and the growth of regional rivalries for power and security. "Thus the emerging polycentric world—composed of many countries, most of them relatively small but capable of deciding to go to war with neighbors—poses enormous dangers." The authors identify patron-client state relationships in which the client can exert substantial influence over the patron's diplomatic and military capabilities as "perhaps the greatest threat to international security in the nuclear age." The relationship between the Soviet Union and Egypt up to the October War of 1973 is a case in point, and that war and relationship serve as the book's most important forum for the authors' views. Notes, index.

3–91 Snow, Donald M. *The Nuclear Future: Toward a Strategy of Uncertainty.* Univ. of Alabama Pr., 1983. 189p.

Snow argues that "strategic uncertainty is the best dynamic around which deterrent strategies must be organized." He spends most of this book describing the current (as of early 1980s) thinking about and organization of deterrence strategies, and examines changes in the strategic environment such as antimissile defense systems which compromise adherence to traditional theories of deterrence. Bibliography, index.

3–92 Steinbruner, John D. and Sigal, Leon V., eds. *Alliance Security: NATO and the No-First-Use Question.* Brookings Institution, 1983. 222p.

Ten essays by American and European scholars on the security issues involved in the debate over the role of nuclear weapons in Europe's defense and about the possibility of relying on non-nuclear defense alone. The opening essay by David N. Schwartz provides "A Historical Perspective" on Western strategic policy from the 1950s, '60s, and '70s. Other contributors discuss NATO ground forces, the status of nuclear deterrence in Europe, domestic and bureaucratic policies of No First Use in Europe, the connection between such policies and arms control, and No First Use outside Europe. Notes, index.

3–93 Stern, Paul C., et al., eds. *Perspectives on Deterrence.* Oxford Univ. Pr., 1989. 343p.

The print result of a late-1986 research workshop on deterrence and related issues. The fourteen papers included are the work of political scientists, psychologists, sociologists, and representatives from other academic disciplines. The primary impetus for the workshop was the desire to investigate critically both conventional assumptions about deterrence (chiefly, that states challenging the status quo are "driven primarily by a quest for gains in international competition, and pursue this quest as if they were unitary rational decision makers,") and opposition to such assumptions, e.g., the belief that domestic motives rather than international ambitions may spur challenges to the status quo. Index.

3-94 Stockton, Paul. *Strategic Stability between the Super-Powers.* International Institute for Strategic Studies, 1986. 90p.

Analyzes alternative means for reducing the likelihood of U.S.-Soviet strategic war in the light of two stability-related goals: protection of U.S. allies from Soviet attack, and limiting the damage the U.S. would suffer in a strategic war. Stockton finds that a defensive posture cannot offer a true escape from deterrence; measures to improve the outcome of war tend to make war more likely; "rationality" in nuclear weapons use is an elusive, and illusionary, objective; and a no-first-use policy appears an impractical means of insulating the U.S.-Soviet strategic relationship from escalatory risks abroad.

3-95 Tucker, Robert W. *The Nuclear Debate: Deterrence and the Lapse of Faith.* Holmes & Meier, 1985. 132p.

Tucker, a professor of International Law and Diplomacy at the Johns Hopkins School of Advanced International Studies, contends that the debate of the 1980s over the "proper role" of nuclear weapons in American strategy "reveals a lapse of faith in the system of deterrence we have lived with for a generation." Notes.

3-96 U.S. Congress. Senate. Committee on Foreign Relations. *Nuclear War Strategy: Hearing before the Committee on Foreign Relations, United States Senate,*

96th Congress, 2d Session, on Presidential Directive 59, Sept. 16, 1980. Government Printing Office, 1981. 40p. Su. Docs. No. Y 4.F 76/2-N 88/15.

A "sanitized" version of a top secret hearing concerning Presidential Directive 59, containing the statements of Secretary of Defense Harold Brown and Secretary of State Edmund S. Muskie. PD-59, ordered by Jimmy Carter, brought a significant change to U.S. nuclear targeting strategy. The change was widely interpreted as stemming from an embrace of the notion of the possibility of a "limited" nuclear war, and as a potential first-strike stance by allowing a stronger focus on military sites. Muskie and Brown attempt to explain why PD-59 is merely a "refinement" of existing deterrent policy in response to changes in Soviet capabilities, and that it does not entail the belief that a "limited" nuclear war is possible, or, if possible, winnable.

3-97 Ury, William. *Beyond the Hotline: Controlling a Nuclear Crisis: A Report to the United States Arms Control and Disarmament Agency.* Houghton Mifflin, 1985. 187p.

Discusses the application of crisis control to reduction of the risk of nuclear war; follows a report of the Harvard Law School's Nuclear Negotiation Project on the topic.

Crisis control involves "improving the ability of nations to halt crises before they become wars, and, better still, to prevent crises from erupting in the first place." Ury speculates on a joint U.S.-Soviet crisis control center that could monitor dangerous situations "and stand ready to defuse a crisis on a moment's notice." He also suggests that other nations, and the U.N., could play effective parts in crisis mediations and peacekeeping to keep regional crises regional, i.e., not directly involving the superpowers.

Ury's discussion of the how and why of crisis control is readable (as he says, this is not a scholarly book), and rooted in case history, especially in the Cuban Missile Crisis. He offers an interesting account of the development of the original Washington–Moscow hotline, which came about in large thanks to the efforts of *Parade* editor Jess Gorkin, who conceived the hotline idea and used his Sunday–supplement magazine in 1959 and the early '60s as a forum on its behalf. Notes, bibliography, index.

3–98 Woolsey, R. James, ed. *Nuclear Arms: Ethics, Strategy, Politics.* ICS Pr., 1984. 289p.

Although there are some departures from the overall approbation for preparing for nuclear warfighting in this volume, that point of view is the one front and center. The contributors, including Colin S. Gray, Brent Scowcroft, Sam Nunn, Charles Krauthammer and Patrick Glynn, are generally critical of the idea of MAD on the grounds that it constitutes an imposition of U.S. perceptions on Soviet nuclear behavior, which allegedly dismisses MAD as irrelevant when the matter comes to actual war. The prevailing concern is a presumed U.S. military inferiority and the nation's bleary strategic vision compared to the U.S.S.R.'s crisp view. One wonders how "soft energy path" advocates Amory and L. Hunter Lovins managed to slip into this collection of military hardcore "solutions." As a bone tossed to the notion of balance, perhaps. Notes, index.

3–99 Zagare, Frank C. *The Dynamics of Deterrence.* Univ. of Chicago Pr., 1987. 194p.

Political scientist Zagare opens with a lament on the "mass of disconnected and seemingly contradictory hypotheses" strewing the landscape of deterrence literature. He believes that "If deterrence were a building, it would probably be condemned." He attempts to put forth a new foundation for the theory of nuclear deterrence using a game theory called "the theory of moves." His conclusions are that capability (the ability to inflict damage), and credibility (the belief by one's opponent that one will inflict damage) are both important factors in deterrence. It appears, however, that "deterrence stability resides 'in the heads' of world leaders" more than it does in the effects of variables easily manipulated by decision makers. Zagare draws on various events with nuclear potential to illustrate his ideas, including the Middle East crises of 1967 and 1973. Stripped of the academic dressing that gives it an acceptable scholarly flavor, Zagare's conclusion is that nuclear deterrence, like poker, is a head game. Any card shark would agree.

CHAPTER 4

Proliferation

4-1 Arnett, Eric H. *Gunboat Diplomacy and the Bomb: Nuclear Proliferation and the U.S. Navy.* Praeger, 1989. 175p.

Arnett, an associate at the Program on Science, Arms Control, and National Security of the American Association for the Advancement of Science, examines the effect of nuclear proliferation on U.S. regional interests, particularly the prospects for projection of naval power. He sees U.S. aircraft carriers, escort ships, and naval installations as vulnerable, in certain situations, to nuclear attack from "proliferants," although he deems it unnecessary for the U.S. "to fight small nuclear wars" against those foes. Satisfactory conventional weapon responses could be made to proliferants' nuclear threats or attacks. Includes speculation on nuclear attack on U.S. forces by Libya, Iran, and India. Notes, bibliography, index.

4-2 Barnaby, Frank. *The Invisible Bomb: The Nuclear Arms Race in the Middle East.* I.B. Tauris, 1989. 223p.

Barnaby stresses the "grave threat to world security" posed by nuclear weapons in the Middle East, and calls escalation of a local nuclear war in the region the most likely way a global nuclear war will begin. He devotes the first part of this book to an analysis of Israel's nuclear status, the next to the Arab states and the PLO ("Could the PLO Go Nuclear?"), and the third to the issue of international control. Barnaby demands that all governments "should face the facts and stop supporting the myth perpetuated by the Israeli and Pakistani Governments that they do not have nuclear-weapon programmes." He characterizes the need to prevent nuclear proliferation in the

Middle East as an urgent task, and one that the five established nuclear weapon powers could and should help effect by acting as if they recognize that there are no rational military uses for nuclear weapons. Notes, index.

4-3 Beckman, Robert L. *Nuclear Non-Proliferation, Congress, and the Control of Peaceful Nuclear Activities.* Westview, 1985. 446p.

Examines the Nuclear Non-Proliferation Act of 1978, along with other laws that seek to tighten the U.S. nuclear export criteria and strengthen the international non-proliferation regime. Covers the entire postwar period, from "The Era of Secrecy" (1945-1954) to the Reagan era. Will be useful for advanced students and scholars studying the topic; others may be visually put off by the text's cramped, dense print. Bibliography, notes, index.

4-4 Beres, Louis Rene, ed. *Security or Armageddon: Israel's Nuclear Strategy.* Lexington, 1986. 242p.

Six Israelis and five American experts in political science and arms control address questions regarding Israel's nuclear arsenal. The points of view range from antinuclear to advocacy of a visible nuclear deterrent, to the present do-they-or-don't-they (will they or won't they?) "bomb in the basement" nuclear guessing game favored by the majority. Beres himself argues that the only way for Israel and the region to escape catastrophe is through negotiated settlements. Topics dealt with include nuclear terrorism, the efficacy of Israel's conventional deterrent, moral considerations of going nuclear, and implications for U.S.-Soviet relations.

4-5 Betts, Richard K., et al. *Nonproliferation and U.S. Foreign Policy.* Brookings Institution, 1980. 438p.

Regional and national studies of the proliferation

threat make up this volume. Covered are Northeast Asia (Japan, Korea and Taiwan), South Asia (India, Pakistan, Iran), the Middle East, Brazil and Argentina, and South Africa. The authors examine then-current policies of the involved countries and the origins of those policies, and pay major attention to factors that could determine future policies. The book's concluding portion analyzes U.S. policy choices in pursuing non-proliferation in these regions, and, although the authors make recommendations, they are not especially optimistic about U.S. ability to prevent proliferation. Notes, index.

4-6 Bhatia, Shyam. *Nuclear Rivals in the Middle East.* Routledge, 1988. 119p.

A gloomy appraisal of what the author calls "a deadly nuclear arms race" in the Middle East. His assessment of the nuclear situation in Israel, Egypt, Libya, Iraq, Iran, and Pakistan leads him to conclude that non-proliferation measures may delay but cannot prevent nuclear weapon research and development in the region. Apart from the Arab-Israeli dispute, ancient enmities provoke an arms race, a race that "will continue until these disputes are settled and lasting political stability is achieved in the Middle East."

4-7 *Blocking the Spread of Nuclear Weapons: American and European Perspectives.* Council on Foreign Relations, 1986. 153p.

Contains the summary reports of two panels, U.S. and European, on prevention of further nuclear weapons proliferation. The U.S. panel, consisting of Gerard C. Smith, Albert Carnesale, James R. Schlesinger, Brent Scowcroft, and several others, enumerates 26 points concerning proliferation prevention, and addresses near-term risks, preserving and extending the international non-proliferation regime, and the roles of countries other than the U.S. Following the U.S. report's case-by-case analysis of nuclear hotspots, the European report, prepared by David Fischer, Harald

Muller, Johan Jorgen Holst, et al., focuses on political perspectives, and the nuclear policies of Western Europe. Numerous appendices contain such material as a comparison of the two reports, the outcome of the 1985 Nonproliferation Treaty Review Conference, and other useful items. Handy, especially for readers new to the topic, because of the easy–to–follow itemized conclusions and recommendations of the two panels.

4–8 Brito, Dagobert L.; Intriligator, Michael D.; Wick, Adele E., eds. *Strategies for Managing Nuclear Proliferation: Economic and Political Issues.* Lexington Books, 1983. 311p.

The proceedings of a conference of the same title, held in April, 1982, at Tulane University. Political scientists, physicists, arms control experts and other specialists discuss such major aspects of proliferation as its relationship with economic development, its effects on stability, regional questions, and forecasting and managing proliferation. The impressive roster of contributors includes McGeorge Bundy, George H. Quester, Bruce Russett, Lewis A. Dunn, and George Rathjens. There is room for diverse opinions; e.g., Russett characterizes Kenneth N. Waltz's rosy view of proliferation ("More may be better" is Waltz's slogan) as "courageous, stimulating, and utterly wrongheaded." Notes, index.

4–9 Dewitt, David B., ed. *Nuclear Non–Proliferation and Global Security.* St. Martin's, 1986. 283p.

A collection of sixteen essays prepared for a preliminary conference on pertinent issues before the Third Nonproliferation Treaty Review Conference in 1985. The authors present credentials from both public and private spheres; they discuss policies and perspectives regarding the International Atomic Energy Agency, nuclear suppliers and emergent suppliers, and provide a good general review of the Nonproliferation Treaty. Notes, index.

4-10 Ehteshami, Anoushiravan. *Nuclearisation of the Middle East.* Brassey's, 1989. 189p.

The creation of Israel and the maturation of Arab states into self-interested regimes have put the region into a seemingly interminable conflict footing, but with the rivalry among the Arab states, contends the author, "forging a nuclear alliance [against Israel] is an impossible dream." "As it stands, though, all the Middle Eastern regimes seeking nuclear technology and materials have begun to create an impressive infrastructure (skilled labour, research reactors, etc.) in a very short time indeed." Suggests that the Middle East was never as politically or ideologically divided as in the 1980s. The author's discussion of nuclear ambitions, and "nuclear war in and for the Middle East" is up to date insofar as possible, and disturbing. Notes, index.

4-11 Finch, Ron. *Exporting Danger: A History of the Canadian Nuclear Energy Export Programme.* Black Rose, 1986. 236p.

Although it has not produced its own bomb, Canada has played a significant part in the global proliferation of nuclear technology. India has used Canadian technology in the development of its bomb, and Canada has been active in attempting to sell the technology to other Third World nations, many noted for their political instability. Finch's history discusses the political background of the Canadian program, the nation's nuclear relations with Taiwan, Argentina, the Republic of Korea and Mexico, and uranium and reactor sales. Bibliography, glossary.

4-12 Goldblat, Jozef, ed. *Non-Proliferation: The Why and the Wherefore.* Taylor & Francis, 1985. 343p.

Why do nations without the Bomb want it? Or want the ability to produce it? Goldblat, the Stockholm International Peace Research Institute's longtime head of arms control and disarmament programs, supports his responses to these questions with papers by some familiar names (and some not so familiar from China, Latin America, and Sweden). Each paper comes with a summary. Goldblat stresses the need to understand motives in proliferation; among NPT signatories that have not chosen to build the Bomb, in spite of their technological prowess, are Canada, Egypt, Taiwan, Switzerland, Sweden, and South Korea. States not party to the NPT, such as Spain and Argentina, may refrain from going nuclear, although failure of superpower arms control talks would help push them toward their own bombs. Notes.

4-13 _____. *Nuclear Non-Proliferation: A Guide to the Debate.* Taylor & Francis, 1985. 95p.

Summarizes findings of the above item. Nations treated in this succinct summary are Argentina, Brazil, Canada, China, Egypt, France, India, Israel, Pakistan, South Africa, South Korea, Spain, Sweden, Switzerland, and Taiwan. Contains numerous appendices, including the text of the Treaty on Non-Proliferation, a 1968 UN Security Council Resolution on security assurances to non-nuclear weapon states, etc.

4-14 _____, ed. *Safeguarding the Atom: A Critical Appraisal.* Taylor & Francis, 1985. 243p.

Focuses chiefly on the International Atomic Energy Agency and its safeguards system designed to prevent nuclear weapons proliferation. David Fischer, who served as an assistant director for the IAEA's international affairs, provides a thorough, critical overview of the safeguards system. Paul Szasz, a UN legal affairs director and former IAEA legal expert, discusses the agency's ability to compel adherence to its safeguards. The range of options is narrow, including suspension of offending members, withholding nuclear assistance, and reporting to the UN. Editor Goldblat concludes with observations on safeguards system improvements and on the system's relationship with the Nonproliferation Treaty. Primarily for those with professional interests in the topic, but useful to the advanced student. Appendices contain various IAEA documents. Glossary.

4-15 *Israel's Bomb: The First Victim: The Case of Mordechai Vanunu.* Spokesman for the Bertrand Russell Peace Foundation, 1988.

Mordechai Vanunu, a former Israeli nuclear plant technician and later lecturer in philosophy, alleged to the London *Sunday Times* in 1986 that Israel's nuclear capacity included thermonuclear weapons, that the nation has a stockpile of up to 200 bombs, and that Israel routinely collaborated with South Africa in nuclear matters. Vanunu was then kidnapped while in Rome by Israel's Secret Service, and imprisoned to await trial for espionage. Although his allegations of Israel's nuclear weapons capacities have not been discounted, Vanunu was reportedly treated with "psychological warfare" in prison. In this short book, Ken Coates discusses "the paranoid responses of the Israeli State" to Vanunu's revelations.

The book also contains reprinted articles from the *Sunday Times*, including "Israel's Nuclear Arsenal," which contains Vanunu's original allegations. The book's concluding chapter, a document written by Vanunu while in prison in 1987, "Against the Nuclear Threat," states, regarding his disclosures, "I acted on behalf of my countrymen and for the sake of all mankind" by showing that the danger "is real and immediate." Vanunu was convicted of treason in March of 1988 and sentenced to an 18-year prison term.

4-16 Joeck, Neil, ed. *Strategic Consequences of Nuclear Proliferation in South Asia.* Frank Cass, 1986. 109p.

Eight contributors, all Americans, discuss proliferation issues in Iran, India, Pakistan and South Asia as a whole. They tend to both global and regional perspectives; the central focus concerns consequences for other nations should India or Pakistan decide to deploy nuclear weapons. The roles of both the U.S. and the Soviet Union in South Asian proliferation receive attention, respectively, from Rodney W. Jones and William C. Potter. It would have been agreeable to see contributions from an individual or two reporting from the scene, so to speak, rather than from Washington or from the University of California. Much of the volume is based on papers presented at an International Studies Association meeting in Washington, DC in 1985. Notes.

4-17 Jones, Rodney W. *Nuclear Proliferation: Islam, the Bomb, and South Asia.* Sage, 1981. 88p.

Jones's discussion of the Bomb's pursuit by Pakistan and its influence on South Asia concludes that proliferation trends in the region "are deeply rooted in security calculations and historical antagonisms." He argues that the most promising approaches to slowing Pakistan's embrace of the Bomb "are likely to be those that avoid excessive or permanent polarization and provide security reassurances and support for Pakistan in such a way as to limit offensive military threats to India." Notes, bibliography.

4-18 _____. *Small Nuclear Forces.* Praeger/Center for Strategic and International Studies, Georgetown University, 1984. 128p.

A study of small nuclear force proliferation in the Middle East and South Asia. Jones recognizes that nuclear proliferation may become a significant factor in political and military relations in the regions under discussion, and focuses on the nuclear capacities and aspirations of the states in question. Effects on regional stability, threats to American military forces, the roles of Western Europe and the Soviet Union, as well as defense planning, crisis management, and policy directions for U.S. security and arms control all receive attention. U.S. security questions entail possible direct military elimination of SNF capabilities by air or missile strike, such as Israel's 1981 strike against Iraq. Notes.

4-19 _____, ed. *Small Nuclear Forces and U.S. Security Policy: Threats and Potential Conflicts in the Middle East and South Asia.* Lexington Books, 1984. 289p.

A dozen essays, most by political scientists, on the problem of small nuclear forces. The contributors review possible threats to U.S. interests in energy resources, security of allied and friendly states, and stability of the entire regions, as well as more specific possible nuclear threats to U.S. military forces. Editor Jones concludes, in contrast to some writers, that "much can be done about the issue of nuclear proliferation." Timely action by the U.S. and other interested nations could, he believes, significantly limit future dangers from SNFs. Bibliography.

4-20 Kapur, Ashok. *Pakistan's Nuclear Development.* Croom Helm/Methuen, 1987. 258p.

Kapur's examination of the Pakistani nuclear program relies extensively on discussions with international experts (not including Pakistani officials themselves). Kapur discusses the external influences, most notably from India, pushing Pakistan toward nuclear capability. He designates the country as a "near nuclear" state, which, as Israel did until its cover was effectively blown by Mordechai Vanunu, practices a policy of nuclear ambiguity. Kapur links the Soviet invasion of Afghanistan with the creation of a climate favorable for Pakistan's development of the Bomb in conjunction with U.S. pressure against Indian proliferation, with non-proliferation in Pakistan taking a back seat to U.S. military and Cold War considerations. Pakistani leaders are now in the position, in the author's estimation, of having to continue their nuclear program or lose face both domestically and abroad, but cannot go nuclear publicly without inviting diplomatic, economic, and military sanctions. Not the least of these would be a resurgent Indian nuclear program and a cut-off of U.S. aid. Notes, index.

4-21 Karem, Mahmoud. *A Nuclear-Weapon-Free Zone in the Middle East: Problems and Prospects.* Greenwood Pr., 1988. 186p.

Karem suggest approaching the effort against nuclear proliferation in the Middle East through implementation of a nuclear-weapon-free zone in the region, a plan supported by existing United Nations resolutions. He indicates the disastrous potential effects of introducing nuclear weapons to the Middle East, and offers a plan for putting his alternative in place. He urges that a clear distinction be drawn between the Arab-Israeli conflict and his proposal: "Efforts should be directed towards separating the military and political conflict from the disarmament proposal for the establishment of a NWFZ in order to save the region from a ruinous nuclear-arms race."

He discusses application of other plans, such as the Treaty of Tlatelolco, which established a nuclear-weapon-free zone in Latin America, to a Middle East solution. His proposal is not unique, but his treatment is careful and well-supported by references. He pays close attention to Israel's nuclear capability and its "policy of implementing a unilateral veto" on neighboring nations with nuclear ambitions; he argues that the NWFZ would serve Israel's needs by preventing the perceived necessity of replicating its 1981 air strike on Iraq's nuclear installation. Bibliography, index.

4-22 Khan, Sadruddin Aga, ed. *Nuclear War, Nuclear Proliferation and Their Consequences.* Clarendon Pr., 1986. 483p.

The proceedings of the Fifth International Colloquium organized by the Groupe de Bellerive, held in Geneva in June of 1985. The three-day conference explored the implications for humanity of nuclear war and nuclear proliferation. The approximately 30 papers in the volume address the performance and future of the Non-Proliferation Treaty, global effects of nuclear war, the arms race, and arms control. Contributors are an international lot with various points of view, and include statesmen, scientists, and other specialists. A taste of the variety: Professor Ali Mazrui discusses the impact of new nuclear weapons states on Third World regional conflicts; John Kenneth Galbraith writes on the American context of the politics of arms control; Qian Jiadong of China outlines his nation's position on non-proliferation, and Carlos Andres Perez of Venezuela offers "A View from the South" on the arms race.

4-23 Leventhal, Paul and Alexander, Yonah, eds. *Preventing Nuclear Terrorism: The Report and Papers of the International Task Force on Prevention of Nuclear Terrorism*. Lexington Books, 1987. 472p.

The task force noted in the book's subtitle convened in 1985, an independent panel of some two dozen authorities from nine countries. They included nuclear scientists, industrialists, military officers, diplomats, and specialists in terrorism. The book opens with the panel's report, noting that terrorists might well be more willing than established states to use nuclear weapons; nuclear deterrence could not work against a group representing little or nothing but its own immaterial interests; "In this case," says the report, "nuclear terrorism could be the most dangerous variant of nuclear proliferation and nonnuclear terrorism."

The report cites national and international measures that might reduce the likelihood of terrorists going nuclear. The longest portion of the book is the collection of studies produced by a variety of experts illuminating aspects of the problem, including the means by which terrorists could attain nuclear capability, responses to terrorist grievances, control of the nuclear fuel cycle, and other matters. Notes, index.

4-24 Meyer, Stephen M. *The Dynamics of Nuclear Proliferation.* Univ. of Chicago Pr., 1984. 229p.

Meyer points out in this revision of his doctoral dissertation that the dissemination of vast quantities of scientific and technical data has given many countries the latent capacity to produce the Bomb; capability has, contrary to the beginning of the nuclear age, "decoupled from prior interest in building nuclear weapons." Meyer's investigation of proliferation--how and why it happens--leads him to conclude that the "cure" lies not in the control of technology, but in the relief of national nuclear propensities. He brings into his account numerous national examples of these propensities, and even works out mathematical formulae for their estimation. (One wonders how necessary or helpful a mathematical formula is to realize that Saddam Hussein, for example, would very much like to have the Bomb.) Chiefly for specialists and advanced students. Bibliography, index.

4-25 Molander, Roger C. and Nichols, Robbie. *Who Will Stop the Bomb?: A Primer on Nuclear Proliferation.* Facts on File, 1985. 150p.

A short overview of nuclear proliferation, with discussion of who has the Bomb, who probably has it, and who wants it. The objective is to inform the concerned citizen, for whom the final chapter, "How to Make a Difference," may be encouraging. Sandwiching the major portion of the book is a fictional treatment of a terrorist nuking of Washington, DC. The first part is narrated by a very old woman, the second by a young girl. The upshot of the strike is movement toward international nuclear control, with the U.S. and the Soviet Union mediating a Middle East peace treaty. Bibliography, index.

4-26 Moore, J.D.L. *South Africa and Nuclear Proliferation: South Africa's Nuclear Capabilities and Intentions in the Context of International Non-Proliferation Policies.* St. Martin's, 1987. 227p.

Discusses South Africa's nuclear capabilities, assesses the number of weapons the country may have produced and existing or potential delivery systems, and the reasons for the apparent lack of unusually stringent non-proliferation measures applied to the nation in spite of its pariah status. South Africa's bargaining strength through its position as a major producer of both natural and enriched uranium, Moore contends, plays an important part; non-proliferation authorities in the West may have been more interested in South Africa's cooperative attitude toward nuclear exports than in its development of a nuclear bomb that would seem to have little or no military value. He argues that the South African nuclear development "is not responding to the possession of nuclear weapons by any possible African adversary." It may be that S.A.'s nuclear developments are chiefly intended to serve the psychological purpose of demonstrating that the white supremacist regime can survive indefinitely thanks to its nuclear potential. The Bomb would serve South Africa as "a weapon of last resort should Western support be withheld." Notes, bibliography, index.

4-27 Muller, Harald. *A European Non-Proliferation Policy: Prospects and Problems.* Oxford Univ. Pr., 1987. 416p.

The result of a project undertaken under auspices of the Centre for European Policy Studies. Following discussion of non-proliferation policy in Europe, the main part of the book dwells at length on analysis of the scope for West European influence on nuclear threshold countries. Eight such nations receive detailed attention; they include India, Pakistan, Iran, Israel, Libya, South Africa, Brazil, and Argentina. A comprehensive and relatively up-to-date treatment; contributors, who have extensive backgrounds in nuclear regulation, suggest tailoring non-proliferation policies to individual national circumstances. Notes, index.

4-28 _____, ed. *A Survey of European Nuclear Policy, 1985-87.* Macmillan, 1989. 158p.

The result of a long-term project of the Centre for European Policy Studies in Belgium, this collection of ten essays by an international group of contributors documents strengths and weaknesses of Western European non-proliferation policy. Four essays focus on themes of nuclear non-proliferation, the rest on individual countries (France, West Germany, Italy, the Netherlands, Spain, and Great Britain). Editor Muller's introduction summarizes Western European non-proliferation policy during the years in question; he sees "marked improvements" in the non-proliferation record, although further reduction in "the obstinate differences in national outlook" is still desirable. Notes, index.

4-29 *New Threats, Responding to the Proliferation of Nuclear, Chemical, and Delivery Capabilities in the Third World: An Aspen Strategy Group Report.* Univ. Press of America, 1990. 273p.

A spin-off of an Aspen Strategy Group workshop held in August, 1989. Participants included, among many others, Strobe Talbott, James Woolsey, Joseph Nye, George Rathjens and Leonard Spector. The report contends that Third World nations pursuing the most sophisticated tools of mass destruction, including nuclear capability, "have been able to operate elaborate networks of clandestine trade" to obtain the necessary materials. On the nuclear front, a simple atomic bomb will no longer satisfy: these states "are now crossing the thresholds into 'boosted' and thermonuclear weapons." The report urges that the U.S. intensify its commitment to non-proliferation, including a heightened engagement with the Soviet Union, Western Europe and Japan toward a more comprehensive approach to the issue. "And most fundamentally, the United States must begin to match its rhetoric with diplomatic action on non-proliferation."

The major portion of the book follows the report, and contains essays on nuclear proliferation, ballistic missiles in the Third World, proliferation in the Middle East, and on other aspects of the race for acquisition of the engines of mass destruction. A useful, up-to-date treatment of the most potentially dangerous development in international relations. Notes.

4–30 Paranjpe, Shrikant. *U.S. Nonproliferation Policy in Action*. Envoy Pr., 1987. 142p.

India exploded its first nuclear bomb in 1974. That explosion was, allegedly, the country's only such test, although India has refused to sign the Nonproliferation Treaty. (Its proximity to "Nuclear Club" member China and to Pakistan with its nuclear ambitions has a lot to do with this refusal, as the author acknowledges.) Paranjpe's study intends "to spell out the Indian nuclear policy and to study the U.S. nonproliferation policy as it has evolved in the context of certain Indian postures and as it has affected India." He concludes that India has come to feel that the U.S. discriminates against India in its nonproliferation stance compared to its treatment of China and Pakistan. A useful source for insights on India's edgy position among neighboring states who have (or may have) the Bomb, and whose intentions are suspect. Bibliography.

4–31 Patterson, Walter C. *The Plutonium Business and the Spread of the Bomb*. Wildwood House, 1984. 272p.

Environmentalist and energy consultant Patterson describes how the use of plutonium as a nuclear reactor fuel became established "in the minds and budgets of nuclear planners around the world," and how the fast breeder reactor fails to correspond in technical or economic reality to the original vision of plutonium as a reactor fuel. The spread of the plutonium "solution" has been manifested in India's bomb, whose "civil" nuclear power program led to that nation's first nuclear weapon. Patterson also describes the international "plutonium diplomacy" and "plutonium addiction" from 1974 on, resulting in a negligible contribution to world energy output, yet some forty tons per year of potential bomb material being stockpiled around the world, "with no idea of what is to become of it or how to keep it from undergoing the grim metamorphosis into bombs." Notes, bibliography, index.

4-32 Paul, T.V. *Reaching for the Bomb: The Indo-Pak Nuclear Scenario.* Dialogue, 1984. 199p.

Paul examines the nuclear proclivities of India and Pakistan. The bulk of his contributions are contained within the first third of the book; the remainder contains a dozen appendices, some of which are useful (an interview with a Pakistani nuclear scientist), others which seem little more than filler, such as a description of a nuclear explosion. Paul concludes that "acquisition of a crude nuclear weapon force capability by India and Pakistan will not help to resolve their outstanding territorial and other disputes." Bibliography.

4-33 Pilat, Joseph F., ed. *The Nonproliferation Predicament.* Transaction Books, 1985. 137p.

A dozen essays by scholars and policy makers clarifying the nonproliferation debate in the U.S. in the middle Reagan years. Seven of the pieces appeared in earlier form in the Sept./Oct. 1983 issue of *Society.* The authors include such familiar names as Joseph Nye, Lewis Dunn, Kenneth Waltz and Leonard Spector. The general consensus is that nonproliferation is in the best interests of the U.S., but the authors differ in what they regard the best ways to support nonproliferation—whether, e.g., through the Reagan administration's position of Nuclear Club cooperation with convincing security assurances to nuclear aspirants, or more vigorous denial of opportunities for Bomb acquisition. The book assumes the reader's general acquaintance with the jargon of the subject. Notes.

4-34 _____ and Pendley, Robert E., eds. *Beyond 1995: The Future of the NPT Regime*. Plenum Pr., 1990. 257p.

The Fourth Review Conference of the Parties to the Treaty on the Nonproliferation of Nuclear Weapons (NPT) took place in 1990, but all interested parties looked ahead to the 1995 conference, whose main purpose will be to decide whether to continue the treaty indefinitely, or to extend it for a fixed period or periods. The editors of *Beyond 1995* have brought together a group of authorities to address the prospects for the treaty beyond that year. They are an international group, including, among others, representatives from Austria, Pakistan, the International Atomic Energy Agency, and the Program for Promoting Nuclear Nonproliferation. Several of the essay titles end with question marks, creating a fit atmosphere of speculation as the NPT's future goes to the line. "The Collapse of the NPT--What If", "What Happens to Safeguards if the NPT Goes?" and "Should India Sign the NPT" are among the interrogative titles. Includes the text of the NPT, which entered into force March 5, 1970. Index.

4-35 Potter, William C., ed. *International Nuclear Trade and Nonproliferation: The Challenge of the Emerging Suppliers*. Lexington Books, 1990. 431p.

Twenty essays grouped into three categories address aspects of the proliferation problem presented by eleven emerging nuclear supplier states. In the opening section, several authors discuss the nature of the problem; following are country-by-country case studies (the countries in question are Argentina, Brazil, India, Israel, Japan, Pakistan, China, South Africa, South Korea, Spain, and Taiwan). The volume closes with reflections on management strategies.

The editor concludes that the new supplier states are for the most part free of existing international export controls; they have, however, shown relative restraint in their nuclear dealings, especially in relation to early nuclear trade practices of the older nuclear nations. Less comforting "is the absence of an internalized commitment to nonproliferation on the part of the emerging suppliers and their increased ability and inclination to export ballistic missile technology as well as sensitive nuclear-related items."

A valuable, up-to-date study featuring the work of several prominent authors. Notes.

4-36 Pry, Peter. *Israel's Nuclear Arsenal.* Westview, 1984. 150p.

Pry, then a Ph.D. student at the University of Southern California, examines the size and sophistication of the Israeli nuclear weapons program, and seeks to answer questions about what foreign assistance Israel may have received in developing its nuclear capacity and the quantity and operational nature of its arsenal. An attempt "to reconstruct the history" of Israel's involvement with the Bomb, Pry's book is a concise but detailed study. His estimates at the time were that Israel had 31 plutonium and 10 uranium atomic bombs, the latter developed from stolen materials. He believes that the Israeli arsenal is a threat, rather than an aid, to stability in the Middle East. (Today's estimates of Israel's shadow nuclear arsenal range up to 200 bombs.) Bibliography, index.

4-37 Reiss, Mitchell. *Without the Bomb: The Politics of Nuclear Nonproliferation.* Columbia Univ. Pr., 1988. 337p.

A revised doctoral dissertation on the extent to which six technically capable countries have not to this point developed nuclear arsenals, or at least refrained from being obvious about it. The abstaining six: Sweden, South Korea, Japan, Israel, South Africa, and India. Reiss's inclusion of Israel in this group is curious, since the majority of informed observers are convinced that Israel has not only built the Bomb, but that it has a nuclear stockpile. Nevertheless, his discussion of Israel's deliberately ambiguous nuclear posture is interesting. In its three parts, the book gives a brief historical overview of the nonproliferation regime; provides case studies of the six nations in question; and evaluates the effectiveness of nonproliferation arrangements in confronting the causes of going nuclear. Supported by in-depth research; there are, e.g., well over 100 notes accompanying the 34-page Israel case study. Index.

4-38 Schear, James A., ed *Nuclear Weapons Proliferation and Nuclear Risk*. St. Martin's, 1984. 185p.

Seven essays on proliferation gathered from the *Adelphi* papers and *Survival*, with the most provocative title that of Kenneth N. Waltz's piece, "The Spread of Nuclear Weapons: More May be Better." Waltz does believe that the slow spread of nuclear weapons will, in fact, promote peace and reinforce international stability. The most important selection, however, is probably Desmond Ball's "Can Nuclear War be Controlled?" which answers that question in the negative: because command and control systems are more vulnerable than the strategic systems they supposedly direct, the "limited" nuclear war advanced by some strategists would likely see the missiles keep flying long after means of controlling their launch within the framework of anything resembling a rational over-all strategy had been destroyed. Notes, index.

4-39 Scheinman, Lawrence. *The International Atomic Energy Agency and World Nuclear Order*. Resources for the Future, 1987. 320p.

The author, a specialist in international law and relations, examines the structure and functions of the International Atomic Energy Agency, which is responsible for combatting nuclear proliferation and for preventing misuse of nuclear facilities and materials intended for peaceful purposes. "To forge ahead successfully" in the struggle against proliferation "requires unstinting support from the nations of the world, a shedding of the conceptual blinders of sovereignty, indeed an understanding that an effective and credible international atomic energy organization enhances their own national sovereignty by providing an added dimension of certainty and security to the environment." Notes, index.

4-40 Sena, Canakya. *Nuclear Weapons?: Policy Options for India.* Sage, 1983. 122p.

New Delhi's Centre for Policy Research solicited this analysis of the Indian nuclear weapons situation. The author discusses pressures for building the Bomb, security scenarios to the year 2000, nuclear threats from Pakistan and China (including scenarios of nuclear escalation with Pakistan), and India's nuclear role in the global nuclear system. The book concludes with a seminar report based on an April, 1982 discussion of India's nuclear policy options. Among other things, the seminar "pointed to the inevitability of a nuclear arms race between India and Pakistan." Notes.

4-41 Simpson, John, ed. *Nuclear Non-Proliferation: An Agenda for the 1990s.* Cambridge Univ. Pr., 1987. 237p.

In four main sections, this collection focuses on the present status of nuclear proliferation, the effects on the nonproliferation regime of superpower and other international relations, on possible ways to tighten the regime, and on challenges and alternatives to nonproliferation under the Nonproliferation Treaty. Contributors include some familiar names in Western nuclear literature (Lewis Dunn, David Fischer, Joseph Pilat), and some, like the Egyptian Mohammed Shaker, who, though he was president of the third NPT Review Conference and author of the massive 3-volume history, *The Nuclear Non-Proliferation Treaty: Origin & Implementation, 1959-1979* (Oceana, 1980), appear much less frequently. A valuable primer, of sorts, on issues that will confront the NPT Review Conference in 1995. Notes, index.

4-42 _____ and McGrew, Anthony G., eds. *The International Nuclear Non-Proliferation System: Challenges and Choices*. Macmillan, 1984. 209p.

Simpson and McGrew, British political scientists, bring together essays by academicians, government officials, and IAEA representatives; the majority of the contributions were first presented at a 1982 London seminar. The emphasis is on U.S. and U.K. nonproliferation policies from 1945 on, and the prevailing sentiment is for international cooperation. Analyzes the issues in considerable depth, within the context of the limitation to the U.S. and U.K. Concludes with a call for reform of a nonproliferation regime in a state of decay. Bibliography, index.

4-43 Snyder, Jed C. and Wells, Samuel F. *Limiting Nuclear Proliferation*. Ballinger, 1985. 363p.

Thirteen papers revised from their original incarnation as contributions to the 1982-83 International Security Studies program "Core Seminar" on nuclear proliferation at the Woodrow Wilson International Center for Scholars in Washington, DC. The book's three sections focus on nuclear threshold states (Iraq, Pakistan and Israel, among others), the "Nonproliferation Regime," which examines the nonproliferation and export policies of the U.S. and the Soviet Union, and "Management Strategies and Policy Alternatives," in which the authors attempt to identify new approaches to the problem. The contributors have significant backgrounds in arms control and analysis, along with expertise in varying regional issues. The chief drawback to an otherwise useful volume is its datedness; most of the literature cited is close to ten years old. Notes, index.

4-44 Spector, Leonard S. *Going Nuclear.* Ballinger, 1987. 370p.

In this third installment of the Carnegie Endowment series on proliferation, Spector dwells on Asia, the Middle East, Latin America and Africa; nine separate countries come into consideration. As Spector notes, even a nuclear war that remained confined to one of these regions could prove devastating; estimates of Israel's nuclear might indicate that it has the weapons to destroy every urban center in the Middle East with a population over 100,000. It looks as though Pakistan will soon be able to wreak nuclear havoc in northwestern India, while South Africa could do the same in Southern Africa. Spector's examination is thorough; each national analysis is preceded by a succinct outline of reactor data, uranium resources, heavy water production, and other data pertinent to production of the Bomb. Spector sees current international non-proliferation efforts as "unequal to the task" of holding the Bomb in check. Glossary, index.

4-45 _____. *The New Nuclear Nations.* Vintage, 1985. 367p.

The second in the Carnegie Endowment's series on proliferation by Spector. He again follows a regional and country-by-country breakdown illuminating the Bomb's spread. Appendices include a primer on nuclear weapons production, along with information on the Nuclear Nonproliferation Treaty, and the Treaty of Tlatelolco, which established a nuclear weapon-free zone in Latin America. Notes, index.

4-46 _____. *Nuclear Proliferation Today.* Vintage, 1984. 478p.

The debut in the series continued by the two books noted immediately above, this one follows much the same region-by-region, nation-by-nation approach as its successors. Well supported with references.

Glossary, index.

4-47 _____. *The Undeclared Bomb*. Ballinger, 1988. 499p.

Although narrow in its chronological scope—the book homes in on events of 1987 and 1988—this study of the nuclear statuses of nations aspiring to (and others already apparently possessing) the Bomb is thorough and informative. Spector assumes that India, Israel, South Africa, and Pakistan have the Bomb; in addition to discussing these nations' delivery systems, he surveys the nuclear scene in Africa, the Middle East, Asia, and Latin America. Extensive notes.

4-48 Sreedhar. *Pakistan's Bomb: A Documentary Study*. ABC Pub. House, 1986. 331p.

22 articles, official statements, and other documents illuminating Pakistan's pursuit of the Bomb. The documents originate from a variety of places—from Germany's *Spiegel*, for example ("The Secret Story of the Pakistan Atom Bomb") to Sen. Allan Cranston's 1984 remarks in the U.S. Congress on Pakistan's nuclear ambitions and activities. Bibliography, index.

4-49 Tiwari, Hari D. *India and the Problem of Nuclear Proliferation*. R.K. Publisher, 1988. 192p.

Endeavors "to critically analyse the nuclear policy of India towards the proliferation of nuclear weapons." Three chapters form the most important portion of the book: "India and Nuclear Test-Ban Negotiations," "India and Nuclear Weapon-free Zones," and "India and the Non-Proliferation Treaty." The author's perception are common among Indian advocates of their nation's "peaceful" nuclear program: he sees the nuclear weapon states as slighting and distrusting India, doubting "the very credentials" of the non-nuclear states regarding the sincerity of their dedication to peaceful intentions for their nuclear programs. Awkwardly written (or badly translated) in the extreme, and showing not even superficial evidence of proofreading by a reader comfortable with English, the book is nevertheless of merit in clarifying Indian perspectives on proliferation. Notes, index.

4-50 Toscano, Louis. *Triple Cross.* Carol Pub. Group, 1990. 321p.

The first in-depth account of Mordechai Vanunu's story. He took close to 60 photos of Israel's Dimona nuclear weapons plant, a plan buried so far below the desert that not even U.S. spy satellites had detected it. Security over the plant was so tight that an Israeli Air Force pilot who accidentally flew overhead in 1967 was shot down by a surface-to-air missile. Toscano contends that the Israeli government allowed Vanunu to tell his story, thus sending a message to the world about its nuclear strength. As Toscano points out, "Vanunu's message has been largely lost on the world," as the U.S. and other countries willingly pretend that Israel does not possess the Bomb, the U.S. engaging in the charade to facilitate its use of Israel as a surrogate for U.S. power in the region.

Told in quasi-novelistic style, the book is an absorbing look at both Israel's national pastime of security and a disenchanted citizen's decision to blow the whistle on one of the nuclear era's outstanding exercises in duplicity. Index.

4-51 Walters, Ronald W. *South Africa and the Bomb: Responsibility and Deterrence.* Lexington Books, 1987. 176p.

Walters states that South Africa's ability to cross the threshold from civilian nuclear power to nuclear weapons capability could be carried out very quickly if the regime's internal security crisis were to mutate into external threat. The South African case "represents a failure of international nonproliferation policy in particular." Walters discusses South Africa's nuclear weapon production capability, its testing, scenarios for nuclear use, relations with the U.S., implications of Western nuclear assistance, and other issues. "With each stage in the escalation of conflict in Southern Africa," he concludes, "all of the people of Africa are increasingly at serious risk that these weapons will be used." Includes an appendix providing a partial list of U.S. nuclear trade license applications for South Africa, 1979–1984. Bibliography, index.

4–52 Weinberg, Alvin, et al., eds. *The Nuclear Connection: A Reassessment of Nuclear Power and Nuclear Proliferation*. Paragon House, 1985. 295p.

Six essays on the links between nuclear power and proliferation. The contributors' papers are each followed by two commentaries by authorities in the field. The papers include speculation on prospects for commercial nuclear power and proliferation to the year 2000; discussion of policy issues regarding the nuclear fuel cycle (which cycle the editors helpfully outline in the introduction); supplier export policies—David Fischer points out that no country holds a nuclear trade monopoly, and that suppliers' ideas differ on a reconciliation of trade and nonproliferation goals; principles for international consensus on safeguards and sanctions, and the possibility of a return to the scheme suggested in 1946 by Dean Acheson and David Lilienthal, who called for limitation of such dangerous nuclear activities as breeder reprocessing to a few countries. Notes, index.

4–53 Worsley, Peter, and Hadjor, Kofi B., eds. *On the Brink: Nuclear Proliferation and the Third World*. Third World Communications, 1987. 278p.

A collection of essays that attempts to change the focus of the debate on nuclear disarmament to include consideration of the Third World dimension, which is generally overlooked in the superpower face-off. Contains some thought-provoking pieces, such as

William Walker's "Exaggerating the Risks of Nuclear Proliferation," in which he itemizes reasons for what he considers the out-of-proportion reaction to the issue of proliferation by observers in the industrialized nations, and Mohamed Babu's "Make Africa a Nuclear-Free Zone." The approximately two dozen contributors—academics, journalists, and government officials—include authors from the U.S., Iran, Tanzania, Cuba, India, and several other nations.

4-54 Yager, Joseph A. *Nuclear Nonproliferation Strategy in Asia.* Center for National Security Negotiations, 1989. 72p.

Both India and Pakistan have the means of producing nuclear explosives; North Korea is apparently engaged in a nuclear program, and South Korea and Taiwan may also move in that direction. Yager argues that the U.S. should broaden its nonproliferation strategy by encouraging India and Pakistan to eschew nuclear weapons production or testing for a specific period; by strengthening the nonproliferation regime through greater involvement of China, and by fostering regional cooperation in peaceful uses of nuclear power. A brief but significant document. Notes.

CHAPTER 5

Strategic Defense, Anti-Satellite Weaponry, and Other Military Incursions into Outer Space

5--1 Adragna, Steven. *On Guard for Victory: Military Doctrine and Ballistic Missile Defense in the USSR.* Pergamon-Brassey's International Defense Publishers, 1987. 93p.

An attempt to examine the Soviet ballistic missile defense effort "through the lens of Soviet military doctrine and strategy," rather than with the assumption that Soviet activity in this area is necessarily a matter of response to U.S. initiatives. What the book is, in fact, is an argument for U.S. perseverance in SDI development on the grounds that the Soviet Union has been pursuing, and will continue to pursue, similar research, and that all Soviet military policies are keyed to the ambition to obtain victory in any conflict, including those of the nuclear sort, and to enjoy dominance over whatever is left after war. Given the author's former status as Director of Research and Analysis of High Frontier, Inc., which operates under the aegis of the right-wing Heritage Foundation, one could hardly anticipate anything less than a position strongly biased in favor of SDI. Notes.

5-2 Anzovin, Steven, ed. *The Star Wars Debate.* H.W. Wilson, 1986. 223p.

Volume 58, number 1 of the H.W. Wilson Company's *Reference Shelf.* As with other topics in this series, the editor gathers pro and con views; this collection of article reprints and excerpts draws on such periodicals as *Foreign Policy, Scientific American,* the *Progressive,* and *Congressional Digest.* Well-known contributors vary from offering enthusiastic endorsement of SDI to outright condemnation. A useful tool for students without easy access to the original sources. Bibliography.

5-3 Arms Control Association. *Star Wars Quotes*. The Association, 1986. 120p.

As it says on the cover, this is a collection of "Statements by Reagan administration officials, outside experts, members of Congress, U.S. allies, and Soviet officials on the Strategic Defense Initiative." Quotations address goals and prospects of SDI, deployment criteria, consequences for arms control, the ABM Treaty, and other areas of concern. For a handful of remarks from the bottomless grab-bag of contradictory claims made by politicians and others about SDI, this is a handy compendium.

5-4 *Ballistic Missile Defense Technologies*. U.S. Congress Office of Technology Assessment, 1985. 325p.

An assessment by the OTA "of the opportunities and risks involved in an accelerated program of research on new ballistic missile defense technologies, including those that might lead to deployment of weapons in space." The report's genesis lay in President Reagan's enthusiastic presentation of his SDI program. As OTA exercises tend to be, this one is a thorough treatment of the questions involved, including technological feasibility; the interrelations between BMD and strategic balance, crisis stability, and deterrence; and "alternative future scenarios." A helpful and detailed executive summary precedes the main body of the report. OTA's findings in a nutshell: the SDI as conceived by the Reagan team won't work. "Assured survival of the U.S. population appears impossible to achieve if the Soviets are determined to deny it to us." Notes.

5-5 Barkenbus, Jack N. and Weinberg, Alvin M., eds. *Stability and Strategic Defenses*. Washington Institute

Pr., 1989. 305p.

The editors and seven other authors contribute seven essays on issues related to strategic defense, especially concerning the feasibility of a shift to an environment dominated by defensive, rather than offensive, orientation. Skeptics dismiss the chances of a transition without provoking a strategic destabilization. Among the subtopics are the role of strategic defenses in first-strike stability, and a model for a defense-protected nuclear weapons build-down. The editors contribute an essay synthesizing transition stability findings (although it is all speculation, so in a real sense little or nothing has been "found.") The volume is based on a 1987 workshop held at the Washington Institute for Values in Public Policy; it includes papers presented at the workshop, along with subsequent work. Index.

5-6 Barnaby, Frank. *What On Earth Is Star Wars?: A Guide to the Strategic Defense Initiative.* Fourth Estate, 1986. 192p.

An introductory guide and critical response to SDI by an author who has consistently advocated nuclear disarmament. Barnaby outlines the existing militarization of space, discusses various components of an SDI system, presents arguments for and against the system, and reflects on the European response to SDI. In his conclusion, he lists strict adherence to the ABM Treaty, preservation of limits on strategic nuclear forces as defined in the SALT II Treaty, and negotiation of a ban on the testing and deployment of anti-satellite weapons as steps required to prevent SDI from provoking an unrestrained nuclear arms race. Brief bibliography.

5-7 Binnendijk, Hans, ed. *Strategic Defense in the 21st Century.* Center for the Study of Foreign Affairs, Foreign Service Institute, U.S. Dept. of State, 1986. 151p. U.S. Supt. of Docs. No. S 1.14/3:St8.

Distinguished by then–U.S. Senator Dan Quayle's observations on the desirability of the U.S. pursuit of SDI, this book compiles remarks and exchanges of fourteen speakers "expert in various aspects of the SDI effort" convened by the Center for the Study of Foreign Affairs in late 1985. Speakers include James A. Abrahamson, Director of the Strategic Defense Organization; Alex Gliksman, Director of Strategic Defense Studies of the U.N. Association of the U.S.A.; arms control expert Gerard C. Smith, and other prominent authorities, including Sen. Quayle, represented here as a result of his Armed Services subcommittee work. Topics covered: research, including Soviet work; arms control implications; SDI and U.S. relations with European allies. Glossary, bibliography, text of the 1972 ABM Treaty.

5–8 Blechman, Barry M. and Utgoff, Victor A. *Fiscal and Economic Implications of Strategic Defense.* Westview, 1986. 152p.

The authors describe four SDI systems, each with a different purpose, ranging from protection of only U.S. nuclear second-strike forces to comprehensive defenses against both Soviet missiles and aircraft, and then estimate costs for each system. They then scrutinize the fiscal results of SDI expenses in a variety of budgetary contexts. They estimate that total investment for the systems, along with ten years' operating cost, "would range between $160 billion and $770 billion at fiscal 1987 prices," and conclude that an income tax surcharge (or equivalent funding device) of approximately $600 per year for a family earning $30,000–$50,000 would be required to support SDI. They believe that the project "might" offer economic pluses over the very long term. Blechman is president of Defense Forecasts, Inc.; Utgoff is a deputy director in the Institute for Defense Analyses. Bibliography.

5–9 Boffey, Philip M., et al. *Claiming the Heavens: The New York Times Complete Guide to the Star Wars*

Debate. Times Books, 1988. 299p.

An outgrowth of a six-part Pulitzer-Prize winning series that ran in *The New York Times* in early 1985; suggests that the future of Star Wars "is both impossible and inevitable." Given the superpowers' immense nuclear arsenals, no foreseeable anti-missile shield can conceivably prevent nuclear devastation in a concerted attack; on the other hand, developing technology does bode ill for the long-range status of the land-based ballistic missile, "a lumbering, old fire-breathing giant that might well be headed for extinction." But not to celebrate too soon: submarine launched and cruise missiles would remain potent nuclear threats. This is a readable, often fascinating portrait of the Star Wars story, covering origins, technology, pro and con arguments, to say nothing of Ronald Reagan's 1940s film "Murder in the Air," in which the president-to-be played an American secret agent fighting communist spies with an electronic weapon, the "Inertia Projector," that knocked enemy planes from the sky. Once again, life imitates art. Or tries to. Index, glossary.

5-10 Bova, Ben. *Assured Survival: Putting the Star Wars Defense in Perspective.* Houghton Mifflin, 1984. 343p.

The only perspective here is the author's. Bova, who is best known for his science fiction, is a gung-ho SDI proponent, and, like many SF writers, loses sight of politics, sociology, history, and even technological reality in the gleam of sexy imaginary hardware. This book is of interest chiefly as a window on the worldview of the credulous enthusiast who took President Reagan's initial Star Wars speech at face value and ran out to proclaim the new Gospel. See Chapter 16, for example, "A Good Strong Roof," in which Bova concocts a Soviet nuclear attack on the U.S. on Dec. 31, 1999: the Soviets fire over a thousand missiles at a thoroughly shielded fortress America; the marvelous gadgetry knocks out all but three warheads. Giddy stuff; wholly unpersuasive except, perhaps, to adolescent SF fans, whatever their age. Bibliography.

5-11 Bowman, Robert. *Star Wars: A Defense Insider's Case Against the Strategic Defense Initiative.* Tarcher, 1986. 180p. Originally published by Wilderness Press in 1985.

As Bowman, president of the Institute for Space and Security Studies, points out, the rationale advanced by Ronald Reagan in his famous 1983 Star Wars speech has been given the boot by technological substance, to the extent that SDI has been transformed from a visionary departure from nuclear deterrence to an enhanced form of deterrence. "The President in 1983 wanted to be able to discard our offensive weapons. Now we want to defend them." Bowman argues that not only would pursuit of SDI throw the ABM Treaty to the winds; it would also compromise the Outer Space Treaty of 1967 and the Test Ban Treaty of 1963. Bibliography, index.

5-12 Brauch, Hans Gunter, ed. *Star Wars and European Defence: Perceptions and Assessments.* St. Martin's, 1987. 599p.

A hefty compendium whose sixteen contributors analyze SDI on a variety of counts, including economic, strategic, political, and technological. Includes attention to Soviet and European ballistic missile defense activities, European perceptions of and reactions to SDI, assessments of the strategic consequences of SDI for Europe, and the ABM Treaty in relation to SDI. The contributors are from Belgium, West Germany, France, Great Britain, and the U.S.; their backgrounds range from academia to employment by the Department of Defense's Strategic Defense Initiative Organization. Bibliography, index.

5-13 Broad, William. *Star Warriors: A Penetrating Look into the Lives of the Young Scientists Behind Our*

Space Age Weaponry. Simon & Schuster, 1985. 245p.

New York Times science reporter Broad offers very much what his subtitle indicates, a human-interest story of the young nuclear scientists of the Lawrence Livermore National Laboratory east of San Francisco. Brilliance, beards, bluejeans and rationalizations—well-crafted and otherwise—are the characteristics of these young masters of the Bomb and its kin: "We're working on weapons of life, ones that will save people from the weapons of death." The same scientist who uttered this remark asks "Why not find technical solutions to a technical problem [i.e., the Bomb]," betraying no trace of understanding that the Bomb itself is the result of socio-political problems, not technology.

Why do these men choose to work on nuclear weaponry? Broad finds numerous reasons; as always, there is plenty of good money to be made by supplying the military with the tools of the trade. But beyond money, there is fun and the pleasure of working in a well-equipped lab with clever colleagues, not to mention the thrill of pursuing projects which but a few years ago existed only in science fiction (Broad embarked on his book shortly after the Livermore Laboratorians turned their attention to the call for strategic missile defense). Not to mention occasional knee-jerk hatred of the Soviets. Bibliography, index.

5-14   Brown, Harold, ed. *The Strategic Defense Initiative: Shield or Snare?* Westview, 1987. 297p.

Former Secretary of Defense Brown gathers ten essays, some previously published, approaching the topic in an exploratory fashion. Brown argues that area defense enabled by SDI is a cost-effective option, but that population defense, the raison d'etre of Reagan's initiative, appears of little potential in the next twenty years. Overall, the collection supports SDI research within a scope in keeping with the ABM Treaty. Among aspects of SDI dealt with here are its relationship to U.S. foreign policy, technical feasibility, economics, politics, and Soviet policy toward SDI and ballistic missile defense. Notes.

5-15   Bruce-Briggs, B. *The Shield of Faith: A Chronicle of Strategic Defense from Zeppelins to Star Wars*. Simon & Schuster, 1988. 464p.

The author argues that history reveals military forces as primarily concerned with defense of the homeland, and that the U.S. has lost sight of this function in its reliance on nuclear deterrence (although it is easy to argue that deterrence is a form of defense). The proper response, then, is further development of SDI. Bruce-Briggs provides a history of U.S. defense strategy, from CONAD (Continental Air Defense Command) of the 1950s to civil defense and the Nike-Zeus antiaircraft missile program.

Bruce-Briggs likes to imply that he is on cozy terms with those with whom he disagrees; Herbert Scoville and Herbert York are both "Herb." Experts he cannot countenance are "experts" in quotes, to suggest that they aren't expert at all, and concerned clergy picketing a defense contractor are "concerned" in quotes, i.e., they are idiots. Describing working class Americans observing protest of the Vietnam War, he writes, "They saw a half-assed war being fought—and apparently lost—with a dip-shit little country they had never heard of." This assumption of the working class worldview strikes the reader as more properly the author's own; his rhetorical stab doesn't work, and its failure is typical of the book as a whole. There is some meat here, but it requires pushing aside a lot of sour trimmings to reach it. Bibliography.

5-16 Brzezinski, Zbigniew, et al., eds. *Promise or Peril, the Strategic Defense Initiative: Thirty-Five Essays by Statesmen, Scholars, and Strategic Analysts*. Ethics and Public Policy Center, 1986. 479p.

An attempt to provide a well-rounded presentation of

the major issues involved in strategic defense which succeeds at achieving a half-roundedness. Beginning with the historical antecedents of the present debate (the lead article is Winston Churchill's 1934 House of Commons speech, "The Need for Air Defense Research,"), the book moves through a variety of views on the technical and strategic possibilities and advisability of SDI, to the moral aspects of strategic defense. Most readers will find some to agree with and much to repudiate here. One could react to Benson D. Adams's fairly astonishing characterization of the RAF fighter fleet as "An Early SDI That Saved Britain" either way, for example. Primarily composed of material reprinted from other sources as far to the right as the Heritage Foundation's *Backgrounder* series, and Reagan Arms Control Director Kenneth Adelman, and as far toward the center as *New Republic,* the *Washington Post,* and Harold Brown. Voices from the left are not in notable evidence. The book originated in a 1985 conference under the auspices of the Ethics and Public Policy Center. Glossary, bibliography.

5–17 Carter, Ashton B. *Directed Energy Missile Defense in Space.* Congress of the U.S., Office of Technology Assessment, 1984. 98p. Supt. of Docs. No. Y3.T 22/2:2 En 2/11.

Carter, an MIT physicist with a background in ABM research, looks at the technological paraphernalia of the proposed SDI system and concludes that the likelihood of developing a system like the one originally announced by Ronald Reagan is slight. He concludes, in fact, that the prospect of SDI serving Reagan's dream of a near-perfect defense system "is so remote that it should not serve as the basis of public expectation or national policy about ballistic missile defense," and that the ABM Treaty forbids deployment of missile defenses based on new technologies. Notes.

5–18 _____ and Schwartz, David N., eds. *Ballistic Missile Defense.* Brookings Institution, 1984. 455p.

Examines strategic, political, and technological issues raised by ballistic missile defense. Close to twenty contributors, including such prominent authorities as Lawrence Freedman, Raymond L. Garthoff, Colin S. Gray, George Rathjens and Leon Sloss discuss the relationship of BMD to strategy, applications of current and future technologies, Soviet views, the role of the ABM Treaty, and BMD in the context of relations between East and West. In the book's final section, nine of the contributors offer their personal views on the issues. Dated, but still interesting. Notes, index.

5–19 Chace, James and Carr, Caleb. *America Invulnerable: The Quest for Absolute Security from 1812 to Star Wars.* Summit, 1988. 316p.

Chace, formerly a managing editor with *Foreign Affairs,* and Carr, once a staff member of the Council on Foreign Relations, do their best to place SDI within a deep historical context. They argue that U.S. presidents have consistently sought the invulnerability referred to in the book's title; their search has led from the near-extermination of the American Indians to the militarization of space, with a response often out of proportion to the "threat." It's an interesting point of view that takes a much larger piece of history into consideration than do most treatments of SDI. Index.

5–20 Chalfont, Arthur Gwynne Jones, Baron. *Star Wars: Suicide or Survival?* Weidenfeld and Nicolson, 1985. 169p.

To answer the title question, Chalfont opts for SDI as a survival device, an enhanced deterrent to Soviet nuclear attack. A former defense writer for *The Times* of London, Chalfont believes that an effective SDI system would bring a heavy measure of doubt to any Soviet attack; the system's ability to destroy incoming missiles would render target selection a hopeless stab in the dark. Thus again, very early in the Star Wars history, even its proponents reduce the vision from the salvation of cities and populations to an augmented form of the nuclear deterrence that has prevailed for decades. Notes, index.

5-21 Charlton, Michael. *From Deterrence to Defence: The Inside Story of Strategic Policy*. Harvard Univ. Pr., 1987. 154p.

This attempt at an "oral history" of nuclear strategy leading to SDI contains transcripts of Charlton's interviews with many prominent architects of that strategy, including Robert S. McNamara, Henry Kissinger, Paul Nitze, Edward Teller, Caspar Weinberger, Jimmy Carter, Brent Scowcroft, and numerous others. The interviews, based on the author's BBC radio series "The Star Wars History," were recorded in the U.S. and Europe in 1985. A nice compilation of statements from an impressively diverse group of major players, the book should be helpful to anyone sorting out the prevailing attitudes toward SDI's potential. Index.

5-22 Cimbala, Stephen J., ed. *Strategic Air Defense*. Scholarly Resources, 1989. 275p.

A useful volume for background reading in developing an understanding of the origins of SDI. Ten contributors including the editor write on the history and decision making of North American air defenses, as well as on air defense technology, strategy, and deterrence. The best starting point might be Owen E. Jensen's essay on the decline of air defense, 1960-1980, a readable analysis of the heyday's slide into the nadir of American air defense. In his concluding overview, Cimbala calls U.S. missile defenses "politically undeployable" unless preceded by a marked Soviet abrogation of the ABM Treaty. He holds, however, that some U.S. air defense modernization should occur, and can be made without moving away from the present basis of offensive deterrence. Notes, index.

5-23 _____. *The Technology, Strategy, and Politics of SDI.* Westview, 1987. 252p.

Cimbala tries to provide a discussion of SDI embracing all three of his title topics, topics frequently discussed in isolation from each other. The eleven essays by strategists and political scientists range from skeptical caution to insistence on SDI's virtue; aspects of SDI addressed include its employment as a protector of strategic forces, SDI and NATO, the impact of SDI on Soviet national security policy, arms control, etc. Not

5-24 Codevilla, Angelo M. *While Others Build: The Commonsense Approach to the Strategic Defense Initiative.* Free Pr., 1988. 256p.

Codevilla, a Hoover Institute fellow and eager devotee of ballistic missile defense, is disgusted with the Reagan administration's less than expeditious pursuit of SDI the system as well as by the Strategic Defense Initiative Organization. He believes that development of an antimissile system must be turned over to the military. "This is how such things have happened in the past, and this is how they must happen in the future, because it is in the nature of things." Bibliography, index.

5-25 Cohen, S.T. *We Can Prevent World War III.* Jameson Books, 1985. Distributed by Kampmann. 129p.

Cohen, credited with invention of the neutron bomb, would avoid WW III, at least as it concerns the U.S., through a policy combining an anti-interventionist approach with vigorous development of SDI. Then, not only would the U.S. not provoke attack through blundering around the world's trouble spots; it would be able to fend off an attack, if it came, by holding up the SDI umbrella. Bibliography, index.

5-26 Council on Economic Priorities. *Star Wars: The*

Economic Fallout. Ballinger, 1988. 234p.

The CEP, an independent research organization, takes SDI to task for what it considers the project's pork barrel nature, its co-option of academic scientists, and the threat of a "Star Wars vision" diverting attention, leadership, and other resources from other important national problems. These objections supplement the Council's belief that not only would SDI fail to achieve a nuclear-free world, but that it could also exacerbate the arms race, destabilize the strategic balance, and lead to other pernicious effects. Notes, index.

5-27 Cowen, Regina; Rajcsanyi, Peter; Bilandzic, Vladimir. *SDI and European Security.* Institute for East-West Security Studies, 1987. 183p. Distributed by Westview Pr.

Three essays look at SDI from European perspectives. The authors, from the U.K., Hungary, and Yugoslavia, examine SDI implications for NATO, U.S.-Soviet relations and arms control, and European attitudes and responses to SDI. The Reagan administration embarked on SDI very much as if Western Europe did not exist. This group of essays is a helpful assist for Americans trying to see why SDI makes many Europeans anxious. Several appendices provide statements from German, Soviet, British, and American officials on aspects of SDI. Notes.

5-28 Daalder, Ivo H. *The SDI Challenge to Europe.* Ballinger, 1987. 185p.

Daalder, a Dutch national, opposes SDI chiefly from the point of view of a European worried about the possible desertion of Western Europe by an America possessing a renewed imperviousness to attack from abroad. If, goes the argument, SDI achieves the goal of an invulnerable U.S., Western Europe may well have to fend for itself against Soviet nuclear or conventional forces. It is not a wholly convincing argument; no one but former President Reagan and a handful of equally starry-eyed visionaries ever believed that SDI could, even at its most successful, allow the U.S. to turn an impervious celestial shield to a nuclear attack. Bibliography, index.

5-29 Dallmeyer, Dorinda G., ed. *The Strategic Defense Initiative: New Perspectives on Deterrence.* Westview, 1986. 112p.

SDI advocates and opponents face off in this collection of essays. There are some familiar names here: "High Frontier" pioneer Daniel O. Graham, arms control expert Gerard C. Smith, strategist Colin S. Gray, and former Secretary of State Dean Rusk, among others. Graham says that SDI "is not a weapons program," and that "SDI is designed to get rid of that militarization of space with non-nuclear defensive systems." Index.

5-30 Drell, Sidney D.; Farley, Philip J.; and Holloway, David. *The Reagan Strategic Defense Initiative: A Technical, Political, and Arms Control Assessment.* Ballinger, 1985. 152p.

From the technical end, this SDI assessment effectively demolishes any wide-eyed acceptance of the Reagan vision of ICBMs rendered "impotent and obsolete" by a defensive system; the book also outlines the negative impact on arms control of SDI, and Soviet perceptions of the venture. The authors urge that priority be given to maintaining the effectiveness of the ABM Treaty "as the clearest demonstration that escape from total political and strategic confrontation is possible and can have practical effect." Notes, index.

5-31 Durch, William J. *The ABM Treaty and Western Security.* Ballinger, 1988. 161p.

Durch, assistant director of the Defense and Arms Control Studies Program at MIT, argues that the ABM

Treaty would still need refurbishing even if SDI did not exist. He reviews the history of U.S. and Soviet strategic defense, examines the Treaty in relation to arms control, and describes different policy paths and options for the U.S. He characterizes the ABM Treaty as "under siege of ideology, technology, and time," yet in his view the Treaty has served U.S. and Western security interests well and can be expected to continue this service into the next century. If the U.S. feels compelled to deploy a ballistic missile defense, he urges that it be devoted to insurance against accidental missile attack; such a system could, he contends, be achieved within current ABM Treaty limits, and could provide some useful "political symmetry" in relation to the existing Moscow system. Notes, index.

5-32 Eglin, James M. *Air Defense in the Nuclear Age: The Post-War Development of American and Soviet Strategic Defense Systems.* Garland, 1988. 307p.

Originally presented as the author's doctoral thesis for Harvard University in 1967, and that date seriously affects the book's currency; this is definitely not the place to come for an evaluation of SDI. It is, however, a useful tool for investigating the early history of serious strategic defense, first enunciated by President Eisenhower in a speech at Ottawa on Nov. 14, 1953, when he said "You of Canada and we of the United States can and will devise ways to protect our North America from any surprise attack by air." Eglin discusses air defense in the U.S. and the Soviet Union from 1946-1960, and provides some treatment of anti-ballistic missile defense issues. Bibliography, but (alas) no index.

5-33 Ennals, J.R. *Star Wars: A Question of Initiative.* J. Wiley, 1986. 236p.

A good source for insights regarding British reaction to Great Britain's participation in SDI research. The most significant section of the book in this regard is a collection of speeches, lectures, and articles written by the author in 1986, featuring such titles as "Star Wars: SDI and the Corruption of British Science." Ennals, a computer scientist, questions the merits of SDI on the basis of his doubts about the computer technology required by the system. Notes, index.

5-34 FitzGerald, Mary C. *Soviet Views on SDI*. Univ. of Pittsburgh Center for Russian and East European Studies, 1987. 70p.

FitzGerald reviews eighteen prominent Soviet periodicals and official statements to clarify Soviet reaction to SDI. She concludes that "the Soviet Union views SDI as an attempt to secure . . . a first-strike capability for the United States." She points to a meshing point of view of Soviet political and military leaders in which a robust offense will continue to render a defensive orientation vulnerable; this offense would include bombers, cruise missiles, and depressed-trajectory ICBMs that SDI cannot stifle.

5-35 Fought, Stephen O. *SDI, a Policy Analysis*. Naval War College, 1987. 88p. U.S. Supt. of Docs. No. D 208.202: St 8/2.

Fought, a Colonel who teaches at the Naval War College, assumes that some versions of SDI are feasible, and proceeds to raise questions about the effects of various types of deployment, their interaction with other elements of the strategic environment, and how the resulting possible outcomes would compare with actual objectives. He argues that a negotiation process should accompany both American and Soviet development of strategic defenses, to address and assuage anxieties on both sides, e.g., American concern over maintenance of survivable land-based ICBMs, and Soviet fears of an American technological leap that would grossly upset the balance of power. Brief bibliography.

5-36 Garthoff, Raymond L. *Policy Versus the Law: The Reinterpretation of the ABM Treaty.* Brookings Institution, 1987. 117p.

Signed and ratified in 1972, the ABM Treaty bans development, testing, and deployment of space-based and mobile antiballistic missile systems or their components. The argument advanced by proponents seeking a back door entry for SDI, and first enunciated in an offhand way by U.S. national security advisor Robert McFarlane in a "Meet the Press" interview in 1985, is that the ABM Treaty does not apply to systems based on new technologies.

In this study, Garthoff examines the negotiating record and ratification proceedings of the treaty, and concludes that the "new technology" rationalization for SDI is without foundation. Garthoff poses the question clearly: "What would the United States have thought if after many years the Soviet Union had suddenly, unilaterally, reinterpreted the ABM Treaty (or any other) to suit a policy purpose of its own contrary to U.S. policy and to the original clear understanding of both parties?" Notes.

5-37 Godson, Dean. *SDI, Has America Told Her Story to the World?: Report of the Institute for Foreign Policy Analysis, Panel on Public Diplomacy.* Pergamon-Brassey, 1987. 73p.

From political stage right comes this lamentation over American failure to convince the Europeans (who have been, we are told, beastly misled by the conniving Soviet) that SDI will be good for them. According to the findings of the Panel on Public Diplomacy, which included representatives from the Heritage Foundation, Boston University, and Tufts University, among other places, "The President's original formulation of March 1983 was, perhaps, too general to form the basis of an information campaign." Among the Panel's suggestions: establish an SDI "High Command" for Public Diplomacy to supervise a public relations campaign that would bring the light of SDI to the dark hinterlands. Notes.

5-38 Graham, Daniel O. *The Non-Nuclear Defense of Cities: The High Frontier Space-Based Defense Against ICBM Attack.* Abt Books, 1983. 152p.

Another of Graham's outings on his antimissile system campaign. The work of a true believer; all objections and questions fall before the obvious correctness of Graham's vision. In addition to living beneath this fantastic umbrella, Graham believes that consumers would be treated to such wonderful SDI-research spin-offs as portable wrist telephones and 3-D holographic teleconferencing.

5-39 _____ and Fossedal, Gregory A. *A Defense that Defends: Blocking Nuclear Attack.* Devin-Adair, 1983. 158p.

Graham and Fossedal argue for the space-based antimissile system that Graham earlier advocated in *The High Frontier.* The system, they say, is more "moral" than MAD, is technologically feasible, and is affordable, provided its pursuit is intense and timely. It will also enable the U.S. to follow a more vigorous (i.e., pushy) foreign policy knowing that the nation can fend off Soviet retribution. Notes, index.

5-40 Guerrier, Steven W. and Thompson, Wayne C., eds. *Perspectives on Strategic Defense.* Westview, 1987. 358p.

Thirty articles, speeches, and other documents illuminating various questions about SDI, from Ronald Reagan's opening 1983 "Star Wars" address to the Union of Concerned Scientists' appeal to ban space weapons in 1986. Those two poles indicate the range of opinion in the collection, from gung-ho support of SDI to its condemnation. A good source of contrasting views as of the book's publication date, including those of Soviet, American, and other Allied governments. General background, technical feasibility, the effects of SDI on strategic doctrine, arms control, and Soviet-American relations are the major issues under consideration. Glossary, index.

5–41 Guertner, Gary L. and Snow, Donald M. *The Last Frontier: An Analysis of the Strategic Defense Initiative.* Lexington Books, 1986. 158p.

Political scientists Snow and Guertner examine the background and prospects of strategic defense, problems associated with demonstrating system effectiveness, interrelationships of offensive and defensive forces and arms control, and "new technologies versus old tactics." Snow is somewhat more amenable to SDI than Guertner, but is wary of the enterprise's financial costs; Guertner dwells on the system's technical, strategic and arms-control related problems. A nicely-balanced treatment that encourages the reader to wrestle with questions the authors raise. An appendix summarizes major administration documents and testimonies on SDI. Notes, index.

5–42 Haley, Edward and Merritt, Jack, eds. *Strategic Defense Initiative, Folly or Future?* Westview, 1986. 193p.

Intended for use as a textbook, this volume contains a number of pro and con positions on SDI's technical and strategic questions and on its implications for U.S.-Soviet and U.S.-Allied relations. Features the usual roster of names: Reagan, Paul Nitze, George Rathjens, Edward Teller (for whom SDI is "The Last, Best Hope"), Sidney Drell, and others. A little dated, but still useful. Bibliographies, glossary.

5–43 Holdren, John and Rotblat, Joseph, eds. *Strategic Defences and the Future of the Arms Race: A Pugwash Symposium.* Macmillan, 1987. 286p.

Deals with the strategic, technological, legal, and political implications of the Reagan SDI vision "as seen through American, European, and Russian eyes." The volume contains two dozen papers based on the Pugwash Symposium on Strategic Defences held in London in December 1985. There are some prominent names among the contributors, but most readers will want to consult more up-to-date publications for an overview of SDI. Useful, however, to those tracking the historical record of the initiative. Index.

5-44 Jasani, Bhupendra, ed. *Space Weapons: The Arms Control Dilemma.* Taylor & Francis, 1984. 255p.

In the first part of this Stockholm International Peace Research Institute study, the author discusses potential targets in space, which include not only reconnaissance satellites, but navigation and meteorological satellites; space-based defensive weapons, anti-satellite weapons, and the 1972 ABM Treaty. The second part contains fourteen papers by as many authors present at a symposium held in Stockholm, Sept. 21-23, 1983, on the militarization of space and arms control. An appendix gives the texts of treaties and treaty proposals pertinent to arms control in space. Clearly dated in its treatment of strategic defense, but a worthwhile source of views on various aspects of the arms race in space. Index.

5-45 Jastrow, Robert. *How to Make Nuclear Weapons Obsolete.* Little, Brown, 1985. 175p.

Dedicated "to the men and women who want to see nuclear weapons disappear from the face of the earth," Jastrow's book firmly buys into the Reagan vision of Soviet missiles as "impotent and obsolete" in the teeth of an American strategic shield in space. The text, which discusses the technological, strategic, and political dimensions of SDI, is accessible, but the book's datedness makes it of not much use other than as a glimpse at an SDI enthusiast's thinking in the middle Reagan years. Notes.

5-46 Jungerman, John A. *The Strategic Defense*

Initiative: A Primer and Critique. Univ. of California Institute on Global Conflict and Cooperation, 1988. 43p.

The author, a physicist at the Univ. of California-Davis, argues that SDI is one more unpromising attempt to solve a political problem through technology; that rather than being a "technically sweet" option, SDI "is fraught with immense difficulties and is vulnerable to countermeasures," and that the political process of arms control and disarmament holds out more room for rational hope than does SDI. Notes, glossary.

5-47 Lakoff, Sanford A. and York, Herbert F. *A Shield in Space?: Technology, Politics, and the Strategic Defense Initiative: How the Reagan Administration Set Out to Make Nuclear Weapons "Impotent and Obsolete" and Succumbed to the Fallacy of the Last Move.* Univ. of California Pr., 1989. 409p.

An effective attack on the SDI that dismisses the proposed system as technologically unworkable, an impetus to destabilization and a renewed arms race, a drag on U.S.-Soviet relations, and a hindrance to effective arms control. Lakoff and York, who was the first director of defense research and engineering for the Department of Defense, share the opinion of many other SDI critics that the search for a technological solution to what is a socio-political problem is bound to fail. The authors elaborate on this criticism thoroughly and persuasively, and provide an interesting analysis of SDI as a defense program that, rather than evolving from needs perceived at the militarily systemic level instead came forth from the imagination of a single individual, Ronald Reagan.

5-48 Lall, Betty G., et al. *Security Without Star Wars: Verifying a Ban on Ballistic Missile Defense.* Council on Economic Priorities, 1987. 106p.

In this study for the CEP, the authors propose a ban on ballistic missile defense and examine verification and cost savings from such an agreement. They suggest, among other points, that the ABM Treaty signatories consider eliminating the existing ABM sites (one per country) approved by the Treaty, that testing of ground-based BMD systems should be banned or limited to testing of traditional technologies, and that the Outer Space Treaty of 1967 be amended to ban all orbiting and testing of weapons in space. Notes, bibliography.

5-49 Lin, Herbert. *New Weapon Technologies & the ABM Treaty*. Pergamon-Brassey, 1988. 95p.

The author, a physicist, examines emerging technologies; he makes specific recommendations on methods of adapting the ABM Treaty to current and developing technologies. "The most important steps," he writes, "are an expression of commitment to the ABM Treaty for the indefinite future, and the endowment of the SCC [Standing Consultative Commission] delegation of both sides with the authority to resolve difficulties and the requisite technical and intelligence support." Notes, index.

5-50 Linenthal, Edward T. *Symbolic Defense: The Cultural Significance of the Strategic Defense Initiative*. Univ. of Illinois Pr., 1989. 139p.

To discover the cultural truth of SDI, states Linenthal, "we must look to the symbols of American technology, space, enemies, and nuclear age mentality." This engrossing discussion of American attitudes, values, and fears effectively uses a large number of both pro- and anti-SDI editorial cartoons culled from the nation's newspapers. Describes SDI as a "symbol of deliverance" from nuclear oppression. A useful and engaging contribution to the SDI debate, but, more expansively, to an understanding of the American nuclear mentality at large. The author teaches religion at the Univ. of Wisconsin-Oshkosh. Notes.

5–51   Longstreth,   Thomas   K.;   Pike,   John   E.;
Rhinelander, John B. *The Impact of U.S. and Soviet
Ballistic Missile Defense Programs on the ABM Treaty.*
3d ed. National Campaign to Save the ABM Treaty,
1985. 99p.

This   report   investigates   superpower   anti–missile
efforts, and evaluates their effects on the ABM Treaty.
The authors describe SDI as "superficially appealing,"
but argue that it "threatens to spur the arms race
forward,   destroy   existing   arms   agreements   and
eliminate any chance for future arms control." They
call the critical issue not whether the U.S. should
move from research to deployment of space–based ABM
systems,   but   "whether   the   United   States   should
structure   its   research   to   lead   to   advanced
development and testing of space–based systems,"
which acts are prohibited by the ABM Treaty. Authors
Pike, Longstreth, and Rhinelander are, respectively,
an Associate Director for Space Policy with the
Federation   of   American   Scientists;   an   Associate
Director of Research & Analysis with the Arms Control
Association, and former legal advisor to the U.S. SALT
I   delegation   which   negotiated   the   ABM   Treaty.
Glossary, bibliography.

5–52 Luongo, Kenneth N. and Wander, W. Thomas, eds.
The Search for Security in Space. Cornell Univ. Pr.,
1989. 334p.

An outgrowth of a seminar for members of Congress
and congressional staff held in 1986. Fourteen essays
or excerpts of reports and books in three main
sections--"U.S. and Soviet Space Weapon Programs,"
"Evaluating SDI Technology," and "Space Weapon Arms
Control"--address   subtopics   in   those   areas.
Contributors   are   generally   well–known   individuals
(e.g., Paul B. Stares, Harold Brown) or institutions
(e.g., the U.S. Arms Control and Disarmament Agency),
with an occasional surprise, such as a statement on
prevention of an arms race in space from the U.S.S.R.
Institute   for   World   Economy   and   International
Relations. Index.

5-53 Manno, Jack. *Arming the Heavens: The Hidden Military Agenda for Space, 1945-1995.* Dodd, Mead, 1984. 245p.

Manno shows how the U.S. space program has historically been dominated by the warrior's vision. He warns that unless we act promptly to block the militarization of space, "Billions will have been spent building the military space hardware and designing the systems before any public debate takes place." A detailed, well-researched study, with an extensive bibliographic essay on various features of the military incursion into space. Index.

5-54 Mikheev, Dmitrii. *The Soviet Perspective on the Strategic Defense Initiative.* Pergamon-Brassey, 1987. 95p.

Marked by its focus on the long-term political and economic effects a U.S. SDI program could bring to bear on the Soviet Union. Expelled from the Soviet Union in 1979, the author is now a naturalized U.S. citizen. He calls SDI "a key element of future U.S. strategy," and contends that even a marginally effective SDI system should be put into place quickly; it would "endlessly complicate Soviet military plans and greatly reduce both the probability of a Soviet first nuclear strike and their ability to exploit politically the threat of such a strike." Mikheev's arguments might be more persuasive if he were not so eager to paint the Western antinuclear-weapons movement as composed of a gang of willing dupes of Soviet manipulation. His characterization of the debate of the nuclear winter issue as "utterly ridiculous" will not help him win serious observers to his point of view. Notes.

5-55 Miller, Steven E. and Van Evera, Stephen, eds. *The Star Wars Controversy: An International Security Reader.* Princeton Univ. Pr., 1986. 327p.

The main portion of this book consists of a half-dozen

essays originally published in the journal *International Security*. Among the contributors, James R. Schlesinger acknowledges in a 1984 speech, "Rhetoric and Realities in Star Wars," that "there is no realistic hope that we shall ever again be able to protect American cities"; Charles L. Glaser discusses "Why Even Good Defenses May Be Bad"; and Sidney Drell, et al., speak of "Preserving the ABM Treaty" in their critique of the Reagan SDI. Background material comprises much of the book; it includes the Office of Technology Assessment's 1984 report *Directed Energy Missile Defense in Space* and the Defense Department's paper of the same year, *The Strategic Defense Initiative: Defensive Technologies Study*. A good look at early reactions to the SDI. Notes.

5-56 Milton, A.F.; Davis, M. Scott; Parmentola, John A. *Making Space Defense Work: Must the Superpowers Cooperate?* Pergamon-Brassey, 1988. 209p.

Two physicists (Parmentola and Milton) and a congressional defense analyst try to help nonspecialists grasp what they believe to be the vital link between policy and technological questions on which SDI decisions depend. The book is a good treatment for the beginning student of SDI; it falls into neither the rah-rah Star Wars camp nor that dismissing all possible virtues of strategic defense. The authors advocate heightened cooperation between the superpowers, and advise cautious treatment of the U.S. commitment to the ABM Treaty. Notes, index.

5-57 Nozette, Stewart, and Kuhn, Robert L., eds. *Commercializing SDI Technologies.* Praeger, 1987. 246p.

In the community concerned with the development of weaponry, there is a school that likes to tout the commercial civilian benefits of massive investments in military ware. In this collection, businessmen, academics, and military types propound on the potential commercial gold to be panned from the SDI program. Editor Kuhn argues that SDI "will catalyze great progress in computing power, directed energy, electronics, electro–optics, automation and robotics," and on and on. It seems reasonable to ask whether this "great progress" might not be achieved more quickly were the billions poured into SDI instead put straight into civilian research. Nevertheless, the experts here discuss SDI and technology transfer, telecommunications, optical technology, space robotics, and other areas perceived as receiving a shot in the arm from this theater of the arms race. Notes, index.

5–58 Nye, Joseph S., Jr. and Schear, James A., eds. *On the Defensive: The Future of SDI*. Univ. Press of America, 1988. 206p.

In spite of the relative relaxation of the Soviet–U.S. tension over SDI, the program is still a viable aspect of the U.S. military program. Whether viable as a solution or as a problem depends on one's point of view. This collection of essays studies various facets of the SDI complex, including factors leading to its emergence, evolution of SDI technologies, key SDI issues for U.S. allies, SDI's effects on arms control agreements, and the effects of SDI on the overall U.S. defense posture. Contributors include such authorities as Ashton B. Carter, Brent Scowcroft, Strobe Talbott, and others. Notes, index.

5–59 _____ and _____, eds. *Seeking Stability in Space: Anti–Satellite Weapons and the Evolving Space Regime*. Univ. Press of America, 1987. 167p.

Satellites have become an essential element of national defense and international security; through satellite observation, the superpowers gain a measure of confidence in knowing that their potential antagonists are not up to threatening business. (The U.S. recently retired the famed SR–71 "Blackbird" spy plane because of the superior job performed by satellites.) Threats to satellites themselves pose serious questions to a stable environment.

This anthology's essays help provide "a comprehensive framework for assessing the security consequences of the ASAT issue and the military uses of space." The book evolved from a 1985 workshop sponsored by the Aspen Strategy Group. Its coverage of anti-satellite weapons includes articles on negotiating constraints, current and future military uses of space, ASAT arms control, and an appendix on the civilian uses of space. Notes, index.

5-60 Parrott, Bruce. *The Soviet Union and Ballistic Missile Defense*. Westview, 1987. 121p.

Parrott, director of Soviet studies at Johns Hopkins University and a specialist in Soviet technology and its political ramifications, has written extensively on arms issues. Here he offers a clear and concise study of the Soviet experience with a ballistic missile defense program, including attention to the effects of the American SDI development on Soviet thinking. An advocate of nuclear deterrence, Parrott argues that U.S. pursuit of SDI, though susceptible to effective countering by Soviet research and weapons development, would destabilize superpower relations. SDI, he argues, is best used as a bargaining tool to effect cuts in Soviet strategic weapons. Bibliography.

5-61 Payne, Keith B. *Strategic Defense: "Star Wars" in Perspective*. Hamilton Pr., 1986. 250p.

Payne is a friend of SDI for enhanced deterrence purposes, as well as for more distant, if more fanciful, objectives. Convinced of the nefarious ambitions of the Soviet Union, he raises anti-SDI arguments for the sake of deflating them; his least persuasive ploy may be the invocation of previous technological feats once dismissed as "impossible" but which later proved workable. Whether an SDI system would "work" or not is probably less important than whether planners and policy makers think it would; subsequent decision making could then lead the U.S. (or the Soviet Union) to begin deployment of such a system—at what price of heightened anxiety in its opponent, and at what likelihood of a military response driven by a sense of "last chance" desperation one can but guess. Payne addresses such concerns here; his conclusions, obviously, do not dissuade him from championing SDI. Notes, index.

5-62 Pratt, Erik K. *Selling Strategic Defense: Interests, Ideologies, and the Arms Race.* L. Rienner, 1990. 177p.

A political scientist, Pratt asks, when considering SDI's departure from the ABM Treaty, "Why did a president of the United States initiate a major scientific and technological effort—the size of eight Manhattan Projects—to develop technologies and capabilities expressly prohibited by an arms control treaty that had been in force for only a decade?" On his way to answering the question, Pratt surveys the origins of U.S. missile defense programs since 1945, and examines the vested interests of those who have sought to promote strategic defense to the public and to the U.S. government. The book will be of primary interest to advanced students of the interaction between political thinking and strategic policy. Extensive notes, index.

5-63 Pressler, Larry. *Star Wars: The Strategic Defense Initiative Debates in Congress.* Praeger, 1986. 179p.

Senator Pressler (R—SD), provides a good account of the legislative debate over SDI, with a focus on the relationship between technological advances and arms negotiations. James Schlesinger astutely raises the question in his foreword whether, if the public comes to recognize SDI's de-evolution to simply an enhancement of nuclear deterrence rather than as the great protector of cities (a de-evolution that is even more the case today than at the time of Pressler's writing), "there would still be sufficient willingness to undergo the heavy expenditures associated with protecting the missile fields." In his description of

Congressional examination of SDI, Pressler focuses on
issues of technology, treaty limitations, anti-satellite
systems, European interests, and other questions.
Bibliography, index.

5–64 Rhea, John. *SDI, What Could Happen: 8 Possible
Star Wars Scenarios.* Stackpole, 1988. 136p.

An imaginative and credible array of scenarios
regarding the future of SDI, from its cancellation to
its "bargaining away" in arms control to its
precipitation of a nuclear war engulfing Europe and
America, leaving 600 million dead. Rhea presents his
scenarios in the form of news stories (on June 20,
1997, for example, the London *Financial Times* headline
reads, "Libyan Cruise Missile Attack Kills Millions in
Israel; U.S., Soviet Forces Put on Full Alert.") Of
particular value in helping readers develop an ability
to imagine possible long-range outcomes of today's
strategic decisions.

5–65 *SDI: Technology, Survivability, and Software.*
Princeton Univ. Pr., 1988. 281p.

A report from the Congressional Office of Technology
Assessment, originally issued by the federal
government in a limited quantity in June of 1988.
Anyone seriously investigating the technological
aspects of SDI must spend some time with this report,
which goes into extensive detail on multiple facets of
ballistic missile defense. Readers will find the opening,
28-page "Summary" a most helpful overview of the
issues more thoroughly addressed in the following
pages. Principal findings indicate a great deal of
skepticism on the part of the report's authors as to
whether an effective SDI system can be put into place
in the near future, and whether such a system could
survive Soviet countermeasures. The report also
indicates that "No adequate models for the
development, production, test, and maintenance of
software for full-scale BMD systems exist." Includes an
excellent glossary and glossary of acronyms and

abbreviations.

5-66 Snyder, Craig, ed. *The Strategic Defense Debate: Can "Star Wars" Make Us Safe?* Univ. of Pennsylvania Pr., 1986. 247p.

Based on a late-1985 conference sponsored by the World Affairs Council of Philadelphia. Contains twenty essays on a variety of SDI topics, including the context of U.S.-Soviet relations, technological issues, effects on strategy and arms control, etc. There are some wildly divergent points of view and personalities represented, from former Secretary of Defense Caspar Weinberger (SDI is "the only hope we have of leading mankind away from the constant threat of nuclear holocaust") to radical gadfly Andrew Cockburn ("The Star Wars folly relies for whatever intellectual coherence it can summon on a number of assumptions, all of them fallacious, about nuclear weapons and Soviet military power.") Other top-of-the-marquee contributors are Richard Pipes, James Schlesinger, Robert S. McNamara, Colin S. Gray, and Paul Nitze. An interesting and even—given the clash of views it offers—exciting collection. Index

5-67 Stares, Paul B. *The Militarization of Space: U.S. Policy, 1945-1984.* Cornell Univ. Pr., 1985. 334p.

Stares's thorough historical survey of the movement of the arms race beyond the earth covers U.S. activity from the Truman era into the Reagan administration. Stares condemns the quest for space-based weaponry on the grounds that nothing will come of it but another round in the arms race. He portrays the militarization of space as anything but a recent innovation, but also indicates that the driving wheel of technological change has lately increased the speed of the race. An expanded adaptation of Stares's doctoral dissertation, the book is heavily based on government documents, as well as on interviews with a large number of government and military officials. Bibliography, index.

5-68 Stein, Jonathan B. *From H-Bomb to Star Wars: The Politics of Strategic Decision-Making*. Lexington Books, 1984. 118p.

Stein looks at two major U.S. weapons decisions, the hydrogen bomb and the Strategic Defense Initiative, in an effort to demonstrate that political considerations, not technological, form the major basis of such decisions. The science fiction quality of President Reagan's strategic defense vision seems to bear out Stein's idea; the Commander in Chief concocted his scheme out of little more than thin air and wishful thinking, certainly not from an informed understanding of presently available technology. The H-bomb example is less compelling, given the "superbomb's" more imminent technological feasibility at the time of the project's go-ahead. Nevertheless, Stein gives a good and concise account of the H-bomb's genesis. Bibliography, notes, index.

5-69 Steinberg, Gerald M., ed. *Lost in Space: The Domestic Politics of the Strategic Defense Initiative*. Lexington Books, 1988. 170p.

Seven essays focusing on the influence of the SDI on U.S. domestic politics, and the impact of those politics on SDI. Editor Steinberg concludes in the final essay "The Limits of Faith," which concerns the conflict between ideological trust in technology and the very real failures of technology, "If SDI fails to provide relief from the threat of nuclear destruction . . . the SDI program will have become a classic example of technological folly. With the failure of the technological fix, perhaps the more difficult but realistic political processes of negotiation and arms control will be strengthened." Other essays cover scientific advice to the President, the bureaucratization of research and development in the Defense Department's new SDI Organization, the role of scientists in the debate, and SDI contracting. Index.

5-70 Teller, Edward. *Better a Shield than a Sword:*

Perspectives on Defense and Technology. Free Press, 1987. 257p.

Speeches, essays, and other documents in this collection cover a four-decade span, some of it reprinted. In spite of nominal attention to SDI, which Teller of course favors, the volume seems, perhaps, more an attempt to cash in on current interest in strategic defense than a real effort to come to grips with the issue. What this potpourri does allow is a good look at Teller's thinking. A champion of more and better bombs and gadgets to the end, he discusses atomic and hydrogen weapons, other atomic scientists (notably J.R. Oppenheimer), Chernobyl, Los Alamos, and many other nuclear topics. Bibliography, index.

5–71 Tirman, John, ed. *Empty Promise: The Growing Case Against Star Wars.* Beacon Pr., 1986. 238p.

A project of the Union of Concerned Scientists, which has been a consistent critic of SDI almost since the Reagan administration's opening efforts to persuade the public of the system's boundless promise. The editor and eight other contributors, all with impressive scientific or diplomatic credentials, look at SDI as it was developing into something other, and a lot less, than the population-saving fantasy originally put forward. The book's three sections deal with political, technological, and strategic issues, all of which "are the weak links that we believe will ultimately undo the Star Wars vision." SDI command and control, software, and Soviet countermeasures are among the subtopics covered. Notes, index.

5–72 Tucker, Robert W.; Liska, George; Osgood, Robert E.; Calleo, David. *SDI and U.S. Foreign Policy.* Foreign Policy Institute, School of Advanced International Studies, Johns Hopkins Univ., 1987. 126p.

Four political scientists discuss possible consequences of space technology for U.S. foreign policy, alliance relations, and strategic stability. Tucker contends that further commitment to defense would not substantially change the nature of deterrence. Liska believes that the unpredictability inherent in an offensive–defensive mix might enhance deterrence, although it might also worsen the risks of pre-emptive attack; Osgood argues that SDI must be approached in the context of an integrated defense and arms–control policy reconciling U.S. and European perspectives, and Calleo maintains that technology cannot solve geopolitical problems; Europe must assume primary responsibility for its own defense. Notes.

5–73 Van Cleave, William R. *Fortress USSR: The Soviet Strategic Defense Initiative and the U.S. Strategic Defense Response.* Hoover Institution Pr., 1986. 60p.

Van Cleave, of the Hoover Institution on War, Revolution and Peace, fears that the Soviet Union will obtain a unilateral defensive capability to accompany its alleged strategic offensive superiority if the U.S. does not follow through on its SDI program. He attempts to explain why SDI will not throw fuel on the arms race, or further militarize space. Notes, bibliography.

5–74 Velikhov, Yevgeni; Sagdeev, Roald; Kokoshin, Andrei, eds. *Weaponry in Space: The Dilemma of Security.* Mir, 1986. 147p.

The translation of *Kosmicheskoe Oruzhie: Dilemma Bezopasnosti.* Interesting as a reaction by Soviet scientists to the early excitement in the Reagan administration over SDI, this study is the product of the Soviet Scientists' Committee for the Defense of Peace Against Nuclear Threat. It examines a number of aspects of space war, including ballistic missile defense, potential uses of space–based weapons against air and ground targets, legal questions, and spin–offs of SDI research efforts, the potential of which the authors dismiss as considerably exaggerated. Notes.

5–75 Waller, Douglas C.; Bruce, James T.; Cook, Douglas M. *The Strategic Defense Initiative, Progress and Challenges: A Guide to Issues and References.* Regina Books, 1987. 172p.

Based primarily on a congressional staff report ordered by Sens. William Proxmire, J. Bennett Johnston, and Lawton Chiles in 1986. The study attempts to highlight important issues related to SDI's progress and problems. The authors discuss SDI in regard to technology and research, arms control, and the political environment. The study urges a skeptical attitude toward claims of "tremendous advances" in SDI research, along with serious questioning of the SDI implementation timetable, production and deployment requirements, and abandonment of the ABM Treaty. A highlight of the book is its 497–item reference guide, grouping books and articles under such SDI issues as "Historical Perspective," "Ethics," "Cost," "SDI Sceptics & Critics" and "SDI Advocates." Glossary.

5–76 Weinberg, Alvin M. and Barkenbus, Jack N., eds. *Strategic Defenses and Arms Control.* Paragon House, 1988. 263p.

The editors advance their belief that strategic defense can be successfully tied to a reduction in offensive systems: the relationship between arms control and strategic defenses is, they contend, "synergistic, rather than antagonistic." Although far from embracing the science fiction fantasy of the original Reagan presentation of SDI, the editors do advocate a "defense dominated world." They see SDI as a protector of missile sites, not cities, for the first form of protection would enhance deterrence, and the second would undermine it. Contributors include political scientists, physicists, and a civil defense specialist. Notes, bibliographies, index.

5–77 Wells, Samuel F., Jr. and Littwak, Robert S., eds. *Strategic Defenses and Soviet-American Relations.*

Ballinger, 1987. 216p.

Six essays and commentaries based on papers presented at an early 1986 conference held by the International Security Studies Program of the Woodrow Wilson International Center for Scholars. Academic and government experts try to fill in the historical context of the SDI debate. Among the arguments put forth are those suggesting that SDI will prompt a Soviet offensive build-up; that there is a need for arms control ideas as much a departure from convention as is SDI; that there is a pronounced gap between available technology and the requirements of an effective SDI system. The continuing note in the collection is one of skepticism about the potential of SDI, although the doubt attaches more to the political realm than to technology. Notes, index.

5-78 York, Herbert. *Does Strategic Defense Breed Offense?* Univ. Press of America/Center for Science and International Affairs, 1987. 60p.

In his relatively brief "1986 Lamont Lecture" which forms the main text of this book, York describes the Reagan SDI vision as one of several comparable initiatives taken up since WW II (these being the development of Soviet air defense, Soviet missile defense, U.S. air defense, 1950-65, and U.S. missile defense, 1958-72). The novel aspect of SDI, as York sees it, is that the defensive "shield" formerly held close to one's body, metaphorically speaking, would be shoved "up against our opponent's nose even in peacetime. Would we consider such an act politically acceptable if the Soviets were to do it to us first?" Albert Carnesale, George Rathjens, and Stephen Rosen respond to issues raised by York in his paper. Bibliography.

5-79 Yost, David S. *Soviet Ballistic Missile Defense and the Western Alliance.* Harvard Univ. Pr., 1988. 405p.

Yost's concern is that Soviet BMD, which he analyzes

in depth, poses a growing threat to NATO's options in military conflict, and argues that the U.S. must develop such a defense to counter that of the Soviet Union. Otherwise, NATO will be left in the lurch. Yost acknowledges the Western Europeans' apprehensiveness about the potential for SDI to loosen U.S.-NATO ties, but, unlike such critics as Ivo Daalder, argues for SDI. The Soviet Union, he contends, can neither be assumed unable to overcome or to match a large-scale U.S. SDI system, or to let its own BMD program lie inert should the U.S. not pursue SDI. "Given the pace of Soviet investments in various forms of strategic defense and in advanced types of offensive strike systems, nuclear and non-nuclear, the true issue may become one of redefining the practical necessities for assuring the security of the Western alliance." Notes, index.

5-80 Zegveld, Walter and Enzing, Christien. *SDI and Industrial Technology Policy: Threat or Opportunity?* St. Martin's, 1987. 186p.

With costs of an operational system estimated at $100–800 billion, the authors conclude that, from a standpoint of industrial technology policy, "SDI is not a cost effective approach and could be defined as counter productive." They discuss SDI's objectives and innovation processes, technological spin-offs, and the government's role in the development of industrial technology. May be the only book extant that seriously and thoroughly addresses the questions it covers. Index.

5-81 Zuckerman, Solly, Baron. *Star Wars in a Nuclear World.* Vintage, 1987. 303p.

Of this book's nine essays, several deal with science advising to the governments of the U.S. and Great Britain. Lord Zuckerman, who has extensive experience as a scientific advisor to the British government and as an authority on nuclear arms and disarmament, writes with astuteness on both political and technical issues. He believes that politicians need to pay greater attention to the scientists who are sent out to make real their visions. The longest of his selections here is an analysis of SDI. He characterizes it as a bargaining chip which can serve best by being thrown away. Even if this system could perform its intended task of destroying incoming land-based ICBMs, the U.S. could be threatened with nuclear ruin through other means. Furthermore, the Soviets would devise measures for defeating a space-based defense system. Lord Zuckerman also questions the economic resolve required to support a fabulously expensive system that yields no concrete results. Notes, index.

CHAPTER 6

Arms Control and Disarmament

6-1 Adelman, Kenneth L. *The Great Universal Embrace: Arms Summitry: A Skeptic's Account.* Simon & Schuster, 1989. 366p.

Adelman, who early in the Persian Gulf War wrote in *Newsweek* about "thanking God" for high-tech weaponry employed by U.S. and allied forces in that war, has been a consistent foe of arms control and disarmament negotiations in spite of his role as Arms Control Director in the Reagan administration. For readers seeking an insider's view of arms deliberations within the Reagan White House, this book will be welcome. Adelman discusses the famous 1986 Reykjavik talks in which Reagan stunned observers with his remarks on eliminating all nuclear weapons, as well as summit meetings in Geneva and Washington between Reagan and Mikhail Gorbachev. Adelman believes that unilateral moves by both the U.S. and the Soviet Union toward reducing the threat of the military stand-off between the two are inevitable; he cites, for example, economic pressures on the Soviet Union leading to military strength cuts in the late 1980s.

6-2 Alternative Defence Commission. *Defence without the Bomb.* Taylor & Francis, 1983. 311p.

"How would Britain defend itself as a nuclear weapon-free country?" That is the prime question at issue here; others concern the nation's position in NATO, and its relationship with the U.S. should it abandon reliance on nuclear weapons. The 16 members of the Alternative Defence Commission, which was set up under the auspices of a charitable educational trust, proceeded on the premise that Britain should renounce the use, or deployment on its territory, of nuclear weapons. Commission members came from peace research groups, religious organizations, government, and various areas of academe. The Commission concluded that nuclear disarmament by Britain would reduce the danger of nuclear war; advanced as alternatives to the Bomb are such suggestions as maintenance of strong conventional forces, protracted guerilla warfare and defense by civil resistance. Notes, bibliography, index.

6–3 _____. *The Politics of Alternative Defence: A Policy for a Non-Nuclear Britain*. Paladin, 1987.

A follow-up to the previous item, this volume shifts the focus from non-nuclear defense to political aspects of security and to the foreign and arms control policies Britain could pursue to promote European and global security. The authors advocate British nuclear disarmament ("abandoning its own nostalgia for great power status"), "accompanied by a major diplomatic and publicity effort to explain to international opinion and to the governments most immediately affected the moral, political, and strategic reasons for Britain's decision." They would promote more widespread disarmament in Europe, including dissolution of the European power blocs. Notes, index.

6–4 Altman, J. and Rotblat, Jozef, eds. *Verification of Arms Reductions: Nuclear, Conventional, and Chemical*. Springer-Verlag, 1989. 228p.

Some two dozen authorities here address eight major areas concerning arms reduction verification. The majority of areas are non-nuclear, but several sections of the book deal specifically with nuclear weapons, including discussion of the INF Treaty, sea-launched cruise missiles, passive detection of nuclear warheads, disposal of fissile material from nuclear weapons, and test ban verification. Contributors represent U.S., Soviet, Eastern and Western European academies and other institutions. Most suitable for advanced students. Notes, index, abbreviation guide.

6-5 *Arms Control and National Security: An Introduction.* Arms Control Association, 1989. 176p.

An excellent overview of issues facing U.S.-Soviet arms negotiators; the book provides first a basic review of the nuclear arms race from its inception to the end of the Reagan administration, then examines the many individual concerns in arms control, including strategic defense, command and control, antisatellite weaponry, nuclear proliferation, weapons testing, and other topics. The book informatively sketches in the various stands taken in U.S. debate over the issues. Contains many good illustrations, and a nicely-executed foldout, "Arms Control and National Security Timeline," pinpointing events and weapons debuts, 1945-1990.

6-6 Barnaby, Frank. *A Handbook of Verification Procedures.* St. Martin's, 1990. 357p.

Seven essays on arms control verification, including use of satellites, verification of a comprehensive test ban, verifying a halt to the nuclear arms race, and other topics. Contributors are physicists, geologists, and professionals in peace and disarmament issues. The book was first intended as a working manual for arms control negotiators and those who would need to implement the procedures, and the depth of commentary reflects the necessities of those in such positions. The detail may overwhelm those new to the topic, but advanced students and scholars will welcome it. Numerous charts, photos, and graphs. Notes, index.

6-7 Becker, Avi. *Disarmament without Order: The Politics of Disarmament at the United Nations.* Greenwood Pr., 1985. 212p.

Is the U.N., with its polemical debates on disarmament, able to promote achievable disarmament and arms control policies? Beker argues that changes in the balance of power within the U.N. reflecting the concept of state sovereignty "elevated into a sacred principle" have shifted the disarmament debate in that institution from East-West to North-South. Disarmament issues in the U.N. have come to represent less a matter of security than a means to reallocate resources toward a more equal world order. This stance, writes Beker, ignores the current global hierarchy and balance of power, "and in the absence of serious confrontation of questions of security and international order, United Nations debates on disarmament are doomed to remain irrelevant to the real world outside." Bibliography, index.

6-8 Bennett, Paul R. *The Soviet Union and Arms Control: Negotiating Strategy and Tactics*. Praeger, 1989. 187p.

Bennett's purpose "is to discern patterns in Soviet behavior and to probe for relationships between shifts in those patterns and possible causes." He attempts to set up a model of Soviet negotiating behavior in various modes ("Bargaining," "Blocking," and "Breakthrough"), and discusses different ways of seeing the underlying motives for this behavior. Does it issue from a rational assessment of interests, or from the multiple effects of domestic political pressures?

Following lengthy discussions of two case studies, the SALT II negotiations and the nuclear weapons and space talks of 1985-1988, he concludes with modifications of the previous models and discusses their employment in the cases studied. Interesting, but the dry academic style will deter most readers. Notes, bibliography, index.

6-9 Berkowitz, Bruce D. *Calculated Risks: A Century of Arms Control, Why It Has Failed, and How It Can Be Made to Work*. Simon & Schuster, 1987. 221p.

Berkowitz believes that "the most important questions

concerning arms control have usually been overlooked," and tries to investigate these questions. Among the points dealt with chapter-by-chapter: Does arms control actually control arms? Can weapons technology be frozen? Why do people believe in arms control? Why don't countries control weapons research and development? Berkowitz offers not an indictment of arms control, but of how it has been pursued so far. He claims that "Arms control—informed by an understanding of which agreements work and which are possible—is absolutely essential in the high-tech nuclear world."

His own strategy for arms control rests on six principles: Arms control is not an end in itself; Bad arms control is worse than none at all; Arms control that depends on retarding technology will fail; Success in one arms control agreement can limit the feasibility of future agreements; Unilateral policies that accomplish arms control objectives are usually better; Arms control negotiation should be pursued quietly among a small group of representatives from each country. Bibliography, index.

6-10 Blacker, Coit D. *Under the Gun: Nuclear Weapons and the Superpowers.* Stanford Alumni Association, 1986. 193p.

A short history of U.S.-Soviet relations in the nuclear age, with an emphasis on arms control. Blacker brings the story up to the beginning of 1986, when those relations were beginning to emerge from a disagreeable trough. A straightforward account by an arms control advocate and associate director of Stanford's Center for International Security and Arms Control. The readable text is complemented by numerous illustrations, including some effective cartoons. Notes, index.

6-11 Blechman, Barry M., ed. *Preventing Nuclear War: A Realistic Approach.* Indiana Univ. Pr., 1985. 197p.

Nine papers by academic and other figures involved in military and political studies. The focus is on advancing practical, nuts and bolts methods of reducing the nuclear threat. The papers were originally prepared for the Nunn-Warner Working Group on Nuclear Risk Reduction, established by U.S. Senators Sam Nunn and John Warner in 1982. Topics include U.S.-Soviet confidence-building measures, weapons test restrictions, on-site monitoring, nuclear terrorism, and other issues.

6-12 _____, ed. *Technology and the Limitation of International Conflict.* Univ. Press of America, 1989. 185p.

A project of the School of the Foreign Policy Institute, School of Advanced International Studies, Johns Hopkins University. The volume compiles various means of using technology to reduce international conflict discussed by the executive committee on Technology and the Limitation of International Conflict organized by that body. Among the papers are those concerning "Rules of the Road" for space operations, monitoring numerical limits in arms control agreements, and reducing the risk of nuclear war with "permissive action links," devices that prevent the accidental or unauthorized detonation of nuclear weapons. Not all nuclear weapon states use such devices, and, in fact, many U.S. nuclear weapons are not so equipped. Includes an appendix of accidents involving U.S. nuclear weapons, 1950-1980, based on information released by the Departments of Defense and Energy in 1981.

6-13 Borawski, John, ed. *Avoiding War in the Nuclear Age: Confidence-Building Measures for Crisis Stability.* Westview, 1986. 234p.

Confidence-building measures, or "CBMs" in the refined jargon of the arms control trade, are an alternative or supplementary approach to achieving the purposes of arms control. CBMs do not aim to limit forces, but are "management instruments" which seek "to control and to communicate about how, when, where, and why military activities are employed." Borawski brings together a dozen experts from government, the military, and academia "to assess the utility of CBMs as applied to a wide variety of arms control considerations." This variety includes such measures as the Hotline, the "Agreement on Measures to Reduce the Risk of Outbreak of Nuclear War" entered upon by the U.S. and the U.S.S.R. in 1971, an East-West center for military cooperation, Soviet views of CBMs, and other issues. An appendix, "A CBM Handbook," provides excerpts from the text of the above-mentioned U.S.-Soviet agreement, along with excerpts from other pertinent international agreements. Bibliography.

6-14 _____. *From the Atlantic to the Urals: Negotiating Arms Control at the Stockholm Conference.* Pergamon-Brassey's, 1988. 261p.

Thirty-three European states joined Canada and the U.S. on Sept. 22, 1986, in the first agreement on security issues between East and West since the 1979 SALT II Treaty. Borawski attempts to demonstrate why this agreement, titled the Conference on Confidence- and Security-Building Measures and Disarmament in Europe (or CDE, as it is known) was considered so important, in spite of its having no bearing on arms reduction and little effect on military activities in Europe. The agreement, the result of nearly three years of negotiation, was dedicated to measures aimed at reducing the risks of confrontation between NATO and the Warsaw Pact. Although the Warsaw Pact's present disappearing act may render this portion of the agreement more interesting as history than as current events, the agreement was also the first in which the Soviet Union agreed to mandatory on-site inspections on its territory. Borawski describes how the CDE evolved, how it performed its mission, and what the future may hold. A series of appendices traces the documentary history of the agreement. Bibliography, index.

6-15 Burns, Richard D., et al. *Disarmament As a Social Process*. Regina Books, 1988. 111p.

A half-dozen essays originally published in the Spring, 1982 issue of *Peace and Change* in observance of the Second United Nations Special Session on Disarmament. Burns contributes two pieces, one offering an historical perspective on arms control and disarmament techniques and methods, the other a selected bibliography on the topic. The most interesting essay may be Alan Geyer's "The Politics of Disarmament in the Third Nuclear Age," in which he identifies this "Third Age" (following the First Age of American nuclear monopoly and the Second of detente coupled with expanding arsenals) as beginning in 1974. The Third Age, the "most dangerous period of post-Hiroshima history," was marked by the demise of detente and serious deterioration of non-proliferation. In spite of the apparent end of the Cold War, the failure of non-proliferation remains very real and dangerous. Would Geyer now refer to the Fourth Nuclear Age as one in which everybody gets the Bomb? Notes.

6-16 Byers, R.B., ed. *The Denuclearisation of the Oceans*. St. Martin's, 1986. 270p.

Contains papers presented at a conference on the topic held in Sweden in mid-1984, sponsored by the Myrdal Foundation and the International Ocean Institute. The conference was called to address prospects for controlling and limiting nuclear weapons at sea; it brought together scholars and experts on the law of the sea and on sea-power and arms control. Arvid Pardo points out in his foreword that the 1982 U.N. Law of the Sea Convention contributes nothing of substance to arms control or disarmament at sea. The seventeen contributors, who include such well-known Americans as William M. Arkin and George Quester, also counts representatives from seven foreign nations, including the U.S.S.R. The volume focuses on regional perspectives in the South Atlantic, the Indian Ocean, the Arctic and the Black Sea, and on a variety of arms control issues. An appendix contains a long chronology of naval nuclear weapons developments, 1946–1985. Notes, index.

6–17 Carnesale, Albert and Haass, Richard N., eds. *Superpower Arms Control: Setting the Record Straight.* Ballinger, 1987. 380p.

An occasionally interesting examination of beliefs about arms control in relation to the actual achievements of the process. Contributors, all but two from Harvard University, discuss the Limited Test Ban Treaty, the superpowers and the Non-Proliferation Treaty, SALT II, and other specific negotiations and issues at large, such as linkage and verification. "Our goal," say the editors, "is to present an accurate and objective picture of arms control's past." Following the individual essays, the editors conclude that "If the history reveals anything, it is that arms control has proved neither as promising as some had hoped nor as dangerous as others had feared." That tepid statement may signify the overall impact of the book. Notes, index.

6–18 Carter, April. *Success and Failure in Arms Control Negotiations.* Oxford Univ. Pr., 1989. 300p.

In this SIPRI study, Carter discusses a variety of impediments to arms control success, from propaganda to the old habitual East-West antagonism. The most significant of these obstacles, she believes, is the technological factor: scientific advances fuel the arms race. The book is especially useful as an overview of arms control on a case-by-case basis from the 1960s on, with attention to such issues as the Test Ban Treaty of 1963, the SALT negotiations, START and INF talks, and other recent arms control issues. Notes, glossary, index.

6–19 Cimbala, Stephen J., ed. *Strategic Arms Control after SALT.* SR Books, 1989. 233p.

Eleven essays including contributions from some of the usual authorities (Keith Payne, George Quester, Louis R. Beres) and from some whose work has been less ubiquitous. Some are less enthusiastic about the achievements of arms control, others more. Especially pertinent in light of cruise missile performance in the Persian Gulf War is David Sorenson's piece on the missile and its role in the near future in "Arms Control and New Weapons Technology: The Case of the Advanced Cruise Missile." Cimbala closes the volume with his essay "The U.S. Prognosis for Arms Control," in which he issues an evaluation of guarded optimism. He characterizes U.S.-Soviet arms discussions of the late 1980s as "no small achievement" in the face of all the forces standing in the way of mutually beneficial agreements between the two countries. Notes, index.

6-20 *Compliance and the Future of Arms Control: Report of a Project Sponsored by the Center for International Security and Arms Control, Stanford University, and Global Outlook.* Ballinger, 1988. 258p.

Because of serious questions raised in the 1980s over Soviet compliance with U.S.-Soviet arms control measures, a working group chaired by Gloria Duffy at the Stanford University Center on International Security and Arms Control reviewed comprehensively both Soviet and U.S. compliance with such measures. Over an 18-month period, the group studied legal, political, and national-security aspects of superpower behavior influencing compliance. This volume presents the group's conclusions. Chief among these is the finding that "allegations that either the Soviet Union or United States routinely violates arms control agreements are false. A net assessment points strongly to a U.S. and Soviet record of compliance, not noncompliance, with the terms of arms control agreements." The review considers alleged or potential violations in the areas of missiles, the ABM Treaty, the SDI system, biological weapons, and others. Appendices list U.S. and Soviet accusations of each other's noncompliance. Could be a useful corrective to charges of noncompliance casually issued by military and political spokespersons with vested interests in the arms race. Notes, bibliography, index.

6–21 Dahlitz, Julie. *Nuclear Arms Control, with Effective International Agreements.* Allen & Unwin, 1983. 238p.

The international legal system, adjudication of arms control agreements, proliferation, and the effects of strategic evolution all receive consideration in Australian lawyer Dahlitz's study. Useful as a history and analysis of arms control by an authority with a commitment to the benefits of arms control; Dahlitz has served the U.N. in an arms control capacity. She states that three common fallacies paralyze effective responses to the nuclear threat. They are the belief that nuclear war isn't "really" going to happen, that nothing can be done to prevent it from happening, and that nuclear war can be prevented by further armament. Dahlitz contends that "the law of the jungle and a disarming first strike capability are incompatible. They cannot exist together in the world." Bibliography, index.

6–22 Davis, Jacquelyn K., et al. *The INF Controversy: Lessons for NATO Modernization and Transatlantic Relations.* Pergamon-Brassey's, 1989. 125p.

A conservative examination of the INF case, from plans for deployment of Pershing II and cruise missiles in Western Europe to the INF Treaty banning such weapons and to ramifications of the entire INF experience for the defense of the West. The authors tip their ideological hand when they refer to "indigenous 'peace' movements" in Europe and elsewhere. Presumably the quotation marks around "peace" indicate that these movements are inauthentic. Contains discussion of the INF issues as dealt with in West Germany, the Netherlands, and Great Britain. Notes.

6–23 Dean, Jonathan. *Watershed in Europe: Dismantling the East-West Military Confrontation.* Lexington Books, 1987. 286p.

Even with the recent cooling in East-West relations, the changes that have taken place in Eastern Europe over the last few years go far to mitigate the threat on which Dean focuses, that of a NATO-Warsaw Pact clash that could easily lead to strategic nuclear war between the U.S. and the Soviet Union. Dean's background as a U.S. arms control negotiator helps bring depth to his discussion of the changing political and military scene in Europe, and is especially advantageous in his treatment of arms control negotiations. He believes that these can serve as a basis for stability during what he foresees as a long, gradual lessening of the potential for armed conflict. Index.

6–24 *Deep Cuts and the Future of Nuclear Deterrence: An Aspen Strategy Group Report.* Univ. Pr. of America, 1989. 75p.

The Aspen Strategy Group, a bipartisan standing committee of the Aspen Institute, draws its members from the U.S. academic, policy, and business communities. This report was prepared by William J. Perry, Brent Scowcroft, Joseph S. Nye, Jr., and Thomas W. Graham. It analyzes public attitudes toward nuclear deterrence following the Reagan-Gorbachev summit in Reykjavik in 1986, when "the idea of nuclear abolition moved from the fringes to the center of political debate." The report argues that public attitudes could be shaped, though not without substantial effort, to accept continued nuclear deterrence at much lower levels of weaponry than presently prevail. It is a position that a majority of strategic experts in the West would also find palatable. Bibliography.

6–25 Diehl, Paul F. and Johnson, Loch K., eds. *Through the Straits of Armageddon: Arms Control*

Issues and Prospects. Univ. of Georgia Pr., 1987. 279p.

A dozen accessible essays on arms control issues, some of the nuclear variety. Contributors are political scientists and legal scholars. Historical perspectives, strategic forces and deterrence, proliferation, space weapons, problems of verification and other concerns receive attention. Dean Rusk's straight-talking introduction ridicules the potential for "crisis management" in a nuclear war, as well as the notion that all-out war could be avoided through selective targeting of military and political command & control targets. Notes, bibliography, glossary.

6-26 Drell, Sidney D. *Sidney Drell on Arms Control.* Univ. Pr. of America, 1988. 219p.

Drell, director of Stanford University's program in arms control, came to widespread attention in the early 1980s through his work on disarmament and Andre Sakharov's *Foreign Affairs* article of 1983, "Dangers of Thermonuclear War: An Open Letter to Dr. Sidney Drell." Gathered here are Sakharov's letter and two papers which inspired it, one originally presented in congressional testimony, the other a 1982 speech in reaction to positions taken by then Secretary of Defense Caspar Weinberger. Also present in the volume are Drell's congressional testimony on SDI, thoughts on the future of arms control, the INF Treaty, verification, and other matters. Given Drell's stature and the historical significance of the Sakharov letter, a valuable book. Readable, too. Notes.

6-27 Dunn, Lewis A. and Gordon, Amy E., eds. *Arms Control Verification and the New Role of On-Site Inspection.* Lexington Books, 1990. 260p.

On-site inspection is crucial for verifying compliance with the Intermediate-Range and Shorter-Range Nuclear Forces Treaty providing for the elimination of U.S. and Soviet ground-based missiles in these categories. The superpowers' acceptance of on-site inspection in the INF Treaty sets a major precedent for future arms negotiations. This book springs from a series of meetings concerning on-site inspection held under the auspices of the Center for National Security Negotiations in 1988 and 1989. Contributions dwell on past experience in on-site inspection, on-site aspects of various nuclear and non-nuclear arms agreements, political and legal issues, and on-site inspection strategy. Contributors include arms control, legal, military and security experts. Notes, index.

6-28 Epstein, William and Webster, Lucy. *We Can Avert a Nuclear War*. Oelgeschlager, Gunn, & Hain, 1983. 181p.

In the 25th anniversary commemorative meeting of the Pugwash Conference on Science and World Affairs, a dozen scholars reflected on aspects of arms control. Papers presented at the conference appear here. Of special interest are Soviet Ambassador to Canada Alexander N. Yakovlev's "War Can Be Averted: A Soviet Perspective," and Notre Dame President Theodore M. Hesburgh's "If We Do Not Eliminate the Nuclear Threat, All Other Problems Will Be Irrelevant."

6-29 Fetter, Steve. *Toward a Comprehensive Test Ban*. Ballinger, 1988. 206p.

Fetter, a physicist, advocates evolution toward a comprehensive nuclear test ban; the evolution would depend on improvement in the apparatus involved in test monitoring. His study will inform the reader of historical as well as contemporary considerations involving verification, nuclear proliferation, and related issues. Fetter seeks to challenge the conventional wisdom of CTB proponents, who believe such a ban would end the arms race and curb proliferation, and CTB critics, who claim the U.S. must keep testing to maintain security and that the Soviets would wrest big advantages from a CTB agreement by cheating. He concludes that a CTB "would serve the security interests of the United States by pointing away from dangerous strategies of nuclear war-fighting and by reinforcing the nonproliferation regime." Notes, index.

6-30 Frei, Daniel. *Perceived Images: U.S. and Soviet Assumptions and Perceptions in Disarmament.* Rowman & Allanheld, 1986. 323p.

Originally published by the U.N. in 1984 as *Assumptions and Perceptions in Disarmament.* Frei seeks to supplement the prevailing "objective" factors of arms control and disarmament, i.e., the beancounting approach to numbers of weapons, their characteristics, technological specifics, etc., with such subjective factors as the psychological dynamics of perceived and assumed threats that help drive the arms race. He tries "to identify views and expectations held by the Soviet and the United States Governments about each other, with special reference to assumptions regarding the sensitive field of security." In his closing list of conclusions and recommendations, he includes such practical adjurations as to shun engagement in wantonly hostile verbiage and not to assume that those not one's friends must be implacable, deracinated enemies. Bibliography.

6-31 Gaertner, Heinz. *Challenges of Verification: Smaller States and Arms Control.* Institute for East-West Security Studies, 1989. 83p.

The author, formerly a Resident Fellow at the Institute for East-West Security Studies, argues that nonaligned and smaller European states can make significant contributions to the verification process on a number of fronts, including a comprehensive nuclear test ban. Notes.

6-32 Garthoff, Raymond L. *Detente & Confrontation: American-Soviet Relations from Nixon to Reagan.* Brookings Institution, 1985. 1,147p.

This massive account contains extensive discussions of nuclear issues, ranging from strategic arms negotiations to the development of specific weapons such as the MX missile and antiballistic missiles. Garthoff is always readable, and has deep personal experience in U.S.–Soviet relations, both as a scholar and in such functions as his role as a member of the SALT I negotiating team.

Garthoff believes that deterrence remains necessary, and that it should exist in an atmosphere of military balance obtained through agreements on arms limitation and reduction. Suggesting the Renaissance ideal of enlightened self interest, he contends that American–Soviet relations must embrace the interests of both nations. "It is not a question of trust, [assuming otherwise is a mistake many opponents of arms negotiations make] or persuasion, but of meeting the interests of the two sides through reciprocal recognition that there is greater advantage in establishing and maintaining particular agreements or understandings than in not doing so." Notes, index.

6–33 George, Alexander L., et al., eds. *U.S.–Soviet Security Cooperation: Achievements, Failures, Lessons.* Oxford Univ. Pr., 1988. 746p.

Twenty-two case studies of U.S.–Soviet efforts to promote stabilization in Europe, to cooperate on arms control issues, and to avoid or manage crises. Each case study is the work of a specialist with pertinent background in international affairs or academic research. On the specifically nuclear front, the cases include nuclear test bans, strategic arms control, U.S.–Soviet cooperation toward nuclear nonproliferation, and efforts to reduce the risk of accidental war. In addition to the case studies, a half-dozen essays by the editors analyze the studies and attempt to draw lessons from them concerning problems and prospects for security cooperation. Notes, index.

6-34 George, James L. *The New Nuclear Rules: Strategy and Arms Control after INF and START.* St. Martin's, 1990. 194p.

George, a Congressional staff member for national security affairs during the SALT debates, also put in a tenure at the Arms Control and Disarmament Agency under Eugene Rostow. He criticizes what he perceives as simplistic distortions of stated refinements of nuclear strategy, contending that whether these refinements are announced by John Foster Dulles, Robert McNamara, or James Schlesinger (or presumably by any other defense official), the architects of the refinements are accused of embracing nuclear warfighting when they are actually seeking more certain deterrent to war.

There is less excuse, perhaps, for the failure of government and military officials to make an equally oblivious blunder in the wake of the INF and (perhaps forthcoming) START agreements, which George contends have changed the "rules" of arms control, yet weapons programs "started and planned during SALT rules of the game are still being built even though the rules have changed." Rather than reliance on quick-fix, scattershot approaches to arms control and disarmament, George insists that the West needs a "Comprehensive Program of Reductions that takes a long term view and is keyed to verifiable Soviet reductions." This "CPD" would be followed in conjunction with a thorough review of existing strategy, toward a strategic revision that would give the West workable options.

6-35 Goldblat, Jozef and Cox, David, eds. *Nuclear Weapon Tests: Prohibition or Limitation?* Oxford Univ. Pr., 1988. 423p.

A good, reasonably up-to-date overview of the many issues involved in nuclear testing. Contributors are an international group with notable expertise in the areas under consideration. These include seismology, covert testing, verification of subsurface detonations, the relation of testing to weapons design, national perceptions of a test ban, and other topics. The whole is much helped by an introductory summary and conclusions.

The outlook for a comprehensive test ban, the editors note, seems slim, but even a ban of tests exceeding 5 kilotons would deny "significant qualitative improvement of nuclear weapons," and would at the same time meet one of the main objections to a comprehensive ban, that the nuclear stockpile would become unreliable through deterioration. Appendices include existing major treaties on nuclear explosions, a year-by-year listing of nuclear explosions nation-by-nation 1945–1987, and other material. A product of a study conducted by the Stockholm International Peace Research Institute and the Canadian Institute for International Peace and Security. Bibliography, index.

6–36 Gormley, Dennis M. *Double Zero and Soviet Military Strategy: Implications for Western Security.* Jane's, 1988. 229p.

A departure from the usual West-centered study in that Gormley first focuses on how the Soviet military might see the INF Treaty's effects on their traditional responsibilities. He determines that contemporary Soviet preferences are for conventional arms orientation, including highly-accurate, long-range conventional firepower. He discusses how Soviet planners might legally compensate for the elimination of shorter range missiles under the treaty, and ponders the implications for Western security and arms control policy. It is the Soviet Union's goal, he believes, to engineer an environment that would leave Western forces critically short of equipment in the wake of a fiercely-fought conventional war. Bibliography, index.

6–37 Haavelsrud, Magnus, ed. *Approaching Disarmament Education.* Westbury House and the Peace Education Commission of the International Peace Research

Association, 1981. 280p.

The editor intends this volume to show a variety of positive approaches to disarmament education, excluding those of a negative and indoctrinating nature. Thus, most of the seventeen contributions approach disarmament in contexts of social justice and development, more in the way of obtaining positive objectives than getting rid of unwanted arms baggage. Contributors are American, Australian, Indian, Norwegian, and other nationalities; they focus on the why, the how, and the substance of disarmament education, on linking science teaching to the topic, and on problems and case studies in both formal and informal education. Notes.

6–38 Halloran, Bernard F. *Essays on Arms Control and National Security*. U.S. Government Printing Office, 1986. 395p. Su. Docs. No. AC1.2: Es7.

The seventeen essays gathered here were selected to commemorate the U.S. Arms Control and Disarmament Agency's 25th anniversary, and "to provide a healthy sampling of the arms control-related speculation and controversy that have occupied us in those years." The collection would not be the worst place for a visitor from another planet to obtain an overview of the nuclear boondoggle that has plagued humanity since 1945. The essays span the nuclear age, beginning with Bernard Brodie's "The Atom Bomb As Policy Maker" from 1948, and concluding with three 1985 pieces by Thomas Schelling, Albert Wohlstetter, and James R. Schlesinger. Whether the topic is deterrence or the danger of nuclear war, the essays succeed in meeting the editor's objectives. Essay sources include the federal government, books, and a small handful of journals, most notably *Foreign Affairs*.

6–39 Harle, Vilho and Sivonen, Pekka, eds. *Europe in Transition: Politics and Nuclear Security*. Pinter, 1989. 184p.

Nine essays by British and Finnish scholars from a 1987 workshop on the political consequences of nuclear disarmament in Europe. The essays identify three main factors in an increasingly comprehensive network of disarmament and arms control agreements: political and economic reform in the Soviet Union and Eastern Europe, encouraging developments in the Conference on Security and Co-operation in Europe, and economic integration in Europe.

6-40 Hartung, William D., et al. *The Economic Consequences of a Nuclear Freeze.* Council on Economic Priorities, 1984. 120p.

The authors look at the possibilities of budget savings from a nuclear weapons freeze, effects on employment, and examine the corporate role in nuclear weapons production and the process of economic conversion. A useful set of arguments to counter claims that a weapons freeze would not work economically. Notes.

6-41 Haslam, Jonathan. *The Soviet Union and the Politics of Nuclear Weapons in Europe, 1969-87: The Problem of the SS-20.* Macmillan, 1989. 227p.

The SS-20, designated by the Soviets as the RSD-10, is a medium-range land-based nuclear missile whose deployment against Western Europe in 1976-77 caused significant apprehension in the West. According to terms of the 1987 INF Treaty, the Soviet Union agreed to withdraw and destroy all the deployed SS-20s, in exchange for similar destruction of Allied Pershing II and cruise missiles. The author's main conclusion to this history of the SS-20 is that the Soviets have learned that "Western Europe has undeniably demonstrated that if its particular security interests are ignored by Moscow and Washington it is fully capable of upsetting the Super-Power apple-cart by mobilising U.S. power to Soviet disadvantage." He calls the Soviet turnabout on the SS-20 "the most significant sign so far of new thinking in Soviet foreign policy." This was written, of course, before

Moscow's observation from the sidelines of the disintegration of the Warsaw Pact and the reunification of Germany, and, alas, before the Soviet clampdown on the Baltic States independence movement. Bibliography, index.

6-42 Hoffman, Mark, ed. *UK Arms Control Policy in the 1990s.* St. Martin's, 1990. 221p.

It is easy for Americans to overlook the significance of the British role in the nuclear state of affairs, given the overwhelming concentration in U.S. media on U.S.-Soviet relations. This little book will help provide some background on the U.K.'s place in the nuclear scheme. It contains a dozen essays that originated in a series of workshops and seminars at the University of Southampton and the London School of Economics. The essays, most by British political scientists, concern alliance politics and arms control, tactical nuclear weapons and European security, British non-proliferation policy, and other nuclear and non-nuclear issues. Editor Hoffman notes that "the discussions in this volume will not bring much comfort to those who have continually sought to reassert the validity of Cold War assumptions. They should provide an impetus to those who see the present phase of East-West relations as offering the possibility of moving significantly beyond the outcomes of detente in the 1970s." Notes, index.

6-43 Jasani, Bhupendra, and Sakata, Toshibomi, eds. *Satellites for Arms Control and Crisis Monitoring.* Oxford Univ. Pr., 1987. 176p.

Describes the technologies required for observation satellites for arms control and crisis monitoring, and examines institutional and political aspects of establishing such verification on an international basis. The first part of the book contains the editor's background presentation of the issues; the next two parts comprise papers given at an international symposium held in Stockholm in 1984. Most readers will be able to negotiate the book's treatment of technological issues. Notes, index.

6–44 Johnston, Carla B. *Reversing the Nuclear Arms Race.* Schenkman Books, 1986. 194p.

Based on the premise that both the U.S. and the Soviet Union want arms control, but are unable to prevent arms escalation. Johnston calls for "an external catalyst" to break the stalemate in arms control and to reverse the arms race; she identifies the American public as the potential catalyst in this matter, applying pressure to policymakers to move away from nuclear arms. Her discussion of the effects public movements can have on public policy contains some useful fodder for those who wish to make similar arguments; her text dwells on the nuclear freeze movement, civil defense, "women and war," and related issues. Bibliography.

6–45 Joseph, Paul and Rosenblum, Simon, eds. *Search for Sanity: The Politics of Nuclear Weapons and Disarmament.* South End Pr., 1984. 604p.

Many informative and provocative articles appear among the 36 entries here, most reprinted from such periodicals as *Bulletin of the Atomic Scientists, Inquiry,* the *Nation,* the *Progressive,* and *Foreign Policy.* Authors such as George Kennan, Daniel Ellsberg, Robert Aldridge, Michael Klare, Desmond Ball and many others discuss arms control, the "Soviet threat," interventionism and nuclear war, and other topics. A little dated in spots, but still a nice collection. Bibliography.

6–46 Kaliadin, Aleksandr N., et al. *Prevention of Nuclear War: Soviet Scientists' Viewpoints.* United Nations Institute for Training and Research, 1983. 90p.

On the various political and strategic issues related to the prevention of nuclear war. Prepared at the

request of the U.N.; considers such issues as nuclear
test bans, banning neutron weapons, non-proliferation,
the roles of international organizations and the public,
and strategic arms limitation. Not without some nods
toward the Soviet political line, but not suffocated by
adherence to the line. The bibliography includes both
Russian and English-language publications.

6-47 Kojm, Christopher A. *The Nuclear Freeze Debate*.
H.W. Wilson, 1983. 221p.

Published as vol. 55, number 2 of *The Reference Shelf*,
this volume gathers excerpts from articles, speeches,
congressional testimony and other sources, along with
some complete reprints of such material, all pertinent
to the then-hot debate concerning a freeze in nuclear
weapons testing, production, and deployment.
Contributors are prominent politicians, arms experts,
and other interested parties. Points of view range
from well to the right to well to the left. Bibliography.

6-48 Krass, Allan S. *Verification, How Much Is Enough?*
Taylor & Francis, 1985. 271p.

Krass terms the most subtle and complex problems of
verification not technical, but political and
psychological. His study, done under auspices of the
Stockholm International Peace Research Institute,
examines in detail both the technical and political
aspects of verification, and reaches a dozen
concluding statements on the issue, referring to such
facets of verification as its necessarily cooperative
nature, the preference for treaties that totally ban
specified activities or weapons, the over-rating of on-
site inspection ("no state will ever knowingly permit
the discovery of a treaty violation on its territory by
foreigners"), and the greatly improved technical
abilities of verification, which, if technology were the
only issue, could enable prompt ratification of a
number of significant treaties. Notes, index.

6-49 Krepon, Michael. *Arms Control in the Reagan Administration.* Univ. Pr. of America, 1989. 314p.

A review by a Senior Associate at the Carnegie Endowment, this volume assesses the Reagan administration's approach to arms control. The book is a collection of over forty of the author's periodical and newspaper articles that appeared during the 1980s, covering the entire range of the Reagan arms agenda, from the MX to SDI. Arranged in chronological order, the pieces offer a fascinating look at the Reagan record on nuclear arms. As Krepon writes in a 1988 essay, "Ronald Reagan is the most anti-communist *and* anti-nuclear president the country has ever had."

6-50 _____. *Strategic Stalemate: Nuclear Weapons and Arms Control in American Politics.* St. Martin's Pr., 1984. 191p.

Krepon analyzes the strategic stalemate and the moribund nature of arms control prevailing at the time of the book's publication. He prescribes phased reductions in nuclear weapons, overall parity and greater survivability in nuclear forces as perhaps modest, but realistic and achievable, objectives. The superpowers must, he believes, "isolate the strategic arms race as much as possible from their other competitive pursuits," while arms controllers and nuclear strategists must attempt a more effective management of their differing views of arms control and nuclear weapons. "The penalties of strategic stalemate," he concludes, "mandate pragmatic, problem-solving approaches, not additional pitched battles." A nicely written, concise book. Notes, index.

6-51 _____ and Umberger, Mary, eds. *Verification and Compliance: A Problem-Solving Approach.* Ballinger, 1988. 308p.

"Easy solutions for verification problems and oversimplified judgments about superpower compliance practices belong to the realm of sales promotion, not policy analysis," says the foreword. The book goes on to illustrate some of the complexities of verification in seven essays on issues raised by mobile and cruise missiles, antisatellite arms control, a test ban, on-site inspections, production monitoring, and counting rules. Seven more essays on enforcing compliance with verification deal with Soviet behavior, SALT II controversies, new technologies and the ABM Treaty, and U.S. government organization for arms control. A better than usual multi-author volume because of its effective editorial structure.

6-52 Laird, Robbin, ed. *West European Arms Control Policy*. Duke Univ. Pr., 1990. 224p.

Six American and European contributors, including the editor, assess the domestic policy processes involved in arms control in the United Kingdom, West Germany, France, and Italy. Laird's introduction helps put the issues into the context of a turbulent time in European history; he argues that in the 1980s, "the European governments have significantly upgraded their arms control expertise and have become more active participants in the arms control process," in spite of the tension that exists between Europeanist and nationalist attitudes. A substantial portion of the book's four main essays concerns nuclear issues. Notes, index.

6-53 Lall, Betty G. and Brandes, Paul D. *Banning Nuclear Tests: Verification, Compliance, Savings*. Council on Economic Priorities, 1987. 83p.

The authors note that significantly improved ability to detect nuclear tests, along with joint U.S.-Soviet intentions to eventually destroy all nuclear weapons are powerful inducements to completely ban nuclear testing. They examine the developing debate during several presidential administrations, offer arguments for and against a comprehensive ban, discuss verification techniques for atmospheric, underground, underwater, and outer space purposes, and look at costs and savings resulting from a comprehensive test ban agreement. They estimate savings at some $4 billion; approximately $50 million would have to be spent on installation and maintenance of additional seismometers. The book contains appendices with texts of existing U.S.-Soviet treaties on banning and limiting nuclear tests. Glossary, bibliography.

6-54 Lamb, Christopher. *How to Think About Arms Control, Disarmament, and Defense.* Prentice Hall, 1988. 300p.

Attempts to simplify the lay reader's efforts to grasp the issues of arms control "by providing the means to identify quickly the premises and assumptions of the principal competing schools of thought on U.S. national security." Chapters deal with arms control and nuclear deterrence, SDI, how politics affect negotiations, the role of technology, and the historical background of arms control. With each chapter's "Discussion Questions" and "Suggested Readings," the book's structure is that of an introductory college text, and it could probably serve capably in that role. Bibliography, glossary, index.

6-55 Litherland, Pat. *Gorbachev and Arms Control: Civilian Experts and Soviet Policy.* School of Peace Studies, University of Bradford, 1986. 103p.

Although the title implies a primary focus on Gorbachev, this short study is chiefly useful for its presentation of the inner workings of the Soviet arms control and disarmament community. The author describes the network of Soviet research institutes that play an auxiliary role in shaping Soviet foreign policy and arms control along with changes in these institutes commencing with Gorbachev's ascent to power. Contains a large number of references to Soviet sources; a good look at Soviet thinking at the time. Bibliography.

6–56 McCain, Morris. *Understanding Arms Control.* Norton, 1989. 239p.

A text that grew from the author's inability to find a good, short introduction to the topic for use in his seminar on arms control at the College of William and Mary. The results of his work should serve the purpose. In three main parts, focusing on nuclear weapons and delivery systems, nuclear strategy, and on the history and current options of arms control. Makes a particular effort to present both sides of responses to such questions as whether the SALT II Treaty should have been ratified, whether the Soviets think they can win a nuclear war, and whether the U.S. needs prompt counterforce capabilities. Notes, glossary, references to further reading. Index.

6–57 May, Michael M.; Bing, George F.; Steinbruner, John D. *Strategic Arms Reductions.* Brookings Institution, 1988. 73p.

Given the clear excess of nuclear weapons held by the U.S. and the Soviet Union, the question rises: how many are required to support effective deterrence? This study examines the effects of a number of reductions of the U.S. and Soviet strategic force configurations, from the present level of about 10,000 warheads on each side. For reductions below 6,000 warheads, "the survivability and alert rates of the forces become more and more important if a disarming first strike is to remain an impossibility and if there are to be enough residual forces to carry out the specified military missions and maintain reserves." Prepared in cooperation with the Lawrence Livermore National Laboratory. Notes.

6–58 Menon, P. K.. *The United Nations' Efforts to Outlaw the Arms Race in Outer Space: A Brief History with Key Documents.* E. Mellen Pr., 1988. 209p.

Calling the progress of the arms race into outer space "a source of deep and urgent concern to the international community, and especially to Third World countries," Menon provides a succinct overview of the military designs now imposed on or envisioned for space, including ballistic missiles, communication satellites, anti-satellite weapons, SDI, and other technologies. He then offers a brief discussion of the legality of such uses, and outlines the problems and accomplishments achieved over the years, from the ban on atmospheric testing in 1963 to concerns expressed in the U.N.'s fortieth General Assembly session in 1984. Much of the book consists of reproduced treaties, including the Outer Space Treaty of 1967, the Moon Agreement of 1979, and the two SALT treaties. Bibliography, index.

6-59 Menos, Dennis. *The Superpowers and Nuclear Arms Control: Rhetoric and Reality.* Praeger, 1990. 179p.

Although Menos, a former Department of Defense analyst, argues that any hope of complete nuclear disarmament "is not only unrealistic but plain foolish," he also contends that the superpowers "have failed beyond belief" in imposing adequate control over these weapons that will not simply go away, and have a lot of trouble acknowledging that a nuclear war must never be fought. He dismisses the INF Treaty as little more than a bit of shallow showmanship indicative of no real desire by either side to alter the fundamental infatuation with nuclear weapons, and accuses both the U.S. and the Soviet Union of pursuing a first-strike capacity: "Achieving a successful first strike occupies a very warm spot in the minds and hearts of the military circles and scientific laboratories of both superpowers."

Unquestionably one of the gloomiest and most pessimistic of recent discussions of nuclear issues; no one who is already discouraged about the prospects for effective nuclear arms control or disarmament is advised to turn to this book, for the effects could be paralyzing. Yet for those who take happy comfort in what may be the illusion of progress--in the INF

Treaty, for example—and relax their individual witness to peace, the book could well rekindle their commitment to the task. Notes, bibliography, index.

6–60 Mickiewicz, Ellen. and Kolkowicz, Roman, eds. *International Security and Arms Control.* Praeger, 1986. 171p.

Contains the transcripts of four public meetings held at the Carter Center in 1985. The meetings resulted from two symposia, chaired by Presidents Ford and Carter, concerning arms negotiations with the Soviet Union, the impact of weapons technology on the arms race, and other issues. The meetings brought together over fifty participants representing nine countries, including the U.S., the Soviet Union, China, and Pakistan. Among the most significant topics addressed are the effects of nuclear weapons technology on international relations, the problem of offense–defense strategies, and the roles of alliances and non–aligned countries. A suitable if somewhat dated source from which to obtain a general grasp of arms control perspectives. Index.

6–61 Miller, Steven E. *The Nuclear Weapons Freeze and Arms Control.* Ballinger, 1984. 204p.

A set of papers presented at a January, 1983 conference at the American Academy of Arts and Sciences in Boston, organized by the Academy and Harvard University's Center for Science and International Affairs. Those investigating the Nuclear Freeze movement of the early 1980s should find this collection useful. There are approximately forty papers dealing with numerous aspects of the Freeze. Represented among the contributors are politicians, Freeze movement advocates, scholars, and others. Notes.

6–62 National Academy of Sciences. Committee on International Security and Arms Control. *Nuclear Arms*

Control: Background and Issues. National Academy Pr., 1985. 378p.

A helpful place for the lay reader to obtain a firm grounding in arms control issues. The coverage includes both strategic and tactical weapons negotiations, test bans, SDI, proliferation, the ABM Treaty, and other topics. The committee responsible for the book was chaired by Marvin L. Goldberger, President of the California Institute of Technology, who states that the volume is not an attempt to reach conclusions or make recommendations on specific arms control issues, but "to present the reader with an overview of the historical development of present U.S. and Soviet positions on specific arms control proposals and to identify the underlying issues on which opinions are so divided." Index.

6–63 Nitze, Paul H. *From Hiroshima to Glasnost: At the Center of Decision: A Memoir.* Grove Weidenfeld, 1989. 504p.

Nitze has had extensive career interests in arms control and disarmament, as well as considerable responsibility for the arms race. He was a member of the U.S. delegation to the Strategic Arms Talks, 1969–1974, served as head of the U.S. negotiating team at the Geneva Arms Control Talks, 1981–1984, and in the early 1950s played a major part in stimulating the U.S. military buildup while Director of the State Department's Policy Planning Staff. In this memoir of his life in public service, he addresses a large number of nuclear issues. A significant first-hand account, with a focus on some of the most important arms control negotiations of the nuclear era. Notes, index.

6–64 *Nuclear Weapons: Report of the Secretary-General of the United Nations.* F. Pinter, 1981. 223p.

The first U.N. study on nuclear weapons in more than ten years, this report originated in a 1978 resolution by the General Assembly calling for information on present nuclear arsenals and other matters. The report covers trends in weapons development, deterrence doctrines, the arms race, and implications of treaties and other negotiations related to nuclear disarmament. Prepared by an international group of experts in 1979 and 1980. Notes.

6–65 Owen, Henry and Smith, John T., eds. *Gerard C. Smith: A Career in Progress.* Univ. Pr. of America, 1989. 131p.

A collection of essays in honor of Smith, who for four decades was intimately involved in arms control efforts under several presidential administrations, recently as Ambassador-at-Large for Non-Proliferation under Jimmy Carter and as a strong opponent of the Reagan administration's efforts to undermine the ABM Treaty. The volume traces Smith's career from early work with the Atomic Energy Commission to his position as head of the Arms Control Association during the Reagan years. A nice little book detailing the efforts of one official to maintain the voice of reason in superpower strategic relations.

6–66 Parsons, William T., ed. *Arms Control and Strategic Stability: Challenges for the Future.* Univ. Pr. of America, 1986. 175p.

Contains sixteen papers from the proceedings of the third annual Seminar of the Center for Law and National Security held at Charlottesville in June of 1984. Contributors include some prominent figures, such as Raymond L. Garthoff, Herbert Scoville, Jr., Michael Krepon, and Ashton B. Carter. Topics tackled include SDI (George A. Keyworth, II, then Science Advisor to President Reagan, calls the initiative "a thoughtful and comprehensive -- and revolutionary -- strategy for changing the course of the world"), a nuclear freeze, verification, confidence-building measures, and nuclear crisis control. Notes.

6–67 Potter, William C. *Verification and Arms Control*. Lexington Books, 1985. 266p.

Eleven papers on the topic provide an acceptable introduction. Subjects covered include Soviet views of verification, monitoring bombers and cruise missiles, the political aspects of verification, and verification of test ban compliance. The overall approach is more analytical than argumentative; useful in conjunction with an examination of the Reagan administration's emphasis on tighter standards of verification than prevailed under previous presidents. A product of a conference on verification and arms control held at UCLA in 1984; contributors are political scientists, physicists, and defense consultants. Notes, index.

6–68 Rosenberg, Daniel. *The Unbroken Record: Soviet Treaty Compliance*. International Publishers, 1985. 113p.

The author attempts to dismantle the notion frequently embraced in the U.S. that the Soviet Union is a dubious partner in the matter of treaties. Of special pertinence are the chapters "Atomic Weapons and the Cold War" and "The Soviet Union and SALT I, SALT II." The book would be more persuasive if the publisher were not an outlet for official Soviet views, but it is still not without interest, and is not too far in its assertions from more presumably objective evaluations such as those contained in *Compliance and the Future of Arms Control* (item 6–20). Bibliography.

6–69 Rostow, Walt W. *Open Skies: Eisenhower's Proposal of July 21, 1955*. Univ. of Texas Pr., 1982. 224p.

At the Geneva summit conference on July 21, 1955, President Eisenhower proposed a system of mutual aerial inspection between the U.S. and the Soviet Union. His proposal, which came to be known as the "Open Skies" proposal, entailed the superpowers' trading one another's "blueprints" of their military establishments, and providing facilities to each other to enable systematic aerial observation of these establishments. Rostow played a personal part in the proposal, and here discusses its origins and aftermath. A major motivator of the proposal was the U.S. ambition to obtain more detailed information about the progress of the Soviet ICBM program. Although rejected by Khrushchev, the proposal was an early incarnation of what has come to be the mutually accepted system of aerial reconnaissance now conducted from satellites rather than balloons or such aircraft as the U-2 or SR-71. Index.

6-70 Rowell, William F. *Arms Control Verification: A Guide to Policy Issues for the 1980s.* Ballinger, 1986. 167p.

Rowell, who teaches operations research at the Air Force Institute of Technology, offers an introduction to the complex topic of verification of compliance with arms control agreements. He gives a brief history of verification, elaborates on its concepts, on the impact of technology and cooperative measures, examines the negotiation of verification, discusses the defense of these negotiations before public and the Congress, and dwells on the complexity of arms control verification. Notes, index.

6-71 Russett, Bruce M. *The Prisoners of Insecurity: Nuclear Deterrence, the Arms Race, and Arms Control.* W.H. Freeman, 1983. 204p.

Social scientist Russett's intention "is to show that most of the fundamental questions about national security and arms control are political rather than technological." He attacks the self-serving myth perpetuated by career arms control and defense experts who contend that the issues with which they wrestle are "too technical" and "too complicated" for the ordinary citizen to grasp. "To the extent that such a vital area of concern remains removed from informed public debate, democratic government is a sham," he claims. His treatment is a good counter to the obfuscation and arcana presided over by too many of the experts; his discussions of the arms race, deterrence, crisis stability, arms control, and other nuclear matters is clear, accessible, and candid. A bit dated, but still worthy. Notes, index.

6–72 _____ and Chernoff, Fred, eds. *Arms Control and the Arms Race: Readings from Scientific American.* W.H. Freeman, 1985. 229p.

Working not from despair, but "from a sense of deep concern," the editors selected sixteen articles appearing in the prestigious journal since 1972. Distinguished by the clarity that is a standard in *Scientific American*, the articles cover SALT and the history of arms control negotiations, European security, and several examinations of nuclear war. Contributors are prominent authorities. Numerous helpful photos and other illustrations.

6–73 Scott, Robert T., ed. *The Race for Security: Arms and Arms Control in the Reagan Years.* Lexington Books, 1987. 297p.

Composed of articles published from 1981–1986 in *Arms Control Today*, the monthly journal and newsletter of the Arms Control Association. Gerard C. Smith sets the tone for the collection in his foreword, when he writes that, in spite of the massive U.S. military buildup of the early to mid–1980s, rather than achieving security, "the Reagan administration has created greater uncertainties about the future direction of the arms race and the possibility of nuclear war." Over forty essays are grouped in five main categories, including those focusing on strategic weapons and strategy, proliferation, testing, and "Rethinking Arms Control." A variety of views are present, not all of which echo Smith's. Among the contributors are some prominent names, such as McGeorge Bundy, Edward M. Kennedy, Leon V. Sigal, and Richard K. Betts. A good look at nuclear arms issues as reflected in events and thinking of the first half of the Reagan years. Index.

6–74 Scribner, Richard A., et al. *The Verification Challenge: Problems and Promis of Strategic Nuclear Arms Control Verification.* Birkhauser, 1985. 249p.

A project of the Committee on Science, Arms Control, and National Security of the American Association for the Advancement of Science, in cooperation with Stanford University's Center for International Security and Arms Control. A reasonable place for the non-specialist to learn about the processes and problems of verification. The book is clearly an introductory text, with discussions of the politics, technology, and history of verification. Its tone is positive, in its contention that verification, though an imperfect science, does not appear to be a limiting factor in achieving meaningful arms control and reduction agreements. The book's utility is considerably augmented by a detailed and substantial glossary and a selected, annotated bibliography. Index.

6–75 Seaborg, Glenn T. and Loeb, Benjamin S. *Stemming the Tide: Arms Control in the Johnson Years.* Lexington Books, 1987. 495p.

With his co-author, Seaborg, chairman of the Atomic Energy Commission 1961–1971, contributes an insider's depiction of the arms control agenda of the Johnson administration. Thanks to Seaborg's position, in which he was privy to many unpublicized events, the book bears a fair share of what will be news to most readers, such as the information that the U.S. pondered bilateral military action, with the Soviet Union, against China in 1964 to prevent China from carrying out its nuclear weapons program.

Among the many other nuclear issues the book addresses are testing, strategic arms negotiations, and the political and technical aspects of nonproliferation. (Those familiar with LBJ's intense dislike of Robert Kennedy will not be surprised to learn that Kennedy's initiatives against nuclear proliferation pushed Johnson to action on that front.) An interesting and detailed account of arms control efforts in the Johnson administration. Bibliography, index.

6–76 Sheehan, Michael J. *Arms Control: Theory and Practice*. Blackwell, 1988. 188p.

The INF Treaty of 1987 was only the second agreement since 1945 to abolish and prohibit an entire category of weapons. Sheehan seeks to answer questions prompted by this dismal record: Why has arms control achieved so little? What impediments have limited its impact? Is the arms control process "fatally flawed?" In answering these questions, Sheehan examines the origins of arms control, the effects of technological change, economic implications of arms control, verification of agreements, and the politics of arms control. He concludes, in spite of the negative tone of his opening questions, that arms control has not been a failure: "Judged in terms of its original objectives, to create a more stable nuclear balance and by so doing to avert war, it has been a complete success." Notes, index.

6–77 Sherr, Alan B. *The Other Side of Arms Control: Soviet Objectives in the Gorbachev Era*. Unwin Hyman, 1988. 325p.

An in-depth study of the Soviet perspectives on arms control. Sherr immerses himself so deeply in his subject that he seems to identify with those perspectives himself, which makes for interesting reading. His discussion ranges from basic motivations to negotiating behavior; his intention is to focus on questions of Soviet aspirations: is the U.S.S.R. ready to join the community of nations (if such community exists), or have its cooperative overtures of the past few years been mere subterfuge to cloak hostile intent?

Sherr maintains that "the Gorbachev leadership

recognizes the growing importance of political/economic considerations, and the relative decline of military ones, with respect to global distributions of power and influence." The West, he believes, can take fair advantage of this recognition through arms control initiatives. Notes, bibliography, index.

6-78 Sims, Jennifer E. *Icarus Restrained: An Intellectual History of Nuclear Arms Control, 1945-1960.* Westview, 1990. 264p.

Although the author's style is not the most felicitous, this adaptation of her doctoral dissertation is a useful one for insights on the period. Following an introductory section in which she makes a case for addressing the intellectual history, in spite of "the lack of enthusiasm" for the topic even among academics in the nuclear field, she discusses arms control as a political instrument and as a security instrument. Sims' view of U.S. arms control thought of the late 1940s and the 1950s rejects the contention that it was characterized by naive, overly idealistic or cynical disarmament proposals. She focuses with some intensity on the Acheson-Lilienthal Report, the Baruch Plan, and other approaches of the period referred to in the book's title, but also spends considerable space on arms control perspectives evolving from 1960. The title's cutoff date, then, is not as closed as it looks. Notes, bibliography, index.

6-79 Sloss, Leon and Davis, M. Scott. *A Game for High Stakes: Lessons Learned in Negotiating with the Soviet Union.* Ballinger, 1986. 184p.

An outgrowth of a series of seminars, "Lessons Learned in Negotiating with the Soviet Union," held under the auspices of the Roosevelt Center for American Policy Studies in 1984. It is a good group of essays featuring work by a number of prominent participants in U.S.-Soviet negotiations in the 1970s and 1980s. The impression that accumulates through

the essays is one of the deep complexity of the
negotiations. Such contributors as Edward L. Rowny,
Paul C. Warnke, Raymond L. Garthoff, Max M.
Kampelman and others reflect on "lessons learned,"
Soviet negotiating practices, the role of Congress in
U.S.-Soviet negotiations, and other aspects of "the
game."

Editor Sloss, chairman of the Board of Trustees of the
Roosevelt Center, concludes that the U.S. "should
approach the process systematically and
professionally, with a long-term plan—not in the
haphazard way that has often been the case in the
past." Bibliography, index.

6-80 Solo, Pam. *From Protest to Policy: Beyond the
Freeze to Common Security*. Ballinger, 1988. 214p.

A useful study of the rise and fall of the nuclear
freeze movement, which petered out into oblivion with
improved U.S.-Soviet relations beginning in the mid-
1980s, along with accompanying fruitful arms
negotiations. Solo's qualifications combine her own
participation in the movement (she was a founder of
the campaign) with a keenly objective critical eye
toward its evolution, including the so-often replicated
phenomenon of leftish political movements, a
splintering into diverse factions seeking leadership. Of
particular damage to the Freeze campaign, insofar as
its ability to gain strength through association with
related movement groups, was its shift in focus to the
legislative stage, away from the grassroots level that
provided its real energy.

6-81 Stanford Arms Control Group. *International Arms
Control: Issues and Agreements*. 2d ed. Stanford Univ.
Pr., 1984. 502p.

A revision of the Stanford Arms Control Group's
volume of the same title published in 1976. An
historical and political analysis of arms control, the
book gives its primary attention to nuclear and

strategic arms. An appendix lists and describes disarmament forums, 1945–1983, from the U.N. Atomic Energy Commission to the Intermediate–Range Nuclear Forces negotiations and the Strategic Arms Reduction Talks. Texts of major arms control agreements through the SALT II Treaty of 1979 are also present. The authors conclude that the lesson to be drawn from a study of arms control negotiations is that "new mechanisms must be developed if we are to rid the world of the scourge of war. As we have sought to point out in this book, the citizen can play a vitally important role in the search for — and the implementation of — these new and necessary mechanisms." Bibliography, index.

6–82 Szilard, Leo. *Toward a Livable World: Leo Szilard and the Crusade for Nuclear Arms Control.* MIT Pr., 1987. 499p.

Collected letters, papers, and other materials documenting Szilard's indefatigable campaign for peace and for a halt to the arms race that he helped create. Among the "fathers" of the Bomb, Szilard stands in marked contrast to Edward Teller, with whom he disagrees on almost every point regarding what must be done to keep their atomic offspring from destroying civilization. Two debates with Teller included here help illuminate these physicists' opposing views. Bibliography, index.

6–83 Talbott, Strobe. *Deadly Gambits: The Reagan Administration and the Stalemate in Nuclear Arms Control.* Knopf, 1984. 380p.

Conceived as a sequel to his *Endgame* (Harper & Row, 1979), which dealt with SALT II, this book concentrates on the first three years of the Reagan Administration, "from the formulation of its proposals in the INF negotiations and START through the suspension of both sets of talks at the end of 1983." He asserts that Reagan and the members of his administration came into office convinced that previous arms control efforts had weakened the U.S., and that they themselves had no real interest in pursuing further negotiations.

The book offers many insights on details of the Reagan arms control and arms build-up agenda, with interesting observations on individuals involved. Among these is Richard Perle, known to his antagonists as the "Prince of Darkness," to whom Talbott assigns major responsibility for the Reagan arms agenda. Caspar Weinberger, whose previous reputation for budget-slicing dissolved in his relentless campaign for greater Pentagon funding also figures large, as, of course, does Ronald Reagan himself.

Talbott gives rich evidence of his ready access, as a diplomatic correspondent for *Time*, to Washington insiders. Informative and readable, a worthwhile book on arms uncontrolled in the Reagan era. Good index.

6-84 _____. *The Master of the Game: Paul Nitze and the Nuclear Peace*. Knopf, 1988. 416p.

Talbott combines a biographical treatment of Nitze with a history of superpower attempts to control and reduce strategic nuclear weapons. Thanks to his journalistic expertise, Talbott's is a far more readable discussion of the complexities and frustrations of superpower arms negotiations than one finds in the vast majority of scholarly works on the subject. For the reader who wants a thorough look at these negotiations, especially during the Reagan administration, this book should prove most satisfactory. Notes, index.

6-85 Thee, Marek, ed. *Arms and Disarmament: SIPRI Findings*. Oxford Univ. Pr., 1986. 491p.

Abridged versions of selected studies on the nature and causes of war. Groups 47 articles into seven major areas: The Quantitative and Qualitative

Dimensions of the Arms Race, Nuclear Armaments, the Military Use of Outer Space, the Contemporary Battlefield, Conceptual and Strategic Issues, Regional Conflicts, and Arms Control and Disarmament. Within these areas are many subtopics of nuclear significance, such as SDI, the neutron bomb, nuclear winter, the "first use" question, nuclear disengagement in Europe, and a comprehensive test ban. An expanded version of a double issue of the September, 1986 *Bulletin of Peace Proposals*. Index.

6–86 Towle, Philip; Elliot, Iain; Frost, Gerald. *Protest and Perish: A Critique of Unilateralism*. Alliance Publishers for the Institute for European Defence and Strategic Studies, 1982. 121p.

The title of this criticism of unilateral disarmament plays on that of E.P. Thompson's and Dan Smith's unilateralist work, *Protest and Survive* (Monthly Review Pr., 1981). The authors find merit in the revivification of the nuclear debate developing in the early 1980s, but argue that "Western armaments can only be reduced slowly as part of a process of verified, multilateral measures." To follow a more vigorous unilateral route would, they fear, weaken the West and invite Soviet attack. They support their position through analysis of Soviet foreign policy, arms control, and unilateralism past and present. Some of their conclusions are well-taken, some less so. It is, for example, questionable that "the grand fundamental cause of all our misfortune" is really "the Marxist-Leninist ideology and its survival as a living force in the Kremlin." Chances are good that the world would have known misery even had Marx and Lenin never lived. One suspects that even total abandonment of such ideology and whole-hearted adoption of democratic capitalism by the Kremlin would not render a world free of the nuclear threat. Notes.

6–87 Tsipis, Kosta, et al., eds. *Arms Control Verification: The Technologies That Make It Possible*. Pergamon-Brassey's, 1986. 419p.

Consists of papers presented at a conference held at MIT in early 1984. Examines the question of the adequacy of the technical means of non-intrusive inspection of the Soviet Union. The first part of the book deals with the process of verification, the second with imaging technologies, and the third, which consumes half the book, with actual monitoring. Some of the two dozen papers are rather general in their discussions of monitoring; others, like Jack Evernden's and Charles Archambeau's "Some Seismological Aspects of Monitoring a CTBT" [Comprehensive Test Ban Treaty] focus on very specific monitoring functions, in this case a new way to treat seismic signals made by distant underground nuclear blasts of modest size. Some difficult reading here for the uninitiated. Annotated bibliography, notes, index.

6–88 *U.N. Disarmament Studies.* Taylor & Francis, 1989. 152p.

The first part of this book deals with a 1988 U.N. study on the climatic and other effects of nuclear war, with discussion of fires and smoke emissions, reductions in sunlight, effects on natural ecosystems and agriculture, and human health and socioeconomic effects. The second part concerns a 1988 U.N. study on the economic and social consequences of the arms race and military expenditures. Notes.

6–89 *Understanding the INF Treaty.* Office of Public Affairs, U.S. Arms Control & Disarmament Agency, 1988(?) 33p.

A handy little guide to the INF Treaty, this pamphlet explains the negotiations, "just what gets eliminated" (and how), answers frequently asked questions about the treaty, etc. Illustrated.

6–90 Van Cleave, William R. and Cohen, S.T. *Nuclear Weapons, Policies, and the Test Ban Issue.* Praeger, 1987. 104p.

Cohen is the inventor of the neutron bomb; Van Cleave is Director of the Defense and Research Studies Program at the University of Southern California, and is a Senior Research Fellow of Stanford University's Hoover Institution. These two spokesmen for the distant right characterize the Soviet Union as beyond trusting, call test bans unverifiable, and insist on U.S. continuation of nuclear tests as essential to U.S. security. Incredibly, the authors "recommend a temporary suspension of the limited test ban to enable the United States to test both in the atmosphere and in space." A stupefying position that, if enacted, would throw to the wind one of the few real achievements of nuclear negotiations since 1945.

6-91 Vigor, Peter H. *The Soviet View of Disarmament.* Macmillan, 1986. 189p.

A readable study by a British Ministry of Defense consultant. His own view of the Soviet attitude toward disarmament is that the Russians are "genuinely interested" in it, and are eager to reach arms control agreements in a businesslike manner. He examines Soviet attitudes toward disarmament both before and after Hiroshima. The U.S.S.R. bases its disarmament policy on narrow, "purely materialistic considerations of Soviet self-interest," he writes, "but then all other countries behave similarly." Vigor relies heavily on Soviet sources, but his analysis, unfortunately, barely penetrates the 1980s. Notes, index.

6-92 Viotti, Paul R., ed. *Conflict and Arms Control: An Uncertain Agenda.* Westview, 1986. 320p.

A significant portion of this collection of essays on arms control is devoted to nuclear weapons and deterrence, with selections on the Reagan administration's negotiations with the Soviet Union, implications of nuclear winter for strategic policy, and the evolution of recent American strategic nuclear and arms control policies. Given the rapid flow of world events, the book's most useful section may be the last quarter, where several contributors look at alternative approaches to arms control, including non-military national defense, and the need to demythologize the heroic and holy myths about war developed in Greek and Hebrew writings, as well as the myth of the "just" war. Notes, index.

6–93 Waller, Douglas C. *Congress and the Nuclear Freeze: An Inside Look at the Politics of a Mass Movement.* Univ of Mass. Pr., 1987. 346p.

Waller, then legislative director for U.S. Congressman Edward J. Markey, makes good on the promise of his title by showing how the nuclear freeze movement culminated in a 1983 House resolution in its favor. Waller points out that the freeze movement was "hatched not in some sterile think tank or the inner sanctum of the State Department. It was a populist initiative, born and nurtured in the grass roots, a very public product." As a public product, it showed the power of concerned citizens to affect government policy. Appendices include the text of the Freeze Resolution passed by the House in May of 1983. Notes, index.

6–94 Wallop, Malcolm and Codevilla, Angelo. *The Arms Control Delusion.* ICS Pr., 1987. 220p.

Senator Wallop and his co-author allege that American arms controllers advocate unilateralism; that the Soviet Union gulled the Reagan administration in Reykjavik; that the Soviets cheat on arms control agreements; that the U.S. has "no alternative" but to invest heavily in the "shield" of strategic defense. A good source for insights on the far right's disenchantment with its former favorite, Ronald Reagan, if not for much else. Notes, index.

6–95 Warner, Edward L. and Ochmanek, David A. *Next Moves: An Arms Control Agenda for the 1990s.* Council on Foreign Relations, 1989. 163p.

The authors explore what they believe will be the most important issues on the arms control agenda well into the 1990s. Their review examines prospects for agreements on limitation of strategic nuclear forces deployed in Europe, anti-satellite and chemical weapons, and nuclear testing. They point out that arms control will always be more a result of political detente than a cause of detente, and indicate a cautious optimism in their conclusion that the changes in attitudes of Soviet leadership at the end of the 1980s will help bring about an atmosphere conducive to long-term achievements in arms negotiations. Bibliography, index.

6-96 Weston, Burns H., ed. *Toward Nuclear Disarmament and Global Security: A Search for Alternatives.* Westview, 1984. 746p.

A solid collection of essays from some of the most influential authors on disarmament, including Robert S. McNamara, McGeorge Bundy, George F. Kennan, Louis Rene Beres, Gerard Smith, Robert J. Lifton, and others of their stature. In four main parts: Confronting the Nuclear Crisis, Rethinking Some Basic Assumptions (about security, deterrence, and "the enemy"), Opting for Nuclear Disarmament, and Pursuing Alternative Global Security. Bibliography.

CHAPTER 7

Ethical, Philosophical, and Religious Perspectives

This volume's consistent practice has been to avoid reiterating citations to material cited in *The Atomic Papers*, but since many books in this section refer to a document treated in that bibliography, let us repeat the citation for the sake of convenience: National Conference of Catholic Bishops. *The Challenge of Peace: God's Promise and Our Response; A Pastoral Letter on War and Peace, May 3, 1983.* U.S. Catholic Conference Office of Publishing Services, 1983. 116p.

7-1 Adeney, Bernard T. *Just War, Political Realism, and Faith.* Scarecrow, 1988. 219p.

Adeney, a theologian and professor of ethics, evaluates the Christian tradition of the "just war" in the light of contemporary technological developments, the Bomb in particular, along with the ethically neutral perspectives of political realism. Following his examination of both historical and technological considerations, including discussion of the war theories of Cicero and St. Augustine, he concludes with a chapter on "The Acute Tension between Morality and Nuclear Policy." He ponders the paradox of the Christian's obligation to oppose nuclear weapons coupled with what he perceives to be the Christian citizen's inevitable share of the apparent present "political necessity" of defending our wealth, our position, and "some of our better values" with the threat of extermination.

Adeney's suggested escape from this binding paradox consists of the encouragement of political policy that supports Christian ideals, such as attention to the need to improve U.S.-Soviet relations; far more radically, he argues that "the Christian must take to the streets. Only the massive protest of people all over the world offers hope that the danger of holocaust may be abated."

A book in the American Theological Library Association's monograph series, originally presented as the author's Ph.D. thesis for the Graduate Theological Union in Berkeley. Bibliography and index.

7-2 Atkinson, David John. *Peace in Our Time?: Some Biblical Groundwork*. Leicester Inter-Varsity Pr., 1985. 221p.

Writing primarily with Christian students in mind, and mainly those among them confused about nuclear issues, Atkinson examines the questions of war and peace in a Christian theological context. His study steers him to conclude that "the peace of God which passes all understanding" is superior to an earthly peace, but nevertheless inspires and drives the believer "to seek peace on earth all the more." Although he does not subscribe to pacifist views, Atkinson rejects the moral grounds of nuclear deterrence, and characterizes the use of nuclear weapons as "utterly immoral." Bibliography.

7-3 Au, William A. *The Cross, the Flag, and the Bomb: American Catholics Debate War and Peace, 1960-1983*. Greenwood Pr., 1985. 278p.

Both Catholics and others interested in the influence of mainstream religious groups on national policy will find Au's book useful. He describes the major schools of Catholic thought--"realist," "nuclear pacifist," and "idealist"--prevailing since the 1960s. He argues that the "Americanism," the support of national goals, which has historically marked Catholic efforts to deal with war must be revised in a way that will free Catholics "to begin an attempt to address the problems of establishing world political community." Notes, bibliography, index.

7-4 Bauckham, Richard J. and Elford, R. Joh, ed. *The Nuclear Weapons Debate: Theological and Ethical Issues*. SCM Pr., 1989. 256p.

Fourteen essays, chiefly by theologians, on nuclear issues. Among the essays one finds attention to the use of the Bible in nuclear debate, the ethics of SDI, the nature of the nuclear threat, the consequences of a failure of deterrence, and an analysis of "Confrontation and Peace in the Nuclear Age." The editors dedicate the volume to the questions "how to turn our nascent world society into a world community," and "how to find meaning in modern life." Notes, indexes, bibliography.

7-5 Berryman, Phillip. *Our Unfinished Business: The U.S. Catholic Bishops' Letters on Peace and the Economy*. Pantheon, 1989. 204p.

Berryman analyzes the two bishops' letters on peace and the economy (*Economic Justice for All: Catholic Social Teaching and the U.S. Economy*, 1986) as a way of discussing a new national agenda aimed at a more reliable global peace and economic equity. "The ultimate test of the bishops' documents is not whether they persuade us to see things as they do, but whether they aid us to become more engaged in dealing with the fundamental issues of our time in the quest for a peaceful world where all persons can attain dignity and fulfillment." Notes, index.

7-6 Blake, Nigel and Pole, Kay, eds. *Dangers of Deterrence: Philosophers on Nuclear Strategy*. Routledge & Kegan Paul, 1983. 184p.

Seven British philosophers argue that conventional attitudes toward nuclear disarmament are "morally defenceless," and are more likely to provoke war than would "a properly managed stance of unilateral nuclear disarmament in Western Europe." Among specific topics up for analysis: nuclear blackmail, games theory and the nuclear arms race, proliferation and deterrence, and "main fallacies" of deterrence. Index.

7-7 _____ and _____, eds. *Objections to Nuclear Defence: Philosophers on Deterrence*. Routledge & Kegan Paul, 1984. 187p.

Ten British philosophers try to keep alive questions about the moral considerations of politics and the Bomb. The philosophers believe that confused thoughts lead to practical mistakes, "and that practical mistakes about nuclear deterrence may mean the end of us all." Leads off with an interesting essay by Anthony Kenny on the old slogan "Better Dead than Red." Referring to the days of martial law in Communist Poland, he asks "can anyone really believe that what the Polish dissidents would really have liked would be for the West to put them out of their agony by dropping a nuclear device with the center of Warsaw as Ground Zero?" Other essays focus on morality and survival, the politics of truth, the ideology of deterrence, and other issues. Notes, index.

7-8 Bridger, Francis, ed. *The Cross and the Bomb: Christian Ethics and the Nuclear Debate*. Mowbray, 1983. 154p.

A response to *The Church and the Bomb* (item 7-14), arguing that nuclear deterrence as well as the use of nuclear weapons can be justified in a Christian analysis, and that "nuclear pacifism" and unilateral disarmament are irresponsible and possibly evil. With the exception of General Sir Hugh Beach, the contributors are theologians, including Dr. Graham Leonard, Bishop of London; Fr. Gerard Hughs, S.J., head of philosophy and lecturer on ethics at London University, and Dr. Francis Bridger, the editor. Notes.

7-9 Casey, Juliana M. *Where Is God Now?: Nuclear Terror, Feminism, and the Search for God*. Sheed & Ward, 1987. 160p.

The author served as a representative on the Catholic Bishops' committee charged with writing the famous (or notorious, depending on one's viewpoint) 1983 pastoral letter on war and peace. She was, in fact, the only woman on the committee, and this uniqueness afforded, or afflicted, her with correspondingly unique perspectives. It is these perspectives Sr. Casey explores, delving into the topics noted in the book's subtitle. "Nuclear terror is the dark night of our world," she writes. "It reduces us to helplessness, it fills us with dread, and we cannot escape it," but peacemaking "leads one...to God." Notes.

7-10 Chapman, G. Clarke. *Facing the Nuclear Heresy: A Call to Reformation*. Brethren Pr., 1986. 274p.

Readers who have waded through many works of nuclear strategy may find themselves emerging from this dry, tangled wood with an impression of having traversed a surreal land. It is a place in which the deaths of millions are swallowed in the prolix verbiage of deterrent logic or "limited" and "rational" nuclear war imagining. One suspects that something is going on at the psychological heart of this literature that its authors do not recognize, and Chapman's analysis of "nuclearism as a religion" may be the book to help penetrate that heart.

Chapman discusses the Bomb as a religious issue in depth, supporting his arguments with numerous biblical references as well as with citations to secular literature. The book is a thought-provoking meditation on religious responses that will help ameliorate the nuclear threat and transform a society whose soul is steeped in violence, that often seems to worship at the altar of destruction. When Ronald Reagan likens the power of prayer to nuclear megatonnage, as he did at a National Prayer Breakfast in 1984, the accuracy of Chapman's reading of our reverence for the Bomb seems unimpeachable. Bibliography, index.

7-11 Chernus, Ira. *Dr. Strangegod: On the Symbolic*

Meaning of Nuclear Weapons. Univ. of South Carolina Pr., 1986. 190p.

A specialist in comparative religion reflects on the question "Why nuclear weapons?" in the belief that "the key to understanding hidden meanings and motivations in religion—and in the nuclear age—lies in the interpretation of symbols." His basic hypotheses include the assertion that nuclear weapons serve important symbolic functions; that the Bomb can profitably be studied much the same way that religious symbolism has been studied; and that it is the symbolic meaning of nuclear weapons that makes them "acceptable, appealing, fascinating, and perhaps even indispensable to us."

Only by the exercise of "total honesty" can humanity free itself from the lure of the Bomb's symbolism, chief among the symbols the Bomb's representation of "awesome and limitless power," a divine attribute that likens it to traditional ideas of Godliness. Chernus's final chapter, in fact, is "The Death-Machine as God." Provocative. Index, bibliography.

7-12 _____ and Linenthal, Edward Tabor, eds. *A Shuddering Dawn: Religious Studies and the Nuclear Age.* State Univ. of New York Pr., 1989. 210p.

Eleven essays divided into four broad categories (History of Religions [sic]; Sociology of Religion; Psychology of Religion; and Reflective Religious Thought) examining such nuclear issues as the Bomb's image in the popular press, the ritualistic aspects of the arms race, psychological challenges, spiritual possibilities of growing up in the nuclear age, and "peacemaking as hopeful activity."

The editors conclude that "if we can understand the nuclear age in all its complex reality—symbolic and metaphoric as well as literal—we can understand the need for a new order and in that very act begin to create the humane order that all the world's religions envision." Contributors are chiefly sociologists and

theologians; they provide a helpful investigation of
the symbolic nature of "nuclearism." Notes.

7-13 Child, James W. *Nuclear War: The Moral Dimension.*
Transaction Books, 1986. 197p.

Calling the Soviet Union "amoral," "bellicose," and
"frightened," Child argues that it is up to the U.S.,
"the world's great, free democracy," "to close the
path to Armageddon." The U.S. does, however, have a
moral right to fight a nuclear war if attacked by
nuclear weapons. Child makes some contentious
remarks suggesting that nuclear war wouldn't be as
bad as depicted in the "hysterical visions" of writers
like Jonathan Schell. After all, humanity has in the
past known considerable suffering; the nuclear
variety, however unpleasant, would amount to more of
the same. Notes.

7-14 *The Church and the Bomb: Nuclear Weapons and
Christian Conscience; The Report of a Working Party
Under the Chairmanship of the Bishop of Salisbury.*
Hodder & Stoughton; CIO Publishing, 1982. 190p.

A seven-member working party chaired by the Rt.
Rev. John A. Baker, Bishop of Salisbury, produced
this book, which originated in a resolution of the
General Synod of the Church of England in 1979. The
resolution called for exploration of discipleship for
peace "effectively and purposefully conducted
throughout the Church of England." The book places
nuclear weapons and deterrence in technological,
historical, and political perspectives, examines such
options toward a more peaceful future as multilateral
and unilateral disarmament, and closes with an
itemized list of recommendations for disarmament,
United Kingdom policies, social and international
aspects of disarmament, and the role of the churches.
Notes, glossary.

7-15 Copp, David, ed. *Nuclear Weapons, Deterrence,*

and Disarmament. Univ. of Calgary Pr., 1986. 269p.

Supplementary volume 12 of the *Canadian Journal of Philosophy*, this book contains ten essays on the title topic. The best-known contributor is Noam Chomsky, whose essay "The Rationality of Collective Suicide" contends that our society is an example of others in history which were "so organized that they drifted towards catastrophe with a certain inevitability, systematically avoiding steps that could have changed this course." Other writers—Canadian, British, and American philosophers—attend primarily to questions of nuclear deterrence and morality. An exception is Ian Hacking's "Weapons Research and the Form of Scientific Knowledge," which attempts to connect the traditional philosophy of science with the issue of weapons research. Index.

7–16 Curry, Dean C., ed. *Evangelicals and the Bishops' Pastoral Letter.* Eerdmans, 1984. 254p.

A diversity of perspectives emerges from this collection of essays in response to the Catholic bishops' pastoral letter. Although in agreement on the letter's importance—as the editor states, the letter "represents the most significant statement on the biblical, moral, and strategic dimensions of war and peace to be written in the nuclear age"—one would not expect a group of Christian evangelicals to react in lock-step to this or any subject in which issues of state and religion are so thoroughly entwined. Fourteen contributors, academicians all, have their say on just war, biblical perspectives on war and peace, the morality of nuclear weapons and nuclear deterrence, and the promotion of peace. Includes a very brief summary of the bishops' letter. Notes.

7–17 Davidson, Donald L. *Nuclear Weapons and the American Churches: Ethical Positions on Modern Warfare.* Westview, 1983. 204p.

Major Davidson, a U.S. Army chaplain, opens with

essays on the development of the just-war tradition and contemporary criteria for such war, but devotes the majority of this study to a documentation of positions on just war and nuclear weapons held by Americans with various religious values, as expressed in statements by religious leaders and in official denominational statements. Roman Catholic and many varieties of Protestant positions (Methodist, Baptist, Episcopal, Lutheran, etc.) receive attention. The book also contains a copy of the letter of inquiry Maj. Davidson sent to surveyed churches soliciting information on their stands concerning just-war theory, the use of nuclear weapons, attitudes toward nuclear deterrence, and other topics. Notes, bibliography.

7-18 Davies, Howard, ed. *Ethics and Defence: Power and Responsibility in the Nuclear Age*. Basil Blackwell, 1986. 296p.

Social scientists, theologians and philosophers contribute to this volume, described by the editor as "about the failure of dialogue [in the nuclear debate] and its military, political and social consequences." The focus is on the nuclear debate in Great Britain. Set up in a series of essays, the book is the joint work of a study group organized by the Church of Scotland in 1983. Among the issues dealt with are the legal status of nuclear weapons, doctrines of nuclear warfighting, public opinion and the media, and the churches' role in nuclear doctrine. In sum, the authors reject current strategy. "The absolute priority for collective human responsibility for the future is to ensure that there will be a future and to combat those tendencies which threaten not just 'ways of life,' be they liberal capitalist or socialist, but the continuity of life itself." Bibliography, index.

7-19 Dougherty, James E. *The Bishops and Nuclear Weapons: The Catholic Pastoral Letter on War and Peace*. Archon, 1984. 255p.

This study of the Catholic bishops' letter is more thorough than most. "The bishops are to be admired for adopting a courageous stance, for raising some tough questions about their own government's policy, and for introducing a strong moral tone into the national debate about nuclear strategies." The author, a political scientist and vice president of the Institute for Foreign Policy Analysis, discusses the Catholic debate over nuclear weapons, pacifism and just war, nuclear deterrence, and the pastoral letter in Catholic doctrinal tradition. A calm, informed, well reasoned response to the bishops' letter; Dougherty is able to identify points of merit in arguments from both left and right. Notes, bibliography, index.

7–20 Dwyer, Judith A., ed. *The Catholic Bishops and Nuclear War: A Critique and Analysis of the Pastoral, the Challenge of Peace.* Georgetown University Pr., 1984. 107p.

Another collection of Catholic reactions to *The Challenge of Peace.* The scale tips toward hostile responses here, with the most notably so that of Michael Novak.

7–21 Eastham, Scott. *Nucleus: Reconnecting Science and Religion in the Nuclear Age.* Bear & Co., 1987. 223p.

Eastham dedicates his book to the "new human reality" that he believes is required for the survival of life on earth, given the threat of destruction embodied not only in nuclear weaponry but in global pollution and political repression. Survival is contingent on "a new or renewed sense of what it means to be human on Earth and under Heaven." Eastham tries "to relocate the center" of the nuclear issue in the human relationship with Heaven and Earth. It is an interesting essay on science, religion, history, and spiritual discipline by a man who has clearly done some serious agonizing over the state of the earth, which he refers to with feminine pronouns, e.g., "Today the Earth is in pain. She suffers mightily...." Notes, bibliography.

7-22 Finnis, John; Boyle, Joseph M., Grisez, Germain. *Nuclear Deterrence, Morality, and Realism.* Oxford Univ. Pr., 1987. 429p.

The authors outline a paradoxical position in which they argue the moral obligation of the West to oppose Soviet ambitions of dominance, the practical necessity of turning to nuclear deterrence to reinforce this opposition, and the moral insupportability of reliance on a means to an end which entails the potential destruction of so many innocents.

The book opens with a discussion of the threats implicit in Western deterrence, moves into "the duty to deter" and an analysis of whether the threat must involve intention and the role of civilians under the threat, and the necessity -- if one subscribes to deterrence -- of the threat of "city-swapping." "By maintaining the deterrent with its murderous intent," states the conclusion, "the world of the West today, protected against the corrupting consequences of Marxist domination, corrupts itself." In an environment in which the demands of morality will not wait, "Our nations ought to renounce nuclear deterrence. They should do so at once. They should do so even though their unilaterally initiated renunciation would almost certainly go unreciprocated by the Soviets."

Rooted in religious faith, this is a carefully argued and powerful statement against reliance on nuclear weapons for security. It will almost surely become one of the standard texts of its kind. Notes, bibliography, index.

7-23 Fischer, David. *Morality and the Bomb: An Ethical Assessment of Nuclear Deterrence.* Croom Helm, 1985. 136p.

Fischer, of the British Ministry of Defence, argues

that deterrence is justified not because it is free of moral problems (those problems are, he acknowledges, enormous), but because it "appears the only way at present available of ensuring that the weapons are never used and that we can continue to enjoy the benefits of both peace and freedom." Nevertheless, although a world free of nuclear weapons remains a utopian vision, "it is a vision that neither our humanity nor Christian hope can allow us entirely to lose from sight." Notes, index.

7–24 Fox, Michael Allen and Groarke, Leo, eds. *Nuclear War: Philosophical Perspectives: An Anthology*. P. Lang, 1985. 278p.

A collection of 26 essays, all but four prepared especially for this book, originating in the editors' belief that "philosophical commentary [on the nuclear threat] seems particularly appropriate given that philosophers possess a unique set of skills which may shed light on a very complex issue." Among the subtopics of the complex threat of the Bomb addressed by the philosophers gathered here are public and governmental misconceptions, or "myths," about nuclear war, indiscriminate killing and the immorality of nuclear war, gender and nuclear politics, "atomic cultism," and other often provocative pieces grouped into such broad categories as "Nuclear Delusions," "The Individual and the State," and "The Pursuit of Peace." This anthology would be useful as a textbook because of the variety of views represented, and because of the "Issues to Think About and Discuss," lists of questions following each major section that would help students organize their own thoughts. Bibliography.

7–25 Gill, Robin. *The Cross Against the Bomb*. Epworth Pr., 1984. 92p.

The author, an Anglican priest and lecturer in Christian Ethics at Edinburgh University, argues that nuclear weapons are inherently evil, and that

Christians cannot properly justify their possession or their use. The book is a specific response to *The Cross and the Bomb* (item 7-8) which seeks to justify nuclear deterrence, the use of nuclear weapons in the context of a traditional Christian just-war theory, and to attack nuclear pacifism and unilateral disarmament. A valuable book to help follow nuclear debate within the Church. Notes, index.

7-26 Gladwin, John, ed. *Dropping the Bomb: The Church and the Bomb Debate*. Hodder and Stoughton, 1985. 144p.

"This book," writes the editor, "introduces concerned lay people to the central issues and to the debate going on in the conscience of the Church." Ten contributors, the majority of them Church officials, discuss the Bomb in relation to Christian beliefs and practices. "General disapprobation of war is not enough," states the Rt. Rev. John A. Baker. "Like it or not, therefore, some Christians have got to understand the technical intricacies not just of armaments but of international politics, negotiations, and so forth. No worth-while moral influence can be exerted without readiness to do this," and this book aims to answer the inquiries prompted by such readiness. Notes.

7-27 Halsell, Grace. *Prophecy and Politics: Militant Evangelists on the Road to Nuclear War*. Lawrence Hill, 1986. 200p.

Halsell's discourse on the religious right's evident enthusiasm for nuclear war as a necessary precursor to the fulfillment of God's plan for planet earth presents a chilling portrait of faith gone awry. The chill really settles in when one reflects on remarks made by Reagan administration officials, including the President himself, giving credence to this extremist view.

The embrace of nuclear climax has been particularly

strong among television evangelists, some of whom have convinced themselves and their followers that right-thinking Christians will somehow be spared the unpleasantness that the rest of us idolaters will suffer: they'll be painlessly spirited away to eternal joy before the bombs start falling. Halsell pays particular attention to the link between this crackpot fundamentalism and the Israel lobby and militant Zionists, and illuminates the connection through interviews with Christians and Jews made during Holy Land tours conducted by Jerry Falwell. Index.

7-28 Hampsch, George H. *Preventing Nuclear Genocide: Essays on Peace and War.* P. Lang, 1988. 170p.

Hampsch, a philosophy professor at the College of the Holy Cross in Massachusetts, offers four essays on nuclear weaponry and related issues of peace and war. Noting the efforts of strategists who attempt to develop means of halting nuclear war before it escalates to utter annihilation (see, for example, the works of J. Cimbala), he argues that "it is far more important, however, that we direct our intellects and our energies principally to the prevention of World War III."

He concentrates on avoidance of war between the superpowers and creation of conditions hospitable to enduring peace between disparate social systems. He turns, as does Sissela Bok, to Immanuel Kant's "Perpetual Peace," and uses Kant's ideas to help advocate a set of goals necessary, in his view, to obtaining a condition resembling that ideal. His discussion also takes up the questions of different interpretations of human rights, the idea of peaceful coexistence between adversaries, and "politically realistic options" to avoid nuclear war. Hampsch writes clearly, brings opposing arguments into his essays, and summarizes them fairly. Notes, bibliography, index.

7-29 Hardin, Russell, et al., ed. *Nuclear Deterrence: Ethics and Strategy.* Univ. of Chicago Pr., 1985. 395p.

Most of the papers here were presented at an Aspen conference of philosophers and strategists. The results: a more or less predictable choosing up of sides, with the strategists focusing on the practical challenges of an assumed opportunistic adversary in the Soviet Union, and the philosophers debating the right and wrong of deterrence, especially as it regards Mutual Assured Destruction. Among the twenty papers contained in the collection, most readers will find several to their tastes, from whatever directions they happen to approach nuclear issues. Index.

7-30 Harries, Richard. *Christianity and War in a Nuclear Age.* Mowbray, 1986. 170p.

The Dean of King's College, London, dwells on the Christian response to a nuclear world. His analysis is serious and careful, critical of both the apocalyptic speakers within the Church who, he believes, pollute the debate with implications of the inevitability (and perhaps religiously acceptable nature) of nuclear war, and anti-nuclearists who argue carelessly about the relationship between swords and plowshares. Individual chapters discuss the teachings of Jesus, love and force, limits of loyalty to the state, nuclear deterrence (Harries finds it both acceptable and necessary; see, e.g., his essay "The Strange Mercy of Deterrence" in *Dropping the Bomb*, item 7-26), and other matters. Notes.

7-31 Holsworth, Robert D. *Let Your Life Speak: A Study of Politics, Religion, and Antinuclear Weapons Activism.* Univ. of Wisconsin Pr., 1989. 225p.

Holsworth focuses on how religious faith has functioned as a spur to political commitment in his home of Richmond, Virginia, where, he writes, the actual evidence of his observations in the early 1980s contradicted the popular notion that in this area, the stronghold of the Rev. Jerry Falwell and the Moral Majority, nuclear enthusiasts and hard-boiled "Christian" nationalists were in the ascendant.

Holsworth identifies as "Personalism" a way of life that can be viewed as individual citizens' attempts "to build a local community which serves as a model for the society they are trying to build; and it can be observed in the way they strive to relate lifestyle choices and child rearing to their beliefs about peace and justice."

Fundamental to the Personalist approach are such issues as personal obligation, a need for harmony between political belief and personal values, and the interdependence of political life, the connection of household with political values, and the interdependence of political and cultural reform. A useful examination of an avenue of spiritual life generally overlooked in the media's decade-long obsession with the radical Christian right. Notes, index.

7-32 Jones, John D. and Griesbach, Marc F., ed. *Just War Theory in a Nuclear Age.* Univ. Press of America, 1985. 214p.

Based on a philosophy symposium at Marquette University in 1983, this collection contains papers presented at the symposium along with edited transcripts of discussion sessions concerning the papers. The contributors deal with such issues as alternatives to nuclear deterrence, the morality of nuclear deterrence, and the role of the Church and Christians in the debate on war and peace. Notes, index.

7-33 Kaufman, Gordon D. *Theology for a Nuclear Age.* Westminster Pr., 1985. 65p.

In this set of lectures delivered in 1984, the author addresses two main issues: the meaning of the nuclear age for humanity's self-understanding, and for the conception of theology as a human activity, and the interpretation of God and Christ in light of these matters. The four lectures, "Nuclear Eschatology,"

"Towards the Reconception of God," "Towards the Reconception of Theology," and "Towards the Reconception of Christ and Salvation," "seek to present the nuclear age as raising extremely serious issues for Christian theology, and they also sketch a way for theology and faith to respond to this challenge." A book of greater use to scholars or to advanced theological students than to the average reader, yet laden with thought-provoking passages for those investigating the nuclear dilemma. Notes, index.

7-34 Kavka, Gregory S. *Moral Paradoxes of Nuclear Deterrence*. Cambridge Univ. Pr., 1987. 243p.

Kavka calls nuclear deterrence justifiable "only when conjoined with a sincere and sustained pursuit of bilateral disarmament." In this interesting meditation, Kavka examines, among other topics, dilemmas faced by concerned citizens as they contend with the nuclear threat (not the least of these dilemmas being "the Superman problem": how does one attempt to live a relatively normal life while seeking to prevent great harm?), dismisses world government as attractive but impossible, and contends that unilateral disarmament is more dangerous than deterrence. Notes, index.

7-35 Kipnis, Kenneth and Meyers, Diana T., ed. *Political Realism and International Morality: Ethics in the Nuclear Age*. Westview, 1987. 271p.

The fourteen selections in this collection of papers were presented at the Tenth Plenary Conference of the American Section of the International Association of Law and Social Philosophy at the University of Notre Dame in 1984. Among them are essays on nuclear deterrence and moral theory, the ethics of deterrence, the tensions between policies of Mutual Assured Destruction (essentially a state of hostage for the populations of the U.S. and the Soviet Union) versus a counterforce strategy, nuclear bluffing, and the relationship between nationalism and the prospects for peace. Contributors are philosophers, legal authorities, and political scientists. Index.

7-36 Knelman, Fred H. *America, God and the Bomb: The Legacy of Ronald Reagan.* New Star Books, 1987. 478p.

A revised edition of the 1985 Prometheus Books publications, *Reagan, God and the Bomb: From Myth to Policy in the Nuclear Arms Race.* Readers who have long suspected or believe that neo-conservative Republicans and right-wing Christian fundamentalists have been sharing the same political bed of theory and eschatology will find nothing here to dissuade them. An in-depth look at what Knelman considers the unspeakable ineptitude and roster of "secret agenda" items of the Reagan presidency, with particular attention to the administration's stands on the arms race, nuclear strategy, strategic defense, etc. Glossary, bibliography.

7-37 Laarman, Edward J. *Nuclear Pacifism: "Just War" Thinking Today.* P. Lang, 1984. 210p.

Originally written as a Ph.D. dissertation, Laarman's book investigates the principle of the "just war," traceable to St. Augustine, in light of the Bomb. His argument, which holds chiefly that the threat of nuclear war poses a deep challenge to those aligning themselves with the just war tradition, includes discussion of nuclear deterrence, nuclear bluffing, the just war tradition and Christianity, and dwells at length on ideas brought forward by Paul Ramsey, beginning with Ramsey's *War and the Christian Conscience* (Duke Univ. Pr., 1961). Of interest primarily to advanced students of ethics and religion. Notes, bibliography.

7-38 Lackey, Douglas. *Moral Principles and Nuclear Weapons.* Rowman and Allanheld, 1984. 265p.

Lackey, a philosopher, contends that "for the ethics of self-scrutiny, the acquisition of strategic weapons

by a sovereign state is as indefensible as the
purchase of a handgun by a private citizen." This
book, which, after chapters on "basic moral
considerations" (principles of just war, moral interests
and national interests, etc.), and a short history of
nuclear weapons, politics, and strategy, moves toward
his arguments for unilateral disarmament. He does not
go the final mile by advocating immediate, complete
disarmament; although he would do away with all
fixed-base ICBMs, much of the U.S. bomber force,
tactical nuclear weapons and the Trident submarine,
he would permit the retention of some nuclear
weapons and delivery systems for the sake of a token
deterrent. Lackey's arguments are interesting both
philosophically and strategically. Bibliography, index.

7–39 Lawler, Philip F. *The Ultimate Weapon*. Regnery
Gateway, 1984. 126p.

Lawler, President of the American Catholic Conference,
discusses the Catholic bishops' pastoral letter on war
and peace for the benefit of those who would prefer
not to read it. His analysis falls firmly into the
conservative camp, and features insistence on prayer
as the most powerful tool for the promotion of peace
("Pray for the conversion of Russia [to Christianity],"
he exhorts), and exclamation-marked observations on
the wonderful possibilities of anti-missile defenses,
together with the bishops' "puzzling" silence on this
technology in their letter. Bibliography.

7–40 McMurrin, Sterling M., ed. *Values at War: Selected
Tanner Lectures on the Nuclear Crisis*. Univ. of Utah
Pr., 1983. 132p.

The essays here attempt to identify the possible
causes of war and explore ways of preventing it.
Freeman Dyson's trio of lectures, "Bombs and Poetry,"
opens the volume; his lectures bring such literary
works and authors as William Bradford, *Winnie-the-
Pooh*, George Herbert, the *Odyssey*, and George
Bernard Shaw into the context of nuclear weapon

debate. He elucidates his "live and let live" strategy elaborated later in *Weapons and Hope* (item 3-37). Joan Robinson's "The Arms Race" concludes the volume; sandwiched in the middle is Raymond Aron's "Arms Control and Peace Research." Notes, index.

7-41   Martino, Joseph Paul. *A Fighting Chance: The Moral Use of Nuclear Weapons.* Ignatius Pr., 1988. 283p.

Martino responds to arguments that nuclear war would violate Christian criteria of a "just war." He believes that rejection of nuclear weapons by Christian leaders "is simply a continuation of our long-standing refusal to face the crucial issue of how to use nuclear weapons morally, in defense of justice and freedom." Some think the "crucial issue" is how to improve international relations and human cooperation at large so that no one would even think about using nuclear weapons, but Martino's interest lies in defending the traditional reliance on these weapons to maintain "peace," as well as to offer a brief for the development and deployment of new, better, "usable" weaponry. He likes the neutron bomb, for example, because it would, he believes, prove an effective tactical battlefield weapon.

Martino concludes that "we must undertake the hard tasks we have neglected in all the years since Hiroshima, those of learning how to use nuclear weapons morally, and of building weapons we can use in good conscience should the need arise." Notes.

7-42 Moulton, Phillips P. *Ammunition for Peacemakers: Answers for Activists.* Pilgrim Pr., 1986. 137p.

The author, a graduate of the Yale Divinity School, believes that those in the peace movement frequently fail to deal adequately with the arguments of those who espouse a "peace through strength" (i.e., military strength) position. Here he tries to present a peace activist's fair assessment of "the other side's" positions in this regard, indicating at the same time why those positions are mistaken. He argues that nuclear weapons are more provocative than deterrent, suggests arms reduction strategies, and discusses the option of replacing the institution of war with reliance on a nonviolent, civilian-based defense. Brief annotated bibliography, notes.

7-43 Murnion, Philip J., ed. *Catholics and Nuclear War: A Commentary on The Challenge of Peace, the U.S. Catholic Bishops' Pastoral Letter on War and Peace.* Crossroad, 1983. 346p.

The U.S. Catholic bishops met in Chicago in May of 1983 to prepare their pastoral letter on war and peace. The letter calls for multilateral disarmament, realistic negotiations toward this action, prayer, discipline, and reverence for human life. It retains approbation for nuclear deterrence. When put to a vote, that letter, reproduced in its entirety in this anthology, received the overwhelming approval, 238-9, of the bishops. Here are sixteen essays by theologians, academicians, and other interested observers commenting on the letter. Authors such as David Hollenbach, George Kennan, Lester C. Thurow and others discuss the letter in its historical context, in relation to the role and tradition of the Church, the doctrine of deterrence, and matters of conscience, prayer, and penance. Considering the nearly 100-page letter's inclusion and the caliber of the commentaries, the book is an especially convenient and instructive place to begin a detailed study of the U.S. Catholic position on nuclear war. Notes.

7-44 Murphy, Matthew F. *Betraying the Bishops: How the Pastoral Letter on War and Peace Is Being Taught.* Ethics and Public Policy Center, Lanham, MD, 1987. 124p.

Murphy, a public information officer at the U.S. Arms Control and Disarmament Agency, argues that the Catholic bishops' pastoral letter is too often not being taught or used in its totality, that it is being used piecemeal and in a distorted fashion to serve the personal purposes of its interpreters. He cites numerous examples of what he considers errant teaching of the pastoral, for using it as a support for a nuclear freeze to teaching that a non-violent response to unjust aggression is the only acceptable one, to confusion over such terms as "first strike" and "first use." Index, bibliography.

7–45 Myers, Robert J., ed. *International Ethics in the Nuclear Age*. Univ. Pr. of America, 1987. 369p.

Eleven contributors look at the ethical and moral considerations of international relations. Four of the essays specifically focus on the moral and strategic problems of nuclear weapons; these include perhaps most notably Sidney Drell on "The Scientists' Dilemma" (scientists are called upon by government to create both offensive and defensive weaponry, but "the scientific community as a whole bears a major responsibility to work to remove the threat of nuclear holocaust by venturing into the unfamiliar and hazardous political arena.") The collection features both conservative and more liberal views from a variety of political scientists, historians, and others. Bibliographies.

7–46 Novak, Michael. *Moral Clarity in the Nuclear Age: A Letter from Catholic Clergy and Laity*. T. Nelson, 1983. 144p.

Novak, who in the 1960s espoused liberal causes, became in the 1970s one of the most noted of Catholic neoconservatives. This book, which in many respects parallels the construction of the Catholic bishops' letter on war and peace, first appeared in the March, 1983 issue of *Catholicism in Crisis*, and then, in a slightly attenuated form, in the April 1, 1983 *National Review*. Novak's essay, signed by a number of prominent conservatives, is essentially a minority opinion countering that expressed in the bishops' letter. In it, Novak invokes the benefits of nuclear deterrence, remarks on Soviet military "superiority," the lack of appeal of a nuclear weapons freeze, and other routine items on the right's ideological menu. A beneficially annoying document.

7–47 Nye, Joseph S. *Nuclear Ethics*. Free Press, 1986. 162p.

Addressed to citizens rather than specialists, Nye's book, as he describes it, "is not really a book about nuclear weapons; it is a helpful book about how citizens in a democracy can carry on moral discourse on a subject that sometimes seems to pose an intractable challenge to our most basic values."

Nye proposes five "moral maxims" for approaching the nuclear dilemma: 1) Self-defense is a just but limited cause; 2) Never treat nuclear weapons as normal weapons [an error that many strategists seem to make]; 3) Minimize harm to innocent people; 4) Reduce risks of nuclear war in the near term; 5) Reduce reliance on nuclear weapons over time. He elaborates on each of these maxims. Index, bibliography.

7–48 *The Nuclear Dilemma: A Christian Search for Understanding: A Report of the Committee of Inquiry on the Nuclear Issue, Commission on Peace, Episcopal Diocese of Washington*. Forward Movement, 1987. 155p.

An Episcopal Committee of Inquiry on the Nuclear Issue appointed by Bishop John T. Walker of Washington produced this document following two years of meetings and research. The statement identifies the nature and existence of nuclear weapons and "the profound distrust and antagonism embedded in the U.S.–Soviet relationship" as the source of the world's nuclear predicament. The Committee concludes that nuclear weapons have no useful military roles; the quest for nuclear superiority is hopeless; the Strategic Defense Initiative is a dangerous delusion.

In addition to urging remedial attention to certain pathological attitudes about the Soviets, the Committee advises that the U.S. pursue or adopt a number of specific steps regarding nuclear weapons, including a test ban, deep reductions in strategic offensive forces, and destruction of obsolete nuclear weapons. The Committee concludes, however, "that it is morally acceptable to possess nuclear weapons for the purpose of deterrence, understanding the implicit and uncertain dangers that they may be used." Bibliography.

7–49 *Nuclear "Normality": The Ethics of Annihilation: Proceedings.* Center on Violence and Human Survival, 1988. 161p.

The transcript of addresses and exchanges at a May, 1987 conference held at the City University of New York. The papers presented fall into three areas: "Fundamentals and Fundamentalism," with examination of religious approaches to the nuclear threat; "Political Morality and the Bomb," and "Toward a New Consciousness," which attempts to reorganize thinking about the threat (a goal of the entire conference). Contributors include such prominent individuals as Rev. William Sloane Coffin, Richard A. Falk, Robert Jay Lifton, and A.J. Mojtabi, whose "Fundamentalism and the Nuclear Threat" is an interesting discussion of that religious persuasion's sometimes alarming and theologically eccentric assignment of a very human event, nuclear war, to the previous roster of natural catastrophes (flood, plague, etc.) interpreted as signs of God's displeasure with human error.

7–50 O'Brien, William V. and Langan, John, ed. *The Nuclear Dilemma and the Just War Tradition.* Lexington, 1986. 260p.

Gathers papers from a 1984 conference held at Georgetown University in response to the Catholic bishops' pastoral letter. The ten contributors, among them David Hollenbach, editor O'Brien, Gerald M. Mara,

John Keegan and others are a diverse group of political scientists, philosophers, historians and theologians. They turn their attention to the matters of just wars, "nuclear shadows on conventional conflicts," democracy and nuclear deterrence, and other issues. Index, notes.

7-51 O'Donovan, Oliver. *Peace and Certainty: A Theological Essay on Deterrence*. Clarendon Pr., 1989. 125p.

An interesting theological essay, buttressed by numerous references to both religious and lay literature, in which the author contends that deterrence has already failed its original objective of serving "as a tight conception of international management." O'Donovan advocates emancipating "our thinking from the dogmas of deterrence," an emancipation that must, he says, be accompanied by a measure of nuclear disarmament. Notes.

7-52 Paul, Ellen Frankel, ed. *Nuclear Rights/Nuclear Wrongs*. B. Blackwell, 1986. 222p.

A collection of essays focusing on what the editor refers to as "the basic moral questions" about the nuclear controversy. The two most fundamental questions—Which defense policies are right? and Which defense policies are wrong?—are approached from various political points of view. Subtopics concern, among others, the killing of "innocent bystanders"; concepts of deterrence; "immoral risks"; and the strategic implications of Marxist-Leninism. The dozen contributors are primarily philosophers and political scientists. Notes.

7-53 Powaski, Ronald E. *Thomas Merton on Nuclear Weapons*. Loyola Univ. Pr., 1988. 169p.

Merton, a Trappist monk and author of the best-selling autobiography *The Seven Storey Mountain*, died in 1968. He was well ahead of his church in his appraisal of the nuclear threat, and was among the first Catholics to condemn any use of nuclear weapons as immoral. Readers who have spent time with Merton's work have found much inspiration within his opposition to both nuclear weapons and to war itself. Powaski based this book on talks given on Merton and the nuclear issue to church groups over a number of years. Calling Merton "the prophet of the nuclear age," Powaski discusses Merton's thought as it concerns the Church's role in peacemaking, the causes and morality of the nuclear arms race, and suitable forms of action to counter the threat. Among these is Merton's powerful insistence on the virtues of solitude, wherein lies the awakening of conscience able to contend against the unquestioning mass mind of society. Bibliography, index.

7-54 Ramsey, Paul. *Speak Up for Just War or Pacifism: A Critique of the United Methodist Bishops' Pastoral Letter "In Defence of Creation."* Penn. State Univ. Pr., 1988. 214p.

In his critical response to the United Methodist Bishops' letter, theologian Ramsey raises a number of questions, including those concerning the meaning of non-violence and assumptions about Christian pacifism and just-war teaching. Unhappy with the bishops' letter, he remains convinced "that, if the church has anything authentic to say on issues of war and peace in the nuclear age, we must not omit any of the heights and depths of the Christian gospel: This is our only distinctive source of moral discernment or claim to anyone's attention." In an epilogue responding to both the bishops and to Ramsey, Stanley Hauerwas (Divinity School, Duke University) argues that the bishops should do a better job of helping Methodists explore issues of just war and pacifism. Dense going for most readers, especially Ramsey's text, which is laden with poorly-placed footnotes and an excessive quantity of parenthetical statements.

7-55 Reid, Charles J., Jr., ed. *Peace in a Nuclear Age: The Bishops' Pastoral Letter in Perspective.* Catholic Univ. of America Pr., 1986. 426p.

Two dozen essays by theologians, historians, government officials and others on the Catholic bishops' pastoral letter. The anthology will be a welcome aid for anyone studying the controversial document, for it contains sharply differing points of view. Alan Geyer, for example, praises the letter as "the most significant entry of Church leadership into American public debate on war and peace in many, many years—perhaps in the whole of American history," while defense consultant Edward N. Luttwak calls the letter "one of those 'faddish' documents that are produced by people who succumb to surrounding social pressures and accept opinions not their own. Because of the bishops, others will fall into error. This will weaken the state." Index, bibliography.

7-56 Schaeffer, Francis A.; Bukovsky, Vladimir; Hitchcock, James. *Who Is for Peace?* T. Nelson, 1983. 112p.

The authors offer a rationale for military preparedness based on biblical perspectives, attack the U.S. Catholic bishops' pastoral letter on war and peace, and "reveal" Soviet manipulation of the world peace movement. (It's the fault of the secular humanists). Strictly for adherents to, or students of, the philosophical presumptions of the American Right.

7-57 Shue, Henry. *Nuclear Deterrence and Moral Restraint: Critical Choices for American Strategy.* Cambridge Univ. Pr., 1989. 435p.

All but one of the nine chapters in this book were written by members of the Working Group on Nuclear Policy and Morality of the Institute for Philosophy and Public Policy, University of Maryland. The authors criticize the current nuclear policies of both superpowers from a variety of vantages, with wide latitude for disagreement. Leon Sloss, for example, makes a case for SDI as an aid to deterrence, while Steven Lee contends that SDI cannot be supported by a moral defense. There does not appear to be anything remarkably original here, but originality of any kind in the nuclear debate is, at this date, not to be expected; the book is not less useful for repeating, with variations, themes played before. Index.

7-58 Sichol, Marcia W. *The Making of a Nuclear Peace: The Task of Today's Just War Theorists.* Georgetown Univ. Pr., 1990. 219p.

Sr. Sichol's study of just war in the nuclear context provides a helpful and detailed comparison of the views on just war held by three of the era's leading scholars of the issue, Paul Ramsey, William O'Brien, and Michael Walzer. She focuses in particular on the three theorists' understandings of the principles of proportionality and discrimination. "Proportionality" may be interpreted as "reasonableness" in the conduct of war, from reasonable use of force to reasonable expectation of success in pursuit of a just cause. "Discrimination" concerns the safety of noncombatants from direct attack, clearly a principle that has been grossly violated in the twentieth century, and one that presents a sticking point in any defense of nuclear war based on just war theory. Sr. Sichol connects the contemporary theorists with classical positions of such authorities as Aquinas and Augustine. A very interesting treatment of a complex set of questions. Notes, bibliography. Absence of an index is a drawback.

7-59 Sider, Ronald J. and Taylor, Richard K. *Nuclear Holocaust & Christian Hope.* Paulist Pr., 1982. 368p.

The book arises from three questions: Can Christians support government policies which rely on the threat of nuclear war? Can they support or engage in war in any form? And how can they act for peace? Arranged in four sections: "The Threat of Nuclear War,"

"Biblical-Theological Perspectives," "What to Do: Concrete Steps Toward Peace," and "Biblical Faith and National Defense," which focuses on the question of non-military defense.

The book opens with yet another of what has become a sub-genre in the nuclear war discipline, the fictional portrayal of a great city's immolation in a nuclear attack. Here the victim is Moscow, fried by a one-megaton warhead. The scenario is familiar but gripping and awful. At one point, a large number of Muscovites are vaporized while waiting in line for a glimpse of Lenin's corpse. Today they might more likely meet their fate while standing in the line outside the Moscow McDonald's yellow arches hoping for a Big Mac, but the physics remain the same even if the cultural icons change.

A special index covers the book's many biblical references.

7-60 United Methodist Church (U.S.) Council of Bishops. *In Defense of Creation: The Nuclear Crisis and a Just Peace.* Graded Pr., 1986. 96p.

The result of two years' study, this document begins with an overview that introduces and summarizes it. The Methodist bishops insist that "the nuclear crisis is a matter of social justice as well as world peace." They reject strategic defense, contend that reliance on nuclear deterrence "has blinded its proponents to the many-sided requirements of genuine security," and, as do a number of other students of things nuclear, identify "nuclearism" as a deeply-rooted pathogen in U.S. society, one that simultaneously promotes denial and hopelessness. The bishops urge United Methodists to take active steps toward peace, and discuss policies for the nation, the Church, and families to follow in this direction. These include a comprehensive test ban, a ban on space weapons, independent U.S. and Soviet initiatives, and peace research, study, and training at all levels of education. Notes.

7–61 Walters, James W., ed. *War No More? Options in Nuclear Ethics.* Fortress Pr., 1989. 115p.

Five American theologians (and one political scientist from the conservative Freedom House) examine questions of nuclear arms, deterrence, and just war. The roster of contributors is sufficiently varied to foster some reflection and debate, rather than mere head-nodding.

7–62 Weigel, George S. *Tranquillitas Ordinis: The Present Failure and Future Promise of American Catholic Thought on War and Peace.* Oxford Univ. Pr., 1987. 512p.

Weigel, a theologian, discusses his perceptions of the historical background of Catholic attitudes toward war and peace in depth, from early times to the present; he dwells on a number of significant figures in that history, from Augustine to Thomas Merton and the Berrigans. He judges that the tradition of Catholic peace-thinking has established a good foundation for a socially and politically effective Catholic peace initiative in the Nuclear Age. His vision of peace activism, however, has little room for some of the leading contemporary Catholic advocates of peace, and his political agenda at large would not distress many traditional conservatives. Bibliography, index.

7–63 Weinberger, David. *Nuclear Dialogues.* P. Lang, 1987. 226p.

Weinberger presents philosophical arguments about nuclear war and weapons in dialogue fashion between fictional characters at an imaginary philosophy conference. Most of the dialogues, whether about the justification of nuclear retaliation, the principles of deterrence, or ways of working for peace, end inconclusively, both because the author intends the book to be used as a teaching tool to provoke open-ended discussion (which it no doubt would), and because "as a consequence of writing dialogues," says

Weinberger, "what settled opinions I had are now unsettled."

7-64 Whitmore, Todd, ed. *Ethics in the Nuclear Age: Strategy, Religious Studies, and the Churches.* Southern Methodist Univ. Pr., 1989. 240p.

One of the products of a two-year workshop, the Colloquium on Religion and World Affairs, held at the University of Chicago's Divinity School. Contains nine essays by theologians on the moral questions of nuclear deterrence, just war, pacifism, and other nuclear issues. The editor identifies the U.S. Catholic bishops' pastoral letter and the growth in ethical concerns among strategists—he cites Joseph Nye's *Nuclear Ethics* (item 7-47) as a prime example—as renewing the prospects for religious scholars to participate in the public debate on nuclear weapons. The scholars appearing here include David Hollenbach, S.J. (Weston School of Theology), James T. Johnson (Rutgers), John H. Yoder (Goshen Seminary and University of Notre Dame), and others. Notes, index.

7-65 Will, James E., ed. *The Moral Rejection of Nuclear Deterrence: The Contemporary Peace Witness of Churches in Eastern and Western Europe, with Insights for U.S. Churches.* Friendship Pr., 1985. 246p.

At issue here are what long-term strategies and short-term tactics the church should use to fulfill the obligation to witness for peace. Contributors from the U.S., Germany, the Netherlands and Poland represent both Protestant and Catholic points of view, and write from positions in the church and academia. They discuss the churches and their ability to influence nuclear disarmament and debate. In his conclusion, editor Will focuses on "Insights for the Churches" that may be drawn from the preceding essays, and applies aspects of the European experience to a broader scope. An appendix contains the "Statement on Peace and Justice" adopted by the Sixth Assembly of the World Council of Churches in 1983. Notes.

CHAPTER 8

New Paths to Peace

8-1 Aizenstat, A.J. *Survival for All: The Alternative to Nuclear War with a Practical Plan for Total Denuclearization.* Billner & Rouse, 1985. 216p.

Horrified by the prospect of nuclear war and exasperated by what he sees as the official ineptitude of efforts to diminish the threat, Aizenstat proposes "The Way Out," a denuclearization plan whose vital features include a Nuclear Control Board and a Joint Nuclear Force which would control nuclear weapons and respond to their threatened use. The plan leads to total nuclear disarmament, with the Joint Force providing protection against any future emergence of a nuclear threat involving illegally concealed weapons. An appendix contains "Basic Provisions of the Treaty on Nuclear Disarmament." It's easy to shrug off such proposals as moonstruck and out of tune with the political and military complexities of the world, but Aizenstat's ideas make far more sense than Ronald Reagan's pipe dream of an invisible protective shield against nuclear attack as enunciated in his original "Star Wars" speech. Withhold skepticism and give this writer a chance to say his piece: it has merits and possibilities. Bibliography, index.

8-2 Allison, Graham T. and Ury, William L., eds. *Windows of Opportunity: From Cold War to Peaceful Competition in U.S. Soviet Relations.* Ballinger, 1989. 345p.

"Peaceful competition" may be an oxymoron, but this collection of essays by American and Soviet writers, completed at the giddy height of *glasnost,* is nevertheless an encouraging exercise in cooperation among representatives of the old Cold War antagonists.

The project began as a mutual effort to explore crisis prevention, but in the relatively hospitable U.S.-Soviet relations of the late 1980s it broadened into an investigation of ways to further improve those relations. The chapters reflect joint work by U.S. and Soviet scholars, among them Georgy Arbatov, Robert S. McNamara, Joseph S. Nye, Jr., the editors, Viktor Kremeniuk, and Albert Carnesale. The book's three main sections focus on the foundations of peaceful competition, historical aspects of U.S.-Soviet relations, including the Cuban Missile Crisis, and opportunities for future efforts. Notes, index.

8-3 Aubrey, Crispin. *Nukespeak, the Media and the Bomb*. Comedia Pub. Group, 1982. 135p.

Essays by ten British peace activists from various walks of life focusing on official and media attention to (or ignorance or stifling of) the U.K. peace movement. There are some interesting items here; one of the most interesting is Michael Tracey's "Censored: The War Game Story," an account of the censorship encountered by Peter Watkins's groundbreaking nuclear war docu-drama *The War Game*, produced for, and banned by, the BBC in 1965. Notes.

8-4 Barash, David P. and Lipton, Judith E. *The Caveman and the Bomb: Human Nature, Evolution, and Nuclear War*. McGraw-Hill, 1985. 302p.

The authors turn in what they call a "nuclear dialectic." The thesis seeks to describe the "Nuclear Neanderthal" mentality; the "antithesis" musters arguments toward overcoming the Neanderthal. In the "synthesis," "A Time for Choosing," they state that "while unable to be saints but refusing to bow down to universal murder, we resolve to overcome the Neanderthal mentality and thereby transcend, if not overcome, our biology itself." Has one advantage over most nuclear literature in that it is, from time to time, amusing, and intentionally so. Bibliography, index.

8–5 Barnett, Lynn and Lee, Ian, eds. *The Nuclear Mentality: The Psychology of the Arms Race.* Pluto Pr., 1989. 176p.

Papers based on presentations at the National Conference of the Medical Campaign against Nuclear Weapons and its Study Group on Psychosocial Issues in the Nuclear Age, held in early 1989 at the Royal College of Nursing in London. The conference was prompted by the resistance of political leaders to change policies of nuclear warfighting and first–use, and the failure of public opinion favoring international cooperation to alter the nuclear status quo. The editors describe the "nuclear mentality" as based on the belief "that only the possession of a threat to use nuclear weapons will maintain peace in the world." The contributors, chiefly from the U.K., have varied backgrounds in psychology, medicine, and defense. They discuss the nature of leadership, psychoanalytical perspectives on political thinking, the assumptions made by nuclear weapons decision makers, children's views, and other psychological issues. A useful response to the question that opens the book: "Peace is abroad. But the arms race continues. Why?"

8–6 Bennett, Gordon C. *The New Abolitionists: The Story of Nuclear Free Zones.* Brethren Pr., 1987. 269p.

An account of the citizen movement to declare cities and other geographical areas legally off–limits to nuclear weapon facilities. The title is illuminated in chapter four, "The Abolitionist Connection," in which Bennett links this movement to that of the 19th–century slavery opponents. Includes case studies, discussion of legal issues, and a list of more than 100 American cities and towns that declared themselves nuclear free zones in the 1980s. Also contains texts of existing nuclear free zone ordinances form Takoma Park, MD and Hoboken, NJ. Notes.

8–7 Blackwood, Caroline. *On the Perimeter.* Penguin, 1985. 117p.

Another look at the women's encampment at Greenham Common, England, in protest of the cruise missile base there. Blackwood indicates her sympathy early in the book in her description of the campers' wretched shelters in both summer and winter (forbidden by law to erect tents, the women protected themselves from the elements with plastic sheets draped over tree branches) and their crude harassment by both local hooligans and government representatives. Noteworthy, if not especially surprising, is Blackwood's observation that "the hatred that seethed round the Cruise missile [and that was directed at the campers] was always expressed in sexual terms." A well-written account that evokes admiration for a group of women of uncommon bravery and commitment. (As of 1987, approximately two dozen women remained in the camp, from the hundreds who occupied six sites at the height of the protest.) See also 8–19, 8–59.

8–8 Bok, Sissela. *A Strategy for Peace: Human Values and the Threat of War*. Pantheon, 1989. 202p.

An expanded version of two lectures delivered by the author at Harvard University in 1985. Her objective is "to propose steps toward a secure and lasting peace that are practical, nonutopian, and in keeping with widely shared human values." She dismisses the idea that a transformation of society can rid the world of the nuclear threat, but believes that a more intense examination of long-standing moral, religious, and political traditions would be beneficial in that regard. She juxtaposes the thought of Carl von Clausewitz and his classic work, *On War*, with Immanuel Kant's essay "Perpetual Peace," and tries to show how these two seemingly antithetical writings complement each other and allow the reader to draw lessons that may, if put into effect, help lessen the chances of global catastrophe. The development of an enlightened trust is highlighted in her argument: "I see all those who strive to reduce distrust as working for peace, even if they produce no immediate and direct effect on the nuclear balance of terror." A clear, insightful book that provides much fuel for further thought.

Notes, index. (See also 8–19, 8–59).

8–9 Boyle, Francis A. *Defending Civil Resistance Under International Law.* Transnational, 1987. 378p.

A professor of international law, Boyle has written for legal journals on nuclear weapons. Here he seeks to provide historical and legal information, along with suggestions for trial materials suitable for use in the court defense of those charged in anti–nuclear civil resistance. (A large part of the book also covers this same territory regarding activism in opposition to South African and Central American policies.) Of interest to both lawyers and anti–nuclear activists who may care to root their actions in legal as well as in moral, political, or religious ground. Bibliography, index.

8–10 Brandon, Ruth. *The Burning Question: The Anti–Nuclear Movement Since 1945.* Heinemann, 1987. 174p.

A short, sympathetic history of the anti–nuclear movement with its main attention on the movement in Great Britain. Brandon homes in on such themes as the relationship between scientists and their war work, methods used by politicians and the military to defuse criticism, and the discrepancy between official pronouncements and detectable reality. Contains some good observations on public attitudes toward those in the peace movement, as the chapter title "Why Do People Hate the Peace Movement?" suggests. Notes, index.

8–11 Burton, John W. *Dear Survivors: Planning after Nuclear Holocaust: War Avoidance.* Westview, 1982. 137p.

An essay "addressed . . . to all of you emerging from shelters" on avoiding war presented as a letter from a survivor of WW III, with the belief "that there are certain basic and universal human needs that have to be satisfied if the individual and group are to be harmonious members of their wider societies." Concludes that the obligation to satisfy these needs without coercive political systems is at the heart of successful avoidance of war; elite society is self-destructive. The body of the book amplifies Burton's last statement: "Participation, recognition, identity, development for all, are not the constituent parts of an ideology. They are the politically realistic constituents of any on-going system."

8-12 Byrne, Paul. *The Campaign for Nuclear Disarmament.* Routledge, 1988. 241p.

Even at its trough, between 1963 and 1979, the CND was one of the most prominent interest groups on the British political scene. Byrne examines the CND from its re-genesis in 1979 to the general election of 1987. He bases his account chiefly on documents made available to him at CND headquarters, on interviews with organization officials and staff members, observations at CND meetings, and a survey of the membership. The survey appears here as an appendix. Among the major topics Byrne examines are the group's objectives, tactics, organizational structure, and impact on British society. Notes, index.

8-13 Caldicott, Helen. *Missile Envy: The Arms Race and Nuclear War.* Bantam, 1986. 346p.

A revised edition of the book first published by Morrow in 1984. Caldicott, an Australian pediatrician and for a long time the most prominent voice in the anti-nuclear group Physicians for Social Responsibility, is one of the best known public advocates of nuclear disarmament. She is nothing if not opinionated and provocative. She notes, for example, that airline pilots must submit to routine medical and psychiatric exams, and urges that world leaders, with their far greater burden of responsibility, undergo similar assessment. She is also intensely emotional and so sincere that only the most cynical reader can fail to be moved.

Too often she lets slip questionable statements. Is it really "the truth that America has placed its destiny in the hands of a few frightened Soviet politicians?" Probably not. Yet Caldicott's intensity, her compassion, and her frequently astute skewering of official absurdity makes her message one that cannot be ignored. Bibliography.

8–14 Cambridge Women's Peace Collective. *My Country Is the Whole World: An Anthology of Women's Work on Peace and War.* Pandora Pr., 1984. 306p.

This collection's purpose "is to reveal the long history of women's protests against war and of their efforts to suggest other ways of resolving conflict." The book grew out of discussions held during meetings in Cambridge, England, of WONT (Women Oppose the Nuclear Threat). Excerpts from books, letters, speeches, articles, and poems are presented in a broad chronological framework, from the Greek poet Sappho (7th–6th century B.C.) to the contemporary scene. A good collection of more than two hundred excerpts. Sources of the excerpts are listed, unfortunately, without page numbers. Bibliography.

8–15 Carlson, Don and Comstock, Craig. *Citizen Summitry: Keeping the Peace When It Matters Too Much to Be Left to Politicians.* Tarcher, 1986. 386p.

The best place to begin this collection of essays might be the penultimate selection, Craig Schindler's and Toby Herzlich's "The Great Turning," written from the hypothetical vantage of the year 2025. Their look backward outlines the shift in international relations from war to peace alluded to in the essay's title. Initially the idea seems an example of wishful thinking, but the authors' summary of changes in thinking from the 1980s on sounds far from impossible.

The peace portrayed by Schindler and Herzlich, and by the whole of *Citizen Summitry*, is founded on the real and the attainable. In five main sections ("Going Beyond War," "Getting to Know the Other Side," "Building a Space-Bridge: A Soviet Contribution," "Transforming Our Consciousness," and "Jumping Ahead and Looking Back at the Future"), approximately 30 contributors dwell on the possibilities and means of peace. The most powerful message is that a growing recognition of our common humanity must, and can, serve as the basis of a healthy change in U.S.-Soviet relations and international conduct at large. The book suggests that this change is more a people-to-people task than government-to-government. An encouraging, positive book, featuring in the page margins many quotations from leaders of state, philosophers and others which illuminate the goals at stake.

8-16 *Choices: A Unit on Conflict and Nuclear War.* National Education Association, 1983. 144p.

An instructional unit developed for use at the junior-high level; intended "to help students understand the power of nuclear weapons, the consequences of their use, and most importantly, the options available to resolve conflicts among nations by means other than nuclear war." The nine lessons deal with such topics as the effects of nuclear weapons, the arms race, the nature and history of war, and methods of reducing the risks of nuclear war. Most valuable, perhaps, may be the last two lessons, which concern the development of independent thinking and the imaginative consideration of alternatives for the future. Illustrations, glossaries, suggested readings. A project of the NEA, the Union of Concerned Scientists and the Massachusetts Teachers Association.

8-17 Cloud, Kate, et al. *Watermelons Not War: A Support Book for Parenting in the Nuclear Age.* New Society, 1984. 163p.

A helpful book by five women, all mothers, who refer to their work as the Nuclear Education Project. *Watermelons Not War* (the title comes from a slogan used in a 1982 Boston disarmament rally) will be a welcome tool to parents, or others who spend much time with children in a caring capacity, as they attempt to deal with youngsters' concerns about war, including but not limited to the nuclear sort. As the authors point out, children's silence on this issue does not mean that they are not thinking about it; a child's silence on a topic sometimes means that it is a very real and threatening matter in his or her life. The book offers many useful suggestions on how to bring a child's concerns about war out into the open, how to steer clear of despair, how children can involve themselves in positive projects that show them they have a voice in the world, and how to respond to such difficult questions as "What would happen if there were a nuclear war and you were killed and I was the only one left?" A good annotated resources list includes material for children.

8-18 Coates, Ken. *The Most Dangerous Decade: World Militarism and the New Non-Aligned Peace Movement.* Spokesman, 1984. 211p.

Readers seeking a left-wing polemic (Coates himself uses the last term to describe his approach) on the nuclear threat and the peace movement in the early to mid-1980s will need look no further than this book. Coates's discussion of a possible nuclear-free Europe, nuclear-free zones, and the peace movement and socialism provides a good overview from within what was in the process of becoming a pan-European phenomenon. Bibliography.

8-19 Cook, Alice. *Greenham Women Everywhere: Dreams, Ideas and Actions from the Women's Peace Movement.* South End, 1984. 127p.

A report on the Greenham Common women's peace camp. Includes numerous lengthy quotations from women involved in the camp; these statements bring home the serious, deeply-conceived objections of the protestors to their government's complicity in exacerbating the threat of nuclear war. Many photos show the Greenham Common women going about their business of peace. Bibliography. See also items 8-7, 8-59.

8-20 Cousins, Norman. *Albert Schweitzer's Mission, Healing and Peace: With Hitherto Unpublished Letters from Schweitzer, Nehru, Eisenhower, Khrushchev, and Kennedy*. Norton, 1985. 319p.

In the five years before Dr. Albert Schweitzer's death in 1965, he sent Cousins a considerable number of letters, most concerned with the world's accumulation of nuclear might. Schweitzer, who seems little-known to the present generation, was very much a Renaissance man of his era. Philosopher, physician, musician, and theologian, he devoted himself to work at his jungle hospital in Lambarene, French Equatorial Africa. The first part of this book is an adaptation of Cousins's *Dr. Schweitzer of Lambarene*, published in 1960; the second, which composes more than half the book, contains previously unpublished correspondence related to Schweitzer's great concern at the end of his life, "the need to free the world of nuclear terror." Schweitzer speaks with a direct logic that cannot be countered by the Byzantine theories of nuclear strategy. In one letter he writes, "And if there is an atomic war because of Berlin, the first thing that will happen is that the two Berlins will cease to exist--thanks to the use of atomic weapons." Index.

8-21 Cuzzort, Raymond P. *Using Social Thought: The Nuclear Issue and Other Concerns*. Mayfield, 1989. 342p.

Cuzzort attempts to show how social theories advanced by such figures as Marx, Weber, George Herbert Mead, and Peter Berger "can be applied to the nuclear issue to deepen and broaden our grasp of the problem." His intent is to show how sociological theory "can inform the imagination and guide it in ways that enhance, rather than constrain, human social vision." A welcome departure from the usual sociology text, and one that might prove useful in undergraduate classes. Notes, index.

8–22 Delf, George. *Humanizing Hell!: The Law v. Nuclear Weapons*. Hamilton, 1985. 367p.

"The agents of nuclear terror, our chosen leaders, present it as regrettable but necessary, lawful, patriotic," writes Delf, who would "seek to throw out the rubbish of corrupt authority, its crumbling institutions and Hollywood fantasies." Bonne chance, brother George. There is a fair quantity of inspired ranting and raving in this book; its essential argument is that nuclear weapons and nuclear deterrence as a policy violate principles of international law, which Delf illustrates with reliance on Nazi war crimes. The book's title comes from a remark made by Admiral Sir John Fisher, during the Hague Conference on the laws of war in 1899: "The humanizing of war! You might as well talk of the humanizing of hell!" Bibliography, index.

8–23 Dyson, John and Fitchett, Joseph. *Sink the Rainbow!: An Enquiry into the "Greenpeace Affair."* V. Gollancz, 1986. 192p.

The *Rainbow Warrior* was a vessel belonging to the environmentalist group Greenpeace. On July 10, 1985, two explosions sank the ship in Waitemata Harbour, Auckland, NZ. One crew member was killed. The French government admitted that the vessel was blown up by its operatives, acting on orders. Greenpeace had for many years led the international protest against French nuclear testing in the South Pacific; the destruction of the *Rainbow Warrior* was a form of preventive retribution. This is a readable account of the case by a maritime historian (Dyson) and a journalist employed in Paris by the *International Herald Tribune*. Includes photos. (See also 8–37, 8–85).

8–24 Ehrlich, Robert, ed. *Perspectives on Nuclear War and Peace Education*. Greenwood Pr., 1987. 242p.

Contains close to two dozen essays, chiefly by college and university faculty, that will be of assistance to those teaching nuclear war issues at the college level. The breadth of approach ranges from how-to (or how not to; some failed attempts in nuclear education receive attention) to the philosophical bases of the discipline. Following several groups of essays on broad views of nuclear war and peace education, the book focuses on nuclear courses in the social sciences, the humanities, in science and technology, as well as interdisciplinary nuclear war courses. Editor Ehrlich closes with an interesting chapter on "Opinions of Nuclear War Educators" with findings based on a survey of participants who attended a George Mason University conference on nuclear education in 1986. The questionnaire he used is reproduced in the book. Notes, index.

8–25 Epstein, William. *The Prevention of Nuclear War: A United Nations Perspective*. Oelgeschlager, Gunn & Hain, 1984. 114p.

Epstein, possessor of a distinguished record as a Canadian diplomat, Chairman of the Canadian Pugwash Group, and a member of the U.N. Secretariat, offers a compact overview of U.N. efforts to promote disarmament and avoid nuclear war. The bulk of the book concerns the U.N.'s historical work in these areas, ranging from establishment of a direct communications link between the U.S. and the Soviet Union to the growing recognition by the U.N. of the need to involve the peoples of the world, as well as their governments, in the quest for disarmament. The final major section tends to "The Current Scene" as it was during the book's preparation, with attention to a nuclear weapons freeze, defense systems, the world disarmament campaign, and other matters. Notes.

8-26 Fahey, Joseph and Armstrong, Richard. *A Peace Reader: Essential Readings on War, Justice, Non-Violence and World Order*. Paulist Pr., 1987. 477p.

Over fifty articles reprinted from scholarly and popular periodicals of diverse nature, from the *Journal of Conflict Resolution* to *Psychology Today* and *Nuclear Times*. In five sections: "Justice for All," "Non-Violence: Philosophy and Strategy," "Other Forms of Conflict Resolution," "War and the Arms Race," and "World Order." Authors range from the universally known (Gandhi, Martin Luther King, Jr.) to the prominent (Warren Burger) to the anonymous; articles are drawn from a wide chronological period. A nice collection, which, with its essay-ending study questions, should satisfy the classroom purposes it was clearly designed to meet. Notes.

8-27 Farren, Pat, ed. *What Will It Take to Prevent Nuclear War?: Grassroots Responses to Our Most Challenging Question*. Schenkman, 1983. 239p.

Approximately 230 statements from U.S., Canadian and British citizens address the title question in space seldom longer than a page. Fear, hope, anguish, resignation, despair, determination—the full range of responses to the Big Question comes through the replies. Some of the respondents are well-known, such as Howard Fast, Noam Chomsky and Denise Levertov, but most are "ordinary" people with a good number of them adolescents. The book is an addictive reading experience, for it takes one to the usually-hidden hearts of others' most terrible apprehensions. It may also give some real insights on how the title question may be answered successfully.

8-28 *Faslane: Diary of a Peace Camp*. Polygon Books, 1984. 86p.

Men and women of the Faslane, Scotland peace camp describe their experience in the camp, which came together in 1983 and 1984 to oppose the Clyde Submarine Base, a site for British nuclear-armed submarine repairs, close by a nuclear weapons storage facility and a proposed Trident submarine development. The site is on the Lower Clyde, 30 miles from the center of Glasgow. Although Scotland's population is just over 5 million, over 200 military bases swamp the country; 40 of them involve nuclear weapons. The book's final words, "Dare to be different. Dare to hope," suggest the attitude of the campers, who subscribe to the belief that "If we cannot carry on as normal under the shadow of the Bomb, then for the time being we have a duty not to carry on as normal."

8-29 Feher, Ferenc and Heller, Agnes. *Doomsday or Deterrence? On the Antinuclear Issue*. M.E. Sharpe, 1986. 154p.

A socio-historical examination of the antinuclear movement, which the authors consider based on ill-founded assumptions. In the view of Feher and Heller, the antinuclear movement gets in the way of an adequate response to "the Soviet threat." The authors, both native Hungarians, speak of "the Soviet empire" as a gang of "ruthless expansionists who grab what they can without risk and never release it." Events since 1986 have proved the authors wrong on this and other counts.

8-30 Fischer, Dietrich, et al.. *Winning Peace: Strategies and Ethics for a Nuclear-Free World*. Crane, Russak, 1989. 272p.

"Si vis pacem, para pacem": If you want peace, prepare for peace. The emphasis here is on what can be accomplished at an individual or local level, from the content of family conversations to recording and sharing one's personal visions, "your images of both the bad and the desirable future." The authors discuss flaws in conventional strategies, the shortcomings of new ones (SDI is part of the problem, not the solution), stress the power of the individual, and encourage a positive response to Einstein's famous remark that "The unleashed power of the atom has changed everything save our modes of thinking, and thus we drift toward unparalleled catastrophe." Lengthy bibliography contains numerous references to German-language sources. Index.

8–31 Flynn, Eileen. *My Country Right or Wrong?: Selective Conscientious Objection in the Nuclear Age.* Loyola Univ. Pr., 1985. 98p.

G.K. Chesterton once said that to claim it is "My country, right or wrong," is somewhat the equivalent of declaring "My wife, drunk or sober." This little book will be welcomed by readers examining their own consciences about taking a stand of conscientious objection to participation in wars that are the product of an intoxicated national leadership. Flynn clearly and simply lays out criteria for judging the justice of a war according to traditional theories of just war. Nuclear war, any nuclear war, fails to meet many of the necessary criteria. Especially recommended to young men and women struggling with the conflict between the patriotic "call to duty" and allegiance to moral obligations that transcend nationality. Bibliography.

8–32 Freeman, Harold. *If You Give a Damn About Life.* Dodd, Mead, 1985. 88p.

In spite of the unfortunate title, with its implication that some, or many, do not "give a damn about life," this short book by MIT Professor Emeritus Freeman quickly succeeds in illuminating the magnitude of the nuclear threat through brief "one-bomb" scenarios depicting the fates of Boston, New York City, Omaha, Chicago, San Francisco, Montreal, Washington, and Moscow under such "limited" attack. Freeman's intent is to awaken readers to the importance of seriously addressing the nuclear threat through a halt of nuclear weapons production, progressive destruction of the existing stock, and conversion of nuclear weapon production facilities to civilian purposes, among other measures. Index.

8-33 French, Dan, et al. *Crossroads: Quality of Life in a Nuclear World*. Jobs with Peace, 1983. 80p.

A curriculum on nuclear war and peace designed for use at the high-school level. The authors developed it "to inform students of the issues of nuclear war and military spending, and to help them overcome feelings of helplessness and powerlessness. The aim is open discussion." Divided into lessons for a ten-day examination of such issues as negotiation and global conflict, national security, military spending and the economy, and the effect of the military budget on overall quality of life. Includes objectives, materials, and activities for the various lessons. Dated in some areas, but still valuable in others. Bibliography.

8-34 Galtung, Johan. *There Are Alternatives!: Four Roads to Peace and Security*. Spokesman, 1984. 221p.; dist. by Dufour Editions.

An effort to explore alternatives to the results of hollow disarmament conferences which "will not stop the arms race." Galtung believes "that arms races cannot go on indefinitely without leading to war." The "four roads" referred to in the subtitle are conflict resolution, balance of power, disarmament, and alternative security policies. Those policies include a shift from an offensive to defensive orientation, non-alignment with the superpowers, enhanced internal strength (economic, ecological, etc.), and development of greater mutual usefulness among nations in cultural, political, economic, and other areas. The final chapter on these alternative policies might be useful in conjunction with Hollins's *Conquest of War*. Galtung, a professional peace researcher and founder of the International Peace Research Institute of Oslo, displays an occasional fondness for formulae and tables whose clarity may elude uninitiated readers. Bibliography.

8–35 Garfinkle, Adam M. *The Politics of the Nuclear Freeze.* Foreign Policy Research Institute, 1984. 258p.

Garfinkle's study of the freeze movement is as much a brief for continued reliance on nuclear deterrence as it is a balanced account of the movement, and is perhaps more useful in the first regard. Also of interest is Garfinkle's sometimes testy analysis of what he perceived to be the various groups which encouraged or opposed the freeze, among them the "Far Right," the "Pragmatic Center," and the "Professional Left." Notes.

8–36 Gerson, Joseph, ed. *The Deadly Connection: Nuclear War & U.S. Intervention.* New Society, 1986. 253p.

Contains articles and speeches by 23 contributors; some of the selections first appeared as talks at "The Deadly Connection" conference held in Cambridge, MA, in late 1982 under auspices of the American Friends Service Committee. The contributors explore the relationship between U.S. nuclear policies and potential U.S. military intervention around the world. Some prominent left–oriented critics, including Daniel Ellsberg, Noam Chomsky, Michael T. Klare, Randall Forsberg and others focus on first–strike policy and U.S. intervention, the dangers of the eroding separation between conventional and nuclear arms, and Third World "nuclear triggers." It is the book's final section, "Toward Strategies for Survival," that accounts for its presence in this bibliography's "Peace" chapter. A provocative treatment of what is almost surely the most likely route for U.S. involvement in any nuclear war. Notes.

8–37 Gidley, Isobelle. *The Rainbow Warrior Affair.* Unwin Paperbacks, 1986. 217p.

Another account of the *Rainbow Warrior* story (see items 8-23, 8-85), blending investigative reporting and quasi-novelization of the events (the reader receives information about individuals' states of mind and specific actions that the author could not have literally known). Readers will need to be careful to separate assumptions from observations.

8-38 Goodman, Lisa M. and Hoff, Lee Ann. *Omnicide: The Nuclear Dilemma.* Praeger, 1990. 153p.

In their analysis of the nuclear threat, the authors link "the pessimism and lack of motivation among youth and the denial of reality among adults to the conscious or unconscious fear of nuclear holocaust." This idea deserves exploration, and the book makes some headway through discussion of questionnaires (reproduced in the text) concerning nuclear war attitudes. Of special interest is an examination of children's ideas about nuclear war. The book concludes with a reasonably optimistic chapter on "Scenarios and Strategies for Peace" in which the authors argue that "the family is the place to begin preparing potential members of the critical mass necessary to institute real change." Notes, bibliography, index.

8-39 Greenwald, David S. and Zeitlin, Steven J. *No Reason to Talk About It: Families Confront the Nuclear Taboo.* Norton, 1987. 270p.

The authors, both family therapists, based this book on their interviews on nuclear war with some two dozen families. The focus is on the "taboo," the avoidance of the topic within family discourse. Greenwald and Zeitlin examine the interviews in some depth, and rely on Erik Erikson's theories of development in the process, but it is the statements of the family members themselves--and the authors sought out people from a variety of economic and ethnic backgrounds--that make the book as interesting as it is. The authors fear that failure to overcome the nuclear taboo will interfere with children's efforts to develop whole identities, and will lead parents into an unhappy, narrow life that leaves a stunted spiritual heritage to their children.

8–40 Gromyko, Anatoly and Hellman, Martin, eds. *Breakthrough: Emerging New Thinking*. Walker, 1988. 281p.

Scholars from the West and from the Soviet Union discuss new ways of thinking about war and peace. It is a good, urgent, clearly-written set of essays in which national agendas take a back seat to concern about global survival. Topics range from discussion of nuclear war through technological glitches to terrorism, improved communication, young people and nuclear war, the myth of rationality in crisis, ecological perspectives, involvement of creative artists in addressing the problems, and others. Some of the better-known U.S. contributors are Paul Bracken, Kenneth E. Boulding, and Sidney Drell. Among the Soviets are Tatiana Kabachenko (Moscow State University), Andrei Y. Melville (Institute of USA and Canada Studies), and Fyodor M. Burlatsky (Soviet Political Science Association). A Russian-language edition was published simultaneously. Notes.

8–41 Grossinger, Richard and Hough, Lindy, eds. *Nuclear Strategy and the Code of the Warrior: Faces of Mars and Shiva in the Crisis of Human Survival*. North Atlantic Books, 1984. 300p.

This special issue of *Io* magazine opens with editor Grossinger's highly personal preface in which he recounts the bomb terrors of his early '60s adolescence, and dismisses as "mindless" literalism much anti-war activism. Anti-war activity is, he believes, most effective when most creative; a dance can do more than a slogan or a bumper sticker. "Nuclear weapons must awaken us to an event outside political parties, even outside consciousness and outside history." True to his belief, the editors have assembled some creative responses to the nuclear threat. Marty Glass's essay "Facing a Few of the Facts" is one of the funniest essays available on the universality of Bomb dread. Not all of the selections are as inspired, and some are fairly routine, but many succeed. Includes the transcript of a long discussion on "The Warrior and the Militarist" among the editors, poet Gary Snyder, psychologist Richard Strozzi-Heckler, and choreographer Karin Epperlein, among others.

8–42 Harris, Ian M. *Peace Education*. McFarland, 1988. 233p.

The author, a Quaker and a professor of community education at the University of Wisconsin-Milwaukee, teaches adult courses on peace education, and has been instrumental in creating a peace studies curriculum on that campus. He addresses his book to a broad audience ranging from academics to peace activists.

The book is a good introduction to his topic, providing a detailed examination of the goals of peace education and proceeding through a discussion of the process's most important issues. These include overcoming obstacles such as enculturated acceptance of violence as a way of life, and curriculum implementation.

Peace Education works as both a philosophical study and as a how-to manual outlining suggestions on how to adapt peace education to many subjects that might not immediately suggest their possibilities in this area, such as music, athletics, and mathematics. Well-suited for use at both high school and college levels, the book contains a wealth of supplementary material, including annotated print, organizational, and other resource directories. Notes, index.

8–43 Higgins, Ronald. *Plotting Peace: The Owl's Reply to Hawks and Doves.* Brassey's, 1990; dist. in U.S. by

Macmillan. 227p.

A veteran of the British Diplomatic Service dismisses the "Hawks versus Doves" debate as sterile and useless, and after outlining predictable left–right, hawk–dove positions on a variety of peace and war issues, advocates the flexibility and pragmatism of the owl, who "tries to see the complex interactions of many factors, rather than be driven by a single pattern of ideas, the temptation alike of doves and hawks." Higgins's is a very interesting discussion, including proposals for reducing nuclear dependency in Europe.

In his epilogue, Higgins writes of the June, 1989 events in Beijing's Tiananmen Square and the Polish Solidarity Movement's electoral victory against a repressive regime. The owl, he claims, "is surprised neither by the pitiful horror of Beijing's rape nor staggering, if still partial, emergence of democracy within the gates of a repressive ideology." Because the owl's vision is accommodating rather than constrained, the possibilities for creative action are broader, and neither cheap euphoria nor opportunistic depression are likely to settle in at a moment's notice. Notes, index.

8–44 Hinton, James. *Protests and Visions: Peace Politics in Twentieth-Century Britain*. Hutchinson Radius, 1989. 248p.

Hinton covers the British peace movement from the Victorian era to the "Second Wave" of the Campaign for Nuclear Disarmament in the 1980s. As a professional historian and peace activist himself, he brought a fitting background to the book; one of his main objectives was to remedy what he saw as the "remarkable absence of debate about peace movement history among peace campaigners." He traces this phenomenon to the negligible institutional existence of the peace movement: it is, rather, an existence manifested in short-lived flurries of activism, or the "protests" referred to in the book's title.

Approximately a quarter of the book is devoted to the post-WW II peace and antinuclear movement. A good tool to open a broad historical view. Notes, index.

8-45 Hollins, Harry B., et al. *The Conquest of War: Alternative Strategies for Global Security.* Westview, 1989. 224p.

A survey of alternatives to "nuclear peace," which the authors call "not a stable and enduring condition but a fragile truce, a cease-fire without a settlement." They consider among other options the United Nations; the plan for a world federalist structure by Harvard lawyers Grenville Clark and Louis Sohn; "qualitative disarmament" to eliminate the war-making capacity of nations; and nonprovocative defense along the lines of Yugoslavia, Sweden, and Switzerland. A chapter on SDI dismisses this system on a variety of counts, from its exorbitant expense to its failure to keep control of events in human hands rather than in computer circuits. Bibliography, index.

8-46 Hudgens, Capt. Tom A. *Let's Abolish War.* Bilr Corp., 1986. Revised ed. 72p.

It is no accident that the word formed by joining the first letters of this book's title words is "LAW." The author, a retired airline pilot and WW II Army Air Corps flying instructor, is now vice president of the World Federalist Association. He advocates world government as the best means to banish "the stupidity of war" from the planet.

This brief book sets out the guiding ideas of world federalism in a lively, understandable way. Hudgens furnishes quotations on the subject from such prominent spokesmen for world government as Norman Cousins, Bertrand Russell, Arnold Toynbee, and Gandhi, and follows them with his own remarks. A good contribution to the idea of peace through internationalism.

8-47 *INFACT Brings GE to Light*. INFACT, 1988. 133p.

From fiscal year 1984 through fiscal year 1986, almost 12 percent of General Electric's sales—over $11 billion—came as a result of nuclear weapons-related work. From ballistic missiles to nuclear-capable delivery systems (the F-15, the F-18, the Trident submarine, etc.), GE makes tools of destruction, bringing to life things hardly in keeping with its corporate slogan.

INFACT has been conducting a nationwide boycott of GE products for several years. The book is a damning documentation of the company's approach to business, even aside from its work in nuclear weapons. Its central part, "GE: Shaping Nuclear Weapons Policies for Profits," is an eye-opening picture of how a powerful company helps shape not only the technology of the arms race and mass destruction, but federal policy itself. This book has been updated with a revised edition (New Society, 1990) that eluded efforts to obtain.

8-48 Jacobs, Marilyn S. *American Psychology in the Quest for Nuclear Peace*. Praeger, 1989. 181p.

A straightforward, brief history of the role of American psychology in the peace and antinuclear movements. Coverage begins with attention to the left of the 1930s, and continues into the 1980s. The author, a psychologist herself, nicely interweaves a literature review with numerous interviews with others in the field. Bibliography.

8-49 Kaltefleiter, Werner, and Pfaltzgraff, Robert L., eds. *The Peace Movements in Europe & the United States*. Croom Helm, 1985. 211p.

Representatives from Western Europe and the U.S. met at a 1984 conference in Kiel, West Germany, to discuss whether the various national peace movements of the period possessed common features. This book, with ten essays based on papers presented at the conference, discusses the movements in Sweden, Norway, the Netherlands, Britain, France, Italy, and the U.S. The editors conclude the volume with a comparative analysis of the movements. Their analysis is simplistic and contemptuous, speaking of the peace movements' ideas as "toys" for the occupation of those who embrace them, in deluded ignorance of the security issues posed by *realpolitik*. The Catholic church in America, for example, is a player in the game, having been "infiltrated by the peace movement." A book of some merit in its examination of the peace movements, but readers should take its editors' biases into consideration. Notes, index.

8–50 Katz, Milton S. *Ban the Bomb: A History of SANE, the Committee for a Sane Nuclear Policy, 1957–1985.* Greenwood Pr., 1986. 215p.

In June of 1957, a group of 27 citizens convened at the Overseas Press Club in New York City to organize a campaign to halt nuclear weapon testing. In the fall, they named their organization the National Committee for a Sane Nuclear Policy, and came to be commonly known as SANE. Katz's book is both a sympathetic history of SANE and its role in American society and an examination of Cold War American liberalism. A well-researched work—Katz turned to SANE itself as well as to such special libraries as the Swarthmore College Peace Collection—*Ban the Bomb* also features reproductions of a dozen SANE ads appearing in the mass media. Most of these date from the 1950s and early '60s, and focus on the health threats of nuclear testing. An interesting treatment. Notes, index.

8–51 Klein, Kenneth and Kunkel, Joseph, eds. *In the Interest of Peace: A Spectrum of Philosophical Views.* Longwood Academic, 1990. 355p.

Two dozen papers originally presented at the Second Annual Conference of Concerned Philosophers for Peace at Temple University in late 1989. Several of the

papers are specifically concerned with nuclear war
and nuclear weapons issues, such as Joseph Kunkel's
appraisal of consequentialist arguments over
deterrence and disarmament, and William Gay's
discussion of the Bertrand Russell–Sidney Hook debate
in 1958 on nuclear war and the Soviet Union. (Russell
argued that nuclear war could destroy all human life,
Hook that communism would do the same to all
freedom.) Notes, bibliography, index.

8–52 Kome, Penney, and Crean, Patrick, eds. *Peace: A
Dream Unfolding*. Sierra Club, 1986. 256p.

A nice collection of statements on the search for peace
and the threat of war drawn from the broad scope of
religious and cultural traditions. Arranged in three
main sections, "The Dream" of peace, "The Nightmare"
of nuclear war, and "The Awakening" to the necessary
global pursuit of peace. The scope of the selections,
which include stories, poetry, nonfiction, selections
from books and periodicals, is broad both in kind and
in chronology, with contributors ranging from
Aristophanes and Lao Tzu to Andrei Sakharov and
Isaac Bashevis Singer. Numerous effective illustrations,
many in color, complement the text; introduction by
Nobel Peace Prize winners Bernard Lown and Evgueni
I. Chazov, founders of International Physicians for the
Prevention of Nuclear War. A beautifully–produced
book; includes many references to nuclear issues.
Index.

8–53 Kovel, Joel *Against the State of Nuclear Terror*.
South End, 1984. 250p.

A psychiatrist's thoroughly–argued discussion of the
origins and species of nuclear fear, coupled with his
prescription for a cure. Kovel contends that the Bomb
is the logical end of technocracy, and believes that
antinuclearism must address more than the threat of
nuclear war. It must go not just to the branches but
to the roots of technocratic hubris, our particularly
Western idea that we were obviously made to dominate

rather than live in harmony with Nature.

The basic need, as Kovel sees it, is for a "prefiguration of what can be, but is not yet." He seeks "a world beyond the nation-state, beyond technocracy, beyond economic domination, beyond racism, beyond sexism, not here and not looming, but not to be put off either." He makes a good case that those who dismiss the vision of such a world have been conditioned by the nuclear state—both the political state and the nuclear state of mind—to reject the vision not because it is impossible to achieve, but because it does not serve the state's pathological purposes.

A book that requires careful reading and pondering; it should help the activist solidify the theoretical basis of his or her worldview, and could help the passive and hopeless (victims of state-induced nuclear terror) overcome their inertia and sense of powerlessness. Notes, index.

8–54 Krieger, David and Kelly, Frank, eds. *Waging Peace in the Nuclear Age: Ideas for Action*. Capra Pr., 1988. 343p.

A collection of 25 essays by 19 authors (only three of whom are women) with backgrounds in academia, the military, and other spheres. The book's main sections feature essays on new ways of thinking about peace, nuclear strategy, ideas for the future (a "Nuclear Age Peace Corps" would educate others on the perils of the arms race), and on the responsibilities and opportunities of the public in the pursuit of peace. A few of the contributors: Robert C. Aldridge, Dietrich Fisher, Gene R. La Rocque, and Ted Turner. Frank Kelly, who served as a campaign director for Averell Harriman's run at the presidency in 1952, offers a challenging piece on "Searching for a President in the Nuclear Age." His suggestions, if followed, could make a real improvement in the quality of the Chief Executive. Notes.

8–55 La Farge, Phyllis. *The Strangelove Legacy: Children, Parents and Teachers in the Nuclear Age.* Harper & Row, 1987. 242p.

La Farge, an editor at *Parents* magazine, looks into the literature on children's and adolescents' attitudes toward nuclear war, and finds that there is "an apocalyptic vision" present in the minds of many young people. She goes on to discuss the impact of this vision, and the importance of meaningful education about nuclear issues at an early age. As one eighth-grade teacher observed after looking at her class and realizing that in four years they would be old enough to vote, the importance of conveying to them the belief that their informed opinions count for something was a shock. "It's really crucial now; it's not a moment too soon." The book contains many quotations from children and adolescents helping dramatize the nature and the depth of their responses to this nuclear world.

8–56 Laffin, Arthur J. and Montgomery, Anne. *Swords into Plowshares: Nonviolent Direct Action for Disarmament.* Harper & Row, 1987. 243p.

Some two-dozen plus essays and poems by American anti-war activists. The contributors include a Catholic nun who has served over two years in jail for her participation in nuclear arms protests, a former missile design engineer who has become a strong critic of U.S. nuclear policy, a grandmother whose family sheltered Jews in Nazi-occupied Holland and who has founded a peace center in Pennsylvania, and a mother of three who served three years in prison for non-violent nuclear protests.

These are but a few of the people whose testimonies of commitment and faith make the book so affecting. Writes one woman, a shelter and soup-kitchen worker who, shortly after her own release from prison saw her husband sentenced to a three-year term: "I struggle with loneliness, fear despair. I search for hope and find none. Where, oh God, are you?" There are a few prominent names among the contributors, but most are ordinary men and women whose selfless dedication to their vision has made them extraordinary.

8–57 Laqueur, Walter and Hunter, Robert, eds. *European Peace Movements and the Future of the Western Alliance.* Transaction Books, 1985. 450p.

Seventeen essays by American and European political scientists, statesmen, theologians and other scholars. The contributors, including Irving Kristol, Henry Kissinger, and Theodore Draper, discuss NATO's history, Nordic peace movements, pacifism in the Netherlands, the role of the church in Great Britain, and other issues. That the editors choose a military specialist (David Thomas) to write (unsympathetically) on the American peace movement may say as much about their own perspectives as the book has to say about the real meaning of the international movement and its possible effects on Western security arrangements. Notes, index.

8–58 Levine, Howard B., et al., eds. *Psychoanalysis and the Nuclear Threat: Clinical and Theoretical Studies.* Analytic Pr., 1988. 290p. Dist. by Erlbaum Associates.

Fourteen psychoanalytic studies concerning the nuclear threat, offered "in the spirit of raising and reraising major questions about psychoanalysis and the world of political thought and action, and, in particular, psychoanalysis and the threat of annihilation of the only world in which we live." The set begins with an historical assessment of Freud's views on aggression and war, and ends with "Hiroshima and Denial," which concerns the ability of one atomic bomb victim to survive psychologically by resorting to denial and repression of her feelings, and her subsequent self-awareness and change in life. Between these essays appears work on strategists and deterrence, gender differences and nuclear issues, nuclear weapons and the need for enemies, and other topics. Contributors are an international group. A good volume on a too-seldom explored and fundamentally important aspect of the nuclear whole. Index.

8-59 Liddington, Jill. *The Long Road to Greenham: Feminism and Anti-Militarism in Britain Since 1820.* Virago, 1989. 341p.

Liddington employs diaries, autobiographies and interviews to produce this history of the women's peace movement in Britain. A good half of the book concentrates on the antinuclear movement leading to the establishment of the Greenham Common peace camp in 1982 at Berkshire, England, base for U.S. cruise missiles. Much of the book focuses on the ideas and relationships linking feminism to maternalism as a "natural" motivation for women to oppose war, the equal rights aspirations of women traditionally excluded from political power, and in the radical feminist position holding that violence is an inherently male phenomenon. Notes, bibliography, index.

8-60 Lifton, Robert Jay and Markusen, Eric. *The Genocidal Mentality: Nazi Holocaust and Nuclear Threat.* Basic Books, 1990. 346p.

Psychologist Lifton, who has done previous work on Nazism, unites with sociologist Markusen to examine parallels between the Holocaust and the threat of nuclear extermination. Drawing on interviews with scientists, military and government officials involved in nuclear decision making, they find much the same sort of emotional distancing and rationalization occurring among the technocrats and policymakers responsible for the rise of "nuclearism" (an exaggerated faith in nuclear weapons) as took place among Nazi engineers of the Holocaust. How precise the parallels actually are between the Holocaust perpetrators and the creators and managers of nuclear weapons is questionable. The Holocaust was a deliberate policy of extermination; nuclear deterrence, a strategy the authors cannot abide, is a deliberate policy intended to prevent extermination. However weak one's trust in deterrence as a durable item, there is clearly a world of difference between the advocate of nuclear deterrence, arms control, and negotiated disarmament and the willing collaborator in a systematic murder exemplified by the Holocaust. The book is, nevertheless, a thoughtful and thought-provoking study that does give numerous insights into the mindsets (there are certainly more than one!) behind the nuclear threat. Index.

8-61 Loeb, Paul R. *Hope in Hard Times: America's Peace Movement and the Reagan Era.* Lexington Books, 1986. 322p.

An affecting, in-depth visit into the lives of ordinary Americans working for peace in the dark and pessimistic days of the early 1980s. From Minneapolis, where Loeb describes the Honeywell Project (a protest against that company's involvement in nuclear weapons production), to South Carolina Baptist peace activists and "The Saga of the Trident Blockade" in Washington State, the book concentrates on a wide variety of citizens who have answered the call to work for peace. It is an inspirational but by no means unrealistic work. "Those who act carry their own doubts, fears, and histories of denial," concludes Loeb. "Yet if they can continue, others can as well. If at last they find strength in rising and speaking, so can we." Bibliography, index.

8-62 London, Herbert I. *Armageddon in the Classroom: An Examination of Nuclear Education.* Univ. Press of America, 1987. 127p.

A tirade against what the author considers the propagandistic, soft-headed, one-sided approach to peace and nuclear war education allegedly carried on in American schools. Most readers will prefer to ignore the main body of the text, which includes such statements as "Peace has throughout history been a utopian vision, a chimera." Ironically useful, however, is the bibliography, which lists in nearly 40 pages a large number of curriculum guides and teacher resources and related materials (books, articles and other documents concerned with peace and nuclear education).

8–63 Lynch, Allen, ed. *Building Security in Europe: Confidence-Building Measures and the CSCE*. Institute for East-West Security Studies, 1986. 181p. Dist. by Westview Pr.

The chief portion of this work concerning the Conference on Security and Cooperation in Europe consists of two essays. Rolf Berg (Deputy Chief of Mission at the Royal Norwegian Embassy in Vienna) contributes "Military Confidence-Building in Europe," and Adam-Daniel Rutfeld (Head of the European Security Department of the Polish Institute of International Affairs, Warsaw) offers "Developing a Confidence-Building System in East-West Relations: Europe and the CSCE." The authors agree that confidence-building measures are not a panacea for problems between East and West, but instruments "for institutionalizing confidence and reducing suspicions in the political, economic and humanitarian, as well as military fields." Appended documents include excerpts from the U.S. "Open Skies" proposal of 1955, various Soviet proposals advanced in 1984 in Stockholm, and other 1984 proposals put forth by neutral and non-aligned countries. The proposals address both nuclear issues, such as nuclear-weapon-free zones in Europe, and non-nuclear, such as the banning of chemical weapons. Notes.

8–64 McAllister, Pam, ed. *Reweaving the Web of Life: Feminism and Nonviolence*. New Society, 1982. 440p.

Fifty-plus essays, poems, stories and a song illuminating aspects of feminist pacifism. Approximately half are reprinted from other sources. Among the selections specifically concerning nuclear war and

related issues are Barbara Reynolds's "Sailing into
Test Waters," an account of her 1958 voyage with her
family and other companions into a nuclear test area
in the Pacific, and Ellen Bass's earnest poem, "Our
Stunning Harvest": "Who are these madmen/whose
lives are so barren, so desperate/they love nothing?"
Some of the other contributors are Alice Walker, Holly
Near, Grace Paley, and Joan Baez. Includes a brief
chronology, 1600–1981, of women's peace actions. Notes,
bibliography, index.

8–65 McCrea, Frances B. and Markle, Gerald E. *Minutes
to Midnight: Nuclear Weapons Protest in America.* Sage,
1989. 200p.

Two sociology professors offer a useful, brief
overview of the title topic. A large part of the book,
too large, perhaps, is devoted to the movement for a
nuclear freeze; in other sections the authors turn
their attention to the atomic scientists' movement and
the *Bulletin of the Atomic Scientists*, and the Ban the
Bomb movement. Bibliography, index.

8–66 McGuinness, Elizabeth A. *People Waging Peace:
Stories of Americans Striving for Peace and Justice in
the World Today.* Alberti Pr., 1988. 388p.

Collects profiles of more than fifty Americans who are
working for peace in many ways and places. The
sense here is one of "everyday people" at the task;
featured are housewives, teachers, local politicians,
grassroots activists, religious leaders and business
people, all of them devoting significant parts of their
lives to the struggle against war, particularly against
the nuclear threat. The sketches of three to six pages
for each person, many with photographs of the
biographees, bring home the lives and the commitment
of their subjects. The kinds of people portrayed, and
their ways of advocating peace, are so varied that
almost any reader would find inspiration in this book.

8-67 Malcolmson, Robert W. *Nuclear Fallacies: How We Have Been Misguided Since Hiroshima.* McGill–Queen's Univ. Pr., 1985. 152p.

A meditation on the nuclear age, reflecting on its origins, the nuclear arms race, and the prospects for the survival of civilization. Counsels such positive steps as international recognition of a shared interest in that survival; reduction of the adversarial relationship between the superpowers; broad recognition of nuclear weapons' absence of military utility; achievement of arms control agreements able to impose constraints on both military scientists and their bureaucratic constituencies; and improvement of cooperative efforts for managing political crises. There is little novel here, but when the ailment remains the same, there is little reason to change the prescription, especially when the afflicted have yet to follow the prescription. Readable, sensible, and informed. Notes, bibliographic essay, index.

8-68 Marullo, Sam and Lofland, John, eds. *Peace Action in the Eighties: Social Science Perspectives.* Rutgers Univ. Pr., 1990. 289p.

The seventeen essays here discuss and analyze the U.S. peace movement in the 1980s. It is a sympathetic collection with contributions chiefly by sociologists. Several of the contributors have significant backgrounds in peace activism, in addition to their formal work in the scholarly arena on peace and war issues. The volume opens with a group of essays tracing the rise, decline, and effects of the American peace movement in the past decade. Among the subtopics considered are the nuclear freeze movement, competition among peace groups, Physicians for Social Responsibility, civil disobedience and the Honeywell Project (the nation's oldest peace group that specifically focuses on weapons research and production), and self-conceptions of peace activists. Notes, bibliography, index.

8–69 Mattausch, John. *A Commitment to Campaign: A Sociological Study of CND*. Manchester Univ. Pr., 1989. 192p. Dist. by St. Martin's Pr.

Based on doctoral research carried out at Edinburgh University, 1982–1986, this book attempts to explain why the Campaign for Nuclear Disarmament only proves attractive to a narrow section of the British public. The author, who has "never met an insincere member of CND," believes that nuclear deterrence is "a dangerous fallacy" which, combined with "the increasing accumulation and proliferation" of nuclear weapons only heightens the probability of nuclear war. Questions Mattausch dwells on include the CND's methods of opposing nuclear weapons, how CND members view the world and their place in it, and how CND relates to other facets of British society. He interviewed many CND members, and seeks to determine how their lives rendered them likely candidates for the organization and for expressing their concern about nuclear weapons in particular ways. Bibliography, index.

8–70 May, Brian. *Russia, America, the Bomb and the Fall of Western Europe*. Routledge & Kegan Paul, 1984. 248p.

Urging that "we should try to step aside from history," and view it with as much detachment as possible, May argues that unilateral nuclear disarmament is essential to Western Europe's avoidance of nuclear war. His analysis of U.S., Soviet, and Western European positions, especially economic problems, leads him to believe that agreement on arms control could be deceptive: a combination of unfulfilled expectations and economic dislocation could lead to nuclear war, as long as weapons remain in hand. He wrote, of course, before the Soviet Union's present calamitous economic problems were fully manifested. Notes, index.

8–71 Meyer, David S. *A Winter of Discontent: The*

Nuclear Freeze and American Politics. Praeger, 1990. 294p.

A good history of the social movement that finally gave mainstream legitimacy to nuclear protest in the U.S. Meyer, a political scientist with a background as a researcher for the Institute for Defense and Disarmament Studies, discusses the interesting career of the Nuclear Freeze movement, which came seemingly out of nowhere shortly after the first Reagan election, and disappeared by his second term. In its brief, dramatic life, the movement organized the largest antinuclear demonstration in U.S. history, approximately 1 million strong marching in New York City on June 12, 1982, to protest Reagan administration nuclear policies. Meyer notes that mainstream politics responded to the freeze movement, and, although "the freeze was fragmented, institutionalized, and coopted by modest restraints in the Reagan program and the administration's increasingly sophisticated political management of dissent," its legacy can be traced in widely-expanded nuclear education and peace studies programs, greater media attention to nuclear issues, and a more politically acceptable response to declarations of nuclear opposition. Notes, index.

8–72 Minnion, John and Bolsover, Philip. *The CND Story: The First 25 Years of CND in the Words of the People Involved.* Allison & Busby, 1983. 158p.

After a brief historical summary of the Campaign for Nuclear Disarmament since its inception in the 1950s, the book offers short articles by forty CND activists elaborating on the organization's principles and its members' experiences. Includes a short resource list of films and books on CND.

8–73 Moore, Melinda and Olsen, Laurie. *Our Future at Stake: A Teenager's Guide to Stopping the Nuclear Arms Race.* Citizens Policy Center, Oakland CA, 1984. 68p. Dist. by New Society.

This short book offers a clear presentation of the nuclear problem and suggestions for relieving it through education, organization, voting, lobbying, and work. Its most valuable feature may be the numerous personal statements from young people. These statements portray individual moments of nuclear truth, when the speakers became aware of the threat, how they felt about it, and what they're doing to overcome it. Each statement is accompanied by a photo of the teenager who makes it. It's a good mix of kids, white, black, Chicano, and it will be easy for young readers to identify with the fears and hopes they express. Throughout the tone is realistic but positive in the belief that all can contribute to the planet's preservation, and enjoy making the contribution.

8–74 New Left Review. *Exterminism and Cold War*. Verso Editions and NLB, 1982. 358p.

This socialist symposium by antiwar activists contains essays written in 1980 and 1981. Edward Thompson's opening piece, "Notes on Exterminism, the Last Stage of Civilization," calls for "a cogent theoretical and class analysis of the present war crisis." He defines "exterminism" as the characteristics of a society "which thrust it in a direction whose outcome must be the extermination of multitudes," and he finds in the Cold War those fatal characteristics. He calls for an alliance of churches, Eurocommunists, workers, Soviet citizens and others to unite against the threat. Several of the volume's remaining 14 essays comment on or take off from Thompson's. Among the best known contributors are Roy and Zhores Medvedev, Marcus Raskin, and Noam Chomsky. Readers curious about or sympathetic with a socialist slant on the nuclear threat should find these essays of interest. Notes, index.

8–75 Norman, Liane E. *Hammer of Justice: Molly Rush and the Plowshares Eight*. Pittsburgh Peace Institute, 1989. 234p.

In September, 1980, Molly Rush and a group of companions illegally entered a General Electric nuclear weapons facility in King of Prussia, PA, and beat with hammers on nuclear warheads being manufactured in the plant. Rush, who spent 78 days in jail for her protest, wrote to her six children from her cell, "I don't think I'm a criminal because we tried to call others accountable. After seeing what I saw first hand, the precision and deep care that goes into producing something capable of 35 Hiroshimas in one small two or three-foot cone—and that's all those hundreds of workers in that one place do, forty hours a week—you know that it *has* to be stopped *soon* before it's too late."

Norman's is a well-researched, journalistic account of one more average citizen who, as the nuclear threat grew in the 1980s, found her love of life provoking her to an act that was technically meaningless, but symbolically immense. Bibliography; numerous illustrations.

8-76 Nye, Joseph S., Jr.; Allison, Graham T.; Carnesale, Albert. *Fateful Visions: Avoiding Nuclear Catastrophe.* Ballinger, 1988. 299p.

Eleven essays by political scientists and other experts on international relations which lay out "fateful visions," involving "the full range of publicly debated visions of a more desirable nuclear future" than an infinitely prolonged peace based on nuclear deterrence, which, however secure it seems at any given moment nevertheless contains all the ingredients necessary for global conflagration. Like the editors' previous book *Hawks, Doves, and Owls* (item 3-5), this collection stems from work done at the Avoiding Nuclear War Project at the Center for Science and International Affairs at Harvard's John F. Kennedy School of Government. Individual essays dwell on lower levels of nuclear weapons, implications of highly-accurate missiles, principles of no first use and disengagement, transformation of the U.S.-Soviet relationship to one of cooperation, and world government, among other topics. The editors' goal is to contribute to "lengthening the fuse and political evolution," the two steps they see as required to reduce the risks of war between the superpowers. Notes, index.

8-77 O'Heffernan, Patrick; Lovins, Amory B.; Lovins, L. Hunter. *The First Nuclear World War: A Strategy for Preventing Nuclear Wars and the Spread of Nuclear Weapons.* Morrow, 1983. 444p.

Opens with a scenario involving a limited but hideously destructive nuclear war between Khomeini's Iran and Saddam Hussein's Iraq, along with Pakistan, India, and terrorist detonations of 5-kiloton bombs in Southern California and Israel. It is a dramatic and credible setting of the stage for the authors' arguments in behalf of "the soft path to peace." The "soft path," as elucidated elsewhere by the Lovinses, calls for an energy policy based not on oil or nuclear sources but on renewable sources such as solar, along with global denuclearization. A useful book for readers exploring the links among the nuclear power industry, weapons proliferation, and nuclear terrorism. Notes, glossary, bibliography.

8-78 Paulson, Dennis, ed. *Voices of Survival in the Nuclear Age.* Capra Pr., 1986. 288p.

A great source of quotable quotes from prominent people in many walks of life whom editor Paulson questioned on their perceptions of and prescriptions for the nuclear menace. Politicians, surgeons, actors, writers, musicians and individuals representing numerous other professions offer their nuclear observations in one to two-page statements. Some of the statements, such as William F. Buckley, Jr.'s, are superficial and lazy, or superficial and hopeless, like psychiatrist Karl Menninger's, but many others are deeply-felt, thoughtful attempts to wrestle with nuclear issues. Given young people's keen interest in the doings of the famous, this book could prove of real utility in provoking discussion and independent thought in high-school classrooms. Illustrations.

8-79 Perry, Thomas L. and DeMille, Dianne. *Nuclear War: The Search for Solutions.* Physicians for Social Responsibility, British Columbia Chapter, 1985. 325p.

The twenty-one selections here, representing proceedings of a conference held at the University of British Columbia in October, 1984, dwell on questions of civil defense, nuclear winter, the psychiatric consequences of nuclear war, the human costs of the arms race, the Canadian role in making a peaceful future, and other issues. Contributors range from Canadian pediatricians to a retired admiral to Dr. Helen Caldicott. The devastating photographs of sick and starving children placed at the center of the book leave no doubt about the editors' position on the costs of the arms race, and the essays reinforce this position, whether in the mathematical formulas of nuclear weapon systems or in exhortations of the present as "a time to act." Notes.

8-80 *Piecing It Together: Feminism and Nonviolence.* Feminism and Nonviolence Study Group, 1983. 58p.

Eight women of the Feminism and Nonviolence Study Group address questions on the roles of women in the peace movement. Of particular interest is the link between violence suffered by individual women at the hands of men, and total war. "It has become clear to us that resistance to war and to the use of nuclear weapons is impossible without resistance to sexism, to racism, to imperialism and to violence as an everyday pervasive reality." Bibliography.

8-81 Porter, Kenneth, et al., eds. *Heal or Die: Psychotherapists Confront Nuclear Annihilation.* Psychohistory Pr., 1987. 132p.

A valuable book for practitioners and students in the

mental health fields, this collection of nine essays and case histories is presented in the activist spirit of psychological engagement suggested by the subtitle. Well-grounded in pertinent literature, and useful not only as a tool to help deal with clients' fears, but as a way for the therapist to come to grips with his or her own nuclear anxieties. Among the selections, Kenneth Porter writes on "The Role of the Psychotherapist in the Nuclear Age," Joanna Macy discusses "Buddhist Resources for Moving through Nuclear Death," and Lloyd deMause proposes a "Nuclear Tensions Monitoring Center." Notes.

8-82 Prins, Gwyn. *The Choice: Nuclear Weapons Versus Security*. Hogarth Pr., 1984. 251p.

Reflections on the lack of utility and counterproductive nature of nuclear weapons from a number of well-known observers, including McGeorge Bundy, John C. Polyani, Raymond L. Garthoff, and George Kennan, among others. Editor Prins tries to set the tone for the book in the introduction by parodying the famous slogans atop the Ministry of Truth in George Orwell's *1984*, but, where Orwell's slogans were ironic, Prins's are sincere: "Power does not equal security"; "Political power does not equal military power"' and "Military power does not equal nuclear weapons." Notes.

8-83 Regehr, Ernie and Rosenblum, Simon, eds. *Canada and the Nuclear Arms Race*. J. Lorimer, 1983. 268p.

Primarily the work of Canadian peace activists, this group of fifteen essays deals with Canada's part in the arms race and the Canadian peace movement. Included are the selections "What Would Happen to Canada in a Nuclear War?" and "Canada as a Nuclear-Weapons-Free Zone." Notes, index.

8-84 _____ and _____, eds. *The Road to Peace*. J. Lorimer, 1988. 206p.

The "preoccupation" of this book is "a reassessment of our continuing struggle with nuclear weapons." The eight contributors, including editors Regehr and Rosenblum, are Canadian activists and professionals in arms control and disarmament. They write on the evolution of nuclear war-fighting strategies, Canada's arms control and disarmament policies, the military use of space, European disarmament, and the prospects for Canada as a nuclear-weapon-free zone. Notes, index.

8-85 Robie, David. *Eyes of Fire: The Last Voyage of the Rainbow Warrior.* New Society, 1987. 168p.

Robie traveled with the *Rainbow Warrior* crew for several weeks until its fateful end as the ship sought to monitor, and interfere with, French nuclear testing. His is an acceptable account of the event, but shows the tracks of a hastily assembled job, along with an orientation toward a New Zealand readership that others may find something of an obstacle. Nevertheless, Robie's proximity to the crew and his geographical perspective on nuclear testing in the region lend the book an immediate authority. First published in 1986 by Lindon Publishing of New Zealand. Illustrated.

8-86 Rochon, Thomas R. *Mobilizing for Peace: The Antinuclear Movements in Western Europe.* Princeton Univ. Pr., 1988. 232p.

Rochon criticizes simplistic accusations of the "it's all a Communist plot" school that were levied against the European antinuclear movement in the early 1980s, as well as more sophisticated analyses made from social science perspectives concerning the movement's origins in political disaffection or in ambitions to change policies rather than institutions themselves. Far from being a tool of Moscow, Rochon contends that the movement embarrassed Soviet leadership, and even reached into Eastern Europe in potentially destabilizing fashion.

He argues further that in proposing that leaders
abolish the threat of nuclear war, the peace movement
demands "a change in the mentality of the political
leaders, nations, and alliances that control the
hardware." He examines the movements in Great
Britain, West Germany, the Netherlands, and France,
and covers such issues as the degree of realism in
movement demands, organization and tactics, and
alliances between the peace movement and major
political and social institutions. Based extensively on
interviews with movement members and on movement
literature. Rochon concludes by calling the peace
movement "particularly well suited to forcing an
examination of the assumptions of existing policy in
areas where that policy causes discontent among a
portion of the population." A worthy study of the
European anti-nuclear weapons movement, especially
when compared to such treatments as those of Werner
Kaltefleiter and Robert L. Pfaltzgraff. Notes, index.

8-87 Rotblat, Joseph and Pascolini, Alessandro, eds.
*The Arms Race at a Time of Decision: Annals of
Pugwash 1983.* St. Martin's, 1984. 291p.

The militarization of space, the strategic nuclear arms
race, problems of regional security, and security-
related Third World issues are the major topics in this
Pugwash volume. The book features the work of three
dozen authors representing the usual broad,
international diversity of Pugwash projects. A
significant book in that the meetings which led to its
contents took place in 1983, the year of the Reagan
"Star Wars" speech, and a time of deepening
pessimism toward the prospects for global war and
peace. The title of one essay by MIT physicist V.F.
Weisskopf indicates the tone of the times: "Avoiding
Nuclear War; There Is Still Hope for Hope." Notes,
index.

8-88 _____ and Valki, Laszlo, eds. *Coexistence,
Cooperation, and Common Security: Annals of Pugwash
1986.* St. Martin's, 1988. 349p.

Over two dozen papers presented at the Pugwash conference in Budapest in 1986, and one from a Pugwash Workshop held in West Germany that year. The contributions focus on the nuclear arms race, European security, the role of non-nuclear weapons states, reduction of East–West tensions through non-military means, and international economic relations. Contributors represent a wide range of academic disciplines and nationalities. As is almost always the case in conference proceedings, some papers are more exciting and better written than others, but the broad range of topics, from nuclear-weapon free zones in Europe to scientific and cultural cooperation should have something to offer most readers. Notes, index.

8–89 Rowe, Dorothy. *Living with the Bomb*. Routledge & Kegan Paul, 1985. 243p.

Rowe, who has also written on psychological depression, tries to describe what, in her view, is happening to the world, and how, facing possible extinction, members of the human community might overcome their individual fears and despair and work for positive change. Rowe takes into her scope not only the Bomb, but threats posed by international debt, overpopulation, and environmental problems as contributing to the end–of–the–world blues. Religious, philosophical, and social concerns underpin her message, which is positive ("We can choose to see ourselves as capable of change") but not altogether optimistic. Notes, index.

8–90 Russell, Diana E.H. *Exposing Nuclear Phallacies*. Pergamon 1989. 335p.

Dedicated "to all the women who are working to save us from a nuclear holocaust," this anthology offers 26 essays on the nuclear threat as perceived and responded to by women. "Feminist anti–nuclear work is as needed now as it ever was," writes the editor in her introduction. "Perhaps this book will help to inspire some women to engage in future efforts similar to the actions described here." Among such actions are those discussed by Helen Caldicott, President Emeritus of Physicians for Social Responsibility; Green politics authority Charlene Spretnak, who discusses cultural forces that lead to war; the editor herself, who writes on sexism, violence, and the "nuclear mentality," and Grace Paley, on the Women's Peace Encampment in Seneca, NY. A nice collection that will be welcomed by anyone investigating, or planning, women's peace and anti-nuclear actions. Includes a "Selected Bibliography on Feminism and the Nuclear Crisis." Index.

8–91 Schell, Jonathan. *The Abolition*. Knopf, 1984. 173p.

Schell follows his landmark book on nuclear war *The Fate of the Earth* (Knopf, 1982) with this study of "The Great Predicament" of a world full of nuclear weapons. He first discusses present attitudes toward the Bomb, "the totality of the peril" inherent in its domination, the most important aspects of the predicament. Critical features of the problem are the suddenness of its arrival, its "apparent everlastingness," and the Bomb's lodging at the center of international decision-making. Schell then puts forth "A Deliberate Policy" to remedy this unhappy nuclear status quo; he would arrange for the "abolition" of nuclear weapons through an international agreement to get rid of them, coupled with attention to the enhanced role of conventional weapons and understandings on possible nuclear rearmament. Schell's diagnosis of the problem is thoughtful, but his prescription for a cure seems out of touch with political reality, one more wishful attempt to dream up a neat fix for an extremely messy problem. Curiously, perhaps, Schell also advocates a strategic defensive capability to underpin a conventional deterrent. Index.

8–92 Schley, Jim, ed. *Writing in a Nuclear Age*. New England Review and Bread Loaf Quarterly, 1984. 239p. Dist. by Univ. Pr. of New England.

A collection of nearly fifty poems, essays and fiction in response to the nuclear threat. Many well-known writers contribute to the anthology, among them Galway Kinnell, Robert Penn Warren, Denise Levertov, David Ignatow, Louise Erdrich, and William Stafford. The level of quality is consistently high; one of the best collective literary efforts to confront the nuclear specter published in the last decade. A reprint of the summer, 1983 issue of *New England Review and Bread Loaf Quarterly*.

8-93 Sloan, Douglas, ed. *Education for Peace and Disarmament: Toward a Living World*. Teachers College Pr., 1983. 288p.

A good collection of two dozen essays addressing both present and past issues concerned with the nuclear threat and the way children are formally introduced to it, whether through the frightening and useless A-bomb raid classroom drills of the 1950s (described by Michael J. Carey) or through more thoughtful and productive approaches to nuclear education. The book first appeared as a special issue of *Teachers College Record* (84, no. 1, fall 1982). It includes contributions by psychologists, sociologists, political scientists, and other scholars and activists, among them authors from Great Britain, Israel, and Romania. The variety of topics and the book's still-timely nature make it worthwhile. Notes, index.

8-94 Speiser, Stuart M. *How to End the Nuclear Nightmare*. North River Pr., 1984. 290p.

The author's lack of faith in all previous approaches to defusing the nuclear threat led him to devise his own plan, which he calls "SuperStock," a system of "universal capitalism" whereby everyone (literally) in the U.S. would own a significant amount of stock in the 2,000 strongest American corporations; this would, in Speiser's opinion, neutralize the conflict inherent in Marxist-capitalist ideology. With the Soviet Union reeling and stumbling toward something resembling a market economy, and with the evident likelihood that for the foreseeable future Soviet nuclear weapons are going to remain generally in place regardless of the economy they guard or threaten, economically-based "solutions" to the threat of nuclear war seem unpromising. Speiser scores some points for enthusiasm and initiative, but his grand scheme smacks more of self-convinced hope than of enlightened insight. Index.

8-95 Storner, Torben, et al., eds. *Peace and the Future: Proceedings of the II International Peace University, Aarhus, October 1985*. Aarhus Univ. Pr., 1986. 267p.

Something like a preface or introduction would have been agreeable here, but we're launched straight into the sixteen selections in this proceedings volume without a word of orientation; nor is there any editorial conclusion or summary. In spite of these oversights, the pieces under consideration will have some use because of the international perspectives of the contributing scholars, who hail from Denmark, Germany, Norway, Hungary, Canada and other nations. They offer a potpourri of articles, ranging from the subject of nuclear-weapon-free zones to a psychoanalytic examination of "narcissistic ideas of defense." Three of the articles are in German. By far the longest piece is Wilfried Bach's "Nuclear Winter: Climatic Effects of a Nuclear War," at close to 70 pages. Notes.

8-96 Sweeney, Duane, ed. *The Peace Catalog*. Press for Peace, 1984. 360p.

A good anthology culling essays and articles from a wide variety of books and journals. Contributors include physicians, scientists, poets, and peace activists, and the range of topics moves from examination of national intentions and personal feelings to education, childraising, nonviolent action, and individual empowerment. The frequent use of quotations from both prominent historical and contemporary figures is handled well. A 53-page directory of over 1,000 peace groups will be badly dated by now, but most of the volume's other material holds up well.

8-97 Taylor, Richard. *Against the Bomb: The British Peace Movement, 1958-1965.* Oxford Univ. Pr., 1988. 368p.

Based on the author's Ph.D. thesis, *Against the Bomb* is one of the most comprehensive histories of the Campaign for Nuclear Disarmament, the first mass anti-nuclear movement. Taylor focuses on the ideological composition and orientations of the main strands within the movement. The first part of the book covers the mainstream of CND; the second the Direct Action Committee and the Committee of 100, the most radical wing of the movement; the third turns to the socialist dimension of the movement. Taylor argues that the CND "acted primarily as a foundation and a catalyst for subsequent movements. It changed the face of radical politics in Britain; but it left the fundamental problems unresolved." Bibliography, index.

8-98 _____ and Pritchard, Colin. *The Protest Makers: The British Disarmament Movement of 1958-1965 Twenty Years On.* Pergamon, 1980. 190p.

A socio-political study of the movement, with a primary concentration on the Campaign for Nuclear Disarmament. The analysis takes into account the movement's nature and purposes, its ideological divisions, and the reasons for its decline (a decline rapidly and dramatically reversed following this study's publication, thanks to the heightened anxiety over nuclear war that commenced with the Reagan administration's arms buildup, and especially with the introduction of cruise and Pershing II missiles to Western Europe). Based on a questionnaire completed by some 400 activists, along with in-depth interviews with over 20 movement leaders. A major source of information on the movement. Bibliography, index.

8-99 _____ and Young, Nigel, eds. *Campaigns for Peace: British Peace Movements in the Twentieth Century*. Manchester Univ. Pr., 1987. 308p. Dist. by St. Martin's.

The history of Great Britain's Campaign for Nuclear Disarmament receives a chapter in this overall study of the British peace movement, as do the churches, the nuclear arms race and the women's roles in the movement. A final chapter examines Britain and the international peace movement in the 1980s. The dozen essays in the book are the work of eight authors with considerable backgrounds, both scholarly and direct, in the peace movement. Notes, index.

8-100 Thompson, Dorothy, ed. *Over Our Dead Bodies: Women Against the Bomb*. Virago, 1983.

British historian Thompson has brought together nineteen selections by women involved in the peace movement. The contributors include historians, novelists, poets, and peace campers who offer both personal statements and examinations of specific problems such as civil defense and the arms race. All but two of the selections—both poems—were written for the book. Illustrates the intensity of concern prevailing in the peace movement in the early 1980s. Bibliography.

8-101 Turner, Paul R. and Pitt, David, eds. *The Anthropology of War & Peace: Perspectives on the Nuclear Age*. Bergin & Garvey, 1989. 208p.

A dozen essays, chiefly by American anthropologists, on anthropological aspects of the Cold War and the nuclear threat. The consensus in the book is that "the differences between the great power blocs are more apparent than real," writes editor Pitt in his introduction. "What divides the world may be essentially cultural and ritual factors which have little relationship to any rational political or social doctrine." The anthropological point of view holds that human action depends far less on superficially stated attitudes, and much more "on frames of mind which are deeply embedded in cultural traits, in language, and, particularly, in ritual." The first five essays dwell on this phenomenon, addressing such ideas as the inducement to military participation in tribal societies, "witchcraft and the Cold War," and the perceptions and values of U.S. military elites. An interesting collection that might have been improved with contributions from some foreign authorities. Bibliography, index.

8–102 Warner, Gale and Shuman, Michael. *Citizen Diplomats: Pathfinders in Soviet-American Relations and How You Can Join Them*. Continuum, 1987. 379p. Dist. by Harper.

One of the most interesting aspects of U.S.-Soviet relations, especially in their too-frequent troughs of hostility and mutual incomprehension, has been the work of "citizen diplomats." These are private citizens who engage in something of an end-run around the obstacles of officialdom to make direct, constructive contacts with "the other side." In this engaging book, the authors present the stories of a variety of these internationally-minded individuals, including the late Armand Hammer, Norman Cousins, Dr. Bernard Lown, nurse Sharon Tennison, and others who have acted on the belief that establishing person-to-person relations is a meaningful contribution to the peace effort. Includes a section on how to participate in such activities in a wide variety of interest areas.

8–103 *We Are Ordinary Women: A Chronicle of the Puget Sound Women's Peace Camp*. Seal Pr., 1985. 115p.

In June of 1983, a group of women embarked on a peace encampment near the Boeing cruise missile factory in Kent, WA. It became known as the Puget

Sound Women's Peace Camp, and joined other such encampments as Greenham Common, England, and the Seneca Women's Encampment in New York in protesting the cruise and Pershing II missiles. This book collects photos, poems, journal entries, and other material concerned with the encampment, with an emphasis on feminist perspectives. "There are no monsters," writes one woman. "Just mistaken people."

8-104 White, Ralph K., ed. *Psychology and the Prevention of Nuclear War: A Book of Readings*. New York Univ. Pr., 1986. 591p.

Close to three dozen contributions, most reprinted or excerpted from other publications, from as many authors examine a large number of war and peace issues in which the role of psychology is significant. Topics range from the personalities of those who control the weapons to nuclear strategy and the effects of living under the nuclear threat. The largest part of the collection, which features work by such diverse writers as Erich Fromm, Charles Osgood, Elise Boulding, Robert Jay Lifton, and Jerome D. Frank, focuses on the present nuclear situation and basic psychological processes related to war. The final part deals with war prevention through negotiations, modification of war-related attitudes, and peace education. Would make a good collection of readings for an undergraduate course. Notes, bibliography, index.

8-105 Wittner, Lawrence S. *Rebels Against War: The American Peace Movement, 1933-1983*. Rev. ed. Temple Univ. Pr., 1984. 364p.

The first edition of this work carried the history of American pacifism from 1941 to 1960; this revision brings the coverage more up-to-date, although the period since 1960 does not receive as detailed attention as the earlier time. The book is a persuasive portrait of pacifists as energetic activists rather than as passive objectors to the distress of war. Includes

attention to nuclear pacifism, in which Wittner shows
that the vitality of the peace movement has been
closely connected to nuclear issues, among them the
original use of the Bomb, nuclear testing, and the
freeze movement. Bibliography, index.

CHAPTER 9

Periodical Guide

This guide focuses on journals, magazines and newsletters with primary or significant emphases on nuclear weapons and peace issues. Most general journals of political science have been omitted from the list, but readers will want to remain alert to the pertinent work that appears from time to time in such titles as *Foreign Affairs*, *Foreign Policy*, *World Politics*, *Orbis*, and many others emphasizing international relations.

Also omitted are numerous periodicals concerned with peace whose publishers did not respond to requests for information or sample copies. Given the shoestring budget supporting many grassroots titles, and the burden faced by editors who are working for love rather than money, the occasional lack of responses is disappointing but not too surprising. It is the nature of the activist press to attempt to do too much with too little in too short a time; great hopes frequently founder on the hard rocks of time and financial demands.

A number of periodicals emanating from the military-industrial complex, and from its attendant observers, have been included. Peace activists too often overlook these materials, which provide useful information on how the "other side" conducts its business; these items will help fill in some informational hollows.

Many newsletter and small-magazine editors, as well as some scholarly journal editors, did respond to requests for information; their cooperation made a real difference in the periodical guide's inclusiveness.

Subscription prices and dates of first publication are noted when ascertained. If there are two subscription costs, the first is for individuals, the second for institutions. Given today's rapid changes in periodical prices, the figures listed here cannot be expected to prevail for long.

When identified as covered by indexing or abstracting services, one or two of the most commonly found such tools are noted.

To facilitate quick identification of individual periodicals, the list is alphabetical by title. A guide by type of publication follows. There is a good deal of overlap of subject coverage in many of these titles; this division, then, is merely for the sake of general orientation.

Arms Control & Disarmament:

Arms Control Today, Arms Control Reporter, Barometer, Bulletin of the Atomic Scientists, Civilian-Based Defense, Council for a Livable World Newsletter, Disarmament: A Periodic Review, LAWS Quarterly, Nuclear Times, PSR Quarterly, Space and Security News

General Titles with Peace and Nuclear Issues Focuses:

Adelphi Papers, Amicus Journal, CPSR Newsletter, F.A.S. Public Interest Report, Greenpeace Magazine, International Atomic Energy Agency Bulletin, Meiklejohn Civil Liberties Institute PeaceNet Bulletin, New Outlook, Nucleus, On Beyond War, Pacific News Bulletin, Positive Alternatives

Grassroots:

Atomic Dispatch, CEASE News, ENDpapers, Fellowship, INFACT, National Association of Radiation Survivors, Nonviolent Activist, Nuclear Resister, Nukewatch Pathfinder, The Objector, PSR Reports, Peace and Freedom, Peace Brigades International Project Newsletters, Peace Conversion Times, Peace Magazine, Psychologists for Social Responsibility Newsletter, Reporter for Conscience' Sake, Surviving Together,

Test Banner, WAND Bulletin, World Peace News

Military and Strategic:

Air Force Magazine, Airpower Journal, Armed Forces and Society, Comparative Strategy, Defense Analysis, Global Affairs, International Security, Jane's Defence Weekly, Journal of Strategic Studies, National Defense, RECON, Research Report of the Council on Economic Priorities, Strategic Review

Peace, Scholarly:

Current Research on Peace and Violence, Conflict Management and Peace Science, Bulletin of Peace Proposals, International Journal on World Peace, Journal of Conflict Resolution, Journal of Peace Research, Peace and Change, Peace and the Sciences, Survival

Religious:

The Advocate, Briefly, Desert Voices, Episcopal Peace Fellowship Newsletter, Ground Zero, Pastoral Care Network for Social Responsibility Newsletter, Pax Christi USA, Peace Office Newsletter, World Peacemaker Quarterly

Indexing and Abstracting Services:

Air University Library Index to Military Periodicals, Peace Research Abstracts Journal

9–1 *Adelphi Papers*. Edited by Col. Michael Dewar. International Institute for Strategic Studies, 23 Tavistock St., London, WC2E 7NQ, England. Irreg. $9.25 ea. 1964–.

This title takes a scholarly, monographic approach, with each issue the work of a single author. In a typical issue of some 70 pages, the author investigates in detail a contemporary problem or question. Recent issues have featured Jeanette Voas's "Soviet Attitudes

towards Ballistic Missile Defence and the ABM Treaty,"
Yezid Sayigh's essay on security in the developing
countries, and Mahnaz Ispahani's discussion of
insecurity in Pakistan.

Some libraries treat the title as a periodical; others,
noting the unique qualities of each issue, treat the
monographs as books. Either way, the *Adelphi Papers*,
with its wide scope and variety of contributors and
its concise yet thorough examination of single issues,
is not to be overlooked by any library planning to
offer a significant collection on peace and nuclear
issues.

9–2 *The Advocate*. Edited by Kathleen Hayes.
Evangelicals for Social Action, 10 Lancaster Ave.,
Wynnewood, PA 19096. Monthly. $20 (membership).
1988–.

A nicely–designed 16–page newsletter including
attention to nuclear issues within its broad embrace of
topics concerned with peace and justice. Describes its
mission as seeking "to contribute to the development
of social awareness and a consistently pro–life social
ethic in the American Christian evangelical community,
in order to, in the words of our slogan, 'promote
shalom in public life.'" Each issue contains a feature
article on an important public policy matter, federal
legislative updates, news on developments abroad, and
other organizational information.

9–3 *Air Force Magazine*. Edited by John T. Correll. Air
Force Association, 1501 Lee Hwy., Arlington, VA 22209.
Monthly. $21. 1942–. Indexed: *America: History and
Life*, *Historical Abstracts*, etc.

A slick organ devoting its approximately 100–page
issues to advocacy of U.S. airpower and allied
industries, *AFM* includes frequent articles on nuclear
topics. The October, 1990 number, for example,
contains a feature speculating on nuclear weapons
falling "into the wrong hands" as a result of Soviet

ethnic unrest, along with a piece on future options
for the U.S. strategic arsenal. Contributors are chiefly
journalists and retired military figures. A good source
of information on new aircraft and Air Force
establishment points of view. Some interesting
historical articles. Up to a dozen brief reviews of
books and occasionally videos.

9–4 *Air University Library Index to Military
Periodicals.*
Edited by Emily J. Adams. Air University Library,
Maxwell AFB, AL 36112–5564. Quarterly; cumulated
annually. 1949–. Free to libraries.

A subject index to approximately 80 English–language
military and aeronautical periodicals. Includes citations
to nuclear warfare and nuclear weapons, SDI, missiles,
strategy, and other pertinent topics. The substantial
book review index could be helpful in locating reviews
not indexed in other sources, and in identifying the
books themselves. A single issue runs to approximately
160 pages; publication lags a year or so behind the
period being indexed. Was *Air University Periodical
Index* until 1962.

9–5 *Airpower Journal.* Edited by Col. Keith W. Geiger.
Air University, Maxwell AFB, AL 36112. Quarterly.
$9.50. 1947–. (U.S. federal depository serial D
301.26/24:2/4). Indexed: *Historical Abstracts, PAIS*, etc.

The professional journal of the U.S. Air Force, *AJ* "is
designed to serve as an open forum for presenting
and stimulating innovative thinking on military
doctrine, strategy, tactics, force structure, readiness,
and other national defense matters." Nuclear–theme
articles are common, but by no means the journal's
dominant feature, which is one focusing on the
operational level of war, from runway requirements to
the psychology of air combat. Articles of the nuclear
genre have dealt with strategic defense, deterrence,
and nuclear strategy. Authors are primarily U.S.
military officers, although the occasional civilian turns

up. Articles are scholarly. A plus is the "Net Assessment" book review section, with up to a dozen or so in-depth reviews of books on military topics. U.S. Depository libraries should surely subscribe, and, at the low price, other libraries and individuals will receive a nicely-produced, well-illustrated magazine.

9-6 *The Amicus Journal.* Edited by Francesca Lyman. Natural Resources Defense Council, 40 W. 20th St., New York, NY 10011. Quarterly. $10/$8. 1979–. Indexed: *Alternative Press Index.*

An attractive and skillfully produced magazine, *The Amicus Journal* is the award-winning journalistic arm of the Natural Resources Defense Council. The editorial focus is on environmental policy at the national and global levels. Not a top choice for collections concerning nuclear weapons or the peace movement, but one does find occasional substantial coverage of nuclear issues, such as Dick Russell's major article on radioactive pollution at U.S. nuclear weapons plants in the fall, 1990 number. A fine addition to libraries because of its broad environmental scope and its good writing, much of it by freelancers. Each issue features a handful of lengthy book reviews.

9-7 *Armed Forces and Society.* Edited by Claude Welch, Jr. Seven Locks Pr., Inc., Box 27, Cabin John, MD 20818. Quarterly. $40. 1974–. Indexed: *PAIS, Social Sciences Index,* etc.

The scope here is very broad, as the subtitle of this scholarly publication indicates: "An Interdisciplinary Journal on Military Institutions, Civil-Military Relations, Arms Control and Peacemaking, and Conflict Management." Within that broad editorial expanse, there is room in most issues for the article on nuclear topics—"The Case for Mobile Missiles," for example, or another piece on extended deterrence and nuclear escalation. Authors are generally political scientists, with sociologists and military officers. They represent diverse nationalities. Book reviews are meaty but late.

9–8 *The Arms Control Reporter: A Chronicle of Treaties, Negotiations, Proposals.* Institute for Defense & Disarmament Studies, 2001 Beacon St., Brookline, MA 02146. Monthly. $325 libraries/$500 profit–making institutions. 1982–.

A useful if, for all but serious research facilities, prohibitively costly looseleaf service providing up–to–date information on the status of arms control negotiations, the positions of governments, the record of events leading to the current situation, and an update on weapons involved in negotiations. Each supplement contains 100–160 pages. The binder arranges material by topic; the 1991 cumulation, e.g., covers close to 40 arms negotiation areas, including short–range nuclear forces, nuclear–weapon–free zones, the Non–Proliferation Treaty, and missile proliferation. Although full of valuable information, the title's cost will inevitably keep it out of the hands of many researchers.

9–9 *Arms Control Today.* Edited by Matthew Bunn. Arms Control Association, 11 Dupont Circle NW, Washington, DC 20036. Monthly except two bimonthly issues, Jan./Feb. and July/Aug. $25/$30. 1972–. Indexed: *PAIS*, etc.

The Arms Control Association, a national membership organization, "seeks to create broad public appreciation of the need for positive steps toward the limitation of armaments and the implementation of other measures to reduce international tensions and promote world peace." Its journal is essential for any serious collection on nuclear weapons and strategic issues in general; *ACT's* typical 40–page issue contains interviews with influential figures, informed articles on such topics as nuclear proliferation, verification, movement toward a comprehensive test ban, strategic defense, etc. The regular departments "News Briefs" and "Factfile" afford quick access to developments in or affecting arms control. One of the most valuable points for the researcher is "Arms Control in Print," a timely, two–page bibliography identifying books, pamphlets, government documents, and articles in various categories. One or two long book reviews per issue allow reviewers to address the topic at hand as well as the books under consideration. Contributors are prominent, and varied in their viewpoints.

9–10 *Atomic Dispatch.* Alliance of Atomic Veterans, P.O. Box 32, Topock, AZ 86436. Quarterly (as funds permit). $20. 1987–.

Director Anthony Guarisco, himself an apparent victim of radiation–induced illness from nuclear testing in the South Pacific, describes the Alliance of Atomic Veterans as "a group of veterans who survived the Japanese, Korea and Vietnam wars only to fall victim of our own U.S. military and the U.S. military industrial complex (war contractors for profits.) Indeed atomic veterans are the 'human face of the nuclear arms race.'" He further describes atomic veterans as "the sacrificial lamb—laid on the altar of the atomic age for the development of nuclear weapons which now hold each of us hostage."

A down–home, grassroots newsletter of the movement to obtain justice for nuclear test victims, *Atomic Dispatch* in its 12 pages discusses news, legislation, historical analysis, and other matters concerning the interests of these atomic veterans. The newsletter's interests transcend simple self–service: in its pages there is a clear statement of a perceived need to reevaluate the way the nation, and the world, go about military business.

9–11 *Barometer.* Edited by Tariq Rauf. Canadian Centre for Arms Control and Disarmament, 151 Slater St., Suite 710, Ottawa, Ontario, Canada K1P 5H3. Quarterly. $30/$45. 1990–.

The Canadian Centre for Arms Control and Disarmament was established in 1983 to encourage informed debate and to provide independent, non-partisan research and information on arms control and disarmament. *Barometer*, although subsidized to some extent by the government, maintains an independent editorial position. An 8–page tabloid printed on quality paper, the paper's emphasis is on Canadian involvement in global issues of arms control and disarmament. 1990 issues contained articles on nuclear testing in the Arctic, IAEA safeguards, trends in the arms trade, Canadian and Soviet cooperation initiatives, and other topics. Occasional book reviews.

9–12 *Briefly*. Edited by Nancy Lee Head. Presbyterian Peace Fellowship, Box 271, Nyack, NY 10960. Quarterly. $25 (membership). 1944–.

A newsletter designed to inform Presbyterian Church members of peacemaking ideas, activities, resources and backgrounds. In its 8 pages, it covers issues on peace in general, including attention to nuclear matters such as the General Electric boycott led by INFACT and nuclear weapons facility investigations. Features notes on resources and kindred organizations. Occasional book reviews.

9–13 *Bulletin of Peace Proposals*. Edited by Magne Barth. Sage Publications, P.O. Box 5096, Newbury Park, CA 91359. Quarterly. $37/$83. 1970–. Indexed: *Historical Abstracts, PAIS*, etc.

Recent issues of this scholarly journal have addressed such topics as religion and armed conflict, the alleged obsolescence of major war between developed countries, international environmental cooperation, current change in Europe, and the arms industry, technology, and democracy in Brazil. It includes the occasional article on nuclear and related issues, such as Sven Hellman's "The Risks of Accidental Nuclear War" in the March, 1990 issue. Authors are an international lot, including those from the U.S., Western and Eastern Europe, Latin America, Africa, Canada, and elsewhere. The journal's motto is "To motivate research, to inspire future oriented thinking, to promote activities for peace." It concentrates on

international policy in the light of general peace
research theory. Perhaps a bit intimidating for
undergraduates and the public at large.

9-14 *Bulletin of the Atomic Scientists.* Edited by Len
Ackland. Educational Foundation for Nuclear Science,
6042 S. Kimbark Ave., Chicago, IL 60637. 10/year. $30.
1945-. Indexed: *General Science Index, Historical
Abstracts,* etc.

The *BAS* debuted in December, 1945. Home of the
famous "Doomsday Clock" logo indicating its editors'
estimation of humanity's proximity to nuclear
annihilation, the magazine is rather more optimistic
about the future than it was a few years ago, or even
at its inception when it warned of atomic catastrophe
being "inevitable if we do not succeed in banishing
war from the world." In its 45th anniversary issue,
editor Ackland wrote, "The race to nuclear destruction
between the world's two military behemoths has been
reversed and the opportunity exists to dismantle the
dangerous Cold War arsenals and superstructures."

If that reversal has taken place, *BAS* can claim as
much credit as any periodical. Throughout its history
it has been at the forefront of "responsible" (i.e.,
professional, expert) forums for addressing the many
and intricate aspects of the nuclear threat.
Proliferation, testing, the arms race, nuclear weapon
facility problems, and many other nuclear issues come
into its scope. With articles by recognized authorities,
a lively format with good illustrations and good book
reviews, *BAS* is a must for all libraries.

9-15 *CPSR Newsletter.* Edited by Gary Chapman.
Computer Professionals for Social Responsibility, P.O.
Box 717, Palo Alto, CA 94302. Quarterly. $50. 1983-.

This newsletter, a desktop-published 30-page
magazine, turns its attention generally to the socially
responsible uses of computers, and has recently
covered such issues as telephone privacy and how

computers contribute to the ecological crisis. It has also published many articles in its history on nuclear war and related topics, including nuclear education, strategy, computer unreliability and nuclear war, SDI, and other topics. Articles contain references, but the style is accessible to the average educated reader; one need not be a computer scientist—or even use a computer—to make sense of it. Recently CPSR called for an end to the "Star Wars" program, and published a response to that call by the Strategic Defense Information Office. Given the importance of computers in contemporary weaponry and defense systems, this newsletter is worth the attention of anyone concerned about the relationship of high technology to war and peace.

9–16 *CEASE News.* Edited by Peggy Schirmer. Concerned Educators Allied for a Safe Environment, 17 Gerry St., Cambridge, MA 02138. 3/year. $5. 1982–.

CEASE is a national network of parents, teachers and other young children's advocates concerned about the dangers of violence, pollution, nuclear power, nuclear war, and a global military budget that drains resources from programs designed to help children and their families. *CEASE News* is a modest but neatly-produced little newsletter reporting organizational activities, and featuring brief articles on various facets of the peace movement. Recent issues have offered articles on the children of Hiroshima, war toys in the classroom, and the Middle East crisis. Includes some book and audiovisual reviews of materials intended either for children or for their adult teachers and guides.

9–17 *Civilian–Based Defense: News & Opinion.* Edited by Melvin G. Beckman, Philip Bogdonoff, and Robert Holmes. P.O. Box 31616, Omaha, NE 68131. 6/year. $15. 1982–.

Intended as a source of information on non–violent civilian–based defense as an alternative policy for national defense, and to provide a vehicle for the exchange of international news, opinion and research on CBD. The newsletter features some interesting articles by international contributors on CBD, a form of "defense" which has been discussed for many decades, and which was reintroduced in the 1950s by such figures as Sir Stephen King–Hall (*Defence in the Nuclear Age*, Fellowship of Reconciliation, 1961), who proposed CBD as the best way to oppose Soviet expansion. The most recent issue focused on the relationship between CBD and the "Velvet Revolutions" that took place in Eastern Europe (some of which, of course, were more velvety than others). Resource notes and occasional substantial book reviews heighten the title's utility. Something of a hybrid between a grassroots and scholarly effort; the spirit is of the former, but the academic qualifications of many contributors lend it an air of the latter.

9–18 *Comparative Strategy*. Edited by Richard B. Foster. Taylor & Francis, 1900 Frost Rd., Ste. 101, Bristol, PA 19007. Quarterly. $89. 1978–. Indexed: *International Political Science Abstracts*, *PAIS*, etc.

Devoted chiefly to American strategic thought "and the influence of history and ideas on the strategic interaction between the free world and the Soviet Union." The editors' division of the world into "free" and "the Soviet Union" says a good deal about the journal's ideological underpinnings, but the range of topics addressed is broad, including nuclear deterrence and nuclear war, arms control, Soviet strategy, military organizations, examination of "great strategists of the past," and many other issues.

It is a scholarly journal; articles are fully–equipped with the standard research paraphernalia, from abstracts to end notes. Contributors are international. A recent issue contained articles by scholars from such varied places as the Hebrew University of Jerusalem and the U.S. Air Force, and on topics as diverse as a comparison of the classic strategists Clausewitz and Sun Tzu, and the relationship between strategic defense and arms control. Few book reviews.

9-19 *Conflict Management and Peace Science.* Edited by Walter Isard. Peace Science Society (International), Dept. of Political Science, SUNY Binghamton, Binghamton NY 13901. Irreg. $20. 1974-. Indexed: *America: History & Life, PAIS,* etc.

It may not publish more than one issue in a year, but this journal nevertheless contributes some worthwhile points of view on nuclear war and peace. This scholarly title has featured articles on long-term effects of nuclear weapons, the high-technology arms race, and the relationship between trade and conflict. For advanced students and scholars; others will be frequently stymied by mathematical formulae in the articles. Contributors are almost exclusively U.S. scholars.

9-20 *Council for a Livable World Newsletter.* Council for a Livable World, 100 Maryland Ave. NE, Washington, DC 20002. Irreg.; free. 198?-.

Although in the words of Council office manager Chris Peterson, "This newsletter is published with no regularity whatsoever," it remains of interest when it does appear. The Council works in behalf of establishing a majority in the U.S. Senate supporting nuclear disarmament and "a big cut in the military budget." The 4-page newsletter contains updates on the current state of that budget, the status of weapons programs, arms control agreements, and other topics. The Council also publishes irregular "Fact Sheets," also free, on specific weapons and military issues, and operates a "Nuclear Arms Control Hotline" (202-543-0006), a 3-minute taped message.

9-21 *Current Research on Peace and Violence.* Edited by Pertti Joenniemi. Tampere Peace Research Institute, Hameenkatu 13 b A, P.O. Box 447, SF-33101, Tampere, Finland. Quarterly. $40. 1971-. Indexed: *Sociological*

Abstracts, Social Science Citation Index, etc.

An interdisciplinary scholarly journal which publishes articles on a wide variety of topics in its 60–70 pages. Recent issues have featured articles on the U.N. and nuclear disarmament, Soviet military doctrine, "peace research as critical research," and other issues. A diversity of viewpoints and contributors, from Scandinavia, North America, Great Britain, and elsewhere, gives the journal appeal to peace activists, scholars and students.

9–22 *Defense Analysis.* Edited by Martin Edmonds. Pergamon Press Journals Div., Maxwell House, Fairview Park, Elmsford, NY 10523. Quarterly. $100. 1985–. Indexed: *Current Contents.*

Published in London, *DA* emphasizes scholarly attention to defense theory. It contains both refereed articles and commissioned works selected by the editors. Each 100+ page issue features approximately five major articles. Recent issues have offered studies of strategic arms control, French nuclear command and control, and NATO security policy. Authors are political scientists, "think tank" representatives (e.g., from the Rand Corporation and the Hudson Institute), sociologists, and other academics. The editors try to provide space for various perspectives from different nations, including the U.K., the U.S., and Europe. Each issue offers a half-dozen or so book reviews, most a good page long.

9–23 *Desert Voices.* Nevada Desert Experience, P.O. Box 4487, Las Vegas, NV 89127. Quarterly. Free (donations welcome). 1988–.

The Nevada Desert Experience describes itself as "a faith-based organization with Franciscan origins working to end nuclear weapons testing through a campaign of prayer, dialog, and nonviolent direct action." Organized in 1984, the Experience conducts prayer vigils at the Nevada Test Site, and sponsors annual commemorations of Hiroshima and Nagasaki in August. "NDE is a voice in the desert calling people of faith to nonviolence in the face of violence, truth in the face of illusion, hope in the face of despair, love in the face of fear." The 6-page newsletter features articles on the comprehensive test ban issue, organizational news, and notes on activities of kindred groups. Occasional book reviews.

9-24 *Disarmament: A Periodic Review by the United Nations.* Edited by Lucy Webster. United Nations Dept. of Disarmament Affairs. Publications Sales Office, Rm. DC2-853, New York, NY 10017. Quarterly. $18. 1978-. Indexed: *PAIS*, etc.

Disarmament is intended to serve as a source of information and a forum for ideas concerning the activities of the United Nations and the wider international community with regard to arms limitation and disarmament issues. The periodical is issued in English, French, Russian and Spanish editions. As one might expect, the breadth of subjects covered is extensive and its contributors international. Recent issues have offered articles on economic conversion in the U.S.S.R., coverage of the Non-Proliferation Treaty Review Conference that took place in the fall of 1990, tactical nuclear weapons, international arms transfers, and other significant topics. Contributors come to their tasks with well-informed backgrounds in the issues. The majority of the articles contain references to other literature. From 20-30 brief book reviews, a list of publications received, recent documents on disarmament, and a chronology of disarmament activities round out each issue. At the price, *Disarmament* is an economical and desirable addition to most libraries.

9-25 *ENDpapers.* Edited by Ken Coates. Bertrand Russell Peace Foundation, Bertrand Russell House, Gamble St., Nottingham NG7 4ET England. 3/year. $35. 1982-.

Features approximately a half-dozen articles in each of its 100–150 page issues. Topics are diverse, recently including commentary on the political changes in Europe, military conversion in the Soviet Union, the global arms trade, the impact of military technology, and environmental issues. Contributors are international, including those from the U.S. and the Soviet Union. Articles may be original or reprints, from such disparate sources as *Parade* and the Soviet journal *International Affairs*. Some articles are scholarly, some journalistic and some opinion pieces. A few lengthy book reviews in each issue. Worth a look when available, but not a priority item for U.S. libraries.

9–26 *Episcopal Peace Fellowship Newsletter.* Edited by Dana S. Grubb. P.O. Box 28156, Washington, DC 20038. Quarterly. $25 (membership). ca. 1965–.

Primarily for the encouragement and information of EPF members and friends, and to keep bishops, church press and others informed of organizational activities and objectives. The Episcopal Church has been an active peace and anti-nuclear weapons advocate for some time; Episcopalians seeking connections with other Church members will find this newsletter helpful.

9–27 *F.A.S. Public Interest Report.* Edited by Jeremy J. Stone and Steven Aftergood. Federation of American Scientists, 307 Massachusetts Ave. NE, Washington DC 20002. 6/year. $25/$50. 1970–.

The journal of the Federation of American Scientists, founded in 1945 by Manhattan Project scientists to promote the peaceful and humane uses of science and technology. Describes itself "as a means to disseminate the research and analysis produced by various projects of the F.A.S. Fund (educational and research arm of the Federation) which deal primarily in the areas of nuclear proliferation, chemical/biological weapons, international scientific exchange, disarmament verification and the environmental and political implications of the U.S. space policy." Occasional book reviews.

9–28 *Fellowship.* Edited by Virginia Baron. Fellowship of Reconciliation, 523 N. Broadway, Box 271, Nyack, NY 10960. 8/year. $15. 1934–. Indexed: *PAIS*, etc.

Contains peace movement news from around the world, news of Fellowship activities, personal accounts of peace activists (such as Joseph J. Fahey's "From Bluejacket to Pacifist" in the March, '91 issue), analysis of military events, as well as discussion of more subtle forms of violence, such as homelessness and war toys. Includes approximately a half–dozen book reviews in each issue, ranging from one or two paragraphs to several hundred words.

9–29 *Global Affairs.* Edited by Charles M. Lichenstein. International Security Council, 1155 Fifteenth St. NW, Suite 502, Washington, DC 20005. Quarterly. $24. 1986–.

The goal of *Global Affairs* is to provide "a forum for responsible and expert views on international security affairs." The journal's 4–10 articles per issue include such pieces as Alexander Webster's "Evaluating the Neutron Bomb" and William R. Van Cleave's "The U.S.-Soviet Military Balance and Arms Control," both in Spring, 1989. The title relies heavily on points of view from the right; contributors frequently represent such conservative bastions as the American Enterprise Institute and the Heritage Foundation. Articles are generally supported with scholarly equipment, but sometimes are not, and thus are reduced to the status of opinion pieces. Contains 4–5 long book reviews and a number of shorter notices. For libraries seeking a vehicle of conservative views.

9–30 *Greenpeace Magazine.* Edited by Andre Carothers. 1436 U St., NW, Washington DC 20009. 6/year. $20. 1981–. Indexed: *Alternative Press Index.*

Next to the Sierra Club, Greenpeace is probably the world's best-known environmental organization. Its magazine is one of the leading journals of environmental activism, providing coverage on a broad range of issues. One of the organization's persistent interests has been pollution from nuclear weapons and nuclear power operations; its ship, the "Rainbow Warrior," was the target of a lethal terrorist bombing by French government functionaries in New Zealand. Among the articles in the magazine, one finds frequent pieces on nuclear topics. Early 1991 issues, for example, featured a devastating account of the aftermath of the Chernobyl disaster ("The Children of Chernobyl"), and a report on Greenpeace actions in the Soviet nuclear weapons test territory in the Berents Sea. Another 1991 article focused on French nuclear testing at Moruroa. A highly desirable addition to any library's peace and environmental offerings.

9–31 *Ground Zero.* Ground Zero Center for Nonviolent Action, 16159 Clear Creek Rd. NW, Poulsbo, WA 98370. Quarterly. Donation.

The root of *Ground Zero's* orientation is secured in the tradition of Christian nonviolence, but, as the "Dear Gandhi" letters column suggests, the point of view is anything but narrowly sectarian, and not without a sense of humor. The 12-page tabloid dwells on peace issues at large, from testimonies to the power of prayer to sustain the peace activist to analysis of current U.S. military projects and protests around the nation. Includes the regular feature "Voices from Prison," in which peace activists jailed for their actions reflect on their situations and the meanings implicit in them. As in most grassroots publications, there is a strong sense of community evoked by *Ground Zero*, in this case a spiritual community. Recommended as a good example of its kind.

9–32 *INFACT: Nuclear Weaponmakers Campaign Update.* INFACT National Field Campaign, P.O. Box 3223, South

Pasadena, CA 91031. Quarterly. $15. 1986–.

For five years INFACT has been leading a consumer boycott of General Electric, one of the nation's leading nuclear weapons contractors. This brief newsletter reports on progress in the campaign and on GE activities on the nuclear front, including current work and historical events, such as the company's involvement in the notorious 1949 release of radioactive iodine into the atmosphere from the Hanford nuclear facility. INFACT has published numerous materials concerning GE and the boycott. The $15 charge is more a donation to the campaign than it is a subscription fee. A significant grassroots contribution to the nuclear debate.

9–33 *International Atomic Energy Agency Bulletin.* IAEC, Wagramer Str. 5, P.O. Box 100, A–1400 Vienna, Austria. Quarterly. Free. 1959–. Indexed: *Biological Abstracts, Chemical Abstracts,* etc.

Published in Chinese, English, French, Russian, Spanish and Japanese editions, the *Bulletin* "aims to inform readers in Member States and other Nations about Agency activities in the application of international safeguards and the peaceful development of nuclear power in various fields." The slick magazine is also an effective way of staying abreast of IAEA publications, described in detail at the front of each issue. Feature articles deal with nuclear accidents, training, and safeguards against nuclear weapons proliferation as an offshoot of civilian nuclear power programs.

9–34 *International Journal on World Peace.* Edited by Panos D. Bardis. Professors World Peace Academy, GPO Box 1311, New York, NY 10116. Quarterly. $15/$30 1984–. Indexed: *PAIS, Sociological Abstracts,* etc.

Another title ranging widely over the world of peace issues. A typical number contains two or three major articles; recent issues have focused on national self-determination, the link between Locke and Kant and ecological theories, the historical paradox of religious sects' lip-service to peace while engaging in war, apartheid, and wars of development in Latin America. A brief "News" section takes an equally broad approach to current political developments, such as the independence movements in the Soviet Union. Includes notes on new books and journals. Book reviews are lengthy, if not plentiful (8–10 per issue). Some of the books chosen for review are curious entries in a journal devoted to peace, e.g., E.D. Hirsch's *Cultural Literacy*, but the reviews also turn up some interesting and generally overlooked titles. Clearly a reflection of its editor's worldview, even to the inclusion of his long "Miscellany" column, in which he may offer anything from his own reflections on global affairs to poems sent in by readers to his "Pandebars," brief poetic musings on whatever catches his fancy.

9–35 *International Security*. Edited by Steven E. Miller. Harvard University Center for Science and International Affairs, 79 John F. Kennedy St., Cambridge, MA 02138. Quarterly. $25/$65. 1976–. Indexed: *Historical Abstracts*, *PAIS*, etc.

Another academic journal with broad subject interests in both contemporary and historical aspects of international security. The winter 1990/91 issue, for example, contains a lengthy section on World War I and a matching section on Europe "after the Cold War." On the narrower field of nuclear weapons and war, the journal frequently carries articles on such matters as nuclear arms negotiations, strategic defense, and weapons ranging from ballistic missiles to bombers and submarines. Authors are chiefly U.S. scholars, although government and military officials appear from time to time. The journal seems receptive to new voices, judging by the occasional inclusion of essays by doctoral students. Sufficiently devoted to scholarship that even letters to the editor come with footnotes.

9-36 *Jane's Defence Weekly*. Edited by Peter Howard. Sentinel House, 163 Brighton Rd., Coulsdon, Surrey CR5 2NH, England. U.S. subscriptions: 1340 Braddock Pl., Alexandria, VA 22314. Weekly. $145. 1980–. Indexed: *Abstracts of Military Bibliography*, etc.

A military newsweekly featuring brief coverage of events on a global scale. Most news articles in the "This Week" section are no more than a page, most shorter. Background analysis, on such topics as Iraq's Scud missile program, are a good deal longer. Sections on "Contracts" and business reveal what companies are being paid to produce anything from helicopter engines to ICBM components. This is hard-core military reporting, and will be useful to anyone keeping track of global military actions, preparations, and investment. One would do well, however, to remember the magazine's adherence to the militaristic view it documents. Was *Jane's Defence Review* until 1984.

9-37 *Journal of Conflict Resolution*. Edited by Bruce M. Russett. Sage Publications, 2455 Teller Rd., Newbury Park, CA 91320. $130. 1957–. Indexed: *PAIS*, *Social Sciences Index*, etc.

JCR's scholarly articles often include those devoted to nuclear deterrence and other facets of strategic arms. The typical *JCR* essay is heavily annotated, laden with mathematical formulae, and more-or-less impenetrable to the lay reader. Desirable for most academic collections; most public libraries can live without it.

9-38 *Journal of Peace Research*. Edited by Nils P. Gleditsch and Stein Tonnesson. Sage Publications, Box 5096, Newbury Park, CA 91359. Quarterly. $37/$83. 1964–. Indexed: *PAIS*, *Social Sciences Index*, etc.

Published under the auspices of the International Peace Research Association, *JPR* "is committed to theoretical rigour, methodological sophistication, and policy orientation." The journal produces an occasional special theme issue; the February, 1991 number is given over to international mediation, and contains ten selections on the topic, including an introduction by former President Jimmy Carter. Other contributors to *JPR* are political scientists, sociologists and psychologists from the U.S., U.K., Scandinavia, and elsewhere.

Articles contain abstracts and end notes. Thematic issues feature an issue-wide bibliography listing citations to all the items referred to in the issue in hand. *JPR* offers numerous articles on specifically nuclear issues; recent essays have dealt with ICBM trajectories, assumptions of British nuclear weapon decision makers, and factors predisposing individuals to support nuclear disarmament. The "Book Notes" section provides fairly substantial reviews of up to a dozen recent books. A good addition to most peace collections.

9–39 *Journal of Strategic Studies*. Edited by Amos Perlmutter and John Gooch. Frank Cass & Co., Gainsborough House, 11 Gainsborough Rd., London E11 1RS, England. Quarterly. $45/$140. 1978–. Indexed in *Current Contents, Sociological Abstracts, America: History and Life,* others.

One might expect that this academic journal would offer primarily British, or at least Western European, views. That is not necessarily the case, since U.S. scholars can be heavily represented in its pages. Articles range across the broad field of military strategy. The journal is especially useful for historical perspectives on nuclear issues; over the last few years articles have appeared on nuclear weapons and the Korean War, U.S.-Soviet arms control efforts in the 1970s, and Eisenhower's attitude toward the atomic bombing of Hiroshima. Contains approximately ten book reviews and numerous short notes on books received.

9–40 *LAWS Quarterly*. Edited by Laura McGough. Lawyers Alliance for World Security, 1120 19th St., NW,

Washington, DC 20036. Quarterly. $20. 1982–.

Recently revamped from a 4-page newsletter to a more substantial 20-page periodical, the *LAWS Quarterly* is designed to assist its parent organization in providing a forum for the analysis and exchange of ideas concerning reduction of the threat of nuclear war, advancing non-proliferation, and enhancing movement towards the rule of law in the Soviet Union. In addition to organizational news, the most recent issue featured essays by a scholar from the Center for International Security and Arms Control of Stanford University and by a former director of the U.S. Arms Control and Disarmament Agency. Previously published as the newsletter of the Lawyers Alliance for Nuclear Arms Control. A desirable addition to law libraries.

9–41 *Meiklejohn Civil Liberties Institute PeaceNet Bulletin.* Edited by Ann F. Ginger. Meiklejohn Civil Liberties Institute, Box 673, Berkeley, CA 94701. Monthly. $12. 1990–.

The Meiklejohn Civil Liberties Institute is active on a variety of fronts; a commitment to peace and social justice is one of them. The *PeaceNet Bulletin* is a 4–6 page newsletter devoted to single-issue analysis of "crucial current events and the central issues of peace law" regarding such topics as the U.S. invasion of Panama, the Persian Gulf War, and nuclear deterrence. The organization's goal "is to fulfill our responsibilities in the nuclear age by helping inform U.S. public discussion and debate on these events and to support appropriate action by U.S. policymakers, organizations, and also specifically by lawyers and lawmakers." Contributors are legal authorities. Chiefly of interest to those in the legal profession who want to explore the opportunities for pursuing peace and justice afforded by their professional expertise.

9–42 *National Association of Radiation Survivors.* Edited by Fred Allingham. P.O. Box 20749, Oakland, CA 94620. Quarterly. $15/$25. 1982–.

Self-description: "To keep our membership and other interested communities apprised of legal, legislative, medical, and scientific information related to exposure to ionizing radiation. Also encourages differing survivor groups to be aware of, and support, each other's issues and activities." Concerned about the radiation exposure of uranium miners, test-site workers, atomic veterans, "downwinders," and others. (Sample issue requested but not received.)

9-43 *National Defense.* Edited by F. Clifton Berry, Jr. American Defense Preparedness Assoc., 2101 Wilson Blvd., Ste. 400, Arlington, VA 22201. 10/year. $35. 1920-. Indexed: *Engineering Index, Chemical Abstracts.*

This slick, professionally produced magazine "focuses on all facets of the North American industrial base, both military and civil," in its own words. "Every issue contains a mix of feature articles and recurring departments examining and reporting on trends and people in the 'business of defense.'"

At first glance the peace activist might dismiss this journal as of interest only to military officials and contractors, but that would be a mistake. *National Defense* focuses on military hardware, to be sure, but within that focus one finds some interesting and useful information, such as an interview with the new Strategic Defense Initiative Organization director, or an essay (with references) on missile proliferation. "Big and medium missiles are getting to the hands of those who might misuse them," says the table of contents blurb on this piece, suggesting questions about what constitutes "proper use" of ballistic missiles. A good source of insights into the thinking of those lodged deep within the military industrial complex. Expects to be covered by an indexing service in the near future; formerly published as *Ordnance.*

9-44 *New Outlook.* Edited by Robert Berls. American Committee on U.S.-Soviet Relations, 109 11th St. SE, Washington, DC 20003. Quarterly. $25. 1990-.

The official journal of the American Committee on U.S.
Soviet Relations. This independent, nonpartisan group
established in 1974 dedicates itself "to strengthen
official and public understanding of U.S.-Soviet
relations by providing accurate information and expert
analysis." Only one issue could be reviewed for this
guide; that one, the Winter, 1990/91 number, contained
in its 90 pages an extensive analysis on "Reform and
the Soviet Armed Forces," addressing the U.S.-Soviet
strategic balance, the Soviet defense conversion
process, "The Troubled Soviet Armed Forces," and
other topics. The report included pertinent Soviet
documents, such as a public opinion poll from August,
1990, indicating that only 12% of Soviet citizens
believe that a threat of military attack against the
Soviet Union existed. The periodical reflects a
thorough journalistic rather than a scholarly
approach. It should prove a useful source of
information and opinion.

9-45 *The Nonviolent Activist: The Magazine of the War
Resisters League.* Edited by Ruth Benn. War Resisters
League, 339 Lafayette St., New York, NY 10012. 8/year.
$15/$25. 1984-. Indexed: *Alternative Press Index.*

A 24-page magazine published by the nation's oldest
secular pacifist organization, *The Nonviolent Activist*
contains political analysis from a pacifist perspective,
feature articles, and information relating to
nonviolence, feminism, disarmament, international
issues, resistance to registration and the draft, war
tax resistance, and other issues. Although it
occasionally runs articles on nuclear topics (such as
"Hiroshima and Nagasaki Remembered" in June, 1990),
the magazine's scope attempts to cover the whole of
the peace and anti-militarist movement insofar as
possible within the space it has to work. Includes one
or two book reviews per issue, up to 600 words long.
Its value is enhanced by annual indexing.

9-46 *The Nuclear Resister.* Edited by Jack and Felice
Cohen-Joppa. P.O. Box 43383, Tucson, AZ 85733. 8/year.

$18/10 issues. 1980–.

The Nuclear Resister, a 16–page tabloid, "works to foster a wider public awareness of imprisoned nuclear resisters, their motivations and their action." It facilitates a support network for such activists in the U.S. Canada, and Great Britain. The paper reports on arrests and jailings of civil disobedients, and provides analysis and commentary on underlying issues, as in the article on "The Militarization of the Academic Community" in the Sept. 21, 1990 issue. Features statements of resisters themselves and a listing of forthcoming nonviolent direct actions at nuclear sites. An excellent source of information and opinion on this most committed segment of the peace movement, particularly in view of the mass media's almost total disregard in this area.

9–47 *Nuclear Times.* Edited by John Tirman. 401 Commonwealth Ave., Boston, MA 02215. Quarterly. $18. 1982–. Indexed: *Alternative Press Index.*

Nuclear Times has evolved to serve as a wide–angle guide to the antiwar and antinuclear movements. It retains a primary focus on nuclear weapons and nuclear war issues, but also features commentary and assessments concerning political and military hotspots around the world (e.g., the Soviet crackdown in the Baltics, militarism in Japan, the Persian Gulf) that harbor the potential for far wider conflict. On the nuclear front, the magazine has recently featured articles on proliferation, nuclear deterrence in the context of the declining Cold War, and nuclear test protests in the Soviet Union. Contributors are journalists, scholars, and activists. Contains a good list of organizational resources keyed to each issue's articles. Belongs in all libraries.

9–48 *Nucleus.* Edited by Steven Krauss. Union of Concerned Scientists, 26 Church St., Cambridge, MA 02238. Quarterly. Donation. 1978–.

Covers arms control, national security and energy policy issues, and nuclear power safety. The oversize 8-page tabloid contains news and analysis of all these issues, and benefits from good graphs, charts, and other illustrations. The Union of Concerned Scientists is dedicated to environmental health, renewable energy, and "a world without the threat of nuclear war." The organization also publishes books and brochures on these issues, along with its 4-6 page "Briefing Papers" on such topics as nuclear proliferation, antisatellite weapons, and other aspects of nuclear war and peace.

9-49 *Nukewatch Pathfinder.* The Progressive Foundation, P.O. Box 5658, Madison, WI 53701. Quarterly. $15.

Nukewatch (the informal name of the Progressive Foundation) came into being in 1979 following a federal court's decree restraining *The Progressive* from publishing information about the U.S. nuclear weapons program. The foundation was founded by the magazine and has developed into an independent action group working for peace and justice. Its newsletter is a 4-page tabloid reporting on organizational activities, including the Nukewatch "H-Bomb Truck Watch," which monitors Department of Energy convoys that transport nuclear warheads and their components throughout the U.S., and the Missile Silo Campaign, designed to map the 1,000 ICBM missiles and 100 launch control centers in the Midwest and Great Plains. A good source of information on the secular arm of the grassroots peace movement.

9-50 *The Objector: A Journal of Draft and Military Information.* Edited by Jeff Schutts. P.O. Box 42249, San Francisco, CA 94142. 6/year. $15/$20. 1980–.

The Objector covers in 12-16 pages Selective Service laws and activities, military regulations and life in the military, issues of conscientious objection, anti-militarism, draft registration and resistance, and other information of concern to those facing compulsory military service. Published by the CCCO, an agency founded in 1948 as the Central Committee for Conscientious Objectors. Includes news of life in the Soviet and other foreign military establishments. Strongly recommended as an information tool in any environment where young men ponder their futures and search their consciences.

9–51 *On Beyond War*. Edited by Mac Lawrence and Marilyn Rea. Beyond War, 222 High St., Palo Alto, CA 94301. 10/year. $25.

The eight-year old organization Beyond War is an educational foundation dedicated to building a cooperative, sustainable world. It is active in a number of areas, including citizen diplomacy with people in the Soviet Union and proposing initiatives for global security and cooperation. The 8–12 page newsletter contains discussions of current conflicts, ideas for positive change, interviews with peace activists and scholars, commentary on socio-psychological aspects of international relations, and occasional book reviews. Beyond War's dominant message is that all humanity shares the same vital need to preserve the planet, and the belief that recognizing the common interest everyone has as a citizen of planet earth in its preservation is a logical and necessary step toward achieving preservation of the planet *and* humanity. "The Earth and all life are interdependent and interconnected," says one Beyond War document. "The well-being of each individual is inextricably linked to the well-being of the whole. All is one." The spirit here is grassroots, but the execution is professional.

9–52 *The PSR Quarterly: A Journal of Medicine and Global Survival*. Edited by Jennifer Leaning, M.D. Published by Williams & Wilkins, P.O. Box 23921, Baltimore, MD 21203. (Editorial offices: 10 Brookline Place West, Brookline, MA 02146). Quarterly. $48/$85. 1991–.

A most welcome new journal begun in the 30th anniversary year of Physicians for Social Responsibility, a national organization of 25,000 health professionals and supporters working to prevent nuclear war and other environmental catastrophes. PSR is the U.S. affiliate of the International Physicians for the Prevention of Nuclear War. The first peer-reviwed periodical coverage of the medical, scientific, public health and bio-ethical problems related to the nuclear age. It features editorials, debate and rebuttal, news notes, letters, book and journal reviews. The 65-page debut issue of March, 1991 contained scholarly articles on the neutron bomb, health effects of radioactive fallout on Marshall Islanders, and other significant contributions to an informed understanding of medical issues in the context of a world bristling with weapons of mass destruction. Any library serving a clientele with an interest in medicine and allied health fields will want to give this title serious consideration.

9–53 *PSR Reports.* Edited by Burton Glass. Physicians for Social Responsibility, 1000 16th St., NW, Suite 810, Washington, DC 20036. 3/year. $80 physicians/$40 associates/$15 students (membership). 1985–. (Was *PSR Newsletter*, 1980–1985).

The official membership newsletter for Physicians for Social Responsibility, this 8-page tabloid informs readers of the organization's campaigns against nuclear weapons testing and production, federal budget priorities and environmental protection and restoration. Some book reviews.

9–54 *Pacific News Bulletin.* Coordinated by Ellen Whelan. Pacific Concerns Resource Center/Pacific News Bulletin, P.O. Box 489, Petersham NSW 2049, Australia. Monthly. $25/$40. 1986(?)–.

Dedicated to "a Nuclear Free and Independent Pacific," the *PNB* promotes an agenda against racism, colonialism and militarism in the Pacific islands. For decades the islands were a "nuclear playground" where the U.S., Great Britain, and France conducted bomb tests with cruel disregard for the rights of native island peoples. In addition to its advocacy of independence and coverage of political and military turmoil in the region, the 16-page bulletin maintains an emphasis on nuclearism, including the campaign against turning the Pacific into a dumping ground for radioactive waste.

9-55 *Pastoral Care Network for Social Responsibility Newsletter.* Edited by G. Michael Cordner, Th.D., P.O. Box 9243, Ft. Myers, FL 33902. Quarterly. $25 (membership). 1984-.

An organizational communication tool serving persons with training and interest in pastoral psychology and issues related to peace with justice and the "integrity of creation." The 16-page newsletter informs members of the network and other interested persons about important related events, issues, resources, and concerns. The strong anti-war theme is accompanied by discussion of such social justice issues as adequate housing. Numerous notes from foreign readers. Resource notes.

9-56 *Pax Christi USA.* Edited by Mary Lou Kownacki, OSB. National Catholic Peace Movement, 348 East Tenth St., Erie, PA 16503. Quarterly. $20 (membership). 1985-.

The primary goal of Pax Christi, the international Catholic peace movement, is "to work with all people for peace for all humankind, always witnessing to the peace of Christ. Its priorities are a Christian vision of disarmament, a just world order, primacy of conscience, education for peace and alternatives to violence." *Pax Christi USA* covers the Catholic peace movement in depth, with articles by and about activists, actions and events, from analysis of the Persian Gulf War to campaigning for a Comprehensive Test Ban treaty. Each 38-page issue contains a variety of feature articles, columns, two or three book reviews, news of Pax Christi organizational matters, and "Network," a resources listing. Essential reading for Catholic peace activists, and a desirable item for libraries that wish to make Catholic peace perspectives more readily available to their users.

9–57 *Peace and Change.* Edited by Robert D. Schulzinger and Paul Wehr. Sage Publications, 2455 Teller Rd., Newbury Park, CA 91320. Quarterly. 1972–. Indexed: *PAIS, America: History and Life,* etc.

Peace and Change publishes scholarly articles on many peace issues, but focuses especially on work concerning the development of a just and human society. The chronological scope is historical as well as contemporary; the January, 1991 issue, e.g., features an assessment of the peace movement in the 1980s and a special section on Bertha von Suttner (1843–1914), author of the famous 1889 antiwar novel *Die Waffen nieder!* (*Lay Down Your Arms*). Contributors, both foreign and U.S., to each issue's 6–9 articles typically represent a variety of disciplines—anthropology, history, literature, political science, sociology, physics, and others. The journal's openness to work from different spheres gives it a healthy and stimulating eclecticism: few readers at all interested in peace topics will fail to find at least one or two articles per issue that strike sparks for them. Book reviews are few; it is an area the journal could bolster.

9–58 *Peace and Freedom.* Edited by Roberta Spivek. Women's International League for Peace & Freedom, 1213 Race St., Philadelphia, PA 19107. 6/year. $30/$60. 1941–. Indexed: *PAIS, Historical Abstracts.*

Billing itself as "the only U.S. magazine devoted solely to the women's peace movement," each issue of *P & F* covers a full spectrum of international peace-related issues, from advocacy of a comprehensive nuclear test ban to children's books, racism, sexism, disarmament, peace education, and WILPF activities. Useful to any peace activist or researcher, *Peace and Freedom* should be a basic item on any woman peace worker's periodical shelf.

9–59 *Peace and the Sciences*. Edited by Peter Stania. International Institute for Peace, Mollwaldplatz 5, A–1040, Vienna, Austria. Quarterly. $240. 1969–.

This journal reports discussions at international meetings of both Western and Eastern scientists organized by its publisher. It also recently inaugurated a more thorough attention to the research activities of the IIP. Chiefly of interest to those looking for a journal with a strong emphasis on European perspectives on peace issues; contributors are, in the vast majority, European, although some U.S. scholars find their way into the journal's pages. Recent issues have dealt in depth with the future of Europe, economic conversion following disarmament, and ecological security. Contains a mix of research and reflective pieces.

9–60 *Peace Brigades International Project Newsletters*. Peace Brigades International, Box 1233, Harvard Sq. Sta., Cambridge, MA 02238. Monthly. $25. 1989–.

PBI sends unarmed international peace teams, on invitation, into areas of repression or conflict, acting on the belief that "citizens can act boldly as peacemakers when their governments cannot." The newsletter provides information about the activities of the teams and the organizations with which they work, as well as background information on the situations in the countries where PBI has projects. Formerly published separately by country, the *Newsletter* began including information about all projects (Central America, Southeast Asia, North America) beginning in the summer of 1991. An effective tool for staying informed about troubled local situations in countries and regions with the potential to serve as catalysts for broader violence and military confrontation.

9-61 *Peace Conversion Times.* Edited by Will Loob. Alliance for Survival, 200 N. Main St., Suite M-2, Santa Ana, CA 92701. 6/year. $25. 1983-.

The Alliance for Progress is a grassroots group whose major goals include the abolition of nuclear arms and power, reversal of the arms race, and an end to military interventions. Primarily active in the city of Los Angeles and Orange County, CA. *Peace Conversion Times* is an 8-page tabloid featuring organizational news and articles on narrower aspects of the broad goals noted above. Included here as a good example of a local peace periodical produced on a slender budget.

9-62 *Peace Magazine.* Edited by Metta Spencer. Canadian Disarmament Information Service, 736 Bathurst St., Toronto, Ont. M5S 2R4, Canada. 6/year. $20. 1985-.

"To inform, enlighten, and inspire. To save Earth from the scourge of war." With this motto, *Peace Magazine* addresses a wide variety of issues and readers. The 32-page magazine endorses multilateral disarmament, but otherwise takes no editorial position and presents a variety of views. Contains a listing of upcoming peace events in Canada, notes on the Canadian peace movement, reviews of books, films, and videos, letters from abroad, and other regular features. Recent issues have offered articles on the Persian Gulf War, the General Electric boycott, Greenham Common, nuclear accidents, and many other relevant issues. A well put-together magazine that will be useful to peace activists and scholars in the U.S., and essential to those in Canada.

9-63 *Peace Office Newsletter.* Mennonite Central Committee, International Peace Section, 21 S. 12th St., Box 500, Akron, PA 17501. 6/year. $10.

The Mennonite Central Committee is "the cooperative relief and service agency of North American Mennonite and Brethren in Christ conferences. It carries on community development, peacemaking and material aid 'in the name of Christ,' in response to His command to teach all nations the way of discipleship, love and peace." The 12-page newsletter features biblical perspectives on war and peace, examination of psychological issues, peace activism among different groups ("Seniors for Peace" is a current project), and reflections on the meaning of peacemaking.

9-64 *Peace Research Abstracts Journal.* Edited by Hanna Newcombe and Alan Newcombe. Peace Research Institute, Dundas, 252 Dundana Ave., Dundas, Ont. L9H 4E5, Canada. Monthly. $210. 1964-.

A very useful tool for peace professionals, this abstracting journal cites and annotates (frequently at considerable length) over 3,000 documents annually. Coverage includes books, scholarly and semi-popular periodicals representing a large number of disciplines, institutional reports, newspapers, films, and other materials. Access is by author and subject indexes and by a code index that classifies entries by subject. Contains extensive coverage of nuclear and related topics. Back issues are available from the publisher. Indispensable for researchers investigating Canada's role in affairs of peace and war because of its strong coverage of Canadian publications, the journal also treats a copious quantity of American and British materials. Some coverage of non-English language documents.

9-65 *Positive Alternatives.* Edited by Jim Wake. Center for Economic Conversion, 222 View St., Suite C, Mountain View, CA 94041. Quarterly. $35. 1990-.

This journal's self-description: *"Positive Alternatives* is the primary publication of the Center for Economic Conversion and is the journal of economic conversion movement. It has a circulation of 7,500. It covers all facets of economic conversion from editorials on alternatives to military dependency, to interviews with key actors in the movement, to case studies, book reviews, reports from the field and updates on CEL's work." Although primarily devoted to promoting economic conversion in the U.S., the journal also turns to other regions, such as Eastern Europe, struggling with the burden of wasteful investment in military projects. Includes one or two book reviews and an annotated resources listing. If this new title survives, it could prove of real value in the present movement by the federal government to close down numerous military bases.

9-66 *Psychologists for Social Responsibility Newsletter*. Edited by Anne Anderson. 1841 Columbia Rd., NW Suite 207, Washington, DC 20009. Quarterly. $35. 1982-.

A 12-page newsletter which, in addition to covering activities of Psychologists for Social Responsibility, focuses on projects in which professional psychologists are involved concerning peace, war, conflict resolution and related topics. The newsletter also features articles on such topics as the psychological case for a comprehensive test ban, profiles of antiwar psychologists, and commentary on current international crises. The organization defines its mission as using psychological principles and tools "to promote conversion from a war system to a world dedicated to peace and social justice." An annotated resource list is a regular feature; occasional book reviews. Psychologists who want to stay abreast of professional developments regarding war and peace will find this title useful; so would lay readers interested in psychology.

9-67 *RECON*. Edited by Chris Robinson. RECON Publications, P.O. Box 14602, Philadelphia, PA 19134. 9/year. $15. 1973-.

This newsletter of approximately 14 pages "covers Pentagon activities around the world. *RECON* exposes little-known events and explains the reasons behind the mass-media headlines." Produced by volunteers, *RECON* reflects its editor's belief that what one reader calls "a goofy bunch of idealists" can help effect positive social change, in spite of the vast financial and political power of the military industrial complex. "We have faith that the change will come," says Robinson. *RECON* often publishes articles on nuclear resistance, nuclear weapons and warfare issues, and SDI. Includes 8-10 paragraph-long book and document reviews in each issue.

9-68 *The Reporter for Conscience' Sake.* Edited by David W. Treber. National Interreligious Service Board for Conscientious Objectors, Suite 750, 1601 Connecticut Ave., NW, Washington DC 20009. Monthly. $20. 1940-.

An update on legislation and developments affecting conscientious objectors to participation in war. Each 8-page issue is likely to discuss individual CO cases, commentary on military action, analysis of pro-military propaganda in the media, a number of brief book reviews and other leads to pertinent literature, coverage of Congressional action, and other matters. A valuable source to help anyone understand contemporary conscientious objection to participation in war, but especially useful to those in a position to counsel young people concerned about the draft and what constitutes their "duty" to their country.

9-69 *Research Report of the Council on Economic Priorities.* Edited by Alice T. Marlin. Council on Economic Priorities, 30 Irving Pl., New York, NY 10003. Monthly. $25. 1969-.

The Council on Economic Priorities is an independent, public interest research organization. A focus on arms control, military spending, and national security has long been one of the Council's interests. Recent issues of the 6-page *Research Report* have dealt with the economic effects of the Cold War's decline, particularly the need for conversion from military to civilian industry in both the U.S.S.R. and the United States. Succinct but informative.

9–70 *Space and Security News.* Edited by Robert M. Bowman. Institute for Space and Security Studies, 5115 Hwy. A1A S., Melbourne Beach, FL 32951. Quarterly. $25. 1984–.

Editor Bowman, the author of *Star Wars: A Defense Insider's Case Against the Strategic Defense Initiative* (item 5–11) is a retired Air Force Lt. Colonel. He conducts an energetic campaign against the militarization of space and the continued funding of defense programs he considers wasteful and a threat to U.S. and global security. Each issue of his 8–16 page *S & S News* contains Bowman's analysis of global events and military programs, chiefly SDI.

Like Thomas Liggett's *World Peace News* (see below), Bowman's periodical reflects the thinking of a former military man who has seen a new light. He describes the publication as providing "an independent voice for the American people on space and other high–tech issues affecting national security. . . . We specialize in those areas where we feel the government has lied to the American people and their elected representatives to Congress. We 'Speak Truth to Power' on issues like 'Star Wars,' the KAL–007 shootdown, the Challenger explosion, nuclear testing, and the war against Iraq. We have vigorously opposed weapons in space since 1980." The format is homey (2–column, typed), the message urgent and clearly–presented.

9–71 *Strategic Review.* Edited by Walter F. Hahn. U.S. Strategic Institute, P.O. Box 618, Kenmore Sta., Boston MA 02215. Quarterly. $15. 1973–. Indexed: *PAIS, Social Sciences Index*, etc.

Subscriptions to *SR* are limited to educational institutions and government agencies. The journal, published in association with the Center for International Relations, Boston University, makes an editorial point of taking "no position other than to provide a forum for discussion of matters of current significance in the politico–military field." This promise of neutrality trips over the title page's credo, which

states that "*Strategic Review* is dedicated to the
advancement and understanding of those principles
and practices—military and political—which serve the
vital interests and security of the United States."
There is no sentimental guff about the global village
to be found in these pages! The roster of
conservative U.S. contributors clarifies the journal's
true agenda, as do the patriotic little stars employed
as a typographic device throughout the title. Each
issue contains five feature essays, frequently bearing
directly on nuclear weapons matters. Will make the
reader either want to stand up and salute or take
cover behind the nearest bulky object. Few but
lengthy book reviews.

9–72   *Survival.*   Edited   by   Hans   Binnendijk.
International Institute for Strategic Studies, 23
Tavistock St., London WC2E 7NQ, England. U.S.
subscriptions to Brassey's, Maxwell House, Fairview
Park, Elmsford NY 10523. 6/year. $30. 1959–. Indexed:
Historical Abstracts.

A scholarly journal devoted to conflict and
peacemaking. *Survival* covers the globe; articles range
from Sri Lanka and Cambodia to Central America and
South Africa. Contains occasional articles on explicitly
nuclear issues, such as coverage of the 1990 Non-
Proliferation Treaty Review and evaluation of SDI
deployment options. Each issue's book reviews are
relatively few, but lengthy, and often focus on works
concerned with nuclear topics.

9–73 *Surviving Together: A Journal on Soviet–American
Relations.* Edited by Harriet Crosby, et al. Institute
for Soviet–American Relations, 1601 Connecticut Ave.,
NW, Suite 301, Washington, DC 20009. 3/year. $25/$30.
1983–.

This journal's parent institute is a nonpartisan
service organization working to improve Soviet-
American relations through better communication,
facilitating working relationships between individual

Soviet and U.S. citizens, cultural exchanges, and other means. *Surviving Together* presents news and editorial opinion on U.S.-Soviet relations and chronicles exchanges between the two countries, especially private-sector contacts. Each 90-page issue's coverage is divided among approximately 20 subjects, such as health, education, world security, environment, city affiliations, and citizen diplomacy. Includes articles reprinted from other sources and those based on information retrieved from interested organizations. Both U.S. and Soviet sources are cited. An effective tool for keeping informed on healthy developments in U.S.-Soviet relations. Features a good number of resource and new book notes. Readable and exciting.

9-74 *The Test Banner.* American Peace Test, P.O. Box 26725, Las Vegas, NV 89126. Monthly. $10. 198?-.

American Peace Test is a grassroots group dedicated to nonviolent action to end the arms race. It advocates a comprehensive nuclear test ban as a first step towards disarmament, and engages in education and outreach to communities affected by nuclear weapons testing and the arms race. The organization's Testing Alert Network monitors U.S. and British tests at the Nevada Test Site and shares information on foreign tests with a global network of activists. *The Test Banner* reports both U.S. and international opposition to nuclear testing, including protests by Soviet citizens. The tabloid is a good tool for keeping up with a variety of testing issues, including environmental and legal matters. Readers seriously interested in participating in the movement for a comprehensive test ban will welcome access to this title.

9-75 *WAND Bulletin.* Women's Action for Nuclear Disarmament. P.O. Box B, Arlington, MA 02174. Quarterly. $30 (membership). 1982-.

WAND was founded in 1980 by Dr. Helen Caldicott as a women's initiative to eliminate weapons of mass destruction and redirect military resources to human and environmental needs. WAND engages in congressional lobbying, grassroots organization, support of women congressional candidates, and other measures serving its objectives. The *WAND Bulletin*, an 8-page newsletter, includes notes from affiliates around the U.S., as well as discussing a variety of political and military issues. A desirable addition to feminist and peace collections.

9-76 *World Peace News: A World Government Report*. Edited and published by Thomas Liggett. 300 E. 33d St., New York, NY 10016. 6/year. $20/3 years. 1970-.

Editor-publisher Liggett, a journalist and decorated World War II Marine Corps fighter pilot, dedicates *WPN* to "All the World-Government News That's Fit to Print and Almost Free of Cant, Hype and Twaddle." The tabloid's single, overriding interest is the objective of its subtitle, world government, and the sooner the better. The whole of *WPN* is given to short news notes and commentary, with occasional longer pieces, analyzing global affairs in light of that objective. Relentlessly critical of efforts to preserve nationalism and the sovereignty of the nation-state; Liggett sees nuclear weaponry as the death knell—one way or another—of the present system of competing states. Each 8-page issue is full of information and opinion of interest to advocates of world government, and in addition to Liggett's includes material by other advocates of the rule of international law. Currently campaigning for Vaclav Havel's designation as U.N. Secretary-General in the belief that Havel has a better understanding of internationalism than "the U.N.'s line of nationalist Secretaries-General." *WPN* is especially interesting for its quick takes on political attitudes expressed by the mass media.

9-77 *World Peacemaker Quarterly*. Edited by Dr. William J. Price. World Peacemakers, Inc., 2025 Massachusetts Ave. NW, Washington, DC 20036. Quarterly. $5. 1979-.

A Christian, non-sectarian newsletter emphasizing the importance of following the teachings of Christ in working for a peaceful world. The newsletter reflects editor Price's statement, drawn from his book *Seasons of Faith and Conscience: Kairos, Confession, & Liturgy* (Orbis, 1991), that "Every act of worship, every occasion where the sovereignty of the Word of God is celebrated, every instance where the realm of God is acknowledged, is always and everywhere expressly political." Church and state may be separate, but World Peacemakers is a group that approaches politics informed by religious conviction. The 20-page newsletter contains essays and notes concerning the spiritual motivations and rationales for turning away from war as a "solution" to international problems.

CHAPTER 10

The Chernobyl Disaster

The reactor meltdown at the Soviet Chernobyl nuclear plant in 1986 was an unparalleled catastrophe in the history of civilian nuclear power. As James Warf notes in *All Things Nuclear*, the amount of radioactivity released in the Chernobyl disaster amounted to 30 to 40 times the quantity released by the Hiroshima bomb. Well over 100,000 people from close to 200 towns and settlements were evacuated because of the radiation danger; the evacuated homes of thousands will be uninhabitable for years to come. Speculation continues about the extent of loss of life.

In spite of its terrible toll on the environment, the radiological effects of Chernobyl represent a minuscule portion of what would be produced in even a very limited nuclear war. This bibliography's focus on the military aspects of nuclear power is set aside here to attend to some of the literature that has followed in Chernobyl's wake. The disaster may very well be, in the words of Robert P. Gale's and Thomas Hauser's book, the "final warning," the last notice to humanity to put its nuclear house in order before the whole risky edifice comes crashing down.

The Chernobyl disaster is the result of peaceful nuclear technology gone out of control. Those who build, manage and pay for nuclear weapons, and those who subscribe to the mythology of peace obtained through nuclear deterrence might well reflect on the lessons of Chernobyl.

10-1 *Cleanup of Large Areas Contaminated as a Result of a Nuclear Accident*. International Atomic Energy Agency, 1989. 135p. Sales agent in U.S.: UNIPUB.

The product of a November, 1987 Advisory Group Meeting on the cleanup of "very large" areas following a nuclear accident. The meeting was attended by 17 experts from IAEA member states. In the Soviet Union, the dose commitment from radioactive fallout deposited on the ground as a result of the Chernobyl disaster is expected to rise to 60% of the total dose. The high rate of exposure from contaminated ground sources would probably be common in other major nuclear facility accidents. This examination of the Chernobyl cleanup goes into considerable detail on measures used in the region and includes photos of cleanup workers in action. Bibliography.

10–2 Gale, Robert P. and Hauser, Thomas. *Final Warning: The Legacy of Chernobyl.* Warner Books, 1988. 230p.

Dr. Gale, chairman of the Bone Marrow Transplantation Unit at U.C.L.A., went to the Soviet Union to assist in the medical aftermath of the disaster. At the time of the book's publication, Gale had made a half-dozen trips to the Soviet Union. His discussion of his work, his patients, his contacts with his Soviet colleagues and other citizens, and his account of the effects of the accident itself are valuable first-hand treatments. He sees his frequent trips to assist the Soviets as advantageous to both superpowers, in the matter of citizen diplomacy, apart from his contributions to the medical efforts in Chernobyl's aftermath. In his conclusion, Gale speaks his position on nuclear power; although he does not propose abandoning it, he makes a number of proposals to lessen the impact of accidents. Gale also provides some interesting insights regarding Soviet perceptions, notably Mikhail Gorbachev's, of American reactions to the disaster.

Turner Broadcasting made a television movie, "Chernobyl: The Final Warning" based on Gale's experiences. First telecast in April 1991, the film benefited from extensive location shooting in the Soviet Union, including scenes inside a Soviet nuclear plant and in a Moscow hospital burn unit. A Soviet crew re-enacted the accident at the plant. An effective production in part, but marred by sentimentality.

10-3 Gould, Peter. *Fire in the Rain: The Democratic Consequences of Chernobyl.* Polity Pr., 1990. 162p.

Gould's is chiefly a book devoted to urging a reawakened assessment of the "benefits" of nuclear power, but his frequent discussion of the environmental consequences of the disaster, particularly the issue of radioactive fallout dumped throughout Europe and its effects on agriculture and food consumption, makes it pertinent for inclusion in a study of the health effects of radiation. Bibliography, index.

10-4 Gubarev, Vladimir. *Sarcophagus: A Tragedy.* Vintage, 1987. 106p.

A literary reaction to the Chernobyl tragedy written only a few months after the event, this play is set in an experimental section of the Institute of Radiation Safety in the U.S.S.R., where a number of Chernobyl radiation victims are delivered for treatment. The author, *Pravda's* science editor, was the first journalist sent to cover the disaster; he found factual news reporting unable to convey the dimensions of terror and pity inherent in the event. The book's title comes from the 300,000-ton concrete and steel tomb that shrouds the plant's reactor core, but it also refers to the concrete sarcophagus that will entomb a dying patient's extremely radioactive body. An interesting example of *glasnost*-era writing, with an American surgeon, Dr. Kyle, apparently modeled on Dr. Robert Gale. The play's eerie, surrealistic tone is, perhaps, the most appropriate one possible to such an unnatural event. First published in the Russian journal *Znamia,* no. 9, 1986.

10-5   Gumprecht, D., et al., eds. *Impact of the*

Chernobyl Nuclear Power Plant Accident on the Federal Republic of Germany: Recommendation of the Commission on Radiological Protection: Assessment, Limitation and Valuation. G. Fischer, 1988. 98p.

Following the cloud of radioactive air which spread over West Germany from Chernobyl, the Commission on Radiological Protection prepared this appraisal and recommendation of precautionary measures against ionizing radiation. The recommendations involve imported foods, feeding of dairy cows, determination of the safety of crops, contamination measurement, potential health hazards to the unborn, etc. Notes.

10–6 Haynes, Viktor and Bojcun, Marko. *The Chernobyl Disaster.* Hogarth, 1988. 233p.

Haynes, a Ukrainian exile and Soviet specialist, and Bojcun, also a Sovietologist, turn in a readable treatment of the effects of the disaster. They document the origins of the meltdown in flawed technology, bureaucratic impatience to develop nuclear power, and managerial ineptitude; they also effectively portray the human face of the tragedy through their attention to the everyday people whose lives were disrupted or destroyed. Bibliography, index.

10–7 Mackay, Louis and Thompson, Mark, eds. *Something in the Wind: Politics after Chernobyl.* Pluto, 1988. 240p.

The link between nuclear weapons and civilian nuclear power is inescapable and is underscored by the adoption of nuclear power facilities in Third World nations with nuclear weapons ambitions. Chernobyl heightened global awareness of the deadly connection between nuclear power that kills by accident and nuclear weapons designed to kill intentionally. This book sets out to show the connections among issues of peace, green politics, and civil liberties as revealed by Chernobyl. Among the essays, Zhores Medvedev writes of the Soviet nuclear program, while other authors examine the movements of "people's detente" and alternatives to "the nuclear fix." What is the cost of this fix, even without its culmination in nuclear war? Medvedev estimates in his essay that the actual monetary cost (to say nothing of the human toll) of the Chernobyl disaster "might well come close to the total investment in the Soviet nuclear power industry since 1954." Notes.

10–8 Marples, David R. *The Social Impact of the Chernobyl Disaster*. St. Martin's, 1988. 313p.

Marples, who teaches Slavic and East European Studies at the University of Alberta, relies extensively on Soviet sources in this study of the health, environmental, economic and political repercussions of the disaster. Whether Chernobyl "was first and foremost a media event," as Marples states, is debatable. The thousands of evacuees who cannot return to their homes and the large number of people who died, or will die, as a result of the accident would probably disagree. Marples does, however, provide a good discussion of media attention, East and West, to the accident. He praises the bravery of those involved in the accident's aftermath, and praises Soviet efforts generally. Yet he questions the thoroughness and honesty of the Soviet public record on the cleanup and radioactive fallout. He is also critical of the premature repopulation of some evacuated villages, as well as the return to service of the Chernobyl plant's first three units.

10–9 Medvedev, Grigori. *The Truth About Chernobyl*. Basic Books, 1991. 274p.

First published in the Soviet Union in 1989, Medvedev's is a thorough and terrible account of the disaster. He writes with unique authority as the chief engineer at the plant during its construction, as an official in the Soviet Ministry of Energy, and as the leader of an examination of the disaster and its causes. One of the first books to turn to for a meticulous detailing of the technical aspects of the accident and for an emotionally grinding statement of the costs in human suffering. Medvedev has abandoned his nuclear engineering career in the wake of Chernobyl. Includes a foreword by Andrei Sakharov and the author's preface to the American edition. Index.

10–10 Medvedev, Zhores A. *The Legacy of Chernobyl.* Norton, 1990. 352p.

Medvedev, a biologist who earlier wrote of a major nuclear accident in the Soviet Union (*Nuclear Disaster in the Urals*, Norton, 1979) here focuses on "the most expensive accident in human history." His analysis draws in depth on Soviet documentation of the accident, and provides a detailed record of its technical aspects, its environmental impact, its effects on agriculture and health, its global effects, and the impact on the Soviet nuclear power program.

Of special interest is the chapter "A History of Nuclear Accidents in the Soviet Union," in which he sheds some light on the officially veiled record of Soviet atomic mishaps. He argues that Chernobyl has brought about an economic and political crisis in the Soviet Union and in countries linked to it economically: "The only way to move forward now is to integrate with those Western economies which have already been restructured, even if this means sacrificing political and ideological dogmas." An important book for grasping the nature and extent of the disaster. Accessible to most readers. Glossary, notes, index.

10–11 Mould, Richard F. *Chernobyl: The Real Story.* Pergamon, 1988. 255p.

An historical account of what happened before, during, and after the accident. Mould, a British medical physicist, cancer statistician, and radiation historian, treats the accident and its causes, the fates of the immediate victims (chiefly firemen), the evacuation of some 135,000 people, radioactive contamination of the food chain, and the aftermath of the accident. He draws heavily on documents provided by Soviet officials and on tape recordings made at the Post-Accident Review meeting, Aug. 25-29, 1986, at IAEA offices in Vienna. The volume is much-enhanced by a wealth of photographs taken at various stages of the accident and in its wake. Notes, index.

10-12 Organisation for Economic Co-Operation and Development. Nuclear Energy Agency. *The Radiological Impact of the Chernobyl Accident in OECD Countries.* Nuclear Energy Agency, OECD, 1987. 184p.

An assessment of the radiological impact of the accident and of the emergency response in OECD countries. The impact in these countries was very uneven; the report concludes that, although serious in the Chernobyl region itself, "these consequences do not raise any major concern for the health of the population in OECD member countries." The report also notes considerable variation in member countries' responses to the accident, "even when they experienced similar levels of contamination." Includes radiation dose estimates and mapping of deposits for the 23 member countries, including the U.S. Numerous tables, maps, graphs. Notes.

10-13 Park, Chris C. *Chernobyl: The Long Shadow.* Routledge, 1989. 207p.

The "long shadow" of Chernobyl fell over the whole of Europe; every nation in Western Europe recorded fallout from the accident. An authority on acid rain, Park provides a retrospective on Chernobyl that describes the accident, its health effects, immediate human problems and long-term problems, and the spread of the radiation across Europe. One small but striking map shows the cloud almost completely enveloping Western Europe. He also speculates on lessons to be drawn from the accident regarding nuclear power's future, international cooperation, and other topics. Bibliography, index.

10–14 Sands, Philippe J., ed. *Chernobyl: Law and Communication: Transboundary Nuclear Air Pollution— The Legal Materials*. Grotius, 1988. 312p.

Vast areas of Europe were exposed to the Chernobyl fallout. The U.K. National Radiation Board has estimated that 1,000 deaths and 3,000 non-fatal cancers will occur in the E.E.C. countries because of the accident. There is no single treaty that covers issues concerning transboundary release of radioactive material, repair of damage resulting from such release, provision of information to other states on such release, or provision of assistance to affected states. Sands gathers numerous legal texts, from the 1960 Paris Convention on Third Party Liability in the Field of Nuclear Energy to the 1987 Resolution on Transboundary Air Pollution of the Institut de Droit International, illustrating points of law pertinent to Chernobyl and other events of its genre. Chiefly of interest to legal scholars and environmentalists. Index.

10–15 Shcherbak, Iurii. *Chernobyl: A Documentary Story*. Canadian Institute of Ukrainian Studies, Univ. of Alberta, 1989. 168p.

First published in 1987 and 1988 in two Soviet periodicals, Shcherbak's treatment entails interviews with many participants in the tragedy, including Valerii Legasov, the First Deputy Chairman of the Kurchatov Institute of Atomic Energy and head of the Soviet delegation to the IAEA in Vienna at the time of the disaster. Dr. Legasov committed suicide in 1988. Shcherbak, a doctor and a prolific novelist, is also chairman of a Ukrainian writers' group concerned with the protection of nature. An essential book for readers seeking to penetrate the heart of the Chernobyl disaster from various perspectives, whether those of firefighters, visiting physicians, or townspeople.

10–16 Silver, L. Ray. *Fallout from Chernobyl*. Deneau, 1987. 237p.

A veteran journalist who covered the Canadian nuclear industry furnishes a readable account of Chernobyl, relying on books (though none of them about Chernobyl itself), articles, scientific papers, and other materials. Silver also carried out numerous interviews, few or none with Soviet sources, judging by the "Acknowledgments" section. Canadian readers will find the book useful because of its emphasis on the Canadian reaction to the disaster. Bibliography, index.

10–17 Wolf, Christa. *Accident: A Day's News*. Farrar, Straus and Giroux, 1989. 113p.

Set during a spring day in 1986, when the narrator's brother is scheduled for brain surgery and when a huge radioactive cloud from Chernobyl is about to engulf Europe. Addressed to her absent brother, the book, which is more a meditation than a novel, dwells on a perceptive woman's powerlessness in the face of events controlled, or set in motion, by others. Short on drama, but deep in doomed and helpless sensibility. "We don't even need a war," says the narrator. "We manage to blow ourselves up in times of peace."

CHAPTER 11

A Nuclear Chronology

The following chronology gives a year-by-year portrait of the march of nuclear weapon and related events. The focus is chiefly on events in and of the United States. Except for a handful of disasters, civilian nuclear power issues have been for the most part omitted from consideration, as have the peaceful uses of nuclear explosives. The chronology tries to cover as many important events as possible, but the relentless accretion of such events since 1945 rules out complete comprehensiveness. One hopes that few events of great significance have been omitted.

In addition to the big historical events, whether treaties, the introduction of major weapons, or international threats and crises, the chronology also includes numerous entries intended to give a sense of the human face of nuclear developments. These entries are particularly common in the late 1940s through early 1960s, when Americans at large were developing the foundations of their nuclear psychology. That in 1950 an amateur radio fan could panic his entire neighborhood with a feigned broadcast of an atomic attack warning may not mean a great deal in the overall historical sweep, but it says a lot about the psychology of people learning to live under the nuclear threat.

The New York Times proved an invaluable tool in constructing this chronology. Most of the direct quotations appeared in *Times* accounts of nuclear affairs. In addition to the *Times*, the chronology draws on many of the books treated in the bibliographic section of this guide, and on the following, especially for pre-1945 entries: Isaac Asimov's *Asimov's Chronology of Science and Discovery* (Harper, 1989) Alexander Hellemans' and Bryan Bunch's *The*

Timetables of Science (Simon & Schuster, 1988); Claire
L. Parkinson's *Breakthroughs: A Chronology of Great
Achievements in Science and Mathematics, 1200–1930*
(G.K. Hall, 1985), and Robert L. Weber's *Pioneers of
Science: Nobel Prize Winners in Physics* (Institute of
Physics, 1980).

1789

Discovery of uranium by the German chemist Martin
Klaproth.

1805

English chemist John Dalton publishes his theory that
there is bonding among atoms in the paper "On the
Absorption of Gases by Water."

1869

The Russian chemist Dmitry Mendeleev devises the
periodic table, which enhances understanding of
element sequence in radioactivity.

1895

Nov. 5: The German physicist Wilhelm Roentgen
discovers a form of radiation that penetrates opaque
substances. Roentgen calls this radiation x-rays. His
own hand is the first human target of x-rays.

1896

February: Inspired by Roentgen's x-ray photography,
French physicist Antoine–Henri Becquerel accidentally
discovers radioactivity in uranium while working with
photographic film.

1897

English physicist Joseph J. Thomson discovers the electron while conducting experiments with electric discharge tubes.

Based on her work with uranium, Marie Curie determines that radioactivity is atomic in origin.

British physicist Ernest Rutherford identifies two kinds of radiation emitted by radium. He calls them alpha and beta. Alpha rays consist of positively charged particles which later prove to be helium nuclei. Beta rays are negatively charged streams of electrons.

1898

Marie Curie coins the term "radioactivity" to refer to the process that takes place when an element self-destructs.

1900

French physicist Paul Ulrich Villard discovers gamma rays. Uncharged, they are related to X rays, and are far more penetrating than alpha or beta rays.

The German physicist Max Planck advances the quantum theory, which represents radiation as coming in individual units known as "quanta" or "photons." The theory is later important to the development of nuclear energy.

1903

Rutherford names the third kind of radioactivity "gamma rays."

1905

Albert Einstein's famous mass–energy equation, $E=mc^2$, indicates that the energy (E) released by converting mass (M) to energy would be the quantity of the mass times the speed of light (C) squared. This is the equation that rules nuclear weapons.

1911

Rutherford demonstrates the existence of the nucleus by bombarding gold foil with alpha particles; most pass through the foil unimpeded, but some are deflected or bounce back upon contact with the gold atom nuclei.

The cloud chamber, developed by the Scottish physicist Charles Thomson Rees Wilson, allows the paths of radioactive particles to become visible and photographed. The cloud chamber plays an important part in further nuclear research.

1914

British author H.G. Wells, always alert to scientific developments, publishes his futuristic novel *The World Set Free*, in which he coins the term "atomic bomb" and does a reasonably creditable job of foreseeing the effects of real–life atomic bombing.

1919

Rutherford discovers the proton.

1927

Five employees of the U.S. Radium Company in New Jersey sue the company after their jaws and spines begin to rot. The women, among a group who applied radium paint to the luminous dials of wristwatches, licked their brushes to points. By 1924, nine of these workers were dead, many others crippled.

1928

Improving on a 1908 design developed by the German scientist Hans Geiger and Rutherford, Geiger and Walther Mueller devise the radioactivity meter named after Geiger.

1929

American physicist Ernest O. Lawrence begins work on the first cyclotron in Berkeley, California. The cyclotron produces protons used to bombard target material in nuclear research.

1932

Feb.: Sir James Chadwick discovers neutrons. Lacking a charge, they are not repelled by atomic nuclei, and are extremely penetrating.

American physicist Carl D. Anderson discovers positrons, positively charged particles with the same mass as negatively charged electrons.

1933

Oct.: It occurs to Leo Szilard that a chain reaction might take place if an element could be found that would emit two neutrons when it absorbed one neutron.

1939

Feb. 11: Otto Frisch and Lise Meitner report their successful splitting of the nucleus of the atom in the periodical *Nature*.

Aug. 2: Einstein signs a letter to Franklin D. Roosevelt advising him of the potential of atomic weapons research.

Oct. 21: Roosevelt appoints a committee to examine the possibilities of building an atomic bomb.

1940

Element 94, plutonium, is created via cyclotron by physicists Glenn Seaborg and Edwin McMillan at the University of California. The readily fissionable plutonium-239 gave an alternative path to nuclear power and weapons in addition to uranium-235.

March: Exiled German scientist Rudolf Peierls and Otto Frisch furnish a 3-page memo to the British government detailing the practical possibilities and the consequences of the atomic bomb.

1941

October: Under the code name "Tube Alloys," Great Britain begins atomic bomb research.

Dec. 6: President Franklin D. Roosevelt signs the order that leads to development of the atomic bomb.

Dec. 21: The Soviet newspaper *Izvestia* publishes the article "Uranium," which discusses the use of uranium-235 to produce a bomb. The article also identifies some top Soviet scientists doing research on the subject.

1942

August: Establishment of the Manhattan Project. The official name of the group, which involves research programs at the University of California, the University of Chicago, the Massachusetts Institute of Technology, and Iowa State University, is the

Manhattan Engineering District.

Dec. 2: In the first nuclear reactor, built in a squash court at the University of Chicago, a nuclear reaction becomes self-sustaining.

Dec. 7: The U.S. Government takes over the Los Alamos Ranch School for Manhattan Project headquarters.

1942–43

The Oak Ridge nuclear facility is developed in Tennessee.

The Hanford Nuclear Reservation is established in Washington State; here nuclear reactors produce plutonium for the Manhattan Project.

1943

Feb. 28: The Allies destroy the Vermork, Norway heavy-water factory being used by Nazi scientists in their atomic bomb program.

A plateau at Los Alamos, New Mexico, is selected as the site for final assembly of the first atomic bombs. 6,000 people under the direction of J.R. Oppenheimer gather to make the bombs.

1944

November: The first spent fuel is obtained from the Hanford reactors.

1945

June 11: The "Franck Report" (after Manhattan Project scientist James Franck) to the U.S. Secretary of War warns against using the Bomb on Japan, partly because such use "will mean a flying start towards an unlimited armaments race."

July 16: The first nuclear test explosion occurs at the Trinity Site near Alamogordo, New Mexico. A bomb containing thirteen and a half pounds of plutonium–239 is detonated atop a 100–foot high steel tower. The heat from the explosion is felt fifty miles away; the light is visible 250 miles away; earth tremors are felt at the same distance. Most of the instruments installed to measure the test are destroyed by it.

July 17: Leo Szilard and 68 other scientists address a petition to the President expressing reservations about using A-bombs on Japan, as well as fears of post-war dangers: "If after the war a situation is allowed to develop in the world which permits rival powers to be in uncontrolled possession of these new means of destruction, the cities of the United States as well as the cities of other nations will be in continuous danger of sudden annihilation."

Aug. 6: The B–29 "Enola Gay," piloted by Paul Tibbets, drops the atomic bomb "Little Boy" on Hiroshima. The Hiroshima bomb contains 132 pounds of uranium, not plutonium. The bomb detonates at 1,900 feet with an explosive force of approximately 15,000 tons of TNT. (Today's estimates are lower than the 20,000 tons estimated at the time). Approximately 69,000 die immediately; 22,000 die soon afterward. In the ensuing months, another 30,000 die. 20,000 are missing. The dead include 23 American prisoners of war.

Aug. 9: "Fat Man" falls on Nagasaki from the B–29 "Bock's Car," killing somewhere around 70,000. "Fat Man" contains plutonium, and goes off at 1,650 feet. It is more powerful than the Hiroshima bomb, with the explosive equivalent of approximately 22,000 tons of TNT (about the same power as the Trinity test blast).

Oct. 4: The Atomic Scientists of Chicago, forerunner of the Federation of American Scientists, advocate international control of atomic energy. "The important question is not whether we should keep the secret of the atomic bomb or give it away, but what the policy of this country should be with the knowledge that in a few years from now there will be a sufficient number of atomic bombs on hand in several countries to cause a world catastrophe."

Oct. 8: Truman announces that the U.S. will not share the "secret" of atomic bomb production.

Oct. 13: The Association of Los Alamos Scientists, composed of several hundred individuals who helped develop the Bomb, denounces Truman's decision to retain the "secret" of the Bomb on the grounds that the decision will hasten the advent of a full-scale atomic war.

Oct. 26: In the November *Atlantic Monthly*, Albert Einstein argues that "the secret of the atomic bomb should be committed to a World Government." Einstein would have this government set up by the U.S., the U.S.S.R., and Great Britain.

Nov. 23: On orders from Gen. MacArthur, Army engineers destroy five cyclotrons in Japan; the cyclotrons were being used for atomic research banned by the General.

Nov. 25: The Association of Oak Ridge Scientists calls the Japanese cyclotron smashing "wanton and stupid" and a "crime against humanity."

Dec. 5: J.R. Oppenheimer tells the Special Senate Committee on Atomic Energy that destruction of the U.S. atomic bomb stockpile should be carried out if required as a step toward world peace.

Dec. 11: Religious cult leader Fr. Divine, who likes to hear it proclaimed that "Father Divine is God!" notes in a sermon published in his newspaper, *New Day*, that he himself is "the author and the finisher of the atomic energy!"

Dec. 18: University of Chicago scientist Dr. John Simpson reports that U.S. atomic bomb plants are working 24 hours a day.

Dec. 20: The Atomic Energy Act of 1946 provides for federal control of atomic energy.

1946

Feb. 19: In preparation for nuclear testing and the beginning of the nuclear arms race, the U.S. moves 120 inhabitants of the Bikini Atoll to Rongerik. Rear Adm C.A. Pownall notes that the Bikini dwellers were permitted to vote on which island they would be moved to.

April 28: United Press reports that the U.S. Army and Navy have ordered a survey of caves for possible military use in atomic war.

May 18: President Truman tells the Rev. Dr. William B. Lampe, moderator of the Presbyterian Church General Assembly, that the Bomb has led humanity into "the new and unpredictable age of the soul."

May 30: Canadian scientist Louis Slotin dies at the age of 35 from exposure to radiation during a May 21 accident at the Los Alamos bomb laboratory. His quick action during the accident saved the lives of several colleagues. Slotin is the first of many workers killed, injured, or contaminated in U.S. nuclear weapons facilities. Not until 1988 does the U.S. nuclear weapons industry's historically abysmal record on safety and environmental pollution become widely exposed to public scrutiny.

June 7: President Truman outlines in a policy statement the "Baruch Plan," named after Bernard Baruch, U.S. delegate to the United Nations Atomic Energy Commission. The plan proposes an international Atomic Development Authority that would oversee atomic energy on a global level. The plan does not succeed.

June 22: Col. S.B. Ritchie reveals U.S. Army plans for

an ocean-crossing missile, able to strike any target on earth within an hour.

July 1: The first post-war U.S. atomic bomb test takes place at Bikini Atoll. A painting of actress Rita Hayworth adorns the bomb, named "Gilda" after a Hayworth film. The B-29 "Dave's Dream" drops the bomb in the vicinity of 73 target ships.

July 24: The second post-war A-test, Test Baker; sailors are saddened at the sinking of the aircraft carrier Saratoga, one of the target ships. The bomb's name is "Bikini Helen."

Aug. 1: President Truman signs the bill authorizing creation of the atomic energy control commission (the A.E.C.). The bill allows the Army and Navy to produce atomic weapons and provides the death penalty for atomic espionage.

Aug. 31: John Hersey's *Hiroshima*, the now-classic portrait of the bombing of the city, is the only article in the *New Yorker*.

Nov. 10: Unitarian Rev. A. Powell Davies denounces as "utterly loathsome" the baking of a cake in a mushroom-cloud shape for U.S. Navy admirals Blandy and Lowry, in St. Louis. Blandy was commander of the Bikini tests. Lowry says that the pastor "probably just doesn't understand the situation."

Nov. 17: In New Jersey, Albert Einstein kicks off a $1 million fund-raising drive by the Emergency Committee of Atomic Scientists to support education regarding the nuclear threat.

Dec. 24: Igor V. Kurchatov's nuclear reactor begins operation in the Soviet Union, some four years after a Soviet decision to pursue the atomic bomb.

1947

Jan. 1: The U.S. Atomic Energy Commission assumes

control of all the nation's atomic energy enterprises.

Jan. 3: British geneticist J.B.S. Haldane warns that bombs may cause gene mutation affecting generations. "The killing of 10 percent of humanity by an attack with atomic bombs might not destroy civilization," he says, "but the production of abnormalities in 10 percent of the population by gene mutations induced by radioactivity may very easily destroy it."

Jan. 28: A.E.C. chairman nominee David E. Lilienthal lambastes the War Department's publication of Prof. H.D. Smythe's report on the bomb, *Atomic Energy for Military Purposes*, as a breach of security.

Feb. 9: Sen. Alexander Wiley (R–WI) proposes that the U.S. set up an emergency "push button" government in case the President, Cabinet, and Congress are obliterated in "one atomic flash."

March 19: Virgil Jordan, president of the National Industrial Conference Board, urges using the Bomb to compel disarmament. "Let us drop them in fact, promptly and without compunction," he says, should U.S.–imposed world peace be resisted.

March 25: The Atomic Bomb Casualty Commission reports abnormalities among infants born to bombing victims of Hiroshima and Nagasaki.

April 9: A U.S. Navy study is reported contending that nuclear missiles with intercontinental range are at least 25 years away.

May 13: Ethel Johns, consultant to the Canadian Nurses' Association, tells 5,000 delegates at the International Council of Nurses meeting that nurses must prepare carefully to offer effective nursing "in so large a calamity" as atomic war.

June 1: President Truman's Advisory Commission on Universal Training outlines an 8-point security program to avert extermination. Unless prompt action is taken, including universal military training for all

American males, the U.S., suggests the commission, will be a sitting duck for atomic attack by 1955.

June 5: The Oak Ridge Engineers and Scientists Association denies charges by Rep. J. Parnell Thomas, chairman of the House Un-American Activities Committee, that Communists have infiltrated Oak Ridge plants.

Sept. 1: In Washington, DC, the Federation of American Scientists warns: "Atomic warfare is intolerably severe. . . . There is no adequate defense against atomic bombs. There will be no defense. Inescapably, then, national security lies in world security and that can be attained only by international action."

Sept. 2: Strategic Air Command chief Gen. George C. Kenney indicates that U.S. atomic bombers are ready for action "against anybody, anytime."

Sept 28: Scientists report that the Bikini Atoll remains completely radioactive a year after the bomb test. All living things in the atoll are contaminated.

Sept. 29: The University of Chicago announces plans to train physicians in the care of atomic war victims. "If an atomic bomb were to hit Chicago," says a University official, "we would have quite a mess on our hands."

Oct. 1: The U.S. Air Force becomes an independent arm of the U.S. military.

Oct. 4: Roger W. Babson, a Massachusetts statistician, predicts atomic war and social collapse within the decade, and opens his "Utopia College" in Eureka, KS. "Kansas will be the Stalingrad of America," says Babson.

Dec. 8: President Truman issues an executive order declaring federal ownership of uranium and other fissionable materials contained in public lands to be leased or sold.

1948

Jan. 13: The President's Air Policy Commission warns that the U.S. Air Force has only five years to prepare for atomic attack.

March 9: *New York Times* military and science writers Hanson W. Baldwin and William L. Lawrence claim that it will take the Soviets 25 years to catch up with the U.S. in A-bomb development.

March 16: Clarence Booth is reported building an "atom bomb proof" house reinforced with thousands of tons of steel and concrete inside a Lakewood, NJ, hillside.

Aug. 21: Gen. Carl Spaatz reveals that the Air Force is working on a long-range missile. "Since there is no existing defense against this type of weapon, it is essential that the United States be the first nation to develop it," says the General.

Sept. 10: Memorandum NSC-30 from the National Security Council assigns responsibility for using nuclear weapons to the Chief Executive.

Oct. 30: Sir George Thomson, former chairman of the British Atomic Energy Commission, assures the British Atomic Scientists' Association that it will be two decades before any nation can compete with the U.S. in atomic bomb production.

Nov. 4: The U.N. General Assembly adopts the U.S. plan for international atomic control. The Soviet Union objects.

Nov. 13: The U.S. Office of Civil Defense Planning submits a 300-page civil defense plan that assumes atomic attack with 100,000 casualties per bomb; the plan calls for the mobilization of 15 million civilians in an emergency.

Dec. 3: Northern New Jersey stages the nation's first atomic bomb attack exercise, based on a hypothetical assault on New York City.

1949

April 4: The North Atlantic Treaty Organization is established.

April 4: Pig No. 311, a survivor of the first atomic test at Bikini in 1946, goes to its new home in the Washington Zoo.

April 6: President Truman says he would use the Bomb if necessary for security. "I wouldn't hesitate," he says.

July 17: American Quakers suggest putting the Bomb under U.N. control as a peace move. The American Friends Service Committee insists that "war between the United States and the Soviet Union is not inevitable."

Aug. 29: The first Soviet nuclear test, "Pervaya Molniya" ("First Lightning") takes place under the direction of Igor V. Kurchatov in the Ustyurt desert.

Sept. 23: President Truman acknowledges the Soviet atomic blast: "We have evidence that within recent weeks an atomic explosion occurred in the U.S.S.R."

Oct. 3: Ferris Booth places an ad in the *New York Times* urging Truman to invoke God to avert atomic war. "God is the only defense against the atomic bomb," claims Booth.

Oct. 7: Speaking to the House Armed Services Committee, Adm. Arthur W. Radford attacks what he believes to be the evolving U.S. strategic policy of massive atomic bombing, the "atomic blitz." He expresses his conviction that area bombing of civilians during WW II, by both atomic and conventional weapons, was a mistake that ignored the objectives of peace.

Oct. 9: Rep. John F. Kennedy claims that indifference to civil defense planning is leaving the U.S. open to "an atomic Pearl Harbor."

Dec. 3: An experiment involving plutonium production for bombs at the Hanford Nuclear Reservation in Washington State spreads radioactive Iodine 131 through Washington and Oregon at levels 1,000 percent greater than those measured during the Three Mile Island reactor accident.

1950

Jan. 31: President Truman directs the A.E.C. to build a hydrogen bomb.

Feb 3: Dr. Klaus Fuchs, German-born British atomic scientist, is arrested in London for giving atomic secrets to the Soviet Union.

Feb. 11: Albert Einstein warns that development of the H-bomb would bring the "annihilation of any life on earth" within technical possibility.

Feb 21: The U.S. Defense Department and the A.E.C. announce that an Army construction force will build a range for periodic atomic tests at Eniwetok.

March 1: Fuchs pleads guilty to 4 counts of betraying U.S. & British secrets to the U.S.S.R. between 1943–1947; is sentenced to 14 years imprisonment. He apologizes for his actions.

March 2: Commenting on suggestions that the seat of government be moved to obtain security from atomic attack, President Truman says he feels safe in Washington, DC.

March 11: The Gallup Poll indicates that 85% of Americans have heard of the H-bomb; half of these believe Russia knows how to build the H-bomb and would use it on the U.S.

March 31: *Scientific American* editor Gerard Piel charges that 30,000 copies of the magazine were burned on orders of the A.E.C. because of H-bomb data contained in an article by Dr. Hans A. Bethe.

April 14: National Security Council Memorandum NSC-68 states that "within the next four or five years the Soviet Union will possess the military capability of delivering a surprise attack of such great weight that the United States must have substantially increased general air, ground, and sea strength, atomic capabilities and air and civilian defenses to deter war. . . ." The chief author of NSC-68 is Paul Nitze, Director of the State Department's Policy Planning Staff. NSC-68 plays a major part in driving the U.S. military buildup of the 1950s.

April 18: W. Stuart Symington, retiring Secretary of the Air Force, warns that the U.S.S.R. has planes able to deliver surprise atomic attack on U.S.

May 12: U.S. officials announce development of small atomic bombs capable of delivery by jet fighter-bombers.

May 26: Nobel Prize-winning British physicist P.M.S. Blackett sees no defense against atomic attack on Great Britain.

June 5: Dr. Norvin C. Kiefer, Director of the Health Resources Division of the Office of Civilian Mobilization, says victims of one atomic attack would need more blood than the U.S. can stock in a year. Two hundred boxcars of medical supplies would be needed for the first week alone.

June 17: The A.E.C. announces that the National Research Council's Atomic Bomb Casualty Commission survey at Hiroshima reveals eye cataracts caused by radiation are the first evidence of delayed effects.

June 25: Korean War starts.

July 4: Colonies of the Ozarks, Inc., forms to build

bombproof homes in the Ozarks. The "colonies" will house 50 residents each; "They will afford some chance for survival and an opportunity to serve in the glorious days ahead," says a company spokesman.

July 7: In the first request for H-bomb funding, Truman asks Congress for $260 million.

July 10: Seattle civil defense officials deal with the hypothetical effects of a simulated underwater atomic bomb blast.

July 12: Rep. Lloyd M. Bentsen, Jr. (D-TX, and 1988 vice-presidential candidate) receives an enthusiastic response in the House when he proposes that Truman demand North Korean withdrawal from South Korea, or have atomic bombs dropped on its cities.

July 19: Arguing that the U.S. must stand "as the champions of decency," General Eisenhower rejects suggestions that the Bomb be used on North Korea.

July 26: West Coast customs inspectors begin to halt foreign ships as they enter the 3-mile limit to search for hidden atomic bombs.

July 27: Truman publicly dismisses the possibility of using the Bomb in Korea.

July 29: A new Washington, DC real estate ad campaign stressing suburban safety begins. "Out beyond range of atom bombs," says one ad. "Out of the radiation zone," says another.

Aug. 10: An A.E.C. spokesman announces that cattle exposed to the Alamogordo, NM blast in 1945 have developed pre-cancerous skin lesions.

Aug. 12: The Defense Department and the A.E.C. publish the 438-page handbook, *The Effects of Atomic Weapons.*

Aug. 18: The Zaro Concrete Co. of Teaneck, NJ, announces formation of the A-Bomb Shelter

Corporation. The company will build affordable backyard bomb shelters.

Aug. 31: The talking blues tune "Old Man Atom" is withdrawn from the market by RCA and Columbia Records following complaints that the song, written by journalist Vern Partlow, parrots the Communist Party "peace line."

Sept. 1: Maj. Gen. Orvil A. Anderson is relieved of command of the U.S. Air War College for advocating a pre-emptive strike against the Soviet Union.

Sept 12: Sen. Olin D. Johnston (D–SC) urges the U.S. to bomb the U.S.S.R. in a speech to the National Federation of Federal Employees. The speech is well received.

Sept 18: Truman submits a master plan for civil defense to Congress.

Sept. 24: Walter Cronkite narrates a CBS television program on what the average person should do to survive atomic attack.

Sept. 27: Truman signs a bill for $260 million for development of the H–bomb.

Oct. 9: At its convention in Los Angeles, the American Legion advocates use of the Bomb to halt Soviet aggression.

Oct. 28: The National Security Resources Board publishes the pamphlet *Survival Under Atomic Attack*, hoping to provide civilians the information required to live through nuclear war.

Nov. 4: Amateur radio enthusiast Stanley Gordon broadcasts a false atomic attack warning, panicking his Bronx neighborhood.

Nov. 15: British sometime-peace activist Bertrand Russell backs use of nuclear weapons against the U.S.S.R. to curb aggression, and urges rapid rearmament.

Nov. 16: The London publication *Intelligence Digest* claims that the U.S.S.R. builds at least four bombs a month, and that it plans an atomic attack on the Middle East.

Dec. 8: Truman agrees to inform Great Britain before using the Bomb.

Dec. 9: The U.S. armed services issue cards on how to act under atomic attack. The 3x2 inch cards advise their bearers not to stand out in the open.

Dec. 16: In a radio address, Prime Minister Attlee assures Britons that the U.S. will not use atomic bombs "lightly or wantonly."

Dec. 22: The U.S. Army announces "dog tag" radiation detectors which, if worn by atomic attack victims, will indicate the victims' degree of radiation exposure.

1951

Jan. 3: The U.S. Senate passes a bill setting up an integrated federal–state civil defense system. The majority of the $3.1 billion program funds are assigned to construction of community A–bomb shelters.

Feb. 1: Gen. Eisenhower tells congressional committees that he would use A–bombs first in war if he thought they would provide a net advantage to his forces.

Feb 2: University of Rochester physicists report that radioactive snow has been falling all week in Rochester, NY.

Feb 6: Paul Aurandt, better known as news broadcaster Paul Harvey, is caught breaking into the Argonne National Laboratory grounds; reportedly he sought to test security measures. The FBI releases him after inquiry.

Feb 6: An atomic test flash in Nevada lights up Los Angeles 300 miles away; witnesses also see it 250 miles south of the Mexican border, and in Boise, ID, 500 miles distant.

Feb. 15: 7th-Day Adventist church leaders announce their plan to turn nearly 3,000 of their churches into atomic war casualty stations.

Feb 26: Former Air Force scientist Dr. Anthony O. Mirarchi announces his suspicions that flying saucers may be carrying out reconnaissance flights over U.S. atomic test sites.

Feb. 26: A television civil defense course for housewives starts in New York City. The "Course in Self-Preservation" focuses on such atomic war concerns as radioactivity and care of burns.

March 6: Julius and Ethel Rosenberg and Morton Sobell go on trial in New York City for atomic espionage.

March 11: Col. William S. Stone of the Army Medical Graduate School advises a meeting of the College of Medical Evangelists against bandaging burns caused by atomic bombs.

March 20: The A.E.C. announces a new series of bomb tests at Eniwetok Atoll to investigate bomb shelter designs.

April 5: Convicted of giving U.S. atomic bomb secrets to the Soviets, Julius and Ethel Rosenberg are sentenced to death by federal judge Irving R. Kaufman. The Rosenbergs' collaborator, Morton Sobell, receives 30 years.

April 16: Rep. Albert Gore (D-TN) suggests using atomic bombs to establish an uninhabitable radioactive zone across Korea to halt North Korean troops.

May 7: President Truman warns the U.S. that a single atomic attack on the U.S. would "cause many more casualties than we have suffered in all the fighting in Korea."

May 12: Rep. Henry M. Jackson (D-WA) says tests at Eniwetok show troops can enter the area immediately after an atomic blast "with no fear of lingering radiation," thus suggesting the merits of battlefield nuclear weapons.

May 20: A Civil Defense administrator reports that over 2 million people have purchased the booklet *Survival Under Atomic Attack*.

June 14: Rep. F. Edward Hebert (D-LA) reports witnessing an Eniwetok blast that demolished everything on the island; "I had a feeling I was standing at the gates of Hell looking into eternity," says Hebert.

July 4: 25,000 watch a mock atomic bomb set off in a Baltimore civil defense show before the regular Independence Day fireworks display.

Sept. 12: Admiral Lynde D. McCormick announces development of an atomic bomb small enough to fit planes on aircraft carriers.

Sept. 29: The Civil Defense Administration urges that all citizens wear radiation-proof chrome-steel I.D. "dog tags."

Oct. 3: The White House announces the second Soviet A-bomb test.

Oct. 27: *Collier's* devotes its entire issue to a fictional atomic war, "Preview of the War We Do Not Want: Russia's Defeat & Occupation, 1952-1960." The hypothetical war includes the A-bombing of Moscow and Washington.

Oct. 30: The flash of light from an atomic test at Yucca Flat is visible close to 300 miles away, in California and Utah, even though the blast occurs in daylight.

Nov. 1: In "Exercise Desert Rock," 5,000 U.S. servicemen watch an atomic test from a distance of approximately 6 miles. The purpose of the test is to determine the effect of atomic blasts on combat installations.

Nov. 2: Scientists report radioactive snow found in upstate New York and radioactive dust "hundreds of times" above normal in Chicago.

Nov. 5: Windows rattle 260 miles away as the U.S. detonates its 21st atomic explosion at Yucca Flat. The explosion is audible for more than 100 miles.

Dec. 9: Radioactive snow falls in France.

Dec. 9: Premature bomb explosions and an ambulance crash injure eight in Lima, Ohio's second atomic-raid test.

Dec. 26: Leo Pauwels of L.A. describes a suit of five pounds of lead and khaki that he has designed as radiation protection for his six-year old son.

Dec 27: During a medical conference, it is revealed that the A.E.C. pays $35 per dog and $3.50 per cat for animals "bootlegged" into its labs.

1952

Jan 30: The Atomic Energy Commission reports "a definite increase in the incidence of leukemia" among Hiroshima survivors.

Feb. 15: "Operation Snowfall," Army winter maneuvers in New York, come to an end. The maneuvers involved simulated atomic bombing.

Feb 17: Prime Minister Churchill implies that Great Britain has the Bomb and announces plans to carry out atomic tests in Australia.

Feb. 25: The Rosenbergs' conviction is upheld by the

U.S. Court of Appeals in New York.

April 22: Over 2,000 soldiers emerge from foxholes and trenches four miles from ground zero shortly after a Yucca Flat A-bomb blast, the largest bomb so far detonated in the U.S. The men enter the target zone within an hour. Parachutists also enter the area as bomber crews fly above. A Pentagon spokesman describes the exercise as psychological indoctrination.

April 30: Prof. Robert R. Newell, director of safety precautions at the Bikini tests, urges California citizens to walk naked in the rain following atomic blasts to reduce fallout effects. "Better keep your shoes on," though, adds the professor.

May 17: The Army announces that troops on the Korean front are rehearsing atomic war defense actions.

May 27: Police hold a Brink's, Inc. driver in Chester, PA, on a disorderly conduct charge for refusing to abandon a truck carrying $1 million during a civil defense test.

June: The Lawrence Livermore Laboratory, one of the primary U.S. nuclear weapons research facilities, is established.

June 1: 1,000 troops proceed into the target area immediately after an atomic test blast at Yucca Flat until halted by radiation. It is the first occasion on which U.S. troops leave their shelters to engage a hypothetical enemy in the blast zone immediately after the explosion.

June 22: *Air Force Magazine* reports that the U.S. plans a guided atomic missile force able to destroy 95% of attacking Soviet bombers.

Oct 3: Great Britain blows up its first bomb at Monte Bello Island, west of Australia. The bomb goes off in a 1,450 ton frigate which is vaporized by the bomb's million-degree heat.

Oct. 7: Truman suggests that Eisenhower cannot be trusted with the "awful responsibility" of managing atomic weapons because of his weak response to "moral pygmies" like Sen. Joe McCarthy.

Nov. 1: The first U.S. hydrogen bomb test ("Mike") takes place at the Eniwetok Atoll in the Pacific. It is a 10.4 megaton blast which vaporizes an island, leaving in its place a crater a mile wide and 175 feet deep. Servicemen who participate in the test feel heat equal to "ten suns" from 35 miles away.

Nov. 13: A radioactive mouse spoils a Trenton, NJ, civil defense show when it contaminates other mice and their cage. Authorities had planned to let the public pick the "hot" mouse out with a Geiger counter.

Nov. 17: The U.S. Supreme Court refuses to review the Rosenberg convictions. The Court also rejects review of Morton Sobell's conviction.

1953

Jan. 7: In his final State of the Union message, Harry Truman warns Joseph Stalin that a war initiated by the U.S.S.R. would bring its ruin. "Lenin was a pre-atomic man," says Truman. "Something profound has happened since he wrote."

Feb. 11: Eisenhower denies clemency to the Rosenbergs.

March 20: Brig. Gen. Thomas K. Vincent, commander of the Army's missile center at Red Stone Arsenal in Alabama, states that the U.S. will have missiles capable of using atomic warheads within a few weeks.

March 24: Nine volunteer officers representing the Army, Navy and Air Force sit though an atomic test in a 5-foot trench 2,500 yards from ground zero at Camp Desert Rock, NV. The volunteers are a half-mile closer to the blast than any previous atomic test veterans. An additional 1,300 troops are 1.5 miles away. 53

planes fly overhead to "condition" airmen.

April 6: High-level commercial flights are banned in a 100,000 square mile area because of radiation danger from a Yucca Flat test detonation at 5,000 feet.

April 18: 2,000 Marines by land and helicopter "capture" an atomized area in a mop-up exercise after a Yucca Flat test blast whose light is visible in Montana, 850 miles away.

April 25: A Yucca Flats test code-named Simon produces such serious fallout that the A.E.C. considers halting nuclear tests at the site. Fallout deposited on Albany, NY, several days later exposes residents to up to 10 times the normal annual radiation dose.

May 8: On Harry Truman's birthday, a B-50 bomber drops an atomic bomb on the Frenchman Flat, NV, test site. Jet drones fly white mice and monkeys through the mushroom cloud a few minutes later; the animals sustain severe radiation injury. An hour after the blast, 2,000 atomic soldiers maneuver in the area.

May 14: Prospectors in the Gallup, NM area complain that atmospheric radiation following tests is so high that their Geiger counters can't distinguish it from radioactivity in uranium ore.

May 19: Radioactive particles fall on communities 100 miles away after a Yucca Flat test. Officials ask 5,000 St. George area residents in southwest Utah to stay indoors for three hours.

May 19: Gordon Dean, chairman of the A.E.C., tells a House subcommittee that the A.E.C. is building atomic bombs so fast it is running out of places to store them.

May 22: Air Force Gen. Nathan F. Twining says that the Soviet A-bomb stockpile may soon be enough to cripple American industry.

May 25: The first launch of an atomic bomb from a

piece of field artillery takes place at a Nevada site. The bomb, launched by the "Atomic Annie" cannon, detonates approximately 7 miles from the launch site. 3,000 atomic soldiers hunker in trenches some 2.5 miles from the explosion, which is about half the strength of the Hiroshima bomb.

May 27: According to A.E.C. records released in 1979, President Eisenhower instructs the agency to keep the public "confused" about nuclear testing to help insure tractable public opinion.

June 19: The Rosenbergs are electrocuted at Sing Sing following on the same day Eisenhower's second refusal to grant clemency. Three shocks are required to kill Julius, five to kill Ethel. The Rosenbergs die the day after their 14th wedding anniversary.

July 10: The Defense Department reveals that single-engine carrier-based fighters (the Douglas AD-4B Skyhawk) can now carry atomic bombs.

Aug. 6: U.S. Army Gen. Mark W. Clark advocates U.S. use of the A-bomb on N. Korea should it violate the truce.

Aug. 8: Soviet Premier Georgi M. Malenkov announces to the Supreme Soviet "that the U.S. has no monopoly in the production of hydrogen bombs."

Aug. 12: The U.S.S.R. detonates its first H-bomb in Siberia.

Aug. 20: *Pravda* announces the successful Soviet H-bomb test.

Aug. 29: U.S. Rep. Ernest Patterson of Connecticut urges seeking weapons more powerful than the H-bomb. "This has more priority than a balanced budget," he claims.

Sept. 13: Operation Monte Carlo, a 4-day nuclear war exercise involving France, Britain, and U.S. troops, concludes.

Sept 17: The federal Civil Defense Administration lists 70 likely atomic targets in the U.S.

Oct. 4: U.S. Rep. W. Sterling Cole, in a "Meet the Press" television interview, warns that the U.S.S.R. can destroy the U.S. with atomic bombs; he calls for an additional $16 billion for defense, "and since we are a God-fearing people, I hope a prayer. I think the condition is that desperate."

Oct. 8: President Eisenhower states at a press conference that the Soviet Union can now launch an atomic attack on the U.S.

Oct 15: Great Britain tests a bomb at Woomera range, Australia.

Oct. 18: Radioactive dust clouds are reported in Canberra, having drifted over the city from the Woomera range test.

Nov. 6: A U.S. military official announces that, in a program begun in 1949, the Navy has trained over 2,000 specialists to defuse dud atomic bombs in war.

Dec. 8: In his "Atoms for Peace" address, President Eisenhower proposes an international atomic energy pool under U.N. supervision devoted to peaceful purposes; he asks nations principally involved in the atomic arms race to contribute from stockpiles of fissionable materials.

Dec 15: The Eisenhower administration issues a directive warning the FBI and other federal law enforcement agencies to watch for small A-bombs smuggled into the U.S. for terrorist purposes in valises or by mail.

Dec. 22: Eisenhower orders suspension of J. Robert Oppenheimer's security clearance because of his previous association with communists. Oppenheimer headed the Los Alamos portion of the Manhattan Project, but opposed development of the hydrogen bomb.

1954

Jan. 7: In his State of the Union message, President Eisenhower announces the "New Look" U.S. military stance based on greater reliance on nuclear weapons and less on manpower.

Jan 16: The A.E.C. denies radiation from May '53 tests killed 1,000 sheep in southern Utah.

Jan. 21: Launching of the USS Nautilus, the first nuclear-powered submarine.

Jan. 28: Cambridge University physicist Otto R. Frisch speculates during a London lecture that blending cobalt into hydrogen bombs could produce radiation so deadly that it might exterminate civilization.

Feb. 15: In congressional testimony released today, a U.S. customs official reveals that Customs Bureau agents are searching the luggage of foreign travelers for smuggled atomic bombs.

March 1: Radioactive fallout from the second U.S. H-bomb test "Bravo" (a 15-megaton blast) at Bikini deposits material in the form of a fine ash on the Japanese fishing boat "Lucky Dragon" and its crew of 23 eighty miles distant, forty miles beyond the official danger zone, as well as on 250 Marshall Islanders.

March 16: U.S. Rep. W. Sterling Cole (R-NY), chair of the Joint Atomic Energy Commission, announces U.S. possession of a hydrogen bomb able to be delivered by airplane anywhere in the world.

March 18: U.S. Rep. James Van Zandt (R-PA) reports that the Bikini blast of March 1 destroyed an area 12 miles in diameter; says the city of Washington and some suburbs would have been destroyed. Remarking on injuries caused by the test, Van Zandt says, "In my opinion somebody is guilty of a blunder."

March 20: The U.S. notifies Japan that the danger area around its Bikini Atoll testing grounds now extends to a radius of 450 miles.

Mar 25: The A.E.C. confirms that strontium 90 could cause bone damage in a statement on Japanese physicians' analysis of victims of fallout from the U.S. test of March 1.

March 28: The Illinois Civil Defense Director calls Chicago "the No. 1 target of the Russians," and characterizes the city's shelters as "death traps." "It would be cruel to allow the public to feel the false security of city bomb shelters," he states.

March 29: Prime Minister Jawaharlal Nehru of India announces his belief that hydrogen bomb testing should cease.

April 6: Sen. Joseph R. McCarthy of Wisconsin charges that American research on the hydrogen bomb was deliberately delayed for a year and a half, apparently due to the presence of "traitors" in the federal government.

April 7: Gen. Charles de Gaulle, disgusted with U.S. treatment of France, says that France must become a nuclear power to assert its independence.

April 9: The U.S. apologizes to Japan for dropping fallout on the "Lucky Dragon."

April 14: Physician, philosopher and humanitarian Albert Schweitzer, winner of the 1952 Nobel Peace Prize, urges scientists to speak out against H-bomb testing.

April 30: Physicians who studied the effects of the bomb on pregnant Nagasaki women report in the *American Journal of Diseases of Children* a high rate of radiation-induced fetal injuries.

May 14: Marshall Islanders petition the U.N. for an end to atomic testing in their territory. They cite illnesses of citizens from Rongelap and Utirik hundreds of miles from the test site including nausea, burns, hair loss and blood disorders.

June 1: J. Robert Oppenheimer's attorneys announce his status as a "loyal citizen" as determined by the Atomic Energy Commission. His security clearance, however, is not restored.

June 2: 12,000 Southern Baptist Convention representatives in St. Louis receive pennies irradiated at Oak Ridge, TN, as symbols of a higher "spiritual power."

June 14: 54 U.S. cities are targets of the country's first nation-wide atomic raid drill. Total "fatalities" are estimated at 12 million. President Eisenhower spends the drill in an underground shelter.

June 15: Publicly-released transcripts of hearings conducted by the A.E.C. special board investigating Oppenheimer reveal that physicist Edward Teller testified that had Oppenheimer and others like him provided "moral support," the U.S. could have procured the hydrogen bomb four years earlier.

Sept. 9: A.E.C. Chairman Adm. Lewis L. Strauss announces in a news conference that he anticipates an early end to the nuclear arms race.

Sept 24: Japanese fisherman Aikichi Kuboyama becomes the first H-bomb fatality when he dies as a result of radiation injuries resulting from the March 1 Bikini blast. His death provokes a national outpouring of grief in Japan, where Kuboyama had come to symbolize the nuclear threat. U.S. Ambassador John Allison sends his regrets and a check for $2,700 to Kuboyama's widow.

Sept. 30: The USS "Nautilus," the first atomic-powered submarine, is commissioned.

Nov. 2: Prime Minister Churchill tells the House of Commons that an "undue number" of bomb bursts might affect the atmosphere seriously for 5,000 years. Some members laugh at his statement.

Dec. 17, 18: NATO gives its commanders the go-ahead to plan for inclusion of nuclear weapons in their defense strategies.

1955

Jan. 12: Sec. of State John Foster Dulles enunciates the U.S. strategic policy of "Massive Retaliation."

Jan. 28: Great Britain dumps containers bearing 1,500 tons of radioactive waste into the Atlantic Ocean.

Feb. 15: The A.E.C. indicates that radioactive fall-out from the March 1, 1954 H-bomb test at Bikini was sufficient to endanger all persons within a 7,000-square-mile area.

Feb. 17: Great Britain announces that it will begin production of its own hydrogen bombs.

March 11: A radioactive cloud 1,000 miles long and 200 miles wide, originating in a March 7 Nevada test, drifts over the eastern U.S.; the Weather Bureau calls it harmless.

March 12: When two scientists from Colorado University note that the atomic tests could pose a danger to the public from radiation, Colorado Gov. Edwin C. Johnson states that the scientists, Ray Lanier and Theodore Puck, should be arrested.

March 16: President Eisenhower states at a news conference that use of tactical nuclear weapons "strictly for military purposes" would receive his approval.

March 22: Fall-out dusts Las Vegas from the 6th test blast in current series. 2,000 Marines hide in trenches 3,500 yards from the blast; ten minutes after the detonation, they advance into the blast zone.

Mar 24: The federal Civil Defense Administration announces plans to develop evacuation and shelter programs for 92 critical target cities.

Mar 29: For the first time, two test blasts go off in one day at the Nevada site. Radiation levels at the hamlet of Alamo, NV, 50 miles away, reach 1.4 roentgens; the A.E.C. takes no special precautions for the residents.

April 1: After the story is reported in the press, the Defense Department acknowledges that some servicemen incurred serious eye injuries during atomic tests in 1952 and 1953.

April 3: The Federal Housing Administration offers to guarantee loans up to $2,500 on private bomb shelters.

April 15: The A.E.C. denies before the Joint Congressional Atomic Energy Committee that radioactive fallout from the atomic tests has caused any health hazards.

May 5: "Doomtown," a mock-up town constructed at the Yucca Flat, NV, proving grounds, suffers the effects of an atomic test with a force of some 30+ kilotons as an armored task force of 460 men maneuvers approximately 3,200 yards from ground zero.

May 5: A number of western states undergo an atomic raid alert when defense units are not notified of a routine training flight of U.S. B–47 bombers approaching from Canada. Office buildings are evacuated, radio stations go off the air, and thousands of Oakland, CA schoolchildren carry out a well-rehearsed A-raid drill that this time seems to be the real thing.

May 8: Twenty-five Japanese women, popularly known as the "Hiroshima Maidens," injured in the Hiroshima attack arrive in the U.S., where they will receive plastic surgery, paid for by private funds, at Mount Sinai Hospital in New York.

May 14: The Warsaw Pact Organization is established.

Aug. 6: An international rally on a nuclear bomb ban opens in Hiroshima immediately following a ceremony to mark the tenth anniversary of the atomic bombing.

Oct 10: The Atomic Bomb Casualty Commission announces the discovery of 11 survivors of both Hiroshima and Nagasaki bombings, the only known survivors of both bombings.

Oct 11: The A.E.C. denies that fallout from spring tests killed cattle at Black Lake, NM.

Oct 21: A.E.C. Commissioner Dr. Willard F. Libby reports that radioactivity in oceans north of the Equator increased 10 times in the past two years as a result of bomb tests; the radiation poses no hazard, he says.

Nov. 26: The Soviet Union acknowledges recent detonation of a hydrogen bomb in the multiple megaton range, the U.S.S.R.'s biggest blast to date.

Nov. 29: The A.E.C. reports that radioactive fall-out from the huge Soviet explosion announced Nov. 26 is widespread in the U.S.

Dec. 16: The United Nations General Assembly approves a disarmament resolution combining the "open sky" proposals of President Eisenhower for mutual air inspection of the U.S. and U.S.S.R., with a Soviet proposal for ground inspectors.

1956

Jan. 19: A.E.C. spokesman Dr. Willard F. Libby assures the public that nuclear weapons testing presents no health hazard to human beings.

Feb. 2: Federal Civil Defense Administrator Val Peterson urges farmers to build atomic shelters for families and livestock.

Feb. 18: Georgi K. Zhukov, Soviet Defense Minister,

tells the Communist Party Congress that nuclear weapons would spread beyond the battlefield and that, if attacked by the West, the Soviet Union would retaliate against the U.S.

Feb. 27: The Federation of American Scientists accuses the Atomic Energy Commission of misleading the American public on the harmful effects of atomic tests.

March 20: Dr. Ralph E. Lapp, an atomic-bomb scientist, testifies before a Congressional subcommittee that officials underestimate the destructiveness of radioactive fallout. Fallout from H-bombs could render an area uninhabitable for years. [This is, in fact, what happened in the Bikini Atoll.]

April 21: Adlai Stevenson tells the American Society of Newspaper Editors in Washington, D.C., that the U.S. should consider a unilateral halt to H-bomb testing. "I question the sense in multiplying and enlarging weapons of a destructive power already almost incomprehensible," says Stevenson.

Apr 22: Rep. August H. Andresen (R-MN) urges Congress to authorize a nation-wide network of "survival food depots" to feed city-dwellers fleeing atomic attack.

April 23: Nikita S. Khrushchev tells a British Industries Trade Fair gathering in Birmingham that the Soviet Union intends to develop an intercontinental missile capable of carrying a hydrogen warhead "that can fall anywhere in the world."

April 25: Eisenhower rejects calls for a halt of hydrogen bomb testing, linking perfection of the bomb with perfection of an ICBM delivery vehicle.

May 25: U.S. Lt. Gen. James M. Gavin tells a Senate subcommittee in secret that he estimates there would be hundreds of millions of casualties from a U.S. hydrogen bomb attack on the Soviet Union, with many of the casualties in non-communist nations.

May 26: The Senate Armed Services Subcommittee on air power releases testimony offered by Strategic Air Command chief General Curtis LeMay. LeMay fears that the Soviet Union will have twice as many long-range bombers as the U.S. by 1959, and an ICBM by 1958; the possible result: a surprise attack on the U.S.

July 18: In a news conference, Secretary of State John Foster Dulles indicates that a "selective" nuclear deterrent could be used in small wars.

July 20: Operation Alert involves mock atomic attacks on 75 U.S. areas; nearly 4,000 radio and television stations throughout the country halt normal broadcasting, and 1,300 AM stations switch to Conelrad frequencies. 10,000 federal employees scatter to 65 secret locations within a 250-mile radius of Washington, D.C. Casualty estimates are withheld for fear of hurting morale.

July 26: SAC's ICBM missile program is announced.

Aug. 4: Secretary of the Air Force Donald A. Quarles states his belief that nuclear weapons could be used in small-scale wars.

Aug. 5: An Hiroshima women's organization survey of people in Hiroshima at the time of the bombing finds 7,668 still suffer from its effects.

Sept. 26: Former New York Governor Thomas E. Dewey says in a speech at the University of Michigan that Adlai Stevenson's stands in opposition to H-bomb testing and the draft would leave the U.S. "naked and alone in a hostile world."

Oct. 2: Sen. Karl Mundt (R.-SD), attacks Adlai Stevenson for advising a U.S. halt to H-bomb tests, as well as the draft, charging that Stevenson's policies would invite attack.

Oct. 3: Vice President Richard Nixon, speaking in Philadelphia, dismisses Adlai Stevenson's position against H-bomb testing as "catastrophic nonsense."

Oct 15: In a Chicago television speech, Adlai E. Stevenson warns of bone cancer and genetic damage from strontium 90 fallout, which he calls "the most dreadful poison in the world."

Oct. 16: Sen. Estes Kefauver (D-TN), who previously advocated continuing hydrogen bomb tests, announces at a press conference that H-bombs could knock the planet 16 degrees off its axis.

Oct. 18: Eisenhower calls Stevenson's H-bomb test and draft opposition "pie-in-the-sky" and "wishful thinking."

Nov. 2: Adlai Stevenson charges in a Detroit speech that the Eisenhower administration is covering up the contamination of American milk with strontium-90 from H-bomb testing.

Nov. 5: Dr. Edward Teller, calling the dangers of radiation "insignificant," urges continued H-bomb testing.

1957

Jan. 11: A U.N. resolution authorizes the International Atomic Energy Agency as a United Nations body. Its mission is to deter nuclear weapons proliferation and to render technical assistance in civilian nuclear power operations.

Jan. 23: President Eisenhower tells newsmen that the U.S. "would almost have to use" nuclear weapons in the event of war in the Middle East.

Feb. 9: Former National Research Council defense expert Willard Bascom urges installing $400 fiberglass shelters in backyards of suburban homes. Bascom designed the shelters himself.

Feb. 18: Civil Defense Administrator Val Peterson tells a House subcommittee that half of the U.S. population would be destroyed in surprise attack regardless of bomb shelters; intercontinental missiles would make evacuation plans pointless. "In the final analysis," he says, "there is no such thing as a nation being prepared for a thermonuclear war."

April 5: West German Chancellor Konrad Adenauer states in a news conference his belief that West Germany must have nuclear weapons.

April 23: Dr. Albert Schweitzer warns of harmful effects from bomb tests in a message to the Nobel Prize Committee. "We are committing this folly in thoughtlessness," contends the humanitarian.

April 24: John H. Harley of the A.E.C. reports a slow but steady rise of strontium 90 in milk. He contends that the presence of the poison is not dangerous.

May 1: The U.S. begins operation of a national warning system for civil defense through the Continental Air Defense Command headquarters in Colorado Springs.

May 15: In Operation Grapple, Great Britain tests its first hydrogen bomb on Christmas Island in the Indian Ocean.

May 22: A 42,000 pound H-bomb, one of the most powerful ever built, falls out of a B-36 bomber and hits the ground near Albuquerque, NM, creating a crater in a non-nuclear explosion.

June 3: Linus Pauling releases a petition bearing the signatures of some 2,000 scientists against nuclear testing.

July 5: The most powerful atomic test of the 52 to date in the U.S., a "shot" of approximately 80 kilotons, is set off at Yucca Flat. Shock waves are felt hundreds of miles away; 2,000 Marines occupy trenches 3 miles from the blast.

July 6-11: The Pugwash meetings on peace begin when approximately two dozen scientists meet at Pugwash,

Nova Scotia. The scientists, representing several nations, issue grave warnings of the damage likely in a nuclear war, and indicate that it would be "difficult to limit a local war once atomic bombs were used."

July 17: President Eisenhower advocates nuclear weapons for NATO.

July 24: The California State Health Department reports that radioactivity in run-off water from Sierra Mountain snow in northern counties makes water unsafe for drinking.

Aug. 25: A dozen U.S. scientists warn that the bones of young people in the Northeastern U.S. may contain up to 25% of the maximum permissible strontium 90 if nuclear tests continue at the present rate.

Aug. 26: The Soviet Union announces the first successful test of an ICBM.

Aug. 31: U.S. troops stage a mock assault on an "enemy" hypothetically struck by a real bomb twice as powerful as the Hiroshima weapon. Blue light from the blast is visible 400 miles away in San Francisco.

Sept. 15: Many television viewers in Hartford, CT, believe that a program intended as a Civil Defense educational tool is announcing actual events when it describes "unidentified airplanes" heading toward the U.S. from across the North Pole.

Sept. 25: The Soviet government reports ground and naval troop exercises in conjunction with an H-bomb test, its first such disclosure.

Oct. 4: The Soviet Union orbits Sputnik 1. The success of this project jolts the world at large, and particularly the U.S., for it demonstrates the imminent Soviet ability to deliver nuclear bombs anywhere on the planet.

Oct. 10: Lt. Gen. C.R. Huebner urges improvement of the U.S. civil defense alert system "whatever the cost." "We have now been shown that a missile fired in Russia can be over New York City...in about thirty-five minutes."

Nov. 15: The head of a U.S. Air Force team investigating nuclear explosions to destroy incoming ICBMs says that "We feel we have ways of destroying nuclear and non-nuclear rockets out in space."

Nov. 22: A committee headed by H. Rowan Gaither, Jr. urges construction of a vast network of fallout shelters at a cost of some $20 billion. The committee includes, among others, arms controller Paul Nitze.

Dec. 17: The first successful test of a U.S. ICBM, the Atlas, occurs at Cape Canaveral, FL.

1958

Jan. 31: The U.S. orbits its first satellite, Explorer 1.

March 11: A B-47 bomber accidentally drops an unarmed A-bomb near Florence, SC; six are hurt and homes damaged when TNT in the bomb's trigger explodes. In later interviews, the bomber crew reports being unaware that the bomb had been dropped until some time after it left the plane.

March 28: Atomic scientist and Manhattan Project veteran Dr. Edward Condon, head of the physics department at Washington University, charges that Edward Teller and U.S. government officials are hiding facts about fallout dangers.

April 1: A Iowa State University chemist reports that farm ponds in southern Iowa show sharp radioactivity increases since 1957 Nevada nuclear tests.

April 3: Dr. Willard F. Libby reports A.E.C. findings revealing the Northeastern U.S. as "one of the hottest places in the world" from a standpoint of radioactivity.

April 13: The Civil Defense Administration announces plans to train 1 million high-school students to operate instruments to measure fallout. "In a nuclear war," says CD chief Leo A. Hoegh, "it isn't the nation that makes the attack that will win; it's the nation that can sustain itself that will win."

April 19: Dr. Willard F. Libby says people could determine when to emerge from shelters if transistor radio manufacturers would build Geiger counters into their sets.

April 30: It is announced that the Office of Defense Mobilization has ordered banks to list plans for protecting personnel, preserving records and continuing operations in nuclear war.

May 15: 150,000 students from 57 Japanese universities boycott classes to protest British and American bomb tests in the Pacific.

July 23: President Eisenhower receives the first copy of a survival booklet to be distributed by Boy Scouts to 40 million U.S. homes. The booklet contains tips on radiation hazards and atomic attack warning signals.

Aug. 1 and 12: Experiments with rabbits during high altitude nuclear explosions over Johnston Island show that such blasts may be blinding at distances as great as 1,000 miles.

Aug. 10: The U.N. Scientific Committee on the Effect of Atomic Radiation reports that "Even the smallest amounts of radiation are liable to cause deleterious genetic, and perhaps also somatic, effects."

Sept. 19: Britain receives its first shipment of American-made IRBMs (intermediate range ballistic missiles) for a British missile base.

Sept. 30: Italian defense officials announce plans for construction of launch sites for U.S. IRBMs.

Oct. 19: The nation's first blast and radiation-resistant

defense control center, a concrete bunker at a rural Illinois intersection, is dedicated. The bunker will serve Chicago, Gary, and Hammond.

Nov. 4: The U.S. Air Force acknowledges publicly for the first time that a nuclear weapon was involved in the crash of an airplane, in this case a B-47 which went down near Abilene, TX.

Nov.-Sept., 1961: The U.S., the Soviet Union and Great Britain observe an unofficial moratorium on nuclear weapons testing.

1959

Jan. 1: A Los Alamos Laboratory technician receives a dose of 1,000 roentgens and dies of radiation poisoning suffered while handling plutonium.

Jan. 7: Civil Defense official Lt. Gen. Clarence R. Huebner says in a speech that most Americans will live in fallout shelters within five years, when most countries will have ICBMs. Americans will venture into the sunshine only at atomic risk.

Feb. 17: The A.E.C. confirms an unusually high amount of strontium 90 in Minnesota wheat grown in 1957. One sample is tested at 140 percent over the permissible level.

March 19: The *New York Times* reveals the Argus Project, in which three nuclear bombs were detonated by the U.S. Navy 300 miles up in August and September of 1958, enveloping the earth in a shell of radiation. The project was linked to weapons research, and provided information on what came to be known as the EMP (electromagnetic pulse) effect.

March 25: The White House denies suppression of information on fallout.

April 22: Staff of the Columbia University Lamont Geological Observatory find the concentration of strontium 90 in bones of North American children up to age 4 doubled from 1955 to 1957.

May 5: The A.E.C. reports that the U.S. and Great Britain, which exploded bombs with a yield of close to 66,000 kilotons since 1945, have created nearly 3 times as much radioactive debris as the Soviet Union.

May 23: The West German Atomic Ministry reports radioactivity in rainfall 60 times the maximum set by the Agency for safe drinking water. The Ministry does not warn citizens who depend on this water to abstain from drinking it.

June 26: The Office of Civil and Defense Mobilization issues a list of 71 U.S. target areas and probable casualties in the event of a limited nuclear war. The list notes the total expected urban deaths in the first day of the war at close to 20 million, with another 17 million fatally injured.

Aug. 30: The Congressional Joint Committee on Atomic Energy estimates 50 million deaths and 20 million serious injuries from a surprise nuclear attack on U.S. metropolitan and industrial targets. The hypothetical attack involves 265 nuclear weapons. (In 1991, the U.S.S.R. has over 30,000 nuclear warheads.)

Oct. 15: A B-52 carrying nuclear weapons collides with a refueling tanker over rural Kentucky; eight die; 2 bombs are recovered from the crash scene.

Oct. 30: The U.S. State Department announces Turkey's agreement to base U.S. IRBMs.

Nov. 12: The A.E.C. announces the third leak of radioactive material in less than two weeks from the Oak Ridge and Los Alamos bomb labs.

Nov. 14: Premier Khrushchev claims that one Soviet factory is producing 250 missiles per year armed with hydrogen warheads.

Nov. 20: The U.N. General Assembly adopts an Asian-

African resolution urging France to refrain from nuclear testing in the Sahara.

Dec. 2: President Eisenhower announces that the Atlas ICBM is operational.

Dec. 30: The first operational, ballistic-missile-firing craft, the Polaris submarine "George Washington," is commissioned.

1960

Feb. 13: France joins the "Nuclear Club" when it tests its first atomic bomb in the Sahara.

March 6: The U.S. Air Force announces plans to install an automatic Atomic Strike Recording System in over 100 major cities. The system will let the Strategic Air Command know which bomber and missile bases are still standing in a nuclear war.

April 9: The A.E.C. claims that a herd of cattle it maintains has grazed on the world's worst fallout area, near Las Vegas, for two years with no ill effects.

May 1: The Soviets shoot down an American U-2 spy plane over their territory.

May 12: Sen. Thomas Dodd (D-CT) urges President Eisenhower to inform the public about the neutron bomb "death ray." "I consider all this hush-hush that surrounds the neutron bomb a glaring instance of the official abuse of secrecy," states Sen. Dodd.

June 1: The U.S. Air Force announces that the first Minuteman ICBM site will be Malmstrom AFB, Montana. 55 missiles will be spread over three counties.

June 4: New York Gov. Nelson Rockefeller urges that huge food reserves be established from farm surpluses, stored at strategic sites throughout the U.S. "to feed our people in the post-attack period in the event of a nuclear attack on this country."

July 20: The submarine "George Washington" fires two Polaris missiles while submerged off Cape Canaveral; one missile hits its target 1,150 miles away less than 14 minutes after launch. It is the first successful launch of a ballistic missile from a submerged vessel.

July 27: The Republican Party platform calls for more and better missiles, bombers, and civil defense.

Sept. 1: The Office of Civil Defense Management announces a new above-ground shelter that doubles as a spare bedroom. Agency director Hoegh calls it "a better investment from the property-value standpoint" than basement shelters.

Sept. 29: John F. Kennedy warns of "the spread of nuclear weapons to several nations, drastically altering the balance of world power and sharply increasing the chances of accidental war."

Oct. 5: The British Labour Party calls for unilateral abandonment of nuclear weapons in Great Britain.

Oct. 11: A home warning system tested by Civil Defense officials in 1,400 homes and 300 business places in Charlotte, MI warns citizens of an "attack" by bombers and missiles crossing the North Pole. Had the attack been real, the town's residents would have had some twenty minutes to put their affairs in order.

Nov. 1: British Prime Minister Harold Macmillan reports agreement for U.S. use of Holy Loch, on the Firth of Clyde in Scotland, for Polaris submarines.

Nov. 15: The "George Washington" sails on patrol from Charleston, SC, armed with 16 Polaris missiles, the first craft so armed.

Dec. 1: The 1st National Bank of Boston opens its underground center in Pepperell for safe storage of its records and those of a banking association in the event of nuclear war.

Dec. 6: Charles de Gaulle's plan to create a French nuclear force becomes codified in French law.

Dec. 6: The U.S. releases photos, for the first time, of atomic bombs of the same types as those dropped on Japan.

Dec. 9: The Office of Civil and Defense Mobilization announces plans to stockpile 10,000 Jewish prayer books for use in nuclear war in emergency hospitals around the U.S.

1961

Jan. 15: The Office of Civil Defense and Mobilization reports plans to furnish 150,000 gas stations with emergency radios and atomic war preparedness posters.

Jan. 17: In his farewell address, President Eisenhower warns the nation against the military-industrial complex.

Jan. 24: A B-52 breaks apart over North Carolina, releasing two 24-megaton bombs, subsequently recovered. Three crewmen die.

Feb. 1: The U.S. Minuteman ICBM is successfully tested for the first time at Cape Canaveral.

Feb. 3: The U.S. Strategic Air Command begins around-the-clock flights of the U.S. airborn nuclear war command post "Looking Glass." The flights remain continuous for 29 years.

Feb. 19: The Office of Civil Defense Management announces plans to teach students in 700 high schools around the U.S. how to build fall-out shelters.

April 10: President Kennedy, in an address to the NATO Military Committee in Washington, sets out the essence of a refined U.S.-NATO nuclear strategy that allows greater conventional response to conventional provocation, while maintaining nuclear options.

April 28: Arrests of demonstrators during this year's Operation Alert civil defense exercise take place in such varied places as Antioch College, New York City, and New Jersey.

May 25: The Kennedy Administration asks $312 million for fall-out shelters in its defense budget.

May 31: Construction of an underground grade school in Artesia, NM, is announced. Built near a strategic air base, the school is intended to test the effects on children of the absence of sunlight and outside air.

July 15: The National Biscuit Company ("Baked by Nabisco") offers to sell survival ration crackers to civil defense organizations at 35 cents a pound. Minimum order is five tons. The biscuits taste like animal crackers.

Aug. 10: Congress approves a $207.6 million fallout shelter program; it is the first major sum approved since the federal civil defense effort began in 1950.

Aug. 31: The U.S.S.R. announces it will resume atmospheric testing; says scientists have created bombs with blast power equal to 20–100 million tons of TNT.

Aug. 31: Responding to Soviet claims about the Russian nuclear arsenal, the Pentagon announces that a 20-megaton bomb exploded on the ground would devastate an area with a 6-mile radius, killing everyone; the bomb's fallout would cover 5,000 square miles. The destruction radius for a 100-megaton bomb would be 12 miles with over 20,000 square miles in the fallout danger area.

Aug. 31: The White House calls the Soviet decision to resume tests "primarily a form of atomic blackmail designed to substitute terror for reason."

Sept. 1: The Soviets test a nuclear bomb in the

atmosphere some 350 miles south of Novosibirsk. It is the first known test by a major nuclear power since 1958.

Sept. 3: John F. Kennedy and British Prime Minister Macmillan ask Khrushchev to accept an immediate mutual ban on atmospheric tests producing fall-out.

Sept. 9: Khrushchev rejects the Kennedy-Macmillan appeal for a test ban.

Sept. 12: 89-year-old British philosopher and pacifist leader Bertrand Russell receives a 7-day jail sentence for inciting "Ban the Bomb" demonstrations.

Sept. 15: The U.S. resumes underground testing in Nevada with its first atomic blast since October, 1958.

Sept. 24: Concerning the latest Berlin crisis, Attorney General Robert Kennedy assures the nation on the television program "Meet the Press" that "the President will use nuclear weapons" if necessary, and that if Khrushchev presses too hard on Berlin, "the world could be destroyed."

Sept. 26: President Kennedy signs a bill creating the U.S. Arms Control and Disarmament Agency.

Sept. 30: In the magazine *America*, Roman Catholic priest Fr. L.C. McHugh contends that a man has the moral right to use violence to bar his neighbor from his fall-out shelter.

Oct. 3: Canada reports that radioactivity readings in Toronto have risen 1,000 times in the last two weeks as a result of current Soviet tests.

Oct. 19: IBM offers its 70,000 U.S. employees $1,000 interest-free loans to build family fallout shelters.

Oct. 30: The Soviets test a mammoth bomb with a yield of 58 megatons—58 million tons of TNT—above the Arctic island of Novaya Zemlya.

Nov. 10: In an "Open Letter to President Kennedy," nearly 200 faculty members of Boston, Brandeis, Harvard and Tufts Universities and MIT oppose shelter programs as preparing the American public "for the acceptance of nuclear war as an instrument of national policy."

Nov. 18: The University of California extension division cancels a lecture series on nuclear war and individual survival for lack of public interest. "One of our mailed announcements came back with 'this is madness' scribbled on it," says a U.C. official.

Dec. 14: The American Medical Association urges the public to "stop worrying about radioactive fallout and concentrate on getting ready for Christmas. There really isn't very much that us average folks can do about it anyway."

Dec. 15: The Pentagon announces plans to stockpile bulgur (crushed wheat) biscuits in community fall-out shelters as the only food item.

Dec. 17: The director of the Atomic Energy Board of South Africa indicates that South Africa can build the Bomb if it wants to.

Dec. 30: The Kennedy Administration publishes a pamphlet, "What to Know and What to Do About Nuclear Attack" for distribution in post offices and civil defense offices around the U.S.

1962

Jan. 6: Human Sciences Research Inc. reports a study for the U.S. Air Force finding that the problem of food and shelter shortages following nuclear war would be relieved by the high death toll.

Feb. 6: The Pentagon begins distributing a handbook with 8 home shelter designs ranging in cost from $75 to $650.

Feb. 7: The Kennedy Administration agrees to let Great Britain fire subsurface shots in Nevada in exchange for providing Christmas Island for atmospheric tests.

March 27: U.S. State Department officials outline for the media conditions under which the U.S. would use nuclear weapons. These conditions include a massive Soviet-led conventional attack on Western Europe.

April 13: Dr. Arthur Schulert reports in the journal *Science* that caribou-eating Eskimos in Alaska have apparently picked up four times as much strontium as average Americans.

April 25: The U.S. resumes atmospheric testing with a blast set off near Christmas Island. It is the first U.S. atmospheric test since October, 1958.

May 31: A new organization composed of Harvard University physicians and medical specialists calling themselves Physicians for Social Responsibility reports in the *New England Journal of Medicine* that "there is no rational basis" for nuclear war survival programs.

June 16: In a commencement address at the University of Michigan, Secretary of Defense Robert S. McNamara indicates an evolution of U.S. nuclear strategy toward counterforce (military) targeting rather than civilian targeting. "If nuclear war should occur," says McNamara, "our best hope lies in conducting a centrally controlled campaign against all of the enemy's vital nuclear capabilities."

Aug. 5: Soviet atmospheric tests resume with a 40-megaton range blast over Novaya Zemlya.

Aug. 26: Korfund Dynamics Corp. of Westbury, Long Island, announces plans to test steel springs under buildings to absorb shock and vibrations from nuclear blasts.

Sept. 28: At a news conference, Defense Secretary McNamara stresses U.S. readiness to use nuclear weapons in defense of West Berlin.

October 22: The Cuban Missile Crisis goes public. A week after Kennedy administration officials determined from photos taken by U-2 reconnaissance craft that Soviet ballistic missiles were being introduced in Cuba, President Kennedy announces a quarantine that would entail turning back any such missile-bearing Soviet ships bound for Cuba. The President also demands that work cease on construction of the missile sites, and that weapons already present must be withdrawn. He warns of "further action" should these steps not be taken.

Oct. 22: U.S. military forces throughout the world are placed on alert.

Oct. 23: The U.S.S.R. accuses the U.S. of "piracy" and transgressions of international law, and warns that the U.S. risks nuclear war over the Cuban missiles.

Oct. 23: Following approval of the proposal by the Organization of American States, the President proclaims a naval blockade of Cuba authorizing the U.S. Navy to stop, search, and seize any vessel carrying contraband, including missiles, their components, and bombers, to Cuba.

Oct. 24: The naval blockade of Cuba takes effect at 10 a.m.

Oct. 24: Low-flying Navy jets determine that work is continuing unabated on construction of the missile sites.

Oct. 25: President Kennedy rejects U.N. Acting Secretary General U Thant's proposal that both the blockade and the arms shipments be suspended for two or three weeks in hopes of a negotiated settlement.

Oct. 26: The White House issues an intelligence report stating that the Soviets are hurrying to achieve "full operational capability" at the missile sites.

Oct. 26: The U.S. Army moves anti-aircraft missiles

into Key West.

Oct. 26: Late editions of many U.S. papers carry reports of the possible invasion or bombing of Cuba.

Oct. 26: Premier Khrushchev sends a letter to President Kennedy offering to withdraw the missiles in return for an end to the blockade and assurances of Cuban safety from invasion by other nations in the hemisphere.

Oct. 27: A second Khrushchev letter arrives offering to trade the Cuban missile sites for NATO missile bases in Turkey.

Oct. 27: A U-2 spy plane is missing over Cuba, presumably shot down; another reconnaissance plane draws anti-aircraft fire. Fidel Castro vows defiance on television. The Pentagon calls up 14,000 air reservists.

Oct. 27: President Kennedy sends the Soviet leader a letter offering to accept his original offer of the 26th.

Oct. 28: Khrushchev informs the President in another letter that he has ordered the missile bases dismantled under U.N. supervision, in return for an end to the blockade and promises not to invade Cuba.

Nov. 8: The Pentagon announces that all known offensive missile bases in Cuba have been dismantled and missiles are being shipped out.

Nov. 8: In London, the independent Institute of Strategic Studies issues a report declaring that the West has 450-500 long-range ballistic missiles; the Soviet bloc has only 75 such missiles.

Dec. 11: The Minuteman ICBM becomes operational.

Dec. 19: The U.S. Air Force announces that the U.S. ICBM force consists of 200 operational missiles.

1963

Jan. 17: Nikita Khrushchev announces that the Soviet nuclear arsenal contains bombs with an explosive power of more than 100 megatons—over 100 million tons of TNT.

April 10: The U.S. nuclear attack submarine Thresher sinks with its 129-man crew in the Atlantic, some 200 miles east of Boston.

April 10: Pope John XXIII issues his encyclical letter "Pacem in Terris," a plea for world peace and for the banning of nuclear weapons.

May 11: Canada accepts U.S. nuclear warheads for use on missiles based in Canada.

June 10: In his commencement address at American University in Washington, D.C., President John F. Kennedy candidly describes the effects on the U.S. should nuclear war take place between the U.S. and the Soviet Union: "All we have built, all we have worked for, would be destroyed in the first 24 hours." In the same speech he announces U.S., British, and Soviet agreement to negotiate a nuclear test ban treaty.

June 20: The U.S. and the Soviet Union sign the "hot line" agreement.

Aug. 5: The U.S., the Soviet Union, and Great Britain enter upon the Treaty Banning Nuclear Weapon Tests in the Atmosphere, in Outer Space and Under Water (more commonly known as the Limited Test Ban Treaty). France and China refuse to sign the treaty.

August 31: The Washington-Moscow "hotline" goes into effect.

Sept. 7: The U.S. Public Health Service reports that strontium 90 in American milk reached a record level in June, nearly double that of a year earlier.

Sept. 11: President Kennedy provides Senate leaders written assurances that ratification of the atmospheric test ban treaty will not entail less vigorous arms development.

1964

Jan. 8: In his State of the Union address, President Johnson announces a substantial cutback in production of fissionable materials and a slowdown in arms manufacture. Johnson states that "we must not stockpile arms beyond our needs."

May 24: Republican presidential hopeful Barry Goldwater suggests that the U.S. use nuclear weapons to defoliate the Vietnamese jungle, thus depriving enemy forces of protective cover.

June 3: In a speech to the U.S. Coast Guard Academy graduating class, Lyndon Johnson states that the U.S. has over 1,000 ICBM and Polaris missiles ready to fly, along with 1,100 strategic bombers.

Aug. 22: Barry Goldwater says he opposed the atmospheric test ban because the treaty prevented the U.S. from gathering data on how nuclear blasts affect communications.

Aug. 26: Presidential candidate Barry Goldwater refers to tactical nuclear weapons as "conventional."

Aug. 27: U.S. Deputy Secretary of Defense Cyrus Vance, in responding to Goldwater's characterization of tactical nuclear weapons as "conventional," states that the typical tactical nuclear bomb has an explosive yield several times that of the Hiroshima bomb.

Sept. 7: President Johnson says in a Detroit speech that "there is no such thing as a conventional nuclear weapon."

October 16: China explodes its first atomic bomb, a 20–kiloton weapon, at Lop Nor, Sinkiang. President

Lyndon Johnson calls the event "a tragedy for the Chinese people."

1965

Jan. 18: President Johnson announces at least temporary withdrawal of a program to build public fallout shelters on the same day that he also announces plans for the Poseidon submarine-launched ballistic missile, with twice the explosive power of the Polaris missile now in service.

May 19: The U.S. Air Force announces that the 800-missile Minuteman I force will be replaced by the bigger, better Minuteman II.

July 13: The U.S. Navy announces plans to develop fluid-shielded aviator goggles to protect pilots' eyes from the intense light of nuclear explosions.

July 29: In Chicago, nuclear scientist Dr. Christjo Cristofv files suit against an animal hospital and the Upjohn pharmaceutical company for $10 million in the accidental death of his cocker spaniel, which, he claims, could detect atmospheric fallout.

Oct. 27: The U.S. Public Health Service reports that a study of 2,000 public school students in Washington County, Utah, the U.S. county that has had most fallout, shows many students have small lumps on their thyroid glands.

1966

Jan. 7: A U.S. B-52 bomber disintegrates over Palomares, Spain, releasing four hydrogen bombs. One is soon recovered; the conventional explosives in two others detonate, spewing plutonium over a wide area. A lengthy search goes on for the fourth bomb, eventually located 2,500 feet below sea level five miles offshore. Not until 44 days after the accident does the U.S. admit that one of its H-bombs is missing.

Feb. 14: 400 flee the A.E.C. Feed Material Production Center in Fernald, Ohio, when uranium hexafluoride gas escapes. Twenty-two years later, the Fernald plant's long-term environmental desecration receives extensive attention in the revelations concerning U.S. nuclear weapons facilities in general.

March 2: Secretary of Defense McNamara states in a news conference that the U.S. will have 2,600 nuclear warheads in its strategic forces by June.

April 25: A subsurface blast in Nevada breaks through a ground fissure and spreads radioactivity over Nevada, Colorado, Nebraska, Utah, and Kansas.

Sept. 7: Charles de Gaulle calls France's current atmospheric test program in the Pacific "a certain assurance of peace" for the French.

Sept. 24: France detonates its first H-bomb in the Tuamoto Islands.

Sept. 28: 17-year old Suzanne Williams, arrested during a pacifist protest of the launching of the Polaris submarine Will Rogers, is released after 68 days in jail for refusing to rise when her case was called in a New London, CT, court.

Sept. 28: Dr. Immanuel Velikovsky says in a speech at Princeton University that humanity bears in its soul the memory of cataclysms that shaped the solar system, and seeks to replicate them with nuclear destruction.

Oct. 27: China conducts a successful ballistic missile test, exploding on target a nuclear weapon in its own territory.

Dec. 9: John Birch Society founder Robert Welch repeats one of his favorite charges, that China does not have the Bomb, regardless of U.S. government statements.

1967

Jan. 27: 62 nations, including the U.S. and the Soviet Union, sign the Outer Space Treaty, which bans placement of weapons of mass destruction in earth orbit.

Feb. 10: The Atomic Bomb Casualty Commission reports on a 20—year study of 100,000 Hiroshima and Nagasaki survivors. It finds the effects "grim beyond doubt, yet not as grim as many had feared."

Feb. 14: 14 Latin American nations sign the Treaty of Tlatelolco, which bans nuclear weapons from Latin America and the Caribbean.

June 17: China explodes a "small" (3—megaton) H—bomb.

Oct. 9: In the *Department of State Bulletin* (57: 443—449), Secretary of Defense Robert McNamara acknowledges in a roundabout fashion that the "missile gap" exploited by the Democratic Party was non—existent, and that the U.S. ICBM buildup that followed in an effort to erase the "gap" was unnecessary.

Nov. 3: Secretary of Defense McNamara speculates that the Soviets may be developing a Fractional Orbital Bombardment System (FOBS), involving the placement of nuclear—armed missiles in low earth orbit, a technique that allows for a shorter flight time than that of an ICBM.

Dec. 13: A Pentagon official reveals U.S. efforts toward a MIRV'd warhead, a warhead bearing multiple, independently—targetable re—entry vehicles.

Dec. 25: The Hiroshima A—bomb hospital, which accepts only patients exposed to the Bomb, reports 62 deaths in 1967 from ailments, including 35 cancer cases, believed caused by the blast. The deaths bring to a total of 531 those recorded by the hospital since its inception in 1956.

1968

Jan. 22: A U.S. Strategic Air Command B-52 carrying four unarmed H-bombs crashes on the Greenland ice, scattering pieces of the bombs.

Feb. 16: President Johnson denies any knowledge of any high-level discussion of the possibility of using nuclear weapons in Vietnam.

June 12: The UN Assembly overwhelmingly approves the Nuclear Nonproliferation Treaty. Taking effect in 1970, this treaty prohibits the nuclear nations from supplying nuclear weapons or nuclear weapons technology to non-nuclear states. It mandates that non-nuclear states remain non-nuclear, and that the International Atomic Energy Agency's safeguards against weapons proliferation be accepted.

Aug. 16: The Poseidon and the Minuteman Space 3 missiles, both built for MIRV'd warheads, are successfully test-fired at Cape Kennedy, Florida.

Aug. 24: France detonates a two-megaton H-bomb near Muroroa in the Pacific, becoming the fifth nation to add the thermonuclear bomb to its arsenal.

Oct. 3: Gen. Curtis E. LeMay, retired Air Force Chief of Staff, announces upon his selection as a vice-presidential running mate by George Wallace that he "would use anything that we could dream up, including nuclear weapons," to win the war in Vietnam.

Nov. 27: Great Britain becomes the first nuclear power to ratify the Nonproliferation Treaty.

1969

Feb. 27: The Pentagon announces it is beginning to clean up Bikini Atoll preparatory to resettlement of inhabitants evacuated in 1946 to permit bomb testing on their home islands.

March 14: President Nixon asks Congress to pursue the Sentinel antimissile system to protect the U.S. nuclear deterrent.

March 30: The Howard Hughes organization threatens the A.E.C. that it will go to court to block any future nuclear tests Hughes experts do not consider safe; Hughes is concerned about environmental effects of radiation, seismic shocks and underground water contamination.

May 7: The Montreal *Gazette,* citing the West German source *Der Spiegel,* says Israel has completed five nuclear bombs without conducting test explosions. Israel denies the charge.

June 19: The U.S. Air Force orders MIRV'd warheads for Minuteman 3 missiles, awarding a contract—without public announcement—to General Electric for initial production of 68 such warheads. These multiple independently-targetable re-entry vehicles allow one missile to carry several bombs bound for various places, and constitute a major new step in the arms race.

June 25: Anti-ABM rallies take place in New York City and Hollywood, California.

July 8: The Senate begins debate on the proposed ABM Safeguard system.

August 6: Senate opponents of the Safeguard fail by one vote to halt the system.

Nov. 6: By a wide margin, the Senate approves a military procurement bill (OK'd by the House the day before) including funds for the Safeguard ABM system.

Nov. 17: The U.S.-Soviet Strategic Arms Limitation Talks (SALT) begin in Helsinki, Finland. It is the first such U.S.-Soviet cooperation at this level.

Nov. 25: President Nixon signs the Nuclear

Nonproliferation Treaty while the treaty is simultaneously ratified in Moscow.

1970

Jan. 13: A private scientific group charges in a report to the Atomic Energy Commission that the Rocky Flats, CO bomb plant, 16 miles northwest of Denver, has been releasing dangerously radioactive plutonium into air, water, and soil; it urges that the plant be phased out of production.

March 5: The Nuclear Nonproliferation Treaty becomes effective. By 1980, over 100 nations ratify the treaty.

March 7: The U.S.S.R. indicates in *Pravda* that it is not seeking nuclear superiority over the United States, and that a continued arms race will not benefit either country.

March 26: In its 500th announced nuclear test, the U.S. detonates a megaton-range bomb below ground in Nevada at Pahute Mesa.

April 11: London's Institute for Strategic Studies reports that the U.S. has 4,235 deliverable nuclear warheads, compared to less than half that number for the Soviet Union.

April 20: Defense Secretary Melvin Laird warns that the U.S.S.R. has been running its strategic nuclear weapons program in "high gear," while the U.S. has been "in neutral gear."

May 15: France begins another series of atmospheric tests in the Pacific with a blast over the Mururoa atoll.

May 26: The Pentagon announces installation of Minuteman III missile launchers at Minot AFB, North Dakota.

June 5: Federal officials announce the award of the $1

billion+ B-1 bomber contract to North American Rockwell Corp.

June 19: The U.S. Air Force announces it has made its first deployment of MIRV'd missiles, a group of ten missiles at the Minot AFB.

July 17: The *New York Times* reports that federal officials assume that Israel either has the Bomb or can quickly build it. Israel denies the report.

Oct. 14: On the same day that the U.N Assembly opens its 25th Anniversary session, the U.S., U.S.S.R., and China all test nuclear bombs. China's is an atmospheric test of an H-bomb.

Nov. 2: The Stockholm International Peace Research Institute reports that the world's nuclear stockpile contains the equivalent of 15 tons of TNT for every person on earth.

Nov. 24: 100 demonstrators attempt to march on the home of Edward ("Father of the H-Bomb") Teller following a "war crimes tribunal" at the University of California's Berkeley campus. Police turn the demonstrators back.

Nov. 24: Reports indicate that secret testimony given before a Senate Foreign Relations subcommittee contended that the 1967 Greek military coup involved surrounding U.S. nuclear missile sites; the sites would have been seized had the U.S. intervened in the coup.

Dec. 18: About 600 workers are exposed to radiation at the Nevada testing site when an underground test blows radioactive dust 8,000 feet into the air. According to the A.E.C., of 210 atomic tests in Nevada since the atmospheric test ban treaty went into effect in 1963, one in twelve tests has leaked radioactivity off site into the atmosphere.

1971

Feb. 11: The U.S. and U.S.S.R. enter a treaty banning nuclear weapons from the ocean floor.

Feb. 20: In a civil defense foul-up, broadcasting stations around the U.S. turn to the emergency status to be used in nuclear war. The blunder stems from an operator's error at the National Emergency Warning Center in Colorado. Numerous stations ceased broadcasting after informing their audiences of the "emergency" declared by the President. It takes 40 minutes to correct the error. Says the operator who made the mistake: "I can't imagine how the hell I did it."

March 4: The U.S. announces suspension of Project Plowshare, which has employed underground nuclear blasts for peaceful purposes since 1958.

March 30: The U.S. deploys the Poseidon submarine-launched ballistic missile.

Aug. 14: Syndicated columnist Flora Lewis reports U.S. military investigation findings of drug abuse among personnel responsible for handling nuclear weapons, including those aboard Polaris submarines, in the Strategic Air Command, and at Nike-Hercules missile installations.

Aug. 3: France's first nine nuclear-armed missiles become operational.

Sept. 14: The federal emergency broadcasting system errs again, sending out an unscheduled nuclear attack notification test, leading ABC radio to suspend broadcasting for half an hour.

Oct. 4: Reports suggest that Israel's costly Jericho ballistic missile, being produced at a rate of up to six per month, is probably designed to carry nuclear warheads.

Nov. 6: In spite of intense opposition reaching the

U.S. Supreme Court, the U.S. tests a 5-megaton warhead below ground at Amchitka Island in the Aleutians. It is the most powerful subsurface test in U.S. history, measuring 7.0 on the Richter Scale.

1972

May 16: In a harbinger of later theories advanced concerning nuclear winter, Dr. L. Machta says in a speech before a symposium on Carbon and the Biosphere that increased volcanic activity is contributing to a consistent drop in the world's temperature over the past 25 years as large amounts of dust form in the atmosphere, blocking sunlight.

May 26: The U.S. and the Soviet Union reach agreements on strategic arms limitations. President Nixon and Leonid Brezhnev sign the SALT I agreements in Moscow; the first of these, the Anti-Ballistic Missile Treaty, limits construction of missile defenses around each national capital and a single ICBM site. The second agreement establishes a 5-year freeze on existing ICBM deployments.

June 6: In congressional testimony Secretary of Defense Melvin Laird reveals that the U.S.S.R. is testing a missile capable of carrying MIRV'd warheads.

June 25: In spite of global protest, France begins yet another series of atmospheric tests in the Pacific.

Aug. 8: The Soviet Union charges in the newspaper *Moskovski Komsomolyets* that Israel is pursuing nuclear weapons research in the Negev desert.

Sept. 30: The U.S. and U.S.S.R. enter the Agreement to Reduce the Risk of Nuclear War Outbreak. The treaty concerns controls over accidental and unauthorized nuclear weapons use.

Nov. 21: The U.S. and U.S.S.R. begin the second phase of strategic arms limitation talks in Geneva. The major objective is to reach a permanent treaty covering arms not now limited, such as heavy bombers and advanced warhead systems.

1973

Jan. 12: White House Press Secretary Ronald L. Ziegler states that "the President has made clear that nuclear weapons were not one of the contingent elements he would use in Vietnam." (See July 21, 1985 for a different perspective.)

Feb. 16: The U.S. Navy announces that Bangor, Washington, has been selected as the first base for the new Trident missile submarine.

March 4: The *New York Times* reports China's work on an ICBM capable of a 7,000-mile range.

June 28: China announces an atmospheric H-bomb test.

May 24: New Zealand calls French contamination of the atmosphere with radioactive fallout "pernicious and inexcusable."

June 22: The International Court at The Hague, on request of Australia and New Zealand, asks France to suspend its nuclear tests in the South Pacific.

July 21: Ignoring international objections, France begins another series of atmospheric tests over Mururoa Atoll in the South Pacific.

Sept. 18: The Colorado Health Department reports finding radioactive contamination in the drinking water of the town of Broomfield, and traces the source to waste dumps at the Rocky Flats nuclear weapons plant five miles away. Tritium—radioactive hydrogen—turns up in the urine of Bloomfield citizens.

Nov. 21: U.S. officials say that the Soviet Union may have provided Egypt with nuclear warheads during the October war with Israel; the warheads were reportedly designed for the Soviet Scud missiles earlier shipped to Egypt.

Nov. 23: The editor of Egypt's semi-official newspaper *Al Ahram* indicates belief that Israel has nuclear weapons, and urges the Arab world to "build, buy or borrow" nuclear weapons as a deterrent to Israel.

1974

Jan. 10: Secretary of Defense James R. Schlesinger announces in a press conference at the National Press Club in Washington the new U.S. strategic thinking regarding flexible options. Mutual Assured Destruction is no longer the guiding light of U.S. policy; the U.S. will instead seek a variety of nuclear options, moving away from the "all or nothing" counter-city approach. Schlesinger's statements clarify the new U.S. policy regarding the possibility of fighting a "limited" nuclear war.

April 26: The Atomic Energy Commission warns in a report of "entirely inadequate" safeguards to prevent theft by terrorists of uranium and plutonium for production of homemade bombs. "We feel that the danger is large and growing," says the report.

May 18: Becoming the 6th nuclear weapons power, India explodes a "peaceful" atomic bomb of 15 kilotons in the Rajasthan Desert.

June 3: Dr. Robert Conard, head of a medical team that has visited Bikini and Eniwetok periodically over a 20-year period, reports that thyroid tumors are common among the island citizens who were doused with fallout from the March 1, 1954 H-bomb test.

June 18: The Stockholm International Peace Research Institute releases a report noting that the U.S. exceeds the U.S.S.R. in deployment of land-based and submarine missiles with MIRV'd warheads. The U.S. outnumbers the Soviets in strategic bombers, 448-130.

July 3: The U.S. and Soviet Union sign the Threshold

Test Ban Treaty limiting nuclear weapons tests to no more than 150 kilotons.

July 10: The vice president of the South African Atomic Energy Board announces that South Africa is able to produce nuclear weapons.

Aug. 22: Alfredo Marques, director of Brazil's Center of Physical Research, announces that Brazil is able to build an atomic bomb.

Sept. 5: Dr. Fred C. Ikle, U.S. Arms Control and Disarmament Agency Director, warns of destruction of the ozone layer and of links in the food chain from environmental effects of nuclear war.

Sept. 15: France detonates the eighth atmospheric test in its current series at Mururoa Atoll.

Sept. 23: France announces future nuclear tests will be underground.

Oct. 25: The Pentagon announces successful test firing of an ICBM from a C-5A cargo plane off the coast of Southern California.

Oct. 26: The first production model of the B-1 bomber is displayed in Palmdale, CA.

Nov. 6: Colorado voters approve by wide margin a proposition giving citizens the right to approve or disapprove experimental nuclear weapons detonations in the state.

Nov. 24: President Ford and Secretary Brezhnev agree on details of the SALT II treaty, including ceilings of 2,400 strategic nuclear delivery vehicles and 1,320 MIRV missiles.

Dec. 1: Israel's President Ephraim Katzir announces that Israel is able to build nuclear weapons. "We have to develop more powerful and new arms to protect ourselves," says Katzir.

1975

Jan. 19: In a reorganization, the U.S. Atomic Energy Commission becomes the Nuclear Regulatory Commission and the Energy Research and Development Administration, later designated the Department of Energy, Aug. 4, 1977.

Jan. 21: U.S. intelligence reports that the Soviet Union has begun deployment of the new Backfire long-range bomber.

Jan. 31: SALT negotiations resume in Geneva.

June 20: Defense Secretary Schlesinger describes the first Soviet deployment of 60 ICBMs with MIRV'd warheads as destabilizing the arms race. The U.S. at this point has close to 1,000 MIRV'd missiles.

June 25: President Ford in a press conference refuses to rule out use of U.S. nuclear weapons should North Korea attack South Korea, reaffirming a similar refusal made by Defense Secretary Schlesinger five days earlier.

July 1: Secretary of Defense James Schlesinger informs newsmen that the U.S. is willing to use nuclear weapons if faced with defeat in conventional war.

Sept. 16: A Senate subcommittee reports that the Pentagon now guesses that a limited Soviet nuclear attack on U.S. military bases would kill up to 22 million people, boosting Defense Secretary Schlesinger's earlier estimate of up to 3 million dead from such an attack.

Oct. 4: Arms Control and Disarmament Agency Director Fred C. Ikle releases a study concluding that a nation conducting a massive nuclear attack, even without nuclear retaliation, could suffer serious ecological and economic damage as a result of destruction of the ozone layer.

Oct. 13: The journal *Aviation Week and Space Technology* reports that China has deployed ICBMs in western China with a range that includes Moscow.

Nov. 18: The Safeguard ABM system at a North Dakota Minuteman site is ordered dismantled by the Senate.

1976

Jan. 19: David E. Lilienthal, the first A.E.C. Chairman, tells the Senate Government Operations Committee that the "impending disaster" implicit in the rapid international spread of nuclear weapons requires that the U.S. immediately impose "a complete embargo of all nuclear devices and all nuclear material."

Jan. 31: South Korean and Western diplomatic sources report that S. Korea has been acquiring capacity to make nuclear weapons, and already has the technical and theoretical ability to build such weapons.

March 5: The first launch of an air-launched cruise missile from a B-52 takes place at the White Sands missile range.

March 15: Washington journalist Arthur Kranish, after attending a CIA briefing, announces in the *Washington Post* that the CIA estimates Israel possesses from 10 to 20 nuclear weapons "available for use."

March 15: The London *Times* reports a non-NATO study alleging that NATO is wholly unprepared, even with the assistance of tactical nuclear weapons, to fend off a rapid Soviet-Warsaw Pact attack.

May 28: President Ford and Soviet leader Brezhnev sign a treaty limiting to 150 kilotons the size of underground nuclear test explosions for peaceful purposes.

June 23: The 160th SALT negotiation takes place in Geneva between U.S. and Soviet representatives.

Aug. 29: U.S. officials report that CIA data indicate that Taiwan is developing the ability to create an atomic bomb through a new program to reprocess spent uranium fuel into plutonium.

Aug. 31: Arms Control and Disarmament Agency Director Fred C. Ikle accuses the Soviet Union of trying to upset the strategic nuclear weapons balance by introducing the new SS-X-20 missile in Eastern Europe. Ikle calls the missile "a massive, unwarranted and unexplained expansion."

Nov. 6: Exiled Soviet scientist Zhores A. Medvedev reports widespread death and injury from a 1958 explosion of buried radioactive wastes near the town of Bloagoveschensk in the Ural mountains. Medvedev subsequently discusses his allegations in his book, *Nuclear Disaster in the Urals* (Norton, 1979). See June 16, 1989, for Soviet confirmation of the disaster.

Nov. 17: China sets off its largest bomb test, a 4-megaton blast; subsequently a massive cloud of radioactive debris from the test drifts toward and then over the U.S.

1977

Feb. 8: Princeton University student and pizza entrepreneur John A. Phillips reports that representatives of both the Pakistani and French governments have requested information concerning his blueprint for building an atomic bomb for $2,000.

Feb. 20: Discussing the California Office of Emergency Services' new handbook on how to determine whether a nuclear terrorist actually has a nuclear bomb, a state spokesman says "The decision on 'what to do' is left in the hands of local officials."

April 7: President Carter says that the U.S. will no longer use plutonium as a reactor fuel, and hopes other nations take similar moves to combat weapons proliferation. "I hope that by this unilateral action we can set a standard," says Carter.

June 5: The *Washington Post* reports that the U.S. is about to begin production of the neutron bomb, which can allegedly kill people without destroying property. (It can't; the neutron bomb, also known as an "enhanced radiation weapon," delivers a significant blast effect along with radiation.) Controversy rages through the rest of the year over the questions of production and deployment of the bomb.

June 9: NATO reports Soviet deployment of the MIRV'd SS–20 IRBM in its western territory. The missile can reach any target in Western Europe.

Aug. 4: The federal government announces that U.S. nuclear facilities cannot account for over 8,000 pounds of enriched uranium and plutonium, but do not believe it was stolen. Maybe, officials say, it became trapped in machinery and wiping cloths.

Aug. 6: Leonid Brezhnev warns the Carter administration that South Africa will soon conduct a nuclear test in the Kalahari Desert; administration officials later say that the warning helped them prevent the test.

Oct. 18: National Public Radio reports that former President Johnson told then–CIA Director Richard Helms not to pursue investigation of the disappearance of 400 pounds of bomb–grade uranium from an Apollo, PA, plant in 1966, even though the CIA believed that Israel received the stolen uranium.

Nov. 15: Reporters Howard Kohn and Barbara Newman charge in *Rolling Stone* that Israel has built a nuclear arsenal of more than 100 bombs through theft of enriched uranium in the U.S. and Europe, and that West Germany and France covered the sale of additional uranium to Israel with phony "hijackings." Israel denies the charges.

Nov. 25: The CIA releases documents supporting Zhores A. Medvedev's claims of Soviet nuclear catastrophe taking hundreds of lives in the Urals. (See Nov. 6, 1976, and June 16, 1989).

1978

Feb. 17: In testimony released by Congress, CIA director Stansfield Turner dismisses Soviet civil defense preparation as inadequate to defend against a retaliatory U.S. nuclear attack.

Feb. 22: Soviet underground deployment of the mobile ICBM, the SS-16, is reported.

March 10: The Nuclear Nonproliferation Act of 1978 becomes law.

April 7: President Carter defers production of the neutron bomb, but says his decision could change if the Soviets do not show restraint in conventional and nuclear arms and force deployment.

April 19: NATO's Nuclear Planning Group, consisting of the defense ministers of the U.S., Britain, West Germany, Italy, Belgium, Denmark, and Turkey, pledges to modernize tactical nuclear weapons in Europe and to maintain the option of deploying neutron warheads.

May 23: The U.N. General Assembly begins a special 5-week session on disarmament.

June 21: The U.S. cruise missile undergoes its initial test at New Mexico's White Sands Missile Range.

June 30: The U.N. Disarmament Conference adopts a final document calling for restraining the arms race. "The ultimate objective of the efforts of states in the disarmament process," says the document, "is general and complete disarmament under effective international control."

Aug. 1: In an unprecedented ruling, Donald C. Coe receives a favorable decision from the Veterans Administration regarding his claim that his exposure to radiation during nuclear tests in the 1950s caused the cancer that he developed over a decade after his retirement from the military.

Aug. 29: The U.S. Arms Control and Disarmament Agency claims that the U.S. has a greater capacity than the U.S.S.R. to destroy targets in a nuclear war.

Nov. 5: The Energy Department reports the first global increase in radioactive fallout in four years, thanks to the November 17, 1976 Chinese atmospheric test.

Dec. 21: Former Interior Secretary Stewart L. Udall files claims against the Energy Department on behalf of 100 Arizona, Utah, and Nevada residents claiming cancer as a result of exposure to fallout from nuclear weapons tests.

1979

Jan. 29: A Department of Health, Education and Welfare study indicates that veterans who participated in the 1957 nuclear test "Smoky" suffer an unusually high incidence of leukemia.

Feb. 1: Carter administration officials report that the U.S.S.R. has begun testing a new long-range cruise missile.

Feb. 14: Federal documents show that over 4,000 sheep grazing downwind from Nevada nuclear tests died in the spring of 1953 after absorbing up to 1,000 times the maximum dose of radioactive iodine permitted human beings.

March 9: A U.S. District Court judge in Milwaukee stops *The Progressive* from publishing Howard Morland's article on how the H-bomb works.

March 28: The Three Mile Island nuclear plant near Harrisburg, PA, suffers the worst reactor accident in U.S. history, involving a potential core meltdown and widespread loss of life.

April 6: In France, saboteurs bomb nuclear equipment destined for Iraq and two other countries. Official speculation focuses on an Israeli group seeking to deny Iraq nuclear weapons capability.

April 6: The U.S. suspends military aid to Pakistan because of that nation's pursuit of nuclear weapons.

April 25: FBI Director William H. Webster warns that by using information from public libraries, a terrorist could build a back-pack nuclear bomb. "You don't have to be Einstein" to do the job, says Webster.

May 10: The Los Alamos Scientific Library closes doors to the public because of the presence of classified material kept in an area accessible to the public.

May 23: In Congressional testimony concerning Dimitri Rotow's discovery in a public section of the Los Alamos Scientific Library of a classified document on H-bomb trigger mechanisms, which he subsequently photocopied and mailed to acquaintances, weapons designer Theodore B. Taylor calls the accidental declassification of the document "the most serious breach of security I am aware of in this country's post-World War II nuclear weapons development programs." The document was publicly, accidentally accessible for four years.

May 30: Defense Secretary Harold Brown charges in a speech at the Naval Academy that the Soviet Union is trying to develop an effective first-strike capability.

June 8: The U.S. launches its first Trident missile.

June 18: President Carter and Brezhnev sign SALT II accords in Vienna, Austria, limiting both nations to the same maximum number of long-range missiles and bombers.

July 11: The U.S. Joint Chiefs of Staff endorse the new SALT agreement, but stress the need for U.S. to modernize its nuclear arsenal.

Aug. 4: The British newspaper *The Sun* notes a high rate of death from cancer among actors and crew members who filmed the movie "The Conqueror" near St. George, UT, when the area was inundated with fallout from a 1953 test. The victims include John Wayne, Agnes Moorehead, Susan Hayward, Dick Powell, and three other members of the crew.

Sept. 17: The federal government abandons its efforts to quash publication of Howard Morland's H-bomb article in *The Progressive*.

Oct. 25: The U.S. announces that a small nuclear blast may have taken place near South Africa in September; a U.S. reconnaissance satellite detected a flash of light characteristic of a nuclear explosion. South Africa denies any knowledge of such an explosion. See July 15, 1980.

Nov. 9: American military forces go on a nuclear war alert when a computer interprets war game data as an actual missile launch by a Soviet submarine.

Dec. 12: NATO announces its decision to base American-built Pershing II and cruise missiles as a tactical force modernization, in spite of objections from Belgium and the Netherlands.

Dec. 26: The Soviet Union invades Afghanistan, prompting the Senate's removal of the SALT II treaty ratification from its agenda.

1980

Jan. 2: On the heels of the Soviet Union's invasion of Afghanistan, President Carter asks that the Senate defer ratification of the SALT II Treaty.

Jan. 24: An earthquake damages the Lawrence Livermore Laboratory, forcing a leak of radioactive water. Official dismiss the leak as no threat to public health.

Jan. 31: In a Jacksonville, FL campaign appearance, Ronald Reagan questions judiciousness of U.S. interference with other nations' development of nuclear weapons. "I just don't think it's any of our business," he says.

Feb. 13: Ralph Nader's antinuclear group Critical Mass releases a report by the Oak Ridge National Laboratory concluding that the nuclear accident in the Urals earlier described by Zhores A. Medvedev was caused by a chemical explosion in radioactive waste tanks, and that the contamination spread over up to a 400-square mile area, forcing evacuation of some thirty villages. See June 16, 1989.

April 9: Approximately 175 people resettle Eniwetok Atoll in the Marshall Islands, where the U.S. carried out 43 nuclear tests, 1948–1958.

April 26: A California study indicates that the rate of serious skin cancer, melanoma, is 500% higher for Lawrence Livermore nuclear weapons lab employees than for other area residents.

April 28: Religious cult leader Leland Jensen and his followers go into fallout shelters around the U.S. to wait for the nuclear war they predict will strike on April 29.

June 3: A false alarm in the North American Air Defense Command headquarters indicates a Soviet ICBM and submarine-launched missile attack on the U.S.; bomber and missile crews prepare for a retaliatory strike.

June 6: Another false alarm signals incoming Soviet missiles, and SAC bombers rev up for a response.

June 17: British officials announce their decision to install U.S. cruise missiles at Greenham Common, Berkshire, and at Molesworth, Cambridgeshire.

July 15: The Presidential Office of Science and Technology Policy reports that the light flash picked up by a VELA satellite over the South Atlantic, Sept. 22, 1979, was probably not caused by a nuclear explosion. The explosion was previously suspected to be of South African origin.

Aug. 5: Federal officials announce President Jimmy Carter's decision to enact Presidential Directive 59. "PD"-59 directs a heightened emphasis on the targeting of Soviet military and political targets, including missile sites and command relocation areas. PD-59 requires U.S. strategic planners to develop the ability to fight a prolonged nuclear war, one of several months' duration.

Sept. 19: A non-nuclear explosion in a Titan 2 missile silo near Damascus, AR, blows the missile's warhead through the silo's concrete roof and into a woods some 250 yards away. The blast wounds 21 Air Force personnel and kills one. Area residents are evacuated.

Sept. 30: In an AP interview, Republican presidential nominee Ronald Reagan advocates a new U.S. arms buildup to pressure the Soviet Union to productive arms negotiations, and says that he would scrap the SALT II treaty.

Oct. 3: The Centers for Disease Control reports in *JAMA*, the journal of the American Medical Association, that there was nearly a 300% increase in leukemia cases among soldiers exposed to radiation in the 1957 Nevada nuclear test known as "Smoky."

Oct. 3: Nigerian President Shehu Shagari suggests that his nation might build nuclear weapons to exert pressure on South Africa.

Oct. 16: China sets off another atmospheric nuclear test.

Nov. 6: President-elect Reagan says in a news conference that arms control negotiations with the U.S.S.R. should be linked to Soviet "policies of aggression."

1981

June 7: Israeli warplanes attack and destroy the Iraqi nuclear reactor near Baghdad. Israel, which received global condemnation for the raid, justified it on the grounds that the facility was intended to aid in the production of nuclear weapons for use on Israel.

June 23: Iraqi President Saddam Hussein requests help of "peace-loving nations" in the Arab quest to obtain nuclear weapons to offset the Israeli nuclear capability.

July 28: The Plowshares Eight, including brothers Philip F. Berrigan and the Rev. Daniel J. Berrigan, are sentenced to prison for their nuclear weapons protest at a Pennsylvania General Electric plant in 1980.

Aug. 8: President Reagan decides to build and deploy the neutron bomb. The neutron bomb is widely misrepresented in the media as one that "destroys people, not buildings." The neutron bomb would, if put to use, cause approximately the same explosive damage as the Nagasaki bomb.

Oct. 1: At a news conference, President Reagan contends that the Soviet Union believes nuclear war is "winnable."

Oct. 2: President Reagan announces elements of the U.S. strategic program, including basing of MX missiles in former Titan and Minuteman silos, development of the B-1 bomber and the B-2 "Stealth" bomber, deployment of submarine-launched cruise missiles, and construction of more Trident submarines.

Oct. 8: President Reagan lifts the ban on reprocessing spent commercial nuclear fuel imposed by President Carter in 1977.

Oct. 16: Regarding a possible war in Europe, President

Reagan remarks to journalists that "I could see where you could have the exchange of tactical [nuclear] weapons against the troops in the field without it bringing either one of the major powers to pushing the button."

Oct. 20: U.S. Army Major Gen. Robert L. Schweitzer is relieved of his job as chief military advisor to the National Security Council after charging in a Washington speech that the Soviet Union is "on the move" and "going to strike."

Nov. 2: In an interview with the West German magazine *Der Spiegel*, Leonid Brezhnev rules out launching a preventive nuclear strike on the West. However, amplifies the Soviet President, "Once begun — in Europe or somewhere else — a nuclear war would unavoidably and irrevocably take on a worldwide character."

Nov. 4: Secretary of State Alexander Haig tells the Senate Foreign Relations Committee that NATO has plans for a nuclear "demonstration shot" to warn against excessive conventional aggression.

Nov. 11: 151 U.S. colleges stage teach-ins on nuclear war.

Nov. 13: The Senate ratifies Protocol I of the Tlatelolco Treaty, denying the U.S. the option to store, deploy, or use nuclear weapons in the Guantanamo Naval Base, Puerto Rico, and the Virgin Islands.

1982

Jan. 29: Adm. Hyman G. Rickover calls for elimination of nuclear weapons and atomic reactors in congressional testimony. "I think we will probably destroy ourselves," says the Admiral.

Feb. 7: Former U.S. Army medic Van Brandon says he was ordered to enter false data to conceal the exposure of soldiers to dangerous radiation levels at four atomic tests in 1956 and 1957. His medical group reportedly kept two sets of radiation exposure ledgers, one recording true exposures, the other a fraud.

March 1-5: The White House orchestrates wargame Operation Ivy League, which entails the hypothetical death of the American President and a full-scale nuclear war. The Reagan administration expresses satisfaction with the exercise.

March 29: The Reagan administration requests over $4 billion for a 7-year civil defense program involving "crisis relocation," the evacuation of large parts of the population to rural areas in the event of nuclear war threat. "This is a complicated business," says a spokesman for the Federal Emergency Management Agency, charged with implementing the scheme.

March 30: Refuting Administration wishes, the Senate votes 88-9 in favor of banning the reprocessing of spent commercial reactor fuel into weapons-grade plutonium.

April 6: Sec. of State Alexander Haig says the Reagan Administration will not renounce first use of nuclear weapons nor agree to a nuclear weapons freeze at present levels. "The essential values of Western civilization" are at stake, suggests the Secretary.

June 3: Secretary of Defense Caspar Weinberger says in a speech at the Army War College that, although the U.S. does have plans for a protracted nuclear war, "Our entire strategic program...has been developed with the express intention of assuring that nuclear war will never be fought."

June 12: Close to one million peacefully protest nuclear weapons in New York City. "It's not just hippies and crazies any more," says one demonstrator. "It's everybody."

June 21: Over 1,300 protestors are arrested in nonviolent demonstrations at the Lawrence Livermore

Laboratory, a major U.S. nuclear weapons research facility. "The business as usual at the laboratory is creating first-strike weapons like the neutron bomb," says protestor Daniel Ellsburg. "It must be stopped."

June 26: Soviet television broadcasts an hour-long debate between Soviet and U.S. physicians on nuclear war.

June 29: Strategic arms reduction negotiations begin in Geneva between the U.S. and U.S.S.R.

July 16: U.S. INF (Intermediate Range Nuclear Forces) negotiator Paul Nitze and his Soviet counterpart Yuli Kuitsinsky conduct their "Walk in the Woods," one of the most famous negotiating sessions of the 1980s. Searching for a deal involving the Soviet SS-20s and the U.S. Pershing II missiles, the two men walk down a Swiss mountain near the French border. On the way down, they sit on a log in the rain and with paper and pencil work out a possible solution to the Euromissile problem. The deal falls through.

July 19: President Reagan decides against resuming negotiations, suspended in 1980, with Great Britain and the U.S.S.R. on a comprehensive nuclear test ban.

Aug. 5: The House of Representatives narrowly rejects (204-202) a call for an immediate freeze in U.S. and Soviet nuclear arsenals.

Aug. 9: The General Accounting Office reports that U.S. monitoring and protection of exports of weapons-grade plutonium is "incomplete and inaccurate."

Aug. 15: The *Los Angeles Times* reports that the Pentagon has finished a master plan for a 6-month nuclear war.

Oct. 4: President Reagan charges in an Ohio speech that the Nuclear Freeze movement is directed by those "who want the weakening of America, and so are manipulating honest people and sincere people."

Nov. 3: Voters in eight states, several major cities and many smaller cities approve referendums calling for a worldwide nuclear freeze. The vote is the largest on a single referendum issue in U.S. history.

Nov. 11: Speaking of the Nuclear Freeze Movement, President Reagan says that "there is no question about foreign agents that were sent to help instigate and help create and keep such a movement going."

Dec. 9: Washington police shoot and kill 66-year-old Norman Mayer, who seized the Washington Monument and threatened to blow it up unless a ban on nuclear weapons is made "the first order of business on every agenda of every organization" in the U.S.

1983

Feb. 11: The U.S.S.R. offers to allow inspection by the International Atomic Energy Agency of some of its civilian nuclear plants. It is a significant step toward on-site inspection of weapons.

Feb. 24: The U.S. Justice Dept. provokes a storm of criticism with its insistence that three documentary films produced by the National Film Board of Canada must be labeled as "political propaganda," the work of "registered foreign agents," for showing in the U.S. Two of the films concern acid rain; the third, "If You Love this Planet," is an anti-nuclear war film.

March 8: In a speech to the National Association of Evangelicals, President Reagan denounces the U.S.S.R. as the "focus of evil in the modern world," and labels the nuclear freeze "a dangerous fraud."

March 16: Soviet General Staff chief Marshal Nikolai Ogarkov says that "The idea of nuclear war has never been tested. But, by logic, to keep such a war limited will not be possible."

March 20: The riveting, well written and quite believable NBC television movie "Special Bulletin," depicting the terrorist nuclear destruction of Charleston, SC, draws criticism from numerous quarters as being "irresponsible" and "frightening."

March 23: President Reagan delivers what soon comes to be known as the "Star Wars" speech, in which he calls for creation of a ballistic missile defense system that will render nuclear weapons "impotent and obsolete."-

April 11: The President's Commission on Strategic Forces (usually referred to as the Scowcroft Commission, after commission head Brent Scowcroft) rejects the notion of a Soviet nuclear advantage over the U.S., and, in a major departure from the multiple-warhead ICBM commitment the U.S. has been following, recommends development of small, single-warhead missiles on the grounds that they will be less likely to invite attack. The report also urges deployment of one hundred MX missiles in existing Minuteman silos, along with arms control negotiations.

April 24: 70 scientists who worked on the Manhattan Project sign a statement urging the superpowers to reduce their nuclear armaments and to work toward total elimination of nuclear weapons. "We are appalled at the present level of the nuclear armaments of the nations of the world," say the scientists, "and are profoundly frightened for the future of humanity."

April 24: More than 80,000 Canadians march against planned U.S. cruise missile testing in Alberta.

May 3: The U.S. Roman Catholic Bishops overwhelmingly ratify a pastoral letter, *The Challenge of Peace: God's Promise and Our Response*, condemning nuclear war and calling on Catholics to help rid the world of nuclear weapons.

May 4: The U.S. House approves a modified resolution calling for President Reagan to negotiate a "mutual and verifiable freeze and reductions in nuclear weapons" with the U.S.S.R.

May 25: The U.S. Senate approves President Reagan's plan to place 100 MX missiles in existing silos, and releases $625 million for the missile's development.

June 20: On Disarmament Action Day, nuclear weapons protestors demonstrate in at least 18 states; arrests total 950 at the Lawrence Livermore Laboratory, where demonstrators try to blockade entrances.

July 15: Canada agrees to permit testing of the U.S. cruise missile on its territory.

July 20: The U.S. House authorizes $2.6 billion for production of the first 27 MX missiles.

Aug. 20: The Energy Department announces plans to conduct a $300,000 cleanup of University of Chicago buildings still contaminated with radioactivity from their use in the Manhattan Project.

Aug. 23: In a Seattle speech to the American Legion convention, President Reagan accuses those in the "so-called peace movement" of waging peace "by weakening the free."

Summer: Publication of Andrei Sakharov's "The Danger of Thermonuclear War" in *Foreign Affairs*, in which he argues that the U.S. should proceed with the MX program, along with other strategic modernizations, if that is what is required to persuade the Soviet Union to negotiate seriously on strategic arms reduction.

Sept. 1: A Soviet jet fighter shoots down Korean Air Lines Flight 007 after the Boeing 747 crosses Soviet air space. 269 lives are lost.

Sept. 23: Following its revelation in the U.S. military paper *Stars and Stripes*, a U.S. military mass burial exercise in preparation for nuclear war in Europe arouses a furor in West Germany.

Oct. 15: Some 10,000 antinuclear protestors peacefully gather at the Rocky Flats nuclear weapons plant near Denver.

Nov. 11: Approximately 12,000 physicists from 43 countries deliver to the U.N. and various governments their signed plea for a halt in nuclear weapons testing, production, and deployment.

Nov. 14: It is reported that the Defense Department has informed Congress that there are 5,845 nuclear warheads in Western Europe.

Nov. 20: Approximately 100 million Americans watch the widely-publicized made-for-television movie "The Day After," which depicts the results of a strategic nuclear war on Kansas.

Nov. 23: The Soviet delegation withdraws from INF talks in Geneva.

Dec. 8: U.S.-Soviet talks on limiting strategic nuclear weapons break off.

Dec. 10: In an address to the Soviet people, U.S.S.R. General Staff Chief Marshal Nikolai V. Ogarkov comments on the film "The Day After," and speaks of the danger of nuclear war and "nuclear madness." "I have seen the film and I believe that the danger it depicts is real," says the general.

Dec. 14: West Virginia authorities report that a man worried about college textbooks being used to help build nuclear weapons has admitted stealing close to 2,000 books from eight libraries.

Dec. 23: *Science* magazine publishes the seminal paper on the nuclear winter theory, "Nuclear Winter: Global Consequences of Multiple Nuclear Explosions," by R.P. Turco, O.B. Toon, T.P. Ackerman, J.B. Pollack, and C. Sagan.

1984

Jan. 1: The first 16 U.S. cruise missiles installed at Greenham Common are now operational.

Jan. 7: The Natural Resources Defense Council estimates that the U.S. nuclear arsenal will grow from 26,000 to 29,000 warheads by 1990. The Council contends that the Energy Department produces 2,000 warheads a year; it makes eight new warheads a day and retires five old ones.

Jan. 12: An article in the *Journal of the American Medical Association* reports that radioactive fallout from nuclear testing in Utah has caused abnormally high cancer rates among Mormons living in the area.

Jan. 13: President Reagan says that the American military buildup has reduced the threat of war, in spite of Democratic presidential hopefuls who have been "yelling that we are threatened by imminent war."

Jan. 15: The Scripps-Howard News Service reports that over 1,700 pounds of enriched uranium, enough to make nearly 100 bombs, has been missing since 1947 from the Oak Ridge, TN nuclear weapons plant.

Jan. 22: A Brazilian official announces his nation's imminent ability to manufacture nuclear weapons by the 1990s.

Feb. 9: A Pakistani nuclear scientist states that Pakistan is able to produce enriched uranium and nuclear weapons.

Feb. 15: A cave-in caused by an underground nuclear test in Nevada injures 14 scientists and engineers.

March 6: A B-52 bomber carries out a cruise missile test in Canada following Canadian Federal Court rejection of a request from antinuclear groups to halt the flight.

April 10: A study by Physicians for Social Responsibility reports that most of the 3,000 students in 14 northern New Jersey high schools believe there will be a nuclear war in the next two decades, and that they will die in it.

April 24: *Jane's Defence Weekly* reports Iran on the verge of nuclear weapons capability.

May 10: A federal District Court rules in Salt Lake City that fallout from Nevada nuclear tests in the 1950s caused nine cancer deaths, and that the government was guilty of negligence in its conduct of the tests.

May 21: Premier Andreas Papandreou of Greece, Prime Minister Indira Gandhi of India, Mexican President Miguel De la Madrid, Tanzanian President Julius Nyerere, Swedish Premier Olof Palme and Argentine President Raul Alfonsin appeal to the U.S., the Soviet Union and other nuclear states to halt the arms race and proceed with moribund arms control negotiations.

June 10: The U.S. Army carries out the first successful test of an anti-ICBM missile as it destroys a Minuteman with a dummy warhead more than 100 miles above the Marshall Islands.

June 17: The Defense Department estimates that the Soviet Union has about 34,000 nuclear warheads.

June 27: The Pentagon announces that the first long-range cruise missiles have become operational on Navy ships.

July 12: Pentagon officials acknowledge that a nuclear war could provoke a "nuclear winter," as charged by astronomer Carl Sagan and others.

Aug. 11: "My fellow Americans," says President Reagan into a live microphone during a radio broadcast voice-check, "I'm pleased to tell you today that I've signed legislation that will outlaw Russia forever. The bombing begins in five minutes." Global amusement at the quip is limited.

Oct. 12: Brown University students pass a referendum requesting the university health service to stock "suicide pills" for use in event of nuclear war.

Dec. 15: Soviet Politburo member Mikhail S. Gorbachev meets British officials in London. "There are no types of armaments that the U.S.S.R. would not agree to see limited and eventually banned," says Gorbachev.

Dec. 25: Nine protesters jailed in Corunna, MI for contempt of court for demonstrating outside a cruise missile engine plant begin a hunger strike.

1985

Jan. 3: An Australian commission opens hearings on British nuclear testing in Australia in the 1950s and '60s.

Jan. 9: William Arkin, head of the Institute of Policy Studies in Washington, reveals that Canada is one of eight countries to be supplied with U.S. nuclear weapons if war occurs or seems imminent. The announcement provokes intense controversy in Canada.

Jan. 23: President Reagan states that his top goal in his second term is reducing and eliminating nuclear weapons.

Feb. 7: The U.S. Air Force announces that women are to serve as launch control officers in Minuteman and MX ICBM bunkers.

Feb. 12: Reagan Administration spokespersons state that the U.S. has plans for deployment of nuclear weapons in Canada, Bermuda, Puerto Rico and Iceland.

Feb. 24: Federal officials and legal documents indicate that Pakistani operatives in the U.S. tried for nine months to illegally procure triggering devices for nuclear weapons.

March 1: The Department of Defense acknowledges the merits of the nuclear winter theory.

March 12: U.S. and Soviet negotiators begin their first formal discussions in more than a year in Geneva.

March 26: In an apostolic letter, Pope John Paul II warns the world's youth that the earth is on its way to becoming "a graveyard of nuclear death."

April 7: Mikhail Gorbachev says that the Soviet Union supports a freeze on strategic nuclear weapons, and places a moratorium on deployment of the SS-20 IRBM in Europe.

May 16: A federal grand jury indicts the owner of Milco International, Inc., on charges of illegal exportation to Israel of 800 devices able to trigger nuclear weapons.

June 10: President Reagan announces his intention to comply with the SALT II agreement, in spite of what he considers its flaws, and following a hot debate over the issue within his administration.

July 9: The National Academy of Sciences assures the public that the 50 million pounds of buried radioactive waste near the Oak Ridge, TN nuclear weapons facility present no health risk.

July 10: French intelligence agents blow up the Greenpeace ship "Rainbow Warrior" in Auckland, New Zealand before it can sail in protest against further French nuclear testing in the South Pacific. The blast kills the boat's photographer.

July 16: An Episcopal peace group holds a service at Trinity Site, New Mexico, scene of the world's first atomic bomb test, on the 40th anniversary of the test.

July 29: Richard Nixon states in an interview with *Time* that he considered using nuclear weapons on four separate occasions during his Presidency. They included the Vietnam War, the October, 1973 war in the Middle East, during a Sino-Soviet border dispute, and the 1971 India-Pakistan war.

June 29: The U.S.S.R. announces that it will suspend nuclear weapons testing beginning August 6, the 40th anniversary of the Hiroshima bombing.

Aug. 23: An MX missile passes its first silo test launch.

Sept. 22: Stanford radiology professor Herbert L. Abrams, citing Defense Department figures, states that thousands of people with psychological or substance abuse problems are responsible for handling U.S. nuclear weapons.

Sept. 25: Jeane J. Kirkpatrick, former U.S. Ambassador to the U.N., defends French motives in the terrorist bombing destruction of the "Rainbow Warrior" on July 10.

Sept. 28: President Reagan hails a new Soviet proposal calling for 50 percent reductions in the superpowers' offensive nuclear weapons. Confusion ensues about what the proposal actually means.

Oct. 11: Scientists at the University of Chicago compare the effects of huge wildfires that apparently contributed to the extinction of the dinosaurs with the theoretical effects of nuclear winter.

Oct. 11: The Nobel Peace Prize goes to International Physicians for the Prevention of Nuclear War, a group founded by American and Soviet doctors.

Nov. 21: In a joint statement following their Geneva summit meeting, Reagan and Gorbachev agree to intensify efforts on arms negotiations. The two leaders "got very friendly," according to President Reagan.

Dec. 31: The Age of Enlightenment News Service clarifies the nuclear war views of Maharishi Mahesh Yogi, guru of transcendental meditation. "If coherence is dominating in world consciousness," he states, "rising emotions of negativity will simply not grow."

1986

Jan. 14: The Natural Resources Defense Council reports that the U.S. conducted close to 20 unannounced underground nuclear tests, 1980–1984.

Jan. 15: Mikhail Gorbachev proposes a schedule for elimination of all nuclear weapons by the turn of the century. Progress on the plan depends on U.S. renunciation of the Strategic Defense Initiative.

March 22: Ignoring a congressional cancellation request, the U.S. conducts its first nuclear test since the Soviet Union extended its test moratorium.

March 29: Mikhail Gorbachev offers to meet Ronald Reagan anywhere in Europe to discuss a nuclear test ban. The White House dismisses the offer as not in U.S. security interests.

April 21: Los Alamos Laboratory scientists claim that new nuclear weapons coming on line will require up to 200 test explosions to perfect, compared to the half-dozen needed for earlier versions.

April 26: The Chernobyl reactor catastrophe begins.

June 20: The U.S. Court of Appeals rules that the Justice Department may compel three Canadian films to be labeled as "political propaganda" if they are to be shown in the U.S. One of the films, "If You Love This Planet," concerns nuclear war.

July 6: For the first time in the nuclear age, Western scientists enter the Soviet Union to monitor its chief underground nuclear test site near Semipalatinsk, 1800 miles southeast of Moscow.

July 8: The Federal Emergency Management Agency's report to Congress contends that U.S. civil defense capabilities are dangerously limited. In a nuclear war, "national survival would be in jeopardy."

Aug. 11: The U.S. announces suspension of its military obligations to New Zealand under the ANZUS treaty because of New Zealand's ban from its ports of ships carrying nuclear weapons.

Aug. 18: Mikhail **Gorbachev** announces continuation of the Soviet Union's year-long suspension of underground nuclear tests until 1987, with a promise that U.S. reciprocation could lead to a formal test ban agreement before the end of the year. "I am appealing to the wisdom and dignity of the Americans not to miss another historic chance on the way toward ending the arms race," says Gorbachev. The U.S. does not reciprocate.

Aug. 23: *Pravda* condemns Prince and other American rock stars who suggest that nuclear war is inevitable.

Sept. 12: 59-year-old Jean Gump, a mother of twelve and a peace activist with the Plowshares group, begins serving an 8-year prison term for assaulting missile hardware at Missouri's Whitney Air Force Base. "We wanted to confront the system," says Ms. Gump.

Sept. 30: Authorities arrest 139 people, including astronomer Carl Sagan, at a nuclear test site in Mercury, NV, for protesting continued U.S. underground testing in spite of the Soviet moratorium. "The White House has been captured by extremists," says Sagan.

Oct. 5: The London *Sunday Times* reports former Israeli arms technician Mordechai Vanunu's charge that Israel has assembled an arsenal of approximately 100 nuclear bombs over the past two decades.

Oct. 6: Following an explosion, a nuclear-missile carrying Soviet submarine sinks in the mid-Atlantic "box" 600 miles east of Bermuda. It is one of the vessels comprising an ongoing presence in the area from which ballistic missiles would be fired at the U.S. in a nuclear war.

Oct. 8: Because of careless handling of plutonium, the Energy Department orders the temporary closing of two nuclear plants in Washington State's Hanford Nuclear Reservation. The facilities produce most of the U.S. supply of weapons-grade plutonium.

Oct. 12: Ronald Reagan and Mikhail Gorbachev conclude two days of talks in Reykjavik, Iceland. Reaction to the discussions fluctuates wildly in ensuing weeks. The meeting is seen both as a complete bust setting back U.S.-Soviet relations, and as a significant step forward in which leaders of the two nations for the first time seriously speculated on major reduction in strategic nuclear forces.

Oct. 24: The House Energy and Commerce Subcommittee on Energy Conservation and Power releases a report showing that federal agencies conducted radiation exposure experiments on people for three decades, beginning in mid-1940s; apparently some were subjected to experiments without offering informed consent.

Nov. 11: The MX missile is operational.

Nov. 14: The "Great Peace March" ends in Washington, DC, as approximately 1,000 people complete a walk against nuclear weapons that began eight months earlier in Los Angeles. "It's really powerful and really sad," says one marcher.

Nov. 28: The U.S., which has, like the Soviet Union, up to this point complied with the unratified SALT II Treaty, transgresses the treaty's limitations when a cruise-missile carrying B-52 bomber enters service.

Dec. 5: The Soviet Union announces intentions to remain in compliance with terms of the SALT II Treaty.

Dec. 13: Nuclear physicist and Korean War veteran Dr. Charles Hyder, in the 82d day of his fast against nuclear weapons across the street from the White House, has lost 100 of his former 310 pounds. He says, "I am happily willing to die of starvation to prevent a nuclear holocaust."

Dec. 30: In a pique over U.S. behavior since the Reykjevik meeting, the Soviets decline to exchange New Year's greetings with the White House.

1987

Jan. 8: Ruling as a result of a suit brought by the National Association of Radiation Survivors, Federal District Judge Marilyn H. Patel fines the Veterans Administration $115,000 for destroying thousands of records pertinent to veterans' claims of exposure to radiation.

Jan. 31: In a Munich speech, Assistant Sec. of Defense Richard Perle ridicules the idea that the world can be made nuclear-weapons free, calling it "foolishness" and "empty propaganda."

Feb. 5: Close to 2,000 demonstrators rally to protest nuclear testing at the Nevada test site.

Feb. 5: The U.S. State Department announces U.S. refusal to participate in an effort begun in 1984 by Australia, New Zealand, and eleven other Pacific nations to establish a nuclear-free zone in the South Pacific.

Feb. 16: Mikhail Gorbachev announces that American negotiators in Geneva are arguing that the ABM Treaty permits extensive tests of the SDI system.

Feb. 27: A Los Alamos National Laboratory report indicates that the U.S. conducted secret nuclear explosions approved by the Eisenhower Administration during the U.S.-Soviet nuclear test moratorium, 1958–1961.

Feb. 28: Mikhail Gorbachev says that the Soviet Union is willing to agree to elimination of Soviet and U.S. medium-range missiles in Europe within five years.

March 30: In a *Time* magazine interview, Pakistan's President Gen. Muhammad ul-Haq Zia claims his country's ability to build nuclear weapons "whenever it wishes."

April 7: Following several years' secret negotiations, the U.S., Canada, Britain, France, West Germany, Japan and Italy agree to control exports of missiles and other technology amenable to nuclear weapons use.

April 20: The U.S. Court of Appeals in Salt Lake City overturns a federal ruling that U.S. negligence during nuclear testing caused cancer in citizens downwind from the Nevada testing grounds. "While we have great sympathy for the individual cancer victims who have borne alone the costs of the A.E.C.'s choices," says the opinion, "their plight is a matter for Congress."

April 27: India says it may end its ban on nuclear weapons owing to the "emerging nuclear threat" posed by Pakistan.

May 11: Police arrest over 700 demonstrators at a Mother's Day protest at the Nevada Test Site.

May 22: Republican contender for presidential nomination Rep. Jack Kemp condemns the idea of eliminating medium-range nuclear missiles from Europe as "a nuclear Munich."

June 1: West German Chancellor Helmut Kohl accepts the "double zero" proposal for removing both medium-range and short-range nuclear missiles from Europe.

June 5: New Zealand adopts legislation banning nuclear-armed ships from its ports, thus formalizing a policy that has been in effect for three years, and which has caused severe strains in U.S.-New Zealand relations.

June 21: Reports of computer simulations at MIT indicate that a Soviet nuclear attack on the U.S. involving only one percent of the Soviet arsenal could destroy U.S. society and leave the survivors at a medieval state of existence for decades.

Aug. 4: The Pentagon acknowledges its decision to redeploy an H-bomb originally in service in the 1960s that is six times as powerful as bombs now on "active duty," and more effective against well-fortified command centers.

Aug. 11: The U.S.S.R. announces deployment of the new rail-mobile ICBM, the SS-24, a MIRV missile with ten warheads.

Sept. 15: The U.S. and the Soviet Union agree on a second "hot line" for the exchange of information on missile tests, troop movements and other issues to help avert accidental nuclear war.

Oct. 1: The U.S. protests Soviet missile tests in the Pacific that drop unarmed warheads 600 miles northwest of Hawaii.

Oct. 22: Auditors tell a House subcommittee that workers at federal nuclear weapons plants are injured and endangered because of lax safety standards.

Dec. 8: U.S. President Reagan and Soviet General Secretary Mikhail Gorbachev sign the Intermediate Nuclear Forces Treaty, providing for the destruction of 1,286 nuclear missiles and over 2,000 nuclear warheads. It is the first treaty between the two nations that actually reduces the size of their nuclear arsenals.

Dec. 13: Sec. of State George Schultz announces that the Reagan Administration will drop its insistence on a broad reinterpretation of the 1972 ABM Treaty to allow in-depth testing of SDI components.

Dec. 18: An article in the journal *Science* reports that a U.S.-Japanese study has determined that radiation doses sustained by A-bomb survivors were lower than historically thought, thus indicating that the effects of radiation at lower doses are more deadly than previously believed.

1988

Jan. 9: The Chinese *People's Daily* reports that China now has a strategic missile force capable of a nuclear counterattack.

Jan. 11: The Supreme Court refuses to hear a civilian appeal of a lower court ruling holding that the federal government cannot be held liable for cancer and other diseases that may have been caused by atmospheric testing, 1951–1962.

Jan. 16: The Natural Resources Defense Council releases a report revealing that the U.S. has carried out over 100 secret underground nuclear tests at the Nevada Test Site in the past 25 years.

Jan. 26–29: Soviet scientists visit the Nevada Test Site to work on nuclear test verification.

Feb. 23: Richland, Washington, high school students decisively reject a proposal to drop a nuclear mushroom cloud as the school's symbol. Richland relies on the Hanford Nuclear Reservation as its chief source of employment. "The whole process was a farce," says one teacher condemning the vote's outcome.

March 24: An Israeli court convicts Mordechai Vanunu of treason and espionage for detailing Israel's nuclear weapons program to the British press.

March 27: Vanunu is sentenced to 18 years in prison.

May 9: Publication of former White House chief of staff Donald Regan's memoirs reveals that Nancy Reagan consulted an astrologer to help determine the best time for President Reagan to sign a nuclear weapons treaty with Mikhail Gorbachev.

May 20: President Reagan signs a bill providing medical benefits for 250,000 veterans exposed to radiation.

May 23: U.S. officials report that Pakistan has tested a missile able to carry nuclear warheads to Bombay and New Delhi.

May 27: The Senate ratifies the INF Treaty, the first

ratification of an arms control treaty since 1972.

May 31: In Moscow, the U.S. and the U.S.S.R. agree on providing advance notice of ballistic missile launches and on the measurement of nuclear tests.

June 1: President Reagan and General Secretary Gorbachev exchange INF Treaty ratification documents.

June 6: The Radioactive Waste Campaign issues a study (*Deadly Defense: Military Radioactive Landfills*, item 2-181) charging U.S. nuclear weapons production facilities with releasing vast quantities of pollutants.

June 15: The House Energy and Commerce Committee charges that the federal government has stifled an investigation of drug trafficking at the Lawrence Livermore nuclear weapons research facility.

July 1: The Energy Department estimates that even a partial cleanup of the radioactive and chemical pollution created by the nation's nuclear weapons plants will cost up to $110 billion.

July 3: A U.S. Navy cruiser shoots down an Iranian jetliner over the Persian Gulf, killing 290 civilians. The Navy contends that the jetliner was mistaken for an F-14 fighter.

July 13: The General Accounting Office says that the cost of the nuclear facilities cleanup will be more in the neighborhood of $175 billion, and probably higher.

Aug. 1: The Soviets begin destroying missiles in accord with the INF Treaty.

Aug. 13: South Africa's foreign minister Botha acknowledges his nation's ability to produce the Bomb. "We have the capability to do so should we want to," says Botha.

Sept. 8: The U.S. begins destroying Pershing II missiles under INF Treaty requirements.

Sept. 27: The China News Agency reports the first successful ballistic missile launch from one of China's nuclear submarines.

Sept. 30: Two congressional committees contend that serious reactor accidents at the federal nuclear weapons Savannah River Plant in South Carolina have been kept secret for as long as three decades; experts say that public health was threatened.

Oct. 3: The Energy Department admits that it and its previous incarnation, the Atomic Energy Commission, were responsible for covering up the nuclear accidents at the Savannah River Plant.

Oct. 8: Reagan Administration officials agonize over the reactors at the Savannah River Plant, shut down for safety purposes since August, fearful that the result may be a breakdown in the nation's nuclear-weapons maintenance program.

Oct. 10: The Energy Department shuts down the Rocky Flats, CO weapons facility because of radioactive contamination of employees.

Oct. 14: A congressional panel charges that the federal government knew for decades that the Fernald, OH nuclear weapons feed plant was releasing immense quantities of radioactive debris into the air, soil, and water. Runoff from the plant contaminated area wells and the Great Miami River with tons of radioactive waste.

Oct. 26: The General Accounting Office confirms that safety problems at the Rocky Flats weapons plant are far worse than the Energy Department has admitted.

Oct. 28: The federal government admits that even small quantities of radioactive material loosed on the environment from the Fernald, OH uranium processing facility pose health hazards.

Nov. 8: The *Washington Post* reports that China has successfully tested a neutron bomb.

Nov. 20: Afraid that the policy threatens the separation of military and civilian nuclear programs, nuclear power experts including former A.E.C. chairman Glenn T. Seaborg criticize President Reagan's directive that the Nuclear Regulatory Commission take over civilian nuclear plants if nuclear war threatens.

Dec. 2: The federal government agrees to pay Ohio compensation for radioactive contamination in the Fernald area.

Dec. 6: The Energy Department warns that pollution from nuclear weapons plants is a serious public health threat; lists 155 cases of contamination at 16 sites, including radioactive pollution of the Snake River Aquifer.

Dec. 16: The Air Force states that the B-2 Stealth bomber will cost over $500 million each.

1989

Jan. 10: West Germany agrees to improve controls on its export of nuclear and chemical materials following a U.S. charge that a West German firm helped Libya build a chemical weapons factory.

Jan. 18: The National Research Council reports that small nuclear reactors would be required to power space-based components of the SDI.

Feb. 27: The Energy Department, the Environmental Protection Agency and the State of Washington agree on a $3 billion cleanup plan for the Hanford Reservation, the most radioactive and toxic of the U.S. nuclear weapons production facilities.

March 18: The Pentagon reveals the "Brilliant Pebbles" missile defense scheme. The plan entails orbiting swarms of little interceptor missiles that could be ordered to destroy incoming ICBMs by ramming them. The initial cost estimate for the BPs is $25 billion.

March 24: Energy Secretary James D. Watkins outlines a five-year plan to determine how to handle the nation's nuclear facilities cleanup.

April 4: Mikhail Gorbachev states in a speech to Cuba's National Assembly that the Soviets do not intend to deploy nuclear missiles in Latin America.

April 19: The U.S. and Great Britain accuse the Soviets of planning to base long-range nuclear missiles at the previous sites of medium range SS-20s junked under the INF Treaty.

May 22: India carries out a successful test of a medium-range, nuclear-capable ballistic missile.

June 6: The Justice Department announces a criminal investigation of possible environmental law violations at the Rocky Flats nuclear weapons plant in Colorado. The violations involve faked documents and concealed contamination.

June 16: The Soviet Union at last acknowledges the blast at the nuclear weapons facility in the Urals which in 1957 led to an evacuation of thousands and the contamination of a huge area of land. The explosion took place in a dry lake bed 12 miles from Kyshtym.

June 18: A report by a House Energy and Commerce subcommittee blames "obsessive secrecy and lack of outside oversight" for safety transgressions at nuclear weapons plants.

June 23: The *Washington Post* reports the Department of Energy's decision to release to independent researchers the health records of 600,000 people employed at nuclear weapons plants since the early 1940s. The decision comes under legal and congressional pressure.

June 30: The Energy Department promises to pay $73 million to residents in the area of the Fernald, OH plant that has polluted the soil and air with tons of radioactive uranium.

July 5: The *Denver Post* reports at least 9 workers exposed to radiation at the Rocky Flats plant, 1981–1987.

July 7–8: For the first time, Americans tour the Kyshtym nuclear weapons plant in the Urals, scheduled for closing in 1991. The tourists, whose visit is coordinated by the Soviet Academy of Sciences and the U.S. environmental group the Natural Resources Defense Council, include physicists, journalists, and members of Congress.

July 13: Officials announce closing of the Fernald, Ohio uranium processing plant because of their inability to make the operation conform to health and safety regulations.

July 13: In SDI research, the Defense Department conducts its first test of a neutral particle beam.

Aug. 8: New Zealand's new Prime Minister, Geoffrey Palmer, announces that he will continue the previous administration's anti-nuclear policy forbidding docking privileges to U.S. warships.

Aug. 31: Idaho Governor Cecil D. Andrus closes his state's borders to radioactive waste shipments from the Rocky Flats Plant.

Sept. 29: The Soviet Union says it detonated an atomic bomb during a Sept., 1954 military exercise in the Urals to test troops' conduct in contaminated terrain.

Nov. 28: Energy Department officials indicate that a nuclear waste dump at Nevada's Yucca Mountain, earlier slated for use by 1998, will not be ready before 2010.

Dec. 1: Energy Secretary James D. Watkins announces the indefinite closure of the Rocky Flats plant, the only source of plutonium triggers for U.S. nuclear weapons, because of plutonium pollution in the plant's ventilating system.

Dec. 8: Federal records furnished to the media by Las Vegas lawyers reveal that Nevada Test Site workers were routinely exposed to dangerous radiation from both atmospheric and underground nuclear tests over a thirty-year span.

Dec. 18: Secret documents released through a congressional report show that the A.E.C. received warnings before 1950 that workers at nuclear weapons facilities were being exposed to dangerous radiation; the A.E.C. did not pass the information on to the workers. "I suggested that they reveal to everybody what the situation was," said one engineer who worked at the Hanford site, "but they didn't tell anybody."

1990

January: Experts determine that Klaus Fuchs' "assistance" to the Soviet H-bomb project was essentially useless, and indicate that much of Edward Teller's work on the H-bomb was flawed. "It is now clear that the 'secrets' regarding the H-bomb known to Fuchs were worse than worthless," state Daniel Hirsch and William G. Mathews in the *Bulletin of the Atomic Scientists*.

March 15: Livingston, Montana officials announce plans to inspect bomb shelters built by the 2,000 members of the Church Universal and Triumphant. The Church owns 33,000 acres, and is responding to the predictions of a spring nuclear attack envisioned by cult leader Elizabeth Clare Prophet.

March 23: An Energy Department official reports that atomic waste tanks stored at the Hanford site could explode, releasing radiation into the atmosphere, because of hydrogen gas buildup in the tanks.

March 28: The U.S. and Britain announce the London arrest of a half-dozen people trying to smuggle nuclear weapons technology from the U.S. to Iraq.

April 10: Eight peace activists, the "Plowshares Eight," among them Daniel and Philip Berrigan and Molly Rush, are sentenced for their 1980 protest at a General Electric nuclear weapons plant in Pennsylvania, where they poured blood on blueprints and damaged nuclear warhead components.

May 8: Iraqi President Saddam Hussein claims that Iraq can now make detonators for nuclear bombs.

May 27: Israel's Supreme Court rejects Mordechai Vanunu's appeal of his conviction and sentence for revealing the extent of the Israeli nuclear weapons program.

June 1: President Bush and Mikhail Gorbachev agree on a framework for reducing strategic nuclear weapons, limiting each side to 1,600 delivery vehicles and 6,000 warheads. The numbers reflect goals of a yet-to-be achieved treaty.

June 5: The U.S. House passes the Radiation Exposure Compensation Act, providing federal aid to civilian victims of radiation from nuclear testing and uranium mining, 1945–1963.

July 6: In the "London Declaration," NATO leaders agree on various strategic and tactical steps to reduce the organization's perceived threat to the Soviet Union. These steps include revised doctrine on nuclear weapons first use and the possible withdrawal of U.S. nuclear artillery shells from Europe.

July 11: Energy Secretary James D. Watkins admits that radiation doses emitted by the Hanford nuclear weapons plant in Richland, WA, were high enough in the 1940s and 1950s to cause cancer in residents of the Pacific Northwest.

July 12: A panel of experts releases a study financed by the Energy Department contending that one in twenty citizens of the 10 counties in the Hanford

nuclear plant area sustained significant radiation
doses, 1945–1947.

July 24: The Strategic Air Command ends the around-
the-clock "Looking Glass" flights of the U.S. airborn
nuclear war command post that had operated
continuously since 1961.

Aug. 3: Soviet accounts of pollution at the Chelyabinsk
nuclear weapons facility are made public in the West.
Workers were reportedly exposed to lethal radiation on
a routine basis in the 1940s and '50s; Lake Karachay,
a dumpsite for the facility's nuclear wastes, packs a
radiation dose of 600 roentgens per hour, enough to
kill a person in weeks following an hour's exposure.

Aug. 25: Veterans of the unit that dropped the
Hiroshima and Nagasaki bombs dedicate a peace
memorial in Wendover, NE, then delete Japanese
speaker Hideaki Kase from the ceremony. He said
earlier that the bombings were not necessary to
assure Japan's surrender.

Oct. 5: Brazil's Science and Technology Minister tells
the *New York Times* that his government in September
discovered and halted a secret 15-year old military
project to develop nuclear weapons. The project,
"Solimoes," which relied on technology siphoned from
a civilian nuclear program developed with U.S. and
West German assistance, was approximately two years
from achieving the Bomb.

Oct. 7: Soviet sources released in the West indicate
that the U.S.S.R. did not possess a deliverable H-bomb
until 1955, two years later than previously believed.
The belief in the 1953 Soviet H-bomb capacity was a
basic component of mistaken U.S. assumptions about
"trailing" the U.S.S.R. in the nuclear arms race.

Oct. 8: The Soviet coast guard seizes and holds a
Greenpeace protest ship near the Soviet nuclear test
site at the island of Novaya Zemla.

Oct. 15: President Bush signs into law the Radiation

Exposure Compensation Act. (See June 5 of this year.)

Oct. 16: The Soviet Union releases the Greenpeace protest vessel and crew seized Oct. 9.

Nov. 18: Intelligence analysts from the U.S., Gt. Britain and Israel conclude that Iraq could produce usable nuclear weapons, including missiles, within a decade.

Nov. 28: Presidents Fernando Collor de Mello of Brazil and Carlos Saul Menem of Argentina agree to renounce the production of nuclear weapons.

Dec. 11: President Bush signs two treaties with the Soviet Union limiting underground nuclear testing.

1991

Jan. 7: Representatives from more than 70 countries begin a two-week U.N. meeting on a comprehensive nuclear test ban.

Jan. 16: President Bush states during a television address that Iraq's nuclear facilities are under attack by U.S. forces.

Jan. 23–26: A Gallup poll conducted during these dates indicates that 45 percent of Americans favor using nuclear weapons in the Persian Gulf War if their use "might save the lives of U.S. troops." At the height of the Viet Nam War, no more than 25 percent of Americans polled expressed a similar opinion.

Feb. 7: The Energy Department sets out four approaches to trim U.S. nuclear weapons production. Proposals range from halving the number of present production facilities to a half-dozen, to involving private enterprise in manufacture of some parts of the weapons.

March 7: Federal controls on export of nuclear-related technology are strengthened through new rules regarding equipment capable of adaptation from civilian nuclear power to nuclear weapons.

March 11: The Brookings Institution releases a study indicating that at least 16 nations, in addition to previously-established nuclear powers, now have ballistic missiles with ranges up to 1,600 miles. The nations in question: Argentina, Brazil, Egypt, India, Iran, Iraq, Israel, Libya, North Korea, Pakistan, Saudi Arabia, South Africa, South Korea, Syria, Taiwan, and Yemen.

March 14-16: U.S.-Soviet START negotiations stumble over conventional forces issues during Sec. of State James Baker's visit to Moscow.

March 20: *JAMA*, the journal of the American Medical Association, reports that Oak Ridge nuclear weapons workers exposed to low-level radiation suffered greater mortality from cancer than previous studies indicated.

March 27: The last U.S. intermediate range missiles to be removed and destroyed in accord with the INF Treaty are announced as having been removed from Sicily's Cosimo airbase.

March 31: The Warsaw Pact ceases its role as a military organization.

April 2: Bush administration officials reveal that the Defense Department has begun work on a nuclear reactor-powered missile designed to lift huge weapons or satellites into space at short notice. The missile would, if perfected, likely lift SDI system components into orbit.

May 6: The last of 846 U.S. missiles marked for destruction under the INF Treaty is eliminated in Longhorn, TX.

May 11: The last existing Soviet intermediate-range nuclear missile is destroyed near Kapustin Yar, with a team of U.S. inspectors and officials present.

June 3: French President Francois Mitterand announces his country's decision to sign the Nuclear Nonproliferation Treaty.

June 12: Business executives Ali A. Daghir and Jeanine C. Speckman are convicted in London of conspiracy to export nuclear weapon trigger technology to Iraq.

June 27: South African President F.W. de Klerk, invoking the end of the Cold War, announces his nation's readiness to agree to the terms of the Nuclear Nonproliferation Treaty.

July 31: Presidents George Bush and Mikhail S. Gorbachev sign the Strategic Arms Reduction Treaty in the Kremlin. The treaty, covering long-range nuclear weapons, remained subject to ratification by the U.S. Senate and the Soviet parliament; it would limit each nation to a maximum of 6,000 nuclear warheads and 1,600 strategic delivery vehicles.

Aug. 2: The U.S. Senate passes a defense budget for fiscal 1992 that partially redefines the mission of SDI from a space-based missile defense to a ground-based system designed to protect against a limited nuclear attack. Inspiration for the change came from the performance of the U.S. Patriot anti-missile missile during the Persian Gulf War.

Aug. 10: China announces its decision "in principle" to sign the Nuclear Nonproliferation Treaty.

Aug. 19-21: In the catalyst for what became the disintegration and official dismemberment of the Soviet Union, a group of Soviet hard-liners mount an ill-organized coup attempt. Public resistance to the coup, led by Russian President Boris Yeltsin, electrifies the world. Questions arise regarding safe control of the Soviet nuclear arsenal during and in the wake of the failed coup.

Aug. 23: According to the *Washington Post*, Soviet coup leaders seized the nuclear launch code briefcase from Mikhail Gorbachev.

Aug. 29: President Nazarbayev of Kazakhstan orders the Semipalatinsk nuclear weapons test site closed.

Sept. 27: President George Bush announces a unilateral reduction of U.S. nuclear weapons in Europe, including tactical missiles, nuclear artillery shells, and cruise missiles. He also announces cessation of work on rail-basing plans for the Peacekeeper (MX) missile, along with a halt to the 24-hour alert status of U.S. strategic bombers. "The future is ours to influence, to shape, to mold," says the President.

Sept. 28: After four days, Iraq ends its detention of a U.N. weapons inspection team in Baghdad, where the inspectors found documentary evidence of a sub rosa Iraqi nuclear weapons program.

Oct. 5: Responding to George Bush's unilateral arms control and disarmament moves announced Sept. 27, Mikhail Gorbachev meets the American steps in most particulars, and exceeds them in others.

Oct. 17: NATO approves a 50 per cent cut in tactical nuclear bombs stored in Europe for use on British and U.S. aircraft.

Oct. 19: The *Washington Post* indicates that Bush administration officials plan to remove all tactical nuclear bombs from South Korea.

Nov. 25: The U.S. Senate votes to spend up to $500 million from the U.S. defense budget to assist in dismantling the former Soviet nuclear and chemical weapons arsenal.

Dec. 21: Eleven former Soviet republics formally align themselves as the Commonwealth of Independent States.

Dec. 25: Mikhail S. Gorbachev resigns his post as the last President of the U.S.S.R., and shortly thereafter signs over the nuclear launch codes formerly under his control to Boris Yeltsin. In his farewell address he states, "We're living in a new world," in which "an end has been put to the cold war and to the arms race, as well as to the mad militarization of the country, which has crippled our economy, public attitudes, and morals. The threat of nuclear war has been removed."

Dec. 30: The former Soviet republics agree that strategic nuclear weapons will remain under a single command. Russian President Yeltsin insists: "Everything agreed to in the strategic arms treaties [with the U.S.] will be respected by Russia and the commonwealth states."

Dec. 31: Enemies since 1945, North Korea and South Korea agree to make the Korean peninsula nuclear-weapon free. The agreement requires North Korea to halt any nuclear weapons program in the works.

Publishers and Distributors

ABBE Publishers Assoc. 4111 Gallows Rd., Annandale, VA 22003.

ABC Pub. House, c/o Advent Books, Inc., 141 E. 44th St., Suite 511, New York, NY 10017.

ABC-Clio. P.O. Box 1911, Santa Barbara, CA 93116.

Aarhus Univ. Pr. Ndr. Ringgade 1, 8000 Aarhus C, Denmark.

Abt Books. 146 Mt. Auburn St., Cambridge, MA 02138.

Addison-Wesley. 1 Jacob Way, Reading, MA 01867.

Air University Pr. Maxwell AFB, AL 36112.

Alberti Pr. 715 W. 17th St., P.O. Box 5325, San Pedro, CA 90733.

Allen & Unwin. 8 Winchester Pl., Winchester, MA 01890.

Alliance Publishers for the Institute for European Defence and Strategic Studies. 12a Golden Sq., London W1R 3AF, England.

Allison & Busby. Sekforde House, 175-179 John St., London EC1V 4LL, England.

American Institute of Physics. 335 E 45th St., New York, NY 10017.

American Library Assoc. 50 E. Huron St., Chicago, IL 60611.

Archon Books. P.O. Box 4327, Hamden, CT 06514.

Arms Control Association. 11 Dupont Circle, NW,

No. 250, Washington, DC 20036.

Arrow Books, Brookmount House, 62–65 Chandos Pl., London WC2N 4NW, England.

Auburn House. 88 Post Rd., W., Box 5007, Westport, CT 06881.

Australian Government Publishing Service. P.O. Box 7, Planetarium Sta., New York, NY 10024.

Avebury. Old Post Rd., Brookfield, VT   05036.

Ballinger Pub. Co. 10 E. 53rd St., New York, NY 10022.

Bantam Books. 666 5th Ave., New York, NY 10103.

Basic Books. 10 E. 53rd St., New York, NY 10022.

Beacon Pr. 25 Beacon St., Boston, MA 02108.

Bear & Co. P.O. Drawer 2860, Santa Fe, NM 87504.

Berg. 175 5th Ave., New York, NY 10010.

Bergin & Garvey. 88 Post Rd., W., Box 5007, Westport, CT 06881.

Billner & Rouse. P.O. Box 20465, Hammarskjold Center, New York, NY 10017.

Bilr Corporation. P.O. Box 22918, Denver, CO 80222.

Birkhauser Boston, Inc. 675 Massachusetts Ave., Cambridge, MA 02139.

Black Rose Books. Univ. of Toronto Pr., 340 Nagel Dr., Cheektowaga, NY 14225.

Blackwell, Basil. 3 Cambridge Center, Cambridge, MA 02142.

Brassey's (UK). Pergamon Pr., Maxwell House, Fairview Park, Elmsford, NY 10523.

Brassey's U.S. Macmillan, Front & Brown Sts.,
Riverside, NJ 08075.

Brethren Pr. 1451 Dundee Ave., Elgin, IL 60120.

Brookings Institution. 1775 Massachusetts Ave., NW,
Washington, DC 20036.

Buchan & Enright. Seven Hills Books, 49 Central Ave.,
Cincinnati, OH 45202.

Butterworth. Reed Pub. Co., 80 Montvale Ave.,
Stoneham, MA 02180.

CSP Publications. 151 Slater St., Ottawa, Ont. K1P 5H3,
Canada.

California Institute of Public Affairs. P.O. Box 189040,
Claremont, CA 95818.

California State University Center for Study of
Armament and Disarmament. 5151 State Univ. Dr., Los
Angeles, CA 90032.

Cambridge Univ. Pr. 40 W. 20th St., New York, NY
10011.

Canadian Institute for International Peace & Security.
(Has ceased publishing.)

Canadian Institute of Ukrainian Studies. 352 Athabasca
Hall, Univ. of Alberta, Edmonton Alta. T6G 2E8, Canada.

Cape, Jonathan. P.O. Box 257, N. Pomfret, VT 05053.

Capra Pr. P.O. Box 2068, Santa Barbara, CA 93120.

Carol Pub. Group. 600 Madison Ave., New York, NY
10022.

Cass, Frank. Biblio Dist. Center, 81 Adams St., Totowa,
NJ 07512.

Catholic Univ. of America Pr. 620 Michigan Ave. NE, Washington, DC 20064.

Center for National Security Negotiations. 1710 Goodridge Dr., McLean VA 22102.

Center for the Study of Foreign Affiars, Foreign Service Institute, U.S. Dept. of State. 2201 C St. NW, Washington, DC 20520.

Center on Violence and Human Survival. CUNY, 444 W. 56th St., New York, NY 10019.

Clarendon Pr. Walton St., Oxford OX2 6DP, England.

Collier Macmillan. 866 Third Ave., New York, NY 10022.

Collins Harvill. 8 Grafton St., London W1X 3LA, England.

Columbia Univ. Pr. 562 W. 113th St., New York, NY 10025.

Comedia Pub. Group. Routledge, Chapman & Hall, 29 W. 35th St., New York, NY 10001.

Common Cause. 2030 M St. NW, Washington, DC 20036.

Cornell Univ. Pr. 124 Roberts Place, P.O. Box 250, Ithaca, NY 14850.

Council on Economic Priorities. 30 Irving Pl., 9th Flr., New York, NY 10003.

Council on Foreign Relations. 58 E. 68th St., New York, NY 10021.

Crane, Russak. Taylor & Francis, 79 Madison Ave., New York, NY 10016.

Croom Helm Australia. P.O. Box 391, Manuka, ACT 2603, Australia.

Croom Helm. Provident House, Burrell Row, Beckenham, Kent BR3 1AT, England.

Crossroad. 370 Lexington Ave., New York, NY 10017.

Daily Telegraph. Telegraph Publications, Peterborough Court, S. Quay, 181 Marsh Wall, London E14 9SR, England.

Deneau. 608 Markham St., Toronto, Ont. M6G 2L8, Canada.

Devin-Adair. 6 N. Water St., Old Greenwich, CT 06830.

Dialogue Pubns., R-686, New Rajendra Nagar, New Delhi 110060, India.

Dodd, Mead. 71 5th Ave., New York, NY 10003.

Dufour Editions. P.O. Box 449, Chester Springs, PA 19425.

Duke Univ. Pr. P.O. Box 6697 College Sta., Durham, NC 27708.

Dutton. 375 Hudson St., New York, NY 10014.

Eerdmans, W.B. 255 Jefferson Ave., S.E., Grand Rapids, MI 49503.

Envoy Pr. 141 E. 44th St., New York, NY 10017.

Epworth Pr. Trinity Pr. International, 3725 Chestnut St., Philadelphia, PA 19104.

Erlbaum Associates. 365 Broadway, Hillsdale, NJ 07642.

Ethics and Public Policy Center. 1030 15th St. NW, Washington, DC   20005.

Faber and Faber. 3 Queen St., London WC1N 3AU, England.

Facts on File. 460 Park Ave. S., New York, NY 10016.

Farrar, Straus and Giroux. 19 Union Sq. W., New York, NY 10003.

Feminism and Nonviolence Study Group. 67B Landor Rd., London SW9 9RT, England.

Firethorn Pr. Sidgwick & Jackson Ltd., 1 Tavistock Chambers, Bloomsbury Way, London WC1A 2SG, England.

Fischer, G. VCH Publishers, 220 E. 23rd St., New York, NY 10010.

Foreign Policy Research Institute. 3615 Chestnut St., Philadelphia, PA 19104.

Fortress Pr. 426 S. Fifth St., Box 1209, Minneapolis MN 55440.

Forward Movement Pubns. 412 Sycamore St., Cincinnati, OH 45202.

Fourth Estate. 113 Westbourne Grove, London W2 4UP, England.

Free Pr. 866 Third Ave., New York, NY 10022.

Freeman, W.H. 41 Madison Ave., New York, NY 10010.

Friendship Pr. 475 Riverside Dr., N. Y., NY 10115.

Fulcrum. 350 Indiana St., Golden, CO 80401.

Gale Research. 835 Penobscot Bldg., Detroit, MI 48826.

Garland. 136 Madison Ave., New York, NY 10016.

Georgetown University Pr. Intercultural Ctr., Rm. 111, Washington, DC 20057.

Gollancz, V. 14 Henrietta St., Covent Garden, London WC2E 8QJ, England.

Gower Pub. Co. Old Post Rd., Brookfield, VT 05036.

Graded Pr. 201 Eighth Ave. S., Box 801, Nashville, TN 37202.

Greenhaven Pr. 577 Shoreview Pk. Rd., St. Paul, MN 55126.

Greenwood Pr. 88 Post Rd., W., Box 5007, Westport, CT 06881.

Grotius. Box 115, Cambridge, CB3 9BP, England.

Grove Weidenfeld. 841 Broadway, New York, NY 10003.

Hamilton Pr. 4720 Boston Way, Lanham MD 20706.

Hamish Hamilton. 375 Hudson St., New York, NY 10014.

Harmsworth, T. 13 Nicosia Rd., London SW18 3RN, England.

Harper & Row. 10 E. 53rd St., New York, NY 10022.

Harvard Univ. Pr. 79 Garden St., Cambridge, MA 02138.

Heinemann, W. 85 Abinger St., Richmond, Victoria 3121.

Her Majesty's Stationery Office. St. Crispins, Duke St., Norwich NR3 1PD, England.

Heretic Books. P.O. Box 247, London N17 9QR, England.

Hill and Wang. 19 Union Sq., W., New York, NY 10003.

Hill, Lawrence. 230 Park Pl., Suite 6A, Brooklyn, NY 11238.

Hodder & Stoughton. Mill Road, Dunton Green, Sevenoaks, Kent TN13 2YA, England.

Hogarth Pr. 30 Bedford Sq., London WC1B 3SF, England.

Holmes & Meier. 30 Irving Pl., New York, NY 10003.

Hoover Institution Pr. Stanford University, Stanford, CA 94305.

Houghton Mifflin. 1 Beacon St., Boston, MA 02108.

Humanities Pr. International. 171 First Ave., Atlantic Highlands, NJ 07716.

Hutchinson Radius. 62-65 Chandos Pl., London, WC2N 4NW, England.

ICS Pr. 23 Kearny St., San Francisco, CA 94108.

Ignatius Pr. 2515 McAllister St., San Francisco, CA 94118.

Indiana Univ. Pr. Tenth & Morton Sts., Bloomington, IN 47405.

INFACT. 256 Hanover St., Boston, MA 02113.

Institute for East-West Security Studies. 360 Lexington Ave., New York, NY 10017.

Institute for Historical Review. 1822 1/2 Newport Blvd., Suite 191, Costa Mesa, CA 92627.

International Institute for Strategic Studies. 23 Tavistock St., London WC2E N7Q, England.

International Publishers. 239 W. 23rd St., New York, NY 10011.

Jameson Books. 722 Columbus St., Ottawa, IL 61350.

Jane's Pub. Co. 115 Fifth Ave., New York, NY 10003.

Johns Hopkins Univ. Pr. 701 W. 40th St., Ste. 275, Baltimore, MD 21211.

Kent State Univ. Pr. 101 Franklin Hall, Kent, OH 44242.

Kimber, William. Denington Estate, Wellingborough, Northants NN8 2QD, England.

Kluwer. 101 Philip Dr., Assinippi Pk., Norwell, MA 02061.

Knopf. 201 E. 50th St., New York, NY 10022.

Kosei Pub. Co. 3-8-4 Botan Koto-Ku, Tokyo 135, Japan.

Lang, P. 62 W. 45th St., New York, NY 10036.

Leicester Inter-Varsity Pr. 38 De Montfort St., Leicester LE1 7GP, England.

Lexington Books. 125 Spring St., Lexington, MA 02173.

Liber Forlag. S-20510 Malmo, Sweden.

Little, Brown. 34 Beacon St., Boston, MA 02108.

Longman. Longman House, Burnt Mill, Harlow, Essex CM20 2JE, England.

Longwood Academic. P.O. Box 2669, Wolfeboro, NH 03894.

Lorimer, J. 35 Britain St., Toronto, ON M5A 1R7, Canada.

Los Alamos Historical Society. P.O. Box 43, Los Alamos, NM 87544.

Loyola Univ. Pr. 3441 N. Ashland Ave., Chicago, IL 60657.

MIT Pr. 55 Hayward St., Cambridge, MA 02142.

McFarland & Co. P.O. Box 611, Jefferson, NC 28640.

McGill-Queen's University Pr. 849, rue Sherbrooke ouest, Montreal, Quebec H3A 2T5, Canada.

McGraw-Hill. 1221 Ave. of the Americas, New York, NY 10020.

Macmillan (UK). Gale Research, 835 Penobscot Bldg., Detroit, MI 48226.

Manchester Univ. Pr. 175 Fifth Ave., New York, NY 10010.

Mayfield Pub. Co. 1240 Villa St., Mountain View, CA 94041.

Medical Follow-Up Agency of the National Research Council. 2101 Constitution Ave. NW, Washington DC 20418

Mellen, E. Pr. Box 450, Lewiston, NY 14092.

Menard Pr. 8 The Oaks, Woodside Ave., London N12 8AR, England.

Mir Publishers. 1-j Rizhsky per 2, 12980 Moscow, USSR.

Morrow. 105 Madison Ave., New York, NY 10016.

Mowbray, A.R. Artillery House, Artillery Row, London SW1P 1RT, England.

Muller, Frederick. Random Century House, 20 Vauxhall Bridge Rd., London SW1V 2SA, England.

National Academy Pr. 2101 Constitution Ave., NW, Washington, DC 20418.

National Defense Univ. Pr. Fort Lesley J. McNair, Fourth and P Sts. SW, Washington, DC 20319.

National Education Association. 1201 16th St., NW, Washington, DC 20418.

National Technical Information Service. U.S. Dept. of Commerce, 5285 Port Royal Rd., Springfield, VA 22161.

Nauka Publishers. Profsojuznaja, 117495 Moscow, USSR.

Nelson, T. P.O. Box 141000, Nelson Pl. at Elmhill Pike, Nashville, TN 37214.

New American Library. 1633 Broadway, New York, NY 10019.

New Society. 4527 Springfield Ave., Philadelphia, PA 19143.

New Star Books. 2504 York Ave., Vancouver BC V6K 1E3, Canada.

New York Univ. Pr. 70 Washington Sq. S., New York, NY 10012.

North Atlantic Books. 2800 Woolsey St., Berkeley, CA 94705.

North River Pr. P.O. Box 309, Croton–on–Hudson, NY 10520.

Northcote. 311 Bainbridge St., Philadelphia, PA 19147.

Norton. 500 Fifth Ave., New York, NY 10110.

Novosti Pr. Imported Pubns., 320 W. Ohio St., Chicago, IL 60610.

Nuclear Energy Agency, OECD. 2, rue Andre–Pascal, 75775 Paris CEDEX 16, France.

Oelgeschlager, Gunn & Hain. 245 Mirriam St., Weston, MA 02193.

Orion Books. 201 E. 50th St., New York, NY 10022.

Oryx Pr. 2214 N. Central Ave., Phoenix AZ 85004.

Oxford Univ. Pr. 200 Madison Ave., New York, NY 10016.

Oxford Univ. Pr., Melbourne. 253 Normanby Rd., S. Melbourne, Vic. 3205, Australia.

Pacific Information Center, University of the South Pacific. Library, P.O. Box 1168, Suva, Fiji.

Paladin. 8 Grafton St., London W1X 3LA, England.

Pandora Pr. 955 Massachusetts Ave., Cambridge, MA 02139.

Pantheon. 201 E. 50th St., New York, NY 10022.

Paragon House. 90 Fifth Ave., New York, NY 10011.

Paulist Pr. 997 MacArthur Blvd., Mahwah, NJ 07430.

Penguin Books. 375 Hudson St., New York, NY 10014.

Pennsylvania State Univ. Pr. 820 N. University Dr., Ste. C, Barbara Bldg., University Park, PA 16802.

Perennial Library. 10 E. 53rd St., New York, NY 10022.

Pergamon-Brassey's. Maxwell Hse., Fairview Pk., Elmsford, NY 10523.

Physicians for Social Responsibility, B.C. Chapter. Box 35426, Sta. E, Vancouver, B.C., V6M 4G8, Canada.

Pilgrim Pr. 475 Riverside Dr., 10th Fl., New York, NY 10115.

Pinter, F. 25 Floral St., London WC2E 9DS, England.

Pittsburgh Peace Institute. 1139 Wightman St., Pittsburgh, PA 15217.

Plenum. 233 Spring St., New York, NY 10013.

Pluto Pr. 955 Massachusetts Ave., Cambridge, MA 02139.

Polity Pr. 108 Cowley Rd., Oxford OX4 1JF, England.

Polygon Books. Box 449, Chester Springs, PA 19425.

Praeger. 88 Post Rd., W., Box 5007, Westport, CT 068981.

Prentice Hall. Rt. 9W, Englewood Cliffs, NJ 07632.

Press for Peace. 2514 S. Grand Ave., Los Angeles, CA 90007.

Princeton Univ. Pr. 41 William St., Princeton, NJ 08540.

Progress Publishers. Imported Pubns., 320 W. Ohio St., Chicago, IL 60610.

Progressive Foundation. P.O. Box 2658, Madison, WI 53701.

Prometheus Books. 700 E. Amherst St., Buffalo, NY 14215.

Psychohistory Pr. 2315 Broadway, New York, NY 10024.

Quartet Books. 12 E. 69th St., New York, NY 10021.

R.K. Publishers. 23 Beadonpura, Karol Bagh, New Delhi 5, India.

Radioactive Waste Campaign. 625 Broadway, 2d fl., New York, NY 10012.

Random House. 201 E. 50th St., New York, NY 10022.

Readers International. P.O. Box 959, Columbia LA 71418.

Regina Books. P.O. Box 280, Claremont, CA 91711.

Regnery Gateway. 1130 17th St., NW, Washington, DC 20036.

Resources for the Future. 1616 P St., NW, Rm. 532, Washington, DC 20036.

Rienner, L. 1800 30th St., Boulder, CO 80301.

Routledge. 29 W. 35th St., New York, NY 10001.

Rowman & Allanheld. 4720 Boston Way, Lanham, MD 20706.

Rowman and Littlefield. 4720 Boston Way, Lanham, MD 20706.

Rutgers Univ. Pr. 109 Church St., New Brunswick, NJ 08901.

SCM Pr. 26–30 Tottenham Rd., London N1 4BZ, England.

Sage Publications. P.O. Box 6944, San Mateo, CA 94403.

St. Martin's Pr. 175 Fifth Ave., New York, NY 10010.

Scarborough House. P.O. Box 459, Chelsea, MI 48118.

Scarecrow Pr. 52 Liberty St., P.O. Box 4167, Metuchen, NJ 08840.

Schenkman. 118 Main St., P.O. Box 119, Rochester, VT 05767.

Scholarly Resources. 104 Greenhill Ave., Wilmington, DE 19805.

School of Peace Studies, Univ. of Bradford. Bradford, West Yorkshire, BD7 1DP, England.

Scribner's. 866 Third Ave., New York, NY 10022.

Seal Pr. 3131 Western Ave., Seattle, WA 98121.

Sharpe, M.E. 80 Business Park Dr., Armonk, NY 10504.

Sheed & Ward. P.O. Box 419492, Kansas City, MO 64141.

Sierra Club. 730 Polk St., San Francisco, CA 94109.

Simon & Schuster. 1230 Ave. of the Americas, New York, NY 10020.

South End Pr. 116 St. Botolph St., Boston, MA 02115.

Southern California Federation of Scientists. 3318 Colbert Ave., Ste. 200, Los Angeles, CA 90066.

Southern Methodist Univ. Pr. P.O. Box 415, Dallas, TX 75275.

Spokesman. Bertrand Russell House, Gamble St., Nottingham, NG7 4ET, England.

Springer-Verlag. 175 Fifth Ave., New York, NY 10010

Stackpole. P.O. Box 1831, Cameron & Kelker Sts., Harrisburg, PA 17105.

Stanford Alumni Assoc. Bowman Alumni House, Stanford, CA 94305.

Stanford Univ. Pr., Stanford, CA 94305.

Starwind Pr. 507 Third Ave., #547, Seattle, WA 98104.

State Univ. of New York Pr. State Univ. Plaza, Albany, NY 12246.

Stein and Day. (Ceased publishing)

Summit Books. 1230 Ave. of the Americas, New York, NY 10020.

Tarcher. 5858 Wilshire Blvd., Ste. 200, Los Angleles, CA 90036.

Tauris, I.B. 110 Gloucester Ave., London NW1 8JA, England.

Taylor & Francis. 79 Madison Ave., New York, NY 10016.

Teachers College Pr. 1234 Amsterdam Ave., New York, NY 10027.

Temple Univ. Pr. Broad & Oxford Sts., Univ. Services

Bldg., Rm. 305, Philadelphia, PA 19122.

Third World Communications. 173 Old St., London EC1V 9NJ, England.

Times Books. 201 E. 50th St., New York, NY 10022.

Transaction. Rutgers Univ., New Brunswick, NJ 08903.

Transnational Publishers. 22 Myrtle Ave., Dobbs Ferry, NY 10522.

Tri-Service. 28 Emerson Court, Wimbledon Hill Rd., Wimbledon, London SW219 7PQ, England.

U.S. Arms Control and Disarmament Agency. Dept. of State Bldg., Washington, DC 20451.

U.S. Army Sergeants Major Academy. Fort Bliss, El Paso, TX 79916.

U.S. Congress Office of Technology Assessment. 600

Pennsylvania Ave., S.E., Washington, DC 20510.

U.S. General Accounting Office. 441 G. St., N.W., Washington, DC 20548.

U.S. Government Printing Office. Supt. of Documents, Washington, DC 20402.

U.S. Naval War College. Newport, RI.

UNIPUB, 4611-F Assembly Dr., Lanham MD 20706.

United Nations. Sales Section. 2 United Nations Plaza, Rm. DC2-853, New York, NY 10017.

Univ. of Alabama Pr. Box 870380, Tuscaloosa, AL 35487.

Univ. of Arizona Pr. 1230 N. Park, No. 102, Tucson AZ 85719.

Univ. of Calgary Pr. 2500 University Dr., N.W., Calgary, Alta. T2N 1N4, Canada.

Univ. of California Institute on Global Conflict and Cooperation. Mail Code Q-068, Univ. of California-San Diego, La Jolla, CA 92093.

Univ. of California Pr. 2120 Berkeley Way, Berkeley CA 94720.

Univ. of Chicago Pr. 5801 Ellis Ave., 4th Flr., Chicago, IL 60637.

Univ. of Georgia Pr. Terrell Hall, Athens, GA 30602.

Univ. of Hawaii Pr. 2840 Kolowalu St., Honolulu, HI 96822.

Univ. of Illinois Pr. 54 E. Gregory Dr., Champaign, IL 61820.

Univ. of Iowa Pr. 119 W. Park Rd., Iowa City, IA 52242.

Univ. of Massachusetts Pr. P.O. Box 429, Amherst, MA 01004.

Univ. of Michigan Pr. P.O. Box 1104, Ann Arbor, MI 48106.

Univ. of Nevada Pr. Mail Stop 166, Reno, NV 89557.

Univ. of New Mexico Pr. Journalism Bldg., Ste. 220, Albuquerque, NM 87131

Univ. of Ottawa Pr. 603 Cumberland, Ottawa, Ont. K1N 6N5, Canada.

Univ. of Pennsylvania Pr. 418 Service Dr., Blockley Hall, 13th Fl., Philadelphia, PA 19104.

Univ. of Pittsburgh Center for Russian and East European Studies. 4E23 Forbes Quad, Pittsburgh, PA 15260.

Univ. of South Carolina Pr. 1716 College St., Columbia, SC 29208.

Univ. of Texas Pr. P.O. Box 7819, Austin, TX 78713.

Univ. of Utah Pr. 101 Univ. Services Bldg., Salt Lake City, UT 84112.

Univ. of Washington Pr. P.O. Box 50096, Seattle, WA 98145.

Univ. of Wisconsin Pr. 114 N. Murray St., Madison, WI 53715.

Univ. Pr. of America. 4720 Boston Way, Lanham, MD 20706.

University Pr. of New England. 17½ Lebanon St., Hanover, NH 03755.

Unwin Hyman. 8 Winchester Pl., Winchester, MA 01890.

Unwin Paperbacks. 40 Museum St., London, WC1A 1LU, England.

Usonia Pr. Box 19440, Diamond Lake Sta., Minneapolis, MN 55419.

Vance Bibliographies. P.O. Box 229, 112 N. Charter St., Monticello, IL 61856.

Verso. 6 Meard St., London W1V 3HR, England.

Viking. 375 Hudson St., New York, NY 10014.

Vintage Books. Mail Drop 28-2, 201 E. 50th St., New York, NY 10022.

Virago. 20-23 Mandela St., London NW1 0HQ, England.

Walker and Co. 720 Fifth Ave., New York, NY 10019.

Warner Books. 666 Fifth Ave., New York, NY 10103.

Washington Institute Pr. 1015 18th St. NW, Washington, DC 20036

Weidenfeld and Nicolson. 91 Clapham High St., London SW4 9TA, England.

Westbury House. Borough Green, Sevenoaks, Kent TN15 8PH, England.

Westminster Pr. 100 Witherspoon St., Louisville, KY 40202.

Westview Pr. 5500 Central Ave., Boulder, CO 80301.

Wildwood House. Gower House, Croft Rd., Aldershot, Hants GU11 3HR, England.

Wiley, J. 605 Third Ave., New York, NY 10158.

Wilson, H.W. 950 University Ave., Bronx, NY 10452.

World Almanac. 200 Park Ave., New York, NY 10166.

World Health Organization. 1211, Geneva 27, Switzerland.

World Without War Council. 421 S. Wabash, Chicago, IL 60605.

Yale Univ. Pr. 302 Temple St., New Haven, CT 06520.

AUTHOR-EDITOR INDEX

TITLE INDEX

Subtitles for most items with distinctive main titles have been omitted. Initial articles have also been omitted.

SUBJECT INDEX TO THE BIBLIOGRAPHY

Taking the current marketing term of choice, the following might be described as a "lite" subject guide. It will help the reader identify some books dealing with specific topics, such as nuclear war scenarios or children's issues, not easily accessed through the subject breakdown by chapter or through the Table of Contents. Some subjects, such as nuclear deterrence, are in plentiful evidence throughout certain chapters, and so have been omitted for the most part from this index.

Index to the Chronology

References in this index include year and, when applicable, month. Specific days have been omitted to avoid clotting the index with a barrage of numbers hostile to the eye. Even in busy nuclear years, most months will not feature more than three or four events, which should make the reader's task of scanning for a specific item relatively easy.

Readers seeking to identify nuclear events occurring in their own locales should look under the names of specific states, countries, cities or institutions (e.g., "University of Chicago"). If the index identifies a U.S. city or institution, an entry for the event in question will also generally appear under the name of the relevant state. Events referred to by entries for Canadian provinces and foreign cities will also generally appear under country names. If not, "See also" notes will ordinarily follow the city entries.

At the risk of pointing out the obvious, many event categories are represented by only a fraction of the total of their kind. Public protests and demonstrations against nuclear weapons and on behalf of peace, for example, have been far more frequent than the relatively few instances noted below might suggest.

Blackett, P.M.S.   May 1950
"Bock's Car" Aug. 1945
Bombers   Aug. 1945; July 1946; Sept. 1947; May 1950;
    April, June 1952; May 1953; May 1955; May 1956; May
    1957; March, Nov. 1958; Oct. 1959; Jan. 1961; Oct.
    1962;   June 1964; Jan. 1966; Jan. 1968; June 1970;
    June, Oct. 1974; Jan. 1975; March 1976; June 1980;
    Oct. 1981; March 1984; Nov. 1986; Dec. 1988; Sept.
    1991 (See also B-1, B-2, B-29, B-36, B-47, B-50,
    B-52, Backfire)
"The bombing begins in five minutes." (Reagan quip)
    Aug. 1984
Boston University   Nov. 1961
Boy Scouts   July 1958
Brandeis University   Nov. 1961
Brazil   Aug. 1974; Jan. 1984; Oct., Nov. 1990
Brezhnev, Secretary Leonid   May 1972; Nov. 1974; May
    1976; Aug. 1977; June 1979; Nov. 1981
"Brilliant Pebbles"   March 1989
Britain (See Great Britain)
Bronx, NY   Nov. 1950
Brookings Institution   March 1991
Broomfield, CO   Sept. 1973
Brown, Sec. of Defense Harold   May 1979
Brown University   Oct. 1984
Bush, President George   June, Oct., Dec. 1990; Jan.,
    July, Sept. 1991

California   1929; 1940; Aug. 1942; Oct. 1950; Oct. 1951;
    April, June 1952; May 1955; July 1957; Nov. 1961;
    June 1969; Nov. 1970; Oct. 1974; Feb. 1977; Jan.,
    April 1980; June 1982; June 1983; Nov. 1986; June
    1988
Cambridge University   Jan. 1954
Canada   July 1957; Oct. 1961; May 1963; Feb., April,
    July 1983; March 1984; Jan., Feb. 1985; April 1987
Canberra, Australia   Oct. 1953
Cape Canaveral, FL (See also Cape Kennedy)   Dec.
    1957; July 1960; Feb. 1961
Cape Kennedy, FL (See also Cape Canaveral)   Aug.
    1968
Caribou, radioactive   April 1962
Carter, President Jimmy   April 1977; April 1978; June
    1979; Jan. 1980

Lima, OH   Dec. 1951
Limited Test Ban Treaty   Aug. 1963
"Little Boy"   Aug. 1945
Livingston, MT   March 1990
"London Declaration"   July 1990
Longhorn, TX   May 1991
"Looking Glass" flights   Feb. 1961; July 1990
Lop Nor, Sinkiang, China   Oct. 1964
Los Alamos Laboratory   1943; May 1946; Jan., Nov.
   1959; April 1986; Feb. 1987
Los Alamos Scientific Library   May 1979
Los Alamos Scientists, Association of   Oct. 1945
Los Angeles   Oct. 1950; Nov. 1986
"Lucky Dragon"   March, April 1954

MIRV warheads   Dec. 1967; Aug. 1968; June 1969; June
   1970; June 1972; June 1974; June 1975; June 1977;
   Aug. 1987
MIT   Aug. 1942; Nov. 1961; June 1987
MX missile   Oct. 1981; April, May, July 1983; Summer
   1983; Feb., Aug. 1985; Nov. 1986; Sept. 1991
MacArthur, Gen. Douglas   Nov. 1945
McCarthy, Sen. Joe   Oct. 1952; April 1954
McMillan, Edwin   1940
Macmillan, Prime Minister Harold   Nov. 1960; Sept. 1961
McNamara, Sec. of Defense Robert S.   June, Sept. 1962;
   March 1966; Oct., Nov. 1967
Malenkov, Premier Georgi M.   Aug. 1953
Malmstrom Air Force Base, Montana   June 1960
Manhattan Project   1942; Aug. 1983
Manhattan Project scientists' disarmament plea   April
   1983
Marshall Islands   March, May 1954
Maryland   July 1951
Massachusetts   Aug. 1942; Dec. 1960; Nov. 1961; May
   1962; June 1987
Massachusetts Institute of Technology (See MIT)
"Massive Retaliation"   Jan. 1955 (See also Strategy)
Mayer, Norman   Dec. 1982
Medvedev, Zhores A.   Nov. 1976; Nov. 1977; Feb. 1980
"Meet the Press"   Oct. 1953; Sept. 1961
Meitner, Lise   1939
Mendeleev, Dmitry   1869
Menem, President Carlos Saul   Nov. 1990

U.S. Air Force   Oct. 1947
U.S. Arms Control and Disarmament Agency   Sept.
   1961; Aug. 1978
U.S. and ANZUS Treaty   Aug. 1986
U.S. Justice Dept.   Feb. 1983
U.S. Radium Co.   1927
U.S. Supreme Court   Nov. 1952; Jan. 1988
University of California   1940; Aug. 1942;   Nov. 1961;
   Nov. 1970
University of Chicago   Aug., Dec. 1942; Dec. 1945;
   Sept. 1947; Aug. 1983; Oct. 1985
University of Michigan   Sept. 1956; June 1962
University of Rochester   Feb. 1951
Ural Mountains   Nov. 1976; June, Sept. 1989
Uranium   1789; 1896; Dec. 1947; Aug. 1977; Jan. 1984
Utah   Oct. 1951; May 1953; Jan. 1954; Oct. 1965; April
   1966; Dec. 1978; Aug. 1979; Jan., May 1984; April 1987
Utopia College, KS   Oct. 1947

Van Zandt, Rep. James   March 1954
Vance, Dep. Sec. of Defense Cyrus   Aug. 1964
Vanunu, Mordechai   Oct. 1986; March 1988; May 1990
Velikovsky, Immanuel   Sept. 1966
Veterans Administration   Aug. 1978; Jan. 1987
Vienna, Austria   June 1979
Vietnam   May 1964; Feb., Oct. 1968; Jan. 1973
Villar, Paul Ulrich   1900
Virgin Islands   Nov. 1981
Voters   Nov. 1974; Nov. 1982

"Walk in the Woods"   July 1982
Wallace, Gov. George   Oct. 1968
Warsaw Pact Organization   May 1955; March 1991
Washington, D.C.   April 1949; March, July 1950; Dec.
   1982; Nov. 1986
Washington Monument   Dec. 1982
Washington State   1942–43; 1944; Dec. 1949; July 1950;
   Feb. 1973; Aug. 1983;   Oct. 1986; Feb. 1988; Feb.
   1989; March, July 1990
Washington University   March 1958
Watkins, Sec. of Energy James D.   March, Dec. 1989;
   July 1990
Wayne, John   Aug. 1979
Webster, William H.   April 1979

ACRONYM LIST

Most acronyms that appear in this guide's entries will be comprehensible in context, but the following brief list may be useful.

ABM   Anti-ballistic missile
AEC   Atomic Energy Commission
ANCOC   Advanced Noncommissioned Officer Course
ANZUS   Australia, New Zealand, and the United States
ASAT   Anti-satellite
BMD   Ballistic missile defense
CTB   Comprehensive Test Ban
DOE   Department of Energy
IAEA   International Atomic Energy Agency
ICBM   Intercontinental ballistic missile
INF   Intermediate range nuclear forces
IRBM   Intermediate range ballistic missile
MAD   Mutual Assured Destruction
MIRV   Multiple independently targetable reentry vehicle
MX   Missile Experimental
NATO   North Atlantic Treaty Organization
NBC   Nuclear, biological and chemical warfare
NPT   Nonproliferation Treaty
NWFZ   Nuclear weapon free zone
PD-59   Presidential Directive 59
SAC   Strategic Air Command
SALT   Strategic Arms Limitation Treaty/Talks
SDI   Strategic Defense Initiative
SIOP   Single Integrated Operational Plan
SIPRI   Stockholm International Peace Research Institute
START   Strategic Arms Reduction Treaty/Talks

ABOUT THE AUTHOR

Grant Burns (B.A., Michigan State University; A.M., A.M.L.S., University of Michigan) is a reference librarian with the University of Michigan-Flint Library. Among his three previously-published books is *The Atomic Papers* (Scarecrow, 1984), an annotated bibliography on nuclear issues. He has contributed a variety of articles to professional journals, including several on the literature of the peace movement.